Margaret Fuller. Daguerreotype, 1846. Courtesy of the Metropolitan Museum of Art, gift of I. N. Phelps Stokes, Edward S. Hawes, Alice Mary Hawes, Marion Augusta Hawes, 1937; and the Schlesinger Library, Radcliffe Institute, Harvard University.

"*My Heart Is a Large Kingdom*"

SELECTED LETTERS OF

Margaret Fuller

Edited by

Robert N. Hudspeth

Cornell University Press

ITHACA AND LONDON

For Cathy and Sharon

First published 2001 by Cornell University Press

Printed in the United States of America

LIBRARY OF CONGRESS CATALOGING-IN-PUBLICATION DATA

Fuller, Margaret, 1810–1850.
  "My heart is a large kingdom" : selected letters of Margaret Fuller
/ edited by Robert N. Hudspeth.
    p. cm.
  Includes bibliographical references and index.
  ISBN 0-8014-3747-4 (cloth)
  1. Fuller, Margaret, 1810–1850—Correspondence. 2. Authors,
American—19th century—Correspondence. 3. Feminists—United
States—Correspondence.   I. Hudspeth, Robert N. II. Title.
  PS2506 .A4 2001
  818'.309—dc21

                                                    00-010239

Cornell University Press strives to use environmentally responsible
suppliers and materials to the fullest extent possible in the publishing
of its books. Such materials include vegetable-based, low-VOC inks
and acid-free papers that are recycled, totally chlorine-free, or partly
composed of nonwood fibers. Books that bear the logo of the FSC
(Forest Stewardship Council) use paper taken from forests that have
been inspected and certified as meeting the highest standards for
environmental and social responsibility. For further information,
visit our website at www.cornellpress.cornell.edu.

Cloth printing   10 9 8 7 6 5 4 3 2 1

FSC FSC Trademark © 1996 Forest Stewardship Council A.C.
     SW-COC-098

CONTENTS

Illustrations

PREFACE

A reader may reasonably ask: Why Margaret Fuller? Why her letters? To answer these questions is to go immediately to the center of American intellectual and literary history. We have, as a culture, been slow to interest ourselves in the lives of women. We have too long thought of "history" only as what men said and did. Only in recent decades have we begun seriously and patiently to listen to the words of women, to think about their experiences, to retell their cultural stories, and to teach ourselves about their assumptions and the conditions of their lives. What we find in *"My Heart Is a Large Kingdom"* is a woman who tried to understand the consequences of that cultural neglect in her own life and in the lives of the women she knew, and who came to analyze them in her *Woman in the Nineteenth Century*. Given the range of her interests and the sophistication of her writing, no other American woman of her time, with the possible exception of Emily Dickinson, so commands our attention.

Not only did she write of the lives of women, she of course lived such a life, and a life of expansive accomplishment it was. Fuller was a cosmopolitan woman who, though she grew up in narrow surroundings, read of Greece and Rome, then became fluent in German, dared to plan a biography of Goethe, and made skillful translations of his poetry. Inevitably she ran up against the limitations her culture placed on women. Though she was educated as young men were educated, she could not have a man's vocation. She was deeply learned and intellectually ambitious, but her world said that all she could do was to marry or teach. Fortunately, she discovered her own ways to use her mind, and it is in her letters that we find most clearly and thoroughly how she did it.

A quick look at her public life makes it clear why she matters. She was— often at the same time—a translator, a literary critic, a feminist theoretician, a travel writer, a journalist, an editor, and a historian. Fuller had a far-ranging mind that was at home with the most modern ideas of her time, and she was a practical woman who put those ideas into print and helped others do so as well; she not only wrote about justice, she worked among the prostitutes of New York City and nursed the wounded Italian patriots who were defending the young Republic of Rome. In both her writing and her personal activities, Fuller pushed herself and those around her to a richer life of engaged thought. It was inevitable that the people she most admired were the thinkers who pushed hardest against their cultures: Goethe, Ralph Waldo Emerson, George Sand, and Giuseppe Mazzini.

Though she detested being a schoolmistress, Fuller was a natural teacher, and the ideal of education runs consistently through her letters. While her life has an incomplete and ad hoc quality because she died so suddenly and prematurely, her literary criticism takes a consistent direction in her efforts to educate American readers about new writers, just as her travel writing was consistently designed to uncover the untold realities of her travels. Her last work was a narrative history of the Italian revolutions, devoted to educating an American audience about the dignity of Italian aspirations.

Fuller's need to educate found a new form of expression when she organized a series of "Conversations" with women in Boston in the 1840s. These sessions were combinations of intellectual testing grounds and feminist self-culture. Fuller thought that women, given the chance, could among themselves develop their own ways of thinking and responding. They could, in short, create their own narratives. In retrospect the idea of a narrative seems to characterize Fuller's life. A passionate reader of novels as a child, she had just completed a narrative history when she died. In the years between we find her reading and writing about autobiographies and histories. She attempted a series of narratives based on the Scriptures (now lost), and she wrote at least one short story.

And so it is that we turn to her letters, for they are her own story, told in her words, on the spot, and with passionate intensity. The texts of the letters in *"My Heart Is a Large Kingdom"* are drawn directly from my six-volume *Letters of Margaret Fuller* (Ithaca: Cornell University Press, 1983–94). The texts are the same save for a few minor corrections.

Fuller and her friends often shared letters, passing them from person to person as if they were items in a semipublic journal. Her letters are moments of consciousness in which we find intriguing mixtures of the profound and mundane, the serious and whimsical, the perceptive and the wrongheaded. Most of all, her letters give us Fuller herself in ways her public writings cannot match. Here she feels free to be tentative, to launch topics without having to see them to their conclusion; she can risk opening herself up emotionally to a variety of men and women, and we find her simultaneously open and guarded. While she was writing passionate love letters to James Nathan, she kept his existence hidden from her friends; when she was about to have her baby, she was emotionally open to her husband but kept him and the child wholly to herself when she wrote to friends in the United States.

Letters from persons long gone have a natural attraction for us, for at their best they put us in touch with the past with a freshness we find nowhere else. We hear Fuller's enthusiasms, her fears, her triumphs, and her sorrows. She was a passionate woman of often conflicting emotions, and she was willing to let that part of her self show in her letters. For her, the personal letter is a literary form: it puts the stamp of personality on a fleeting moment; it brings news, both about herself and about her world. For Fuller, her letters make it possible to merge the personal and impersonal, to tie herself firmly to a time and place. Although we know that in any letter Fuller is controlling the information, letting her correspondent know and see what she thinks right to reveal at the moment, at our distance we can see the letters in a broader context. We can see, for example, that it was only when she encountered Italy directly after meeting Mazzini that she had a defining moment of the sort that John Brown made for Thoreau, a moment when the need for political action became clear and inescapable. An otherwise abstract process takes form when we read her letter to the Italian leader, written as it was at the very time of crisis when "liberty" had meaning for specific people in a specific place. Thus it is that we both read Fuller as she wrote herself into her letters and see how that self reveals qualities about the nineteenth century. We read, in other words, both her time and ours, for it is only in more fully grasping her world that we know how we became who we are.

At her death, her friends immediately understood the value (and the danger, they thought) of her letters. From the first, the friends who edited *Memoirs of Margaret Fuller Ossoli*—James Clarke, Waldo Emerson, and William Channing—used her letters extensively. They also, to our dismay, abused the letters, for they rewrote some, mutilated many, and ignored others that they considered too revealing. This use of her letters stood in our way for many years, and it was only with the six volumes of *The Letters of Margaret Fuller* that we could begin to undo the damage. While I am quite aware that *"My Heart Is a Large Kingdom"* is yet another editor's selection and thus another version of Margaret Fuller, I have worked hard to present a comprehensive, balanced selection that meets Fuller on her own ground. I have attempted to mirror her interests, her friendships, her ideas, her longings, and her successes. Finally, this vol-

ume has the virtue of being the first—and the only—collection of her letters based solely on the actual manuscripts written in her hand. The voice
here is hers alone.

We can now hear the voice to which Fuller's correspondents responded. Fuller thought her voice her best medium. She valued spon-
taneity and improvisation, which are, after all, the qualities of good letter
writing. Much of what she knew she did best in talking spills over into her
letters, and so they make an ideal introduction to her. After reading this
selection of her correspondence a reader will want to explore her life and
her world in greater detail. "*My Heart Is a Large Kingdom*" is a beginning to
an understanding of *the* American woman of the nineteenth century.
Suggestions for further reading are offered in the Bibliographical Essay.

I have sparsely annotated this edition because *The Letters of Margaret
Fuller* has an elaborate apparatus of textual and explanatory notes. I have
introduced only a few explanatory notes. The Biographical Sketches give
standard biographical information about each recipient. Readers who
want to see more extensive documentation may find it in *The Letters of
Margaret Fuller.*

I have followed the format of the complete edition: dates and locations
are printed flush right; salutations are flush left, closings flush right. I
have lowered Fuller's superscripts. I have retained Fuller's spellings; editorial additions are contained in square brackets. Square brackets with an
empty space indicate missing matter in the text. Each letter is followed by
the location of the manuscript, identified by the standard Library of
Congress symbol. The symbols are explained in the list of abbreviations.

ROBERT N. HUDSPETH

Ontario, California

ACKNOWLEDGMENTS

For permission to publish letters of Margaret Fuller, I am grateful to Willard P. Fuller. For permission of the owners of the physical letters, I am grateful to the following institutions: the Barnard College Archives; the Bodleian Library of Oxford University; the Trustees of the Boston Public Library, Rare Books and Manuscripts Department; the William Wetmore Story Papers, Rare Books and Manuscripts Library, Columbia University; the Fruitlands Museums, Harvard, Massachusetts; the Stiftung Weimarer Klassik, Goethe- und Schiller-Archiv; the Houghton Library, Harvard University; the Ralph Waldo Emerson Memorial Association and the Houghton Library, Harvard University; the Collections of the Maine Historical Society; the Massachusetts Historical Society; the Middlebury College Library; the Berg Collection of English and American Literature and the Duyckinck Family Papers, Manuscripts and Archives Division, the New York Public Library, Astor, Lenox and Tilden Foundations; the Caroline Wells Healy Dall Papers, the Schlesinger Library, Radcliffe Institute; the Manuscript Collection, Rhode Island Historical Society; the Special Collections, Stanford University Libraries; the Harry Ransom Humanities Research Center, the University of Texas at Austin; the Margaret Fuller Papers, Clifton Waller Barrett Library of American Literature (MSS 7196), Special Collections Department, University of Virginia Library; the Wellesley College Library, Special Collections; the Yale Collection of American Literature, Beinecke Rare Book and Manuscript Library.

I gratefully acknowledge the assistance of the following librarians: Jean Ashton of the Rare Book and Manuscript Library of Columbia University Library; Susan Brady of the Beinecke Rare Book and Manuscript Library of Yale University; Bob Buckeye of the Middlebury College Library; Peter

Drummey of the Massachusetts Historical Society; Carol Falcione of the Barnard College Library; Wayne Furman of the Berg Collection of the New York Public Library; Edward Gaynor of the University of Virginia Library; Susan Glover Godlewski of the Boston Public Library; Marie-Hélène Gold of the Schlesinger Library, the Radcliffe Institute; Rebecca King of the Schlesinger Library, Radcliffe Institute; Sylvia McDowell of the Schlesinger Library, Radcliffe Institute; Betsy Martin of the Unitarian Universalist Association; Leslie A. Morris of the Houghton Library, Harvard University; Ruth R. Rogers of the Wellesley College Library; Timothy Rogers of the Bodleian Library of Oxford University; Christa Rudnik of the Stiftung Weimarer Klassik, Goethe- und Schiller-Archiv; Richard D. Stattler of the Rhode Island Historical Society; Roberto G. Trujillo of the Stanford University Library; Michael A. Volmar of the Fruitlands Museums; Tara Wenger of the Harry Ransom Humanities Research Center of the University of Texas at Austin; and Roberta Zonghi of the Boston Public Library.

I am grateful for the skillful research assistance of Linda Mammano. Barbara H. Salazar of Cornell University Press skillfully edited the volume. As she has done for many years, my wife, Kay Hudspeth, helped with this edition in concrete and intangible ways. My daughters, to whom this book is dedicated, grew up with Margaret Fuller as a presence in our family.

BIOGRAPHICAL SKETCHES

ALCOTT, A. BRONSON (1799–1888)   An imaginative teacher, Alcott began a school at Boston's Masonic Temple in 1834. Fuller was his assistant from December 1836 to April 1837. He later moved to Concord, then, in 1844, established Fruitlands, a utopian farm in Harvard, Massachusetts. In 1859 he became superintendent of the Concord schools.

ARNIM, BETTINA BRENTANO VON (1785–1859)   A peripheral figure in Goethe's literary circle, Bettina Brentano married Ludwig Joachim von Arnim in 1811. Her books *Goethes Briefwechsel mit einem Kinde* and *Die Günderode* were fabrications, though during Fuller's lifetime both were widely read and admired. Fuller translated part of the latter as *Günderode* in 1842.

BROWNING, ELIZABETH BARRETT (1806–61)   Elizabeth Barrett began publishing poetry in 1826. In 1846 she married Robert Browning, and they lived in Florence, where Fuller knew them in 1849–50.

BRUCE, GEORGIANA (1818–87)   Bruce, who was born in England, lived for a time at Brook Farm before she became an assistant at the women's prison at Sing Sing.

CASS, LEWIS, JR. (1813?–78)   Son of a prominent Michigan Democrat politician, Cass was appointed the American chargé d'affaires to the Papal States.

CHANNING, WILLIAM H. (1810–84)   A nephew of Dr. William Ellery Channing, William Henry graduated from Harvard in 1829 and from the Divinity School in 1833, and was ordained in Cincinnati in 1839. He later formed the Society of Christian Union in New York City, and then, in 1854, moved to England. One of Fuller's closest friends in the 1830s and 1840s, Channing was an ardent socialist.

CHAPMAN, MARIA WESTON (1806–85)   Maria Weston married Henry Grafton Chapman in 1830. She was a leader of the Boston Female Anti-Slavery Society, one of the editors of the *Non-Resistant,* and an occasional editor of William Lloyd Garrison's *Liberator.*

CLARKE, JAMES F. (1810–88)   Clarke, a distant cousin of Fuller, was her closest friend and confidant during the 1830s. With him she studied German language and literature. Clarke graduated from Harvard in 1829 and from the Divinity School in 1833. He went to Louisville and served the Unitarian church there until 1840. He returned to Boston in 1841 and organized a new congregation, the Church of the Disciples. In 1835 Clarke founded and edited a literary-religious magazine, *The Western Messenger,* in which Fuller published essays and poems. In 1839 Clarke married Anna Huidekoper.

CLOUGH, ARTHUR HUGH (1819–61)   After graduating from Oxford, Clough became principal of University Hall, London. His poem "Bothie of Toper-na-fuosich" was well regarded. He met Fuller in Rome in May 1849.

DAVIS, GEORGE T. (1810–77)   Like James Clarke, Davis was a distant cousin and a member of Harvard's class of 1829. He became a lawyer and settled in his native Greenfield, Massachusetts. Davis later served in the U.S. House of Representatives and devoted himself to journalism. The details of his friendship with Fuller are scanty, but it is clear that at one time she loved him deeply and was wounded when he rejected her for Harriet T. Russell, whom he married in 1834.

DUYCKINCK, EVERT A. (1816–78)   The editor of Wiley and Putnam's Library of Choice Reading, Duyckinck was a central figure in the Young America movement. In 1847 he founded the magazine *Literary World.* He furthered the career not only of Fuller but of Herman Melville.

DWIGHT, JOHN SULLIVAN (1813–93)   Dwight graduated from Harvard in 1832 and pursued his interest in German literature by editing *Select Minor Poems Translated from the German of Goethe and Schiller* (in which he published Fuller's translations). A graduate in 1836 of the Divinity School in Cambridge, he served only one year at Northampton before leaving the ministry. Dwight lived at Brook Farm and later became a noted Boston music critic.

EMERSON, RALPH WALDO (1803–82)   The most important writer of his generation, Emerson was friend, fellow editor, and symbol for Fuller. From 1836 until her departure for New York City in 1844, Fuller wrote and visited

Emerson frequently. She and he were instrumental in founding the *Dial*, whose editor he became in 1842 upon her resignation. Though ever wary of his closest friends, Emerson called out Fuller's emotional warmth, especially in the early 1840s. His work on the posthumous *Memoirs* simultaneously helped keep her influence alive and diminished her complexity.

FULLER, ABRAHAM WILLIAMS (1784–1847) Timothy Fuller's next younger brother and executor, Abraham was a lawyer but made his modest fortune in real estate. Margaret quarreled bitterly with him over his attempts to dictate to her and her mother after her father's death.

FULLER, ARTHUR BUCKMINSTER (1822–62) Despite a severe eye wound as a young man, Arthur graduated from Harvard in 1843 and from the Divinity School in 1847. He was ordained as a Unitarian minister in Manchester, New Hampshire, in 1848. Arthur served as a chaplain in the Civil War until 1862, when he resigned to enlist in the Union Army. He died the next day at the battle of Fredericksburg.

FULLER, ELLEN KILSHAW (1820–56) Margaret's only surviving sister was a lovely young woman with a strong temper who was ill with tuberculosis her entire adult life. In 1841 she married the poet Ellery Channing, with whom she lived unhappily.

FULLER, EUGENE (1815–59) The next oldest after Margaret, Eugene graduated from Harvard in 1834, studied law with George Farley in Groton, Massachusetts, and became a lawyer, but left the bar to become a newspaperman in New Orleans. On 21 June 1859 he was lost overboard from a ship.

FULLER, MARGARETT C. (1789–1859) The daughter of Peter and Elizabeth Jones Weiser Crane of Canton, Massachusetts, Margarett married Timothy Fuller in 1809 and bore nine children, of whom seven survived.

FULLER, RICHARD FREDERICK (1824–69) Margaret's favorite brother, Richard graduated from Harvard in 1844, studied law with George Davis, and then graduated from the Harvard Law School. He was a melancholic man who took affront quickly, but he staunchly acted as his sister's helper when she was in Italy.

FULLER, TIMOTHY (1778–1835) Her father was the son of a minister. He graduated from Harvard in 1801, studied law, and served in the Massachusetts Senate. In 1817 he began the first of his four terms as United States representative from Cambridge. After his retirement from Washington in 1825, he was elected to the Massachusetts House. Failing to win the expected patronage of John Quincy Adams, whom he had supported in the election of 1824, Fuller retired, first to return to his law practice and then to become a farmer in Groton, where he died suddenly of cholera.

GREENWOOD, CATHARINE AMELIA (1810–67)   Greenwood was one of Fuller's closest girlhood friends. In 1834 she married George Bartlett, a Boston physician.

HEDGE, FREDERIC HENRY (1805–90)   One of Fuller's close intellectual friends, Hedge, after study in Germany, graduated from Harvard in 1825 and from the Divinity School in 1828. He became a Unitarian minister but was known early in his career as an accomplished scholar who helped introduce German thought to the United States. When Emerson formed the group later known as the Transcendental Club, he called it Hedge's Club, for the group met when Hedge came to town from his pastorate in Bangor, Maine. Later in life Hedge was on the Harvard faculty, first as professor of ecclesiastical history and then as professor of German.

HOAR, ELIZABETH SHERMAN (1814–78)   The daughter of Samuel Hoar of Concord, Elizabeth was engaged to Charles Emerson when he died in 1836. Waldo Emerson thereafter considered her a sister. She and Fuller were close friends.

HOWITT, MARY BOTHAM (1799–1888)   Mary Botham, a prolific writer of poetry and children's stories and a translator, married William Howitt in 1821. Fuller met her in London and later corresponded with her from the continent.

JAMESON, ANNA BROWNELL (1794–1860)   Mrs. Jameson was an Irish writer who knew Ottilie Goethe and helped to popularize German culture with her 1834 *Visits and Sketches at Home and Abroad.*

LORING, ELLIS GRAY (1803–58)   A wealthy and socially prominent Boston lawyer, Loring helped to found the New England Anti-Slavery Society.

LORING, LOUISA GILMAN (1797–1868)   She married Ellis Loring in 1827.

MAZZINI, GIUSEPPE (1805–72)   A heroic figure to Fuller, Mazzini was an Italian revolutionary patriot who had been exiled to France and then to England, where she met him in 1846 at Thomas Carlyle's home. Shortly after his triumphant return to Rome to lead the newly founded republic, Mazzini visited Fuller. She unfailingly championed him and his vision in her dispatches to the *New-York Tribune,* saying: "He is one of those same beings who, measuring all things by the ideal standard, have yet no time to mourn over failure or imperfection."

NATHAN, JAMES (1811–88)   A shadowy, important man in Fuller's life, Nathan was one of a series of men whom she loved in vain. A German businessman, he came to the United States in 1830, left in 1845, and later settled in Hamburg. Fuller immediately fell in love with him when they met on New Year's Eve 1845, but he appears first to have misunderstood her and later to have fled her emotional intensity.

NEWCOMB, CHARLES KING (1820–94)   One of several young men whom Emerson thought a genius but who never fulfilled his promise, Newcomb graduated from Brown in 1837, tried his hand at writing (Emerson published one of his essays in the *Dial*), and lived for a time at Brook Farm. He later became a businessman in his native Providence.

OSSOLI, GIOVANNI ANGELO (d. 1850)   Fuller's husband was the son of Marchese Filippo Ossoli, the head of a noble Roman family. During the revolution Giovanni and his brother Giuseppe took opposite sides: Giovanni was a member of the Civic Guard while Giuseppe was in the papal service. Giovanni and Fuller probably, though not certainly, married in 1849.

PEABODY, SOPHIA (1809–71)   Sophia was one of three daughters of Nathaniel and Elizabeth Palmer Peabody of Salem. All three were friends of Fuller. Sophia married Nathaniel Hawthorne in 1842.

RIPLEY, GEORGE (1802–80)   Ripley graduated from Harvard in 1823 and from the Divinity School in 1826. He became the minister at Boston's Purchase Street Church until he left the ministry in 1841 to found Brook Farm. In 1827 he married Fuller's friend Sophia Dana (1803–61). After Brook Farm failed, Ripley became a writer for the *New-York Daily Tribune*, a position Fuller had held.

ROTCH, MARY (1777–1848)   A member of a prominent Quaker family in New Bedford, Mary Rotch was called Aunt Mary by both Fuller and Emerson.

SHAW, SARAH (1815–1902)   The daughter of Nathaniel Russell and Susan Parkman Sturgis, Sarah married Francis George Shaw (1809–82). Children of Boston gentry, they became ardent abolitionists and socialists. Their son was Robert Gould Shaw, the leader of the black regiment that fought at Fort Wagner. Fuller knew Sarah and her family from childhood.

SPRING, MARCUS (1810–74)   Spring was a dry goods merchant who became a prominent reformer. It was on his estate that the Raritan Bay Community was founded. In 1836 Spring married Rebecca Buffum (1811–1911), daughter of Arnold Buffum, a founder of the New England

Anti-Slavery Society. The Springs persuaded Fuller to accompany them to Europe in 1846 and probably paid part of her expenses.

STORY, EMELYN (1820–94)   Emelyn Eldredge married William Wetmore Story in 1843. Fuller knew them both in Boston, though she was cool toward them. In Italy, however, she and Emelyn became fast friends. It was to her that Fuller entrusted her son's birth certificate during the peril of the French invasion of the Roman Republic in 1849.

STURGIS, CAROLINE (1819–88)   Fuller's closest friend, Caroline Sturgis was the daughter of a wealthy Boston merchant, William Sturgis, and his wife, Elizabeth Davis. In 1847 Caroline married William Aspinwall Tappan. The couple settled in Lenox, Massachusetts, where they became the center of an intellectual community that at one time included Hawthorne, who rented their home. Caroline Tappan later wrote children's books.

THOREAU, HENRY D. (1817–62)   Fuller liked Thoreau personally, but she was a stern critic of the young man's writing. She rejected his essay "The Service," but she did publish five of his poems in the *Dial.*

TRACY, ALBERT HALLER (1793–1859)   A native of Connecticut, Tracy moved to New York in 1811 and entered Congress as a member from Buffalo in 1819. He and Fuller's father were friends. After leaving the House in 1825 (the same year Timothy Fuller retired), Tracy declined offers of cabinet posts and unsuccessfully sought a Senate seat from New York.

WARD, ANNA BARKER (1813–1900)   Anna Hazard Barker was the daughter of Jacob Barker of New Orleans, who made, lost, and remade fortunes. A woman of great beauty and grace, Anna remained Fuller's lifelong friend even after Anna married Samuel G. Ward, whom Fuller also loved.

WARD, SAMUEL G. (1817–1907)   Son of a prominent banker with Baring Brothers, Sam Ward showed early promise as a painter but instead followed his father into Baring's. Fuller, who for years called him Raphael, idealized and loved him deeply. His marriage to Anna Barker in 1840 was a crisis in Fuller's life, but it did not end her friendship with the Wards. Later, in her Italian years, Fuller relied on Ward for financial advice and a loan.

WHITMAN, SARAH HELEN POWER(1803–78)   The daughter of Nicholas and Anna Marsh Power, Sarah Helen married John Winslow Whitman in 1828. After his death in 1833 she became a writer and the center of a lively intellectual community in Providence when Fuller taught there. In 1848 Whitman was briefly engaged to Edgar Allan Poe (who addressed his "To Helen" to her).

Abbreviations

The locations of the manuscripts of the letters in this volume are identified by the standard Library of Congress symbols:

CSt   Stanford University Library

CtY   Yale University Library

MB   Boston Public Library, Department of Rare Books and Manuscripts

MCR-S   Radcliffe College, Schlesinger Library

MeHi   Maine Historical Society Library

MH   Harvard University, Houghton Library

MH-AH   Andover-Harvard Library, Harvard Divinity School

MHarF   Fruitlands Museums, Harvard, Massachusetts

MHi   Massachusetts Historical Society

MWelC   Wellesley College Library

NN-B   New York Public Library, Henry W. and Albert A. Berg Collection

NN-M   New York Public Library, Manuscripts and Archives Division

NNC   Columbia University Library

NNC-B   Barnard College Library

NNPM   Pierpont Morgan Library, New York City

RHi   Rhode Island Historical Society

TxU   University of Texas, Harry H. Ransom Humanities Research Center

ViU   University of Virginia Library

VtMiM   Middlebury College Library

I

Hold On in Courage of Soul

1818–1839

Hold on in courage of soul.

————————

When Sarah Margaret Fuller was born, on 23 May 1810, her father was a successful lawyer who had moved to the outskirts of Cambridge, Massachusetts. His first child, she was an object of his love and devotion, which he expressed by expecting much of her. Timothy Fuller shaped his daughter's mind as he would try to shape the minds of his sons, but only she was fully fit to profit from the regimen that he imposed. She early learned languages; she read widely in popular literature, in political economy, philosophy, history, poetry, and drama. Margaret had the advantage of Timothy's own classical training at Harvard and his insistence that things be done in an orderly manner. She grew up with a combination of tutelage at home and private schools in Boston and Groton, and, finally, she underwent an intense course of self-instruction. Although she later remembered those days as harsh and deforming, for she had nightmares and periods of anxiety, the letters she wrote at the time make it abundantly clear that she also danced at Harvard balls, shared enthusiasms with a circle of young women, and was thoroughly at home in the local social life. She even fell in love with George Davis, a distant cousin, but he disappointed her.

Her intellectual development did not slow down, for in her teens she became intensely interested in German literature and rapidly cultivated fluency in the language. This was a time when German had come to dominate the scholarly world of theology, but Fuller was more interested in the literary works of Goethe, Novalis, Schiller, and others. She was, of course, self-taught, but she was able to talk to and correspond with Frederic Henry Hedge, a deeply learned minister who had studied in Germany. She asked his advice, read what he suggested, and then challenged him to give her new directions.

Even more important was her friendship with yet another distant cousin, James Freeman Clarke, who shared her passion for German literature. Fortunately for us, Clarke left New England to take a pastorate in Louisville, thus making it necessary for Fuller to write often and in detail to him. It is through these letters that we now get the best insight into the mind of a brilliant young woman as she expands her knowledge and develops her own critical power. But it was not literature alone that prompted the letters, for Fuller was willing to keep Clarke up to date about the goings on in Cambridge and Boston, and so we have a corresponding record of life among their friends in New England.

But Margaret's father put an end to that life when he moved the family to Groton, some forty miles from Cambridge. Fuller felt isolated and balked, so she turned to her books, even more determined to keep abreast of the world of letters. All too soon, however, disaster fell: her father suddenly died of cholera on 1 October 1835. Though he had been successful, Timothy had not left the family on a sound financial basis, so the family faced an immediate need for action. Margaret had just been invited to go abroad in the company of Samuel G. Ward (a young man who became her second love) and John and Eliza Farrar, a Harvard professor of mathematics and his wife. Fuller, of course, had to decline the trip and look for employment. Her only choice was teaching, for she was not yet practiced enough to think of herself as a professional author, and even if she were rash enough to try, the probability of making a living with her pen was small. So teach she did.

Her first opportunity came when she found that Bronson Alcott needed an assistant at his Temple School in Boston. An educational reformer and philosopher, Alcott had tried to teach in radically new ways, among them the use of Socratic dialogues with his pupils. Elizabeth Peabody had been Alcott's first teacher and recorder of the talks with the children, but the subject matter sometimes bordered on sexuality and the manhood of Jesus—topics that could and did cause scandal—so Peabody resigned. Fuller took the position in 1836, only to find Alcott interesting but improvident, for he could not pay her for her efforts. It was, then, with some relief that she received an offer to teach in Providence, where Hiram Fuller (no relation) had established a school on Alcott's principles but on a firmer financial basis. He offered Fuller a handsome salary of $1,000 a year and the freedom to teach the girls in the school as she wished. In midsummer 1837 she accepted the offer.

In one way it was not a propitious time for Fuller to leave Massachusetts, for she had finally made the acquaintance of the man most electrifying to young intellectuals—Ralph Waldo Emerson, at whose home she spent a satisfying visit in July 1836 and again in May and June 1837. But because

Emerson lived in Concord, they could stay in touch only by letters, so Fuller began another significant correspondence.

She was a successful teacher in Providence, and she became a part of a lively intellectual circle of men and women, but she liked neither the city nor the teaching. She fretted under the daily routine of instruction, and she was impatient with the complacent, rather conservative bent of her Providence acquaintances. Inevitably she gave it all up, even though the financial reward was substantial. Early in 1839 she went back to Boston, where she gave private lessons and translated Johann Peter Eckermann's *Gespräche mit Goethe,* a "table talk" book of conversations with the master. Fortunately for Fuller, George Ripley had begun a series of translations of German works, Specimens of Foreign Standard Literature, and he accepted her work for publication.

At the same time Fuller planned a new project: in November 1839 she organized a series of "Conversations" for women in Boston. Participants paid $10 to join. Fuller would begin each session by offering an opinion and then draw out her participants in a conversational give-and-take. The series was highly successful, for it gave Fuller an income, and it was very attractive to the women, some of whom were also prominent intellectuals; others were the wives of public men in the Boston area. Fuller was a natural conversationalist, so she was able to exploit this modification of the lecture format for five years. She gave semiannual courses and opened some of them to men—unhappily, it turned out, for the men, as might have been predicted, dominated the discussions and silenced the women. But her Conversations limited to women seem to have been consistently successful and strengthened her public presence.

During those years Fuller's friendship with Sam Ward grew into love, but, like Davis before him, Ward did not respond to her. She thought Ward a promising young painter and encouraged him to develop his talent, but he was in fact headed to Baring Brothers to join his father as a banker. Even more confounding was the fact that Ward fell in love with one of Fuller's close friends, Anna Barker, a beauty from New Orleans whom Fuller deeply admired. Sam and Anna married on Ward's birthday, 3 October 1840, a date Fuller noted each succeeding year.

Readers will find in the letters in this section a record of Fuller's growth from childhood to maturity. These letters show clearly how important German literature was to her and how liberated she felt in exploring it. The letters chart the emotions of a woman trying to find her place in a world that offers her few opportunities. She loves and loses two men, her father dies, and she makes her first, successful ventures outward into a professional life as conversationalist and writer.

1.   To Timothy Fuller

Cambridgeport. 16 Dec. 1818.

Dear Papa.

I was very sorry to hear of your accident.[1] I dreamed the night Mamma recieved your letter that you were sick and your life was despaired of when you suddenly recovered. I hope the latter will be accomplished not the former. Papa I do not suppose you think it a good excuse to say that I could not write. No Papa nor do I either for I could have done it. But I have been like Basil in the "Tomorrow" and have determined to be so no longer. I am resolved to write you every week. I have requested Mamma often to let me learn to make puddings and pies. Now I will tell you what I study Latin twice a week and Arithmetick when Aunt Elizabeth is here. If you have spies they will certainly inform you that we are not very dissipated. We have been three times to Dr. Williams and once to Mr Gannetts Aunt Elizabeth often goes to Boston. Eugene has got well but William Henry is rather fretful today. Eugene was very much pleased to recieve your letter but I found it began to grow dirty and took it into custody. Mamma has given me one of the arches to put my letters in for I hope you will write to me when you are not more usefully employed. I do not see how I have contrived to write without being forced to search my brain for something to say except your letter furnished a variety of topicks for I cannot write a long letter seldom more than a page and a half neither do I see how you and Mamma write so much. Perhaps I shall now though. It will take you fifteen minutes to read this letter and me an hour to write it. You say a relation of your pain would be uninterresting to any but an affectionate wife. Do not forget that I am Your afectionate Daughter

SARAH M FULLER

(MH: fMS Am 1086 [9:4])

1. On his trip from Boston to Washington, Fuller's stage had overturned.

2.   To Timothy Fuller

Cambridge. 16 January 1820

My dear father

I received your letter of the 29th about a week ago[.] I should have written to you much sooner but have been very busy. I begin to be anxious about my letter of the 28th which you do not mention having received in any of your letters. If it has not miscarried it reached you a fortnight ago. Your letter to me was dated the day after mine was written but you do not mention it in any of your letters to Mamma.—

I attend a school which is kept by Aunt Abigail for *Eugene* and *myself* and my *cousins* which with writing and singing schools and my lessons to Uncle Elisha takes up *most* of my time—

I *have* not written to Miss *Kilshaw yet as* there is no opportunity of sending our letters.[1] *Deep rooted* indeed is my affection for her May it flourish an *ever* blooming flower till our kindred spirits absolved from earthly day mount together to those blissful regions where never again we shall be seperated. I am not romantic, I am not making professions when I say I love Ellen better than my life. I love her better and reverence her more for her misfortunes. Why should I not she is as lovely as sweet tempered as before. These were what I loved before and as she possesses all these now why should my love diminish. Ought it not rather to increase as she has more need of it. It is for herself alone I grieve for the loss of fortune She will be exposed to many a trial a temptation she would otherwise have escaped Not but I know she will go through them all No But I shall feel *all* her sorrows—

You will let me read Zeluco?[2] will you not and no conditions. Have you been to the theatre this winter? Have they any oratorios at Washington?— I am writing a new tale called The young satirist. You must expect the remainder of this page to be filled with a series of unconnected intelligence My beautiful pen now makes a large mark I will write no farther. 17th January 1820

Yesterday I threw by my pen for the reason mentioned above. Have you read Hesitation yet. I knew you would (though you are no novel reader) to see if they were rightly delineated for I am possessed of the greatest blessing of life a good and kind father. Oh I can never repay you for all the love you have shown me But I will do all I can

We have had a dreadful snowstorm today. I never look around the room and behold all the comforts with which Heaven has blessed me without thinking of those *wretched* creatures who are wandering in all the snow without food or shelter. I am too young No I am not. In nine years a great part of my life I can remember but two good actions done those more out of sefishness than charity. There is a poor woman of the name of Wentworth in Boston she would willingly procure a subsistence but has not the means. My dear father a dollar would be a great sum to this poor woman. You remember the handsome dollar that I know your generosity would have bestowed on when I had finished my Deserted Village I shall finish it well and desire nothing but the pleasure of giving it to

her. My dear father send it to me immediately I am going into town this
week I have a thousand things to say but neither time or paper to say
them in.

Farewel my dear Father I am Your affectionate daughter

MARGARET FULLER

P S I do not like Sarah, call me Margaret alone, pray do!

(MH: fMS Am 1086 [9:11])

1. Ellen Kilshaw, whom Fuller called "the first angel of my life," lived in Liverpool but had
visited her sister in Cambridgeport, where she met the Fullers.

2. John Moore, *Zeluco: Various Views of Human Nature Taken from Life and Manners, Foreign
and Domestic* (London, 1789).

3.   To Margarett C. Fuller

Boston. December 9th. 1821

Dearest mother,

I received or rather grandmother did my fathers letter on the 7th. I do
not think his plan of making you his secretary a very feasible plan. I fancy
you will be too much engaged besides you do not write half so fast as he
can, and are not sufficiently fond of letter writing; do tell my father that I
expect some letters from him. You know mother that I am not a very good
dancer. I wish to go to Mr Park's dancing school. I do not think it would
interfere with my studies as it will keep only Thursday an[d] Saturday and
I should have all the evenings to myself. I wish you would let me know
your determination as quickly as possible as this quarter will finish a week
from next Tuesday. Uncle Williams is better, but he says it is very hard for
him to lie in bed so, and so hungry too. Poor Susan is confined to her bed.
Last Teusday night she had shivering fits, she went to bed but was attacked again in the morning, and is now quite ill. I went to Mr
Frothingham's on Thanksgiving day and heard Mr Everet.[1] I liked his sermon or rather lecture much except two or three expressions which I
could not understand such as "the active centres of fermentation and in
my opinion his pronunciation was not very good. The meeting house was
very much crowded and there was some excellent singing. They say that
the choir at Mr. F's is the best in Boston. I believe I did not tell you in my
former letter that uncle Abraham had carried me and aunt Sarah and the
two girls to the ampitheatre. The performance was Blue Beard, in which
we had the pleasure of seeing fire, smoke, battles, death, blood, skeletons
and all the ghostly preparations.[2] But there were many beautiful horses

and some of the performances really wonderful. One of the little ponies being ordered to jump through a balloon went and stuck his nose through the paper and then not liking the sport ran back. An Arabian horse kept excellent time to the tune of Nancy Dawson. By the way uncle Abraham says that he had as lieve see Mr Whittiers children take a cane and ride around the room as hear me play on the piano and that it came as near to these performances as my music did to that of Mrs Holman and Mrs French. Uncle Elisha asked me if I talked to him about it on purpose to quarrel with him I shall not ever play before him I fancy tho' he says I may when he is asleep. My best love to papa I am your affectionate daughter

SARAH M FULLER.

(MH: fMS Am 1086 [9:20])

1. Nathaniel Langdon Frothingham (1793–1870) was the minister at Boston's First Church; his brother-in-law, Edward Everett (1794–1865), was famous as an orator. Then professor of Greek at Harvard, Everett was later a member of both houses of Congress, governor of Massachusetts, ambassador to Great Britain, and president of Harvard.

2. *Bluebeard,* a popular melodramatic opera by George Colman the younger (1762–1836), had first been performed in London in 1798.

4. To Timothy Fuller

Cambridge. 25th. Jan. 1824.

My dearest father,

I was delighted a short time ago by receiving a letter from you. I should very much prefer going to Mr Emerson's on every account, and if I go to Miss Prescott's I must be compelled to give up seeing you at all.[1] But if you wish it, I am willing to go, only, I hope you will not keep me there very long. I would give you the particulars of Miss Pratts party, as you desire, but it is so long ago I have really forgotten them. I was very happy, I am passionately fond of dancing and there is none at all in Cambridge except at the Cotillon parties. I thank you most sincerely, my beloved father, for the interest you take in my pleasures. Be assured, I will do all that is in my power to manifest my gratitude for the indulgence and kindness you have ever shown in endeavoring to gratify even my slightest wishes. I think there never was so kind and affectionate a father as you and I am most profoundly and ardently sensible of it. At Miss Wells's there was dancing to the piano, singing, music, and chess. I played "Mary list awake," Bruce's address to his army,"—and "Oh this is the spot." Miss[e]s Gray and Wells accompanied me on the flute and flageolet. Miss Channing Miss Cochran and Miss Brewster, who have all delightful voices sang and played. I was particularly pleased with Miss Cochran's singing, for though her voice is neither very powerful, nor of great compass; I think it is the most soft and melodious I ever heard. Miss Howard did not sing well at all. There was great difficulty in prevailing on her to sing and when she did, she played without any apparent diffidence to the middle of the tune, when she suddenly b[r]oke off and buried her face in her hands. Every one thought that she was very silly and affected, and some gentlemen told me she always did just the same thing, and they supposed she thought it graceful and practised it at home for effect. Misses Spooner and Pratt played for us to dance, and my partner for the two first dances was Mr Ripley, who had the first part last Commencement, and as you thought spoke so finely. Afterwards I danced with Messrs Lunt, Newell, Emerson and Denny, Adeline Denny's brother. There is to be a Cotillon party this week. If you were at home, I am sure Mother would be willing that I should go, when she knew you I wished it. Elisabeth Ware, Charlotte M'Kean, Abba D'Wolfe, the Misses Hilliard indeed all the young ladies of my age in Cambridge except Harriette Alston H Fay and poor Sarah M. Fuller are going, and Sarah M. is going to Groton next summer and in all human probability will not go to a dance this two years. If there was time for Mother to receive a letter from you, signifying your desire, that I should go, I am sure she would let me, but that cannot be, as the party is on Thursday.

You have I suppose received a letter from Uncle Elisha, giving you the particulars of his being exposed to the infection of the small pox. But I do not believe he can have caught it. Uncle Abraham has written to him advising him not to avoid it by any means. Uncle A has been inoculated for the kine pock again, and mother thinks she shall be so too. Mother was very unwell yesterday, she seemed very feverish and I feared that she would be sick, but she appears much better to day. Have you any objection to my having my music bound. I can get it done in two volumes, half binding for two dollars. I am extremely obliged to you for your permission to buy a Graeca Minora. Dearest father, yr most affectionate daughter

Sarah Margaret Fuller.

(MH: fMS Am 1086 [9:24])

1. Her father did send her to Groton to attend the school of Susan Prescott (1796–1869).

5. To George T. Davis

Cambridge. 23d Jany. 1830

My dear Cousin,

You profess yourself satisfied with my religious opinions— Yet most persons would consider them as amounting to what you deprecate believing, even "temporarily," ie, Deism. I do not myself consider them in this light, because I do not *dis*believe or even *carelessly set aside* Revelation; I merely remain in ignorance of the Christian Revelation because I do not feel it suited to me at present. And the reason you yourself have given; "The philosophers" you say "appealed to the intellect,—Christ to the sympathies"— And these sympathies I do not wish to foster— Shall I quicken the heart to a sense of its wants when I can so ill supply those of the mind?— I shall write no formal answer to what you say, but any-thing that occurs to you will be welcome interesting to me. And sometimes I shall speak. At any rate I like to have your thoughts by me in their own garb and colors—I am too apt to retain only impressions from a conversation.— I thought there was *much* in your views of Leonard Wood's character, though indeed you did seem to have measured him rather by the standard of personal comparison than by that of perfection. This is natural enough!— But there is great beauty and truth in what you say— "Too intellectual to be sympathizing" And I was struck too by what you say of the acceptance in which Heaven holds generous faith.— I have read Leonard Woods's letter often and cannot but think of his prophetick fear that half stimulating contact might produce that sameness in the intellectual world, never to be dreaded in the material.

I believe I understand about Mr Wilde; I hope you will tell me a great deal when you come back. James did sketch a little but not with spirit.— In truth I did not know when I began how exhausted I was. I have taken a long walk the first for a fortnight, paid two decent visits, and one at Mrs Higginson's very long and most pleasantly exciting— Then my Journal does exhaust me. I felt charmed by the image presented by Neal in Miller's obituary; ie Miller seeing his life for months, the substance of his existence, his present Soul whelmed in the vasty deep when others but wondered at his grief in loving his thick logbook.[1] I thought to put my soul *without* me too— and began to keep a Journal this year in *fearless sincerity*. It is my very life in all its moods and tenses, strength and folly, beauty and deformity. But the habit of keeping it gives an aching intensity to my thoughts. In pursuing this Record I feel all the pains and fascinations of the most intimate confidential intercourse without its sweetness, its composing and sustaining influences. But I shall keep it through the year unless I find it goes nigh to break my heart or turn my brain— Tis indeed a most fascinating employ and the return to *any* common employment is generally highly distasteful to me. I felt greatly inclined to write to you this eveg but I must defer the rest till tomorrow. I have just read a letter from Marian Marshall to Amelia; she seems *good* and happy Amelia is reading Brown's novels. If I get excited writing tomorrow I should forget these little items. Marian inquires after you; she has met a "James Clarke man" now.

Sunday eveg— I have been reading the foregoing two pages— and far from thinking them most "excellent" they seem to me very very dull— but I am at present excited and hope your receptive feelings will be more propitious. You will be pleased to hear that I have been most happy. Henry Hedge came for me about four oclock this afternoon and I went with him home to his father's whence I have just returned. And I never can feel more perfect enjoyment from any one's conversation. I return satisfied on many points and shall feel the pleasurable effects of the conversation for weeks. I feel as if I had taken into my mind his new metaphysicks, experience new beautiful things he has seen and known, and new beautiful imaginings. There was no one there and Mrs [Hedge] after observing "that Henry and Margaret thought themselves such high geniuses that nobody could get up to or comprehend them" was so kind as to interfere no further. But what did I mean to tell *you*? Oh! I asked Henry "whether, if he had not chosen the profession of a Christian Divine, he should not have contented his youth with Natural religion and remained ignorant of Christianity."— He said he should have waived the subject to later years probably, because he had an impression that Christianity appealed rather to the sympathies than the intellect; but he was mistaken, that he had found in this religion a home for theories cherished before, nearly all of novel or peculiar that he had added, with the most beautifully profound views of life.— I thought you might like to hear his opinion of this.— Ah! What pleasure to meet with such a daring yet realizing mind as his!—But the fine things which I heard and the also fine things which I myself said, thought, and shall think shall be inscribed on the pages of my journal since I cannot keep my records in "hearts" as you do. However my memoranda shall be always with me and at my command. I doubt your being as well assured of yours.— Talking of hearts La belle I fancy is submitting the well filled leaves of hers to the comprehending eye of Mr Hutchinson who is reported to have said "that he had for the first time found an echo to his feelings in those of Miss Fay"— You see I persist in giving you les nouvelles de vos amies despite your *remarks*. This letter is hardly worth sending and scarcely legible for I hold the paper in one hand and write with the other, however, be merciful for the sake of your cousin

M.

(MCR-S)

1. James William Miller published the *Boston Literary Gazette,* which he had merged with John Neal's *Yankee.* An opium addict, Miller died in 1829. In his obituary, Neal favorably compared Miller's journal to De Quincey: "every wild vision of his heart, every strange colour and shape of his fiery and bewildered imagination had a place there." Neal later published Fuller's story "Lost and Won."

6.   To Amelia Greenwood

Lynn Oct 17 1830

My dear, amiable, arrogant friend,

I just met the gentle Jamis who says there's a letter in the P.O. from thee to me, whereupon je vous ecris (rhyme you may par parenthèse)— I went thereunto yesterday and not finding said epistle according to thy promise did in a rage vow to leave thee, promise breaker, in ignorance of all the interesting tidings to me appurtaining but I find you as heretofore better than my thought. I am *"perfectly happy"* Deep in a vale the cottage stands of David and Almira" I spend all the sunny hours in rambling over richly wooded hills which overlook your pet ocean! The house is, to my taste, charming and a lovely brook fusses and babbles before it— Almira is enchantingly droll and piquante— Elisabeth is more sweet and lovely than ever and I in highest glee— We have seen some very decent world's people; I have no books but in lieu have amused the odd minutes in exploring Mr and Mrs B's private correspondence. I was right glad to see James Stuart's bright handsome face. He was not gay though. Tomorrow we are going to Nahant, Mr Dodge's &c I believe. James Clarke looks wondrous well; like former times today; I have no ideas in my head and cannot give you what I don't possess. If you'd ride down some afternoon I know Almira would be glad to see you; why cant you come with Marian if she's well enough?

Love to Ann—

M.

(MH: Autograph File)

7. To James F. Clarke

[11 February 1831]

"I'll gang, I'll gang, Lord William, she said For ye've left me nae ither guide."[1]

And I may say so to you, my cousin, inasmuch as I have no way to answer your very kind and polite invite save by coming into town. Had you awaited my decision, I believe I should have contented myself with a *lecture* by way of evening amusement, being very desirous to inform myself tonight respecting tomorrow's eclipse, that I might not meet that delightful incident as an *entire* stranger and still more because my hon. papa (who little knows that when I leave home tis but to *vary* the *scene* of drudging my fingers with needles and my head with ideas) (well! This *is* a sentence; I always had supposed my style to be clear and concise; where was I) oh?) my papa coming home last night full of the anticipation of folding to his heart his long-lost daughter M. met her on the threshold just departing to that scene of *riot* and heartless dissipation a *levee;* and on the occasion gave vent to some expressions of disappointment and anguish which cut me to the heart. True! they did not prevent my going out *when I was dressed,* but they *would* have prevented my *dressing* to go out tonight (*especially* as there is nobody at home to fix my hair) tonight could I have let you know— Oh dear! I *must* come to the point. The state of things is this— My mamma is dining in town at this moment. She was to have come out in the stage; I will ride to her in a sleigh wherein she may ride out and if she will dress my hair; I will thereafter come to your house where I will have left this note on my way to Avon Place. But as to *conversation,*— I shall expect you to protect me from having a word of French spoken to me it would frighten me; I am too sensitive and enthusiastick to converse in any foreign tongue— "But there is something more," to use your own lucid form of connection; I am obliged by your mother and sister's politeness but believe I shall stay the *night* with Elizabeth.[2]

Now my dear James; dont you ever write a note again without giving a person a chance to answer it— And let me tell you I expect a little more ceremony even from you, mon ami, *bien*-connu— Is that French? No, yes, no matter— In English let me say— read Lamb and never more subscribe "*Yours &c!* to your

 affectionate cousin

                M.

(MHi)

1. From "The Douglas Tragedy," a ballad that Walter Scott published in his *Minstrelsy of the Scottish Border.*

2. Elizabeth Wells Randall (1811–67), daughter of Dr. John Randall of Boston, figures prominently in the letters between Fuller and Clarke. Clarke came to love Elizabeth, but Fuller, though a close friend to both of them, interfered in the match. Elizabeth later married Alfred Cumming of Georgia, who became the governor of the Utah Territory.

8. To James F. Clarke

7th August 1832.

Dear James,

Where are you, and what doing? and *why* dont you come here? I feel quite lost; it is so long since I have talked myself— To see so many acquaintances, to talk so many words and never tell my mind completely on any subject. To say so many things which do not seem *called out* makes me feel strangely *vague* and *moveable.*—

'Tis true the time is probably near when I must live alone to all intents and purposes— separate entirely my acting from my thinking world, take care of my ideas without aid (c'est a dire except from the "illustrious dead") answer my own questions, correct my own feelings and do all that "hard work" for myself— How tiresome 'tis to find out all one's self-delusion— I thought myself so very independant because I could conceal *some* feelings at will and did not need the *same* excitement as other young characters did— And I am not independant nor never shall be while I can get any-body to minister to me. But I shall go where there is never a spirit to come if I call ever so loudly— But I dont wish to anticipate the time when stones and running brooks shall be my only companions— and I wish to talk with you now about the *Germans*

I have not got any-body to speak to that does not talk common place— And I wish to talk about such an uncommon person—About Novalis!—[1] a wondrous youth— and who has only written *one volume.* That is pleasant! I feel as if I could pursue my natural mode with him, get acquainted, then make my mind easy in the belief that I know all that is to be known. And he died at twenty-nine, and as with Korner your feelings may be single, you will never be called upon to share his experience and compare his future feelings with his present.[2] And his life was so full and so still.

—Then it is a relief after feeling the immense superiority of Goethe.[3] It seems to me as if the mind of Goethe had embraced the universe— I have felt that so much lately in reading his lyric poems— I am enchanted while I read; he comprehends every feeling I ever had so perfectly, expresses it so beautifully, but when I shut the book, it seems as if

I had lost my personal identity— All my feelings linked with such an immense variety that belong to beings I had thought so different. What can I bring? There is no answer in my mind except "It is so" or "It will be so" or "No doubt such and such feel so"— Yet while my judgement becomes daily more tolerant towards others the same attracting and repelling work is going on in my feelings. But I persevere in reading the great sage some part of every day, hoping the time will come when I shall not feel so overwhelmed and leave off this habit of wishing to grasp the whole and be content to learn a little every-day as becomes so mere a pupil. But now the one-sidedness, imperfection and glow of a mind like Novalis's seem refreshingly human to me. I have wished fifty times to write some letters giving an account first of his very pretty life and then of his one volume as I re-read it chapter by chapter— If you will pretend to be very much interested perhaps I will get a better pen and write them to you. But you know I must have people interested that I may speak. And I wish to ask you, now I think of it whether you feel as I expect people to feel about the *tasteless want of reserve* exhibited in my hand-writing. I see I shall never improve— Now though I sat down with the best resolves I have written this letter just as usual. And so in my journal and even extract-books If I were a princess I would have a secretary and never write another line— I always fancy whoever reads this handwriting must see all my faults. And I dont like to have them seen without my consent.—

I called on *Miss Smith* when in town but forgot to ask about your letter in proper times. Mark this— Amelia was charmed with your visit which you thought such a failure— "Such is the nature of social intercourse" Did you ever receive my invite for that Sunday eveg to meet Helen It is well you did not come. She was very angry with me again and probably you might have come in for a share— So much thunder and lightning is rather fatiguing— I dont think I shall venture near her soon

Mr Henry has returned to Cambridge and many other little things have happened which I cant take the trouble to write— Miss Woodward told me she had lately seen and liked you very much "Indeed she had always been interested in you on account of your family &c" Did you like *her*?— Have you seen Elizh—She is well and divides her time between hard piano practice and the study of *Johnson* and Mrs *Chapone*!—

This is a sad blotting half-sheet I have taken, but I shall send this whole scrawl. I feel so much more natural since I began to write that I dare say I have nothing more to tell you and you need not come here. But write if you have encountered any-thing new or pretty. I must not expect die Grosse und Schöne.— With love to Sarah[4] if she be with you yours

M.

James Freeman Clarke. Courtesy of the Unitarian Universalist Association archives.

(MHi)

1. Friedrich, Freiherr von Hardenberg (1772–1801), known as Novalis, published his *Hymnen an die Nacht* in 1800. After his death, Friedrich Schlegel and Ludwig Tieck gathered his writings in a two-volume edition, *Novalis Schriften* (Berlin, 1802), which contained aphorisms and two fragmentary novels, *Die Lehringe zu Sais* and *Heinrich von Ofterdingen*.

2. Karl Theodor Körner (1791–1813), author of five tragedies and five comedies, had been killed in the Napoleonic Wars.

3. Both Fuller and Clarke were avidly reading widely in the work of Johann Wolfgang Goethe (1749–1832). While she never finished her planned biography of him, she did translate his conversations with Johann Peter Eckermann and she published an extensive article on him in the *Dial*.

4. Clarke's sister, Sarah Ann (1808–96), an artist who was Fuller's close friend.

9.   To James F. Clarke

[2? July 1833]
Tuesday aft

I send inclosed a somewhat and tautological epistle dating Sunday.[1] I have been still more moonstruck since, for last eveg surpassed Sunday's in beauty as much as that does a hideous, glaring January noon— Eclipse of the Moon on one side Heavens dome Opposite incessant glows of the very finest lightning above those deep blue, (but then black) hills which you remember and the air one continued sigh of delight. Verily the beauties of nature may be sympathized withal, nor can such hours of communion leave behind dregs and bitterness they *are* "marvellously good." I think I should prefer a desert for my dwelling place to a convent.

And to-day is so luxurious, so warm so fragrant. O! it would be Elysium to have just performed some great and glorious deed, or to have just finished some beautiful work the Apollo Belvidere for instance or Shakespeare's Tempest and to pause this day and feel creation and one's self a worthy part thereof. But it is sad to stand by Nature's side and feel one's self a bungling pupil, not gifted to bring into life and shape one of her beautiful thoughts or pay back aught for her bounteous instruction. But why do I write this now— I am not feeling, only remembering it. For I have been working in nature's garden, digging round and watering two or three plants not fragrant indeed, no nor stately, but she placed them there and probably intended them to grow by some means. "The nearest duty" is comfortable doctrine whether true or no? Mais assez de cela?—

You are right to send the "*scratches*"!— the kind of Faith is right. Also I am glad that you have this new interest. An elegant female writer hath observed "that every new torch kindled in the mind's cavern makes those already lit burn more brightly" This figure of speech is not, I presume, philosophically correct but the idea is so. The head of Prometheus is *fine* but of these anon—when I see you c' est à dire. Alas—Helas!—I shall not be able any more to say "when I see you"— I could be sentimental quite à la Morgan about it—² *Is* not that sketching number in Blackwood *very* good? "I ask for information. I like the review of Mr Motherwell (odious rustick name) better than his poetry though some of *that* pleased me too— But the article on Cornwall and Devon made me laugh to die and think tis as good as the old Noches—so degagée and overflowring!³ Voici Titan! I have not been able to get into Richter's stream—⁴ I read here and there before E, whom I may call my external sensibility arrived—But she and Jean Paul to-gether were de trop. Too rambling and melting— I found necessary to balance and harden myself with some good onward books all plan and method else I should have been dissolved by this time, and such a catastrophe would not suit the style of the 19th century, however natural it seemed in ancient days.— I do not even know why the book is called Titan so if you do pray tell me for I fancied a reason.

I have had a letter from H. Hedge in which he says you are better qualified to translate transcendentalism than he had supposed. You are a good-for nothing young man not to write about Eugene. What do you suppose I care for aught else in comparison?— If it is bad why *dont* you tell it—?

M.

(MH: bMS Am 1569.7 [463])

1. Fuller first wrote "somewhat silly" but canceled the "silly." She then wrote above the line: "inexpressive rather. Though I said silly when I read it over, I do suppose perhaps I should not dispatch it if I really thought so."

2. Sydney Owenson Morgan (1783?–1859) had published a popular novel, *The Wild Irish Girl* (1806), and *Dramatic Scenes from Real Life* (1833), either of which Fuller may mean here.

3. Clarke had sent her a copy of *Blackwood's Edinburgh Magazine* that had an article of advice on amateur sketching and one on William Motherwell (1797–1835), a Scottish poet. The issue also had a travel article, "Devonshire and Cornwall Illustrated. No. 1."

4. Johann Paul Friedrich Richter (known as Jean Paul) (1763–1825) published his novel *Titan* in 1800–1803. It is marked by its linguistic inventiveness, play, and obscurity.

10.   To Frederic H. Hedge

Groton 4th July. 1833.—

I think I cannot commemorate the anniversary of our independence better than by writing to you, since all of freedom that has fallen to my lot, is that of thought and unrestrained intercourse with my friends. The citizens of this place, I grieve to state, are quite ungrateful for the blessings of their estate— No speech, no procession, no glorification of any kind, not so much as a cannon to please the boys with its bobbing report— I am only reminded of the occasion by loud shouts from the juvenile citizens of this family who cannot sufficiently express their joy at being released for one day from all obligation to "intellectual progress."

Your letter was very grateful to me and I confess I had not expected such a token of remembrance. Since I came here I have had much reason to believe that there exists more warmth of feeling in the little world wherein I have been living than I had supposed. I expected that my place would be immediately filled by some person "about my age and height." I have not found it so. My former intimates *sigh* at least, if they do not pine, for my society I rejoice to see that it is so for their sakes more than my own. They must be living since they can feel peculiar wants. I could not expect that you should miss me—but since you do, why not come here? The journey is short, the weather is delightful, the country in perfect beauty, and either Lucy or Mary will, I am sure, be inclined to acompany you.[1] Both will be welcome.

I do, indeed, wish you might succeed your Father. The place would suit you exactly and I know of none other that would. Could you once be brought into unison with your day and country without sacrificing your individuality all would be well. Let me once more intreat you to *write,* to bring your opinions into collision with those generally received. Nobody can be more sensible than myself that the pen is a much less agreeable instrument for communication than the voice, but all our wishes will not bring back the dear talking times of Greece and Rome. And believe me, you cannot live, you cannot be content without acting on other minds "it's no possible." I should be very willing to join in such a society as you speak of and will *compose a piece,* if you will give me a subject— Why will you not continue Novalis's novel, I should think your experiences might suffice. As to my German studies, I have not done much. My time has been much broken up, although not frittered away (to use a favorite expression of my mothers.). I have with me those works of Goethe which I have not read and am now perusing Kunst and Alterthum and Campagne in Frankreich.[2] I still prefer reading Goethe to anybody and as I proceed find more and more to learn.— feel too that my general idea of his mind was less perfect than I supposed and needs testing and sifting. I brought your beloved Jean Paul with me, but have been obliged to send him back before I was half through Titan.

I found considerable difficulty in reading it, my knowledge of German is so imperfect and there are so many compound and coined words in his works that 'twas almost like learning a language: thus perhaps I cannot judge so well, but I think he and I shall not be intimate. I prefer wit to hu-

mour, and daring imagination to the richest fancy, his infinitely varie-
gated and I confess most exquisitely coloured web fatigues my attention. I
like widely extended plan, but the details more distinc[t.] Besides his philosophy and religion seem to be of the sighing sort, and having some tendency that way myself I want opposing force in a favorite author. Perhaps
I have spoken unadvisedly— if so I shall recant on further knowledge.—
You kindly offer me books— I have some of yours which should by rights
have been returned, but I wish to make some further translations from
them. I shall not keep them always— and should like Serapions Bruder,
which you mention.[3] I have never seen it.—

I highly enjoy being surrounded by *new* and beautiful natural objects.
My eyes and my soul were so weary of Cambridge scenery— my heart
would not give access to a summer feeling there. The evenings lately have
been those of Paradise and I have been very happy in them: The people
here are much more agreeable than in most country-towns—there is no
vulgarity of manner, but little of feeling and I hear no gossip— They are
very kind to us and if they do not give great pleasure will not, I believe annoy or pain me. I have met with few characters strongly marked enough
to be amusing, but I am not yet *intimate* with any of the lower class. I have
not the advantages of a clergy man. The length of this letter gives it right
to be called a lady's if not a ladylike letter. Farewell. Commend me to
Lucy and your family. Sincerely your friend

MARGARET F.

(MH: fMS Am 1086 [10:96])

1. Hedge's wife, Lucy Pierce (1808–91), and his sister Mary (1803–65).
2. Goethe's *Über Kunst und Altertum* was published between 1816 and 1832; *Campagne in Frankreich 1792* was written in 1820–21 and was later included in *Aus meinem Leben*.
3. E. T. A. Hoffmann, *Serapionsbrüder* (1819–21).

11. To James F. Clarke

Boston 7th Oct 1833.

My dear Friend,

I received your two good letters at Cambridge where I have been passing these ten days last past.—

As to Amelia's engagement I ought not to say much about it— You were
right in supposing I was not a confidante in the matter, nor do I regret
it!— Amelia seems perfectly happy— I confess Dr. B. does not seem to me

such a finishing portion as I should wish to see a friend of mine supplied withal. But perhaps I am wrong when she is so blest I cannot bear to think it all delusion. So I stand and wait hoping to discover many charms and fine traits in this [*illegible*]. This is profoundly confidential between us.

I saw Mr. Elliott frequently and think him a marvellous proper youth— He talked of you with an affectionate enthusiasm which gratified me. Mr. Osgood too was eloquent in your praise—[1] Mrs. Farrar made many inquiries and I read her proper excerpts from your letters—[2]

I was very happy in Mrs Farrar's house— There all goes on in harmonious gentle movement. She was so kind, so entertaining— *he* so sweet, so bright— I saw all the people I used to know but as my pulse doth now more healthfully keep time I find myself better able to enjoy them after their own fashions than in former days— Helen Davis made a party for me and invited your sister and Elizabeth R. to meet me!! Mrs Farrar, Mrs Devens, and Miss Ware had also their soirées— saw Henry Hedge several times to some effect— I had one quite good talk with Mr Ware about Miss Martineau—[3] one with Mr Palfrey about Mr Robbins (who is likely to have Brattle St and is pronounced to have many virtues and *no* faults —of manner.)[4] Mr Felton lent me his Flaxmans which I drew in at the eyes with unfeigned delight) Did you know Flaxman was a Swedenborgian, and did you guess it from his angels?—[5]

One pleasant day I passed at Mr T. Lee's in Brookline. Twas the loveliest day and I enjoyed every-thing. Mr Bancroft dined there, talked much, earnestly, and well— Of Wilhelm Meister he spoke with a reverent desire to do justice, but could not keep to the true standard—His tastes kept getting in the way.[6]

Mr Lee (who pleased me much) is a Realist of the first water and was brought out in bold relief relief by the opposing lights of Mr Farrar and Mr Bancroft.

I recommend to your attention a review of Goethe in the last Edinburgh— It is so very candid the reasonings are so free and so just. You will observe that the writer is repelled by those sides of G's character with which *you* have the closest affinity.—[7] Ah I am too tired I am going to Cambridge to *drink* honied what? from the lips of Hon E. Everett— *Sip* I should have said— If I am awake when I return shall then finish.

8th Octr. Morng. I was in very good spirits when I wrot[e] last night but this morng my attention has been forcibly recalled to some painful domestick circumstances I must write to you, dear friend, for you are the only one I have on earth young enough to sympathize with me and firm in faith enough to sustain me.

O pray for me— Hard as has been the part I have had to act, far more so than you ever knew; it is like to become much more difficult. Pray that

I may go through all with cheerful spirit and unbroken faith— that any talents with which Heaven has endowed me may be ripened to their due perfection and not utterly wasted in fruitless struggles with difficulties which I cannot overcome. Pray that I may deserve to feel self-complacency— If I could only have that!—

I think I am less happy in many respects than you but particularly in this. You can speak freely to me of all your circumstances and feelings can you not?— It is not possible for me to be so profoundly frank with[?] any earthly friend. Thus my heart has no proper home only can prefer some of its visiting-places to others and with deep regret I realize that I have at length entered upon the concentrating stage of life— It was not time; I had been too sadly cramped— I had not learned enough and must always remain imperfect. But so it is and now I must be as painfully seeking for the centre of my orbit as I was formerly to "wander into the vague" with which you used to reproach me. Enough! I am glad I have been able to say so much.

You know that Elizabeth is going with your mother to Georgia. I am very glad. William P. keeps coming here and making appeals to her feelings. But it is good for her to see that he can act thus without any serious intent. She must regard him in his true light sometime though she cannot now prevail on herself to condemn him. She is delighted at the thought of change. I have read your Robert Hall piece and like it much—[8] Send me a sermon if you have opportunity— I heard a beautiful one from Mr Ware on "religion considered as a restraint and as an excitement.— You will *need* the skill of Champollion to decipher this— By the way, if I can be free and serene enough these winter months which I am to pass in seclusion at Groton I shall read many books about Egypt.!— Mrs Farrar has given me Schiller's works— I was delighted, after all I think I can get more intimate with my dead than with my living friends— Yet I should like to see you and have not been able to supply your place as yet— Adieu—

M.

E. wishes you not to pay the postage of your letters, for the rest see No 2 my Louisville corres— with some additional fuss of her own about "fears tis improper to speak of it at all" &c—

(MHi)

1. Two friends of Clarke's who become clergymen: William Greenleaf Eliot (1811–87) and Samuel Osgood (1812–80).

2. Elizabeth Rotch (1791–1870) married Professor John Farrar of Harvard in 1828. She had taken a special interest in Fuller for many years and remained a devoted friend.

3. Henry Ware, Jr. (1794–1843), was professor of Pulpit Eloquence and Pastoral Care at Harvard. Harriet Martineau (1802–76) was an English reformer and woman of letters. Fuller, who was probably at this time reading her pamphlets on political economy, met her in 1834, when she visited New England.

4. Fuller here passes along ministerial gossip to Clarke: John Gorham Palfrey (1796–1881) was the former minister at Boston's Brattle Street Church. Chandler Robbins (1810–82), Clarke's classmate as an undergraduate and at the Divinity School, did not, however, go to Brattle Street, for he became Emerson's successor at Second Church.

5. Cornelius Felton (1807–62) was professor of Greek from 1832 to 1860, when he became Harvard's president. John Flaxman (1755–1826) was an English engraver who read Swedenborg's works.

6. Thomas Lee (1779–1867) was a wealthy philanthropist; George Bancroft (1800–1891) studied in Germany after his graduation from Harvard. Later a noted historian and Democratic politician, Bancroft provoked Fuller into writing her first published piece, a letter to a newspaper opposing his view of Brutus.

7. William Empson, in the April issue, said that Goethe "breathed over [the legend's] leading figures a poetical and living interest which they never before possessed."

8. Clarke reviewed *The Works of Robert Hall* in the September *Christian Examiner*.

12.   To Richard F. Fuller

Boston 17th Octr 1833

My dear Richard,

As Ellen and Arthur both have letters I think it right to address you and Lloyd, although you are *juniors*.[1] I hear from Father that you are a very good boy— I hope you will not forget your resolves about study but that when I return you will have a grand account to give me of what you have learned— I think a great deal of my brothers and always paint them to myself as neatly dressed, speaking in a polite gentlemanly way to one another or learning some good thing. Dont let me feel disappointed and sad when I come home. Frank Rotch, only eleven years old, has made such progress in Mathematicks that his Master sent him back to his parents saying that he had no boys who could keep up with little Frank. When shall we have any thing so pleasant said of Richard?— Two years hence?

I have looked at some building-blocks—but find that the really good ones, those which have little books with them showing how to build the foreign churches &c are 1-25 a set— I fear we cannot afford this— What do you think about it? The cheaper-sets are mere baby's toys and would give no knowledge of Architecture.

Give love to all I do love. I should be glad to get a neatly written letter from you— Do you write a copy every day?— Your afft sister

M

(MH: fMS Am 1086 [9:33])

1. Their youngest brother, James Lloyd (1826–91), was either emotionally disturbed or mentally retarded.

13. To James F. Clarke

Boston 25th Octr 1833.

I must write to you, dear James, I feel such a want of enthusiasm this eveg—and you are the only person I can think of whose recollection makes me feel pleasantly.— I have been passing several days in what is called a very gay manner, and the jarred and saddened state in which this always leaves me brings your remembrance very forcibly upon me— 'Tis unaccountable that I should always feel so inclined to tell you my mental wants and troubles when I know you cannot minister any remedy which I cannot procure for my self— I can only suppose it is because I feel that you are upon the right path and that therefore your words and thoughts soothe me indirectly for they breathe the perfumes of a healthful atmosphere and fertilized soil.— How very silly? This does not bear rereading immediately.— I am not going to tell you what vexes me but you must write and direct to me at Boston, care of Henry H. Fuller—that I may receive the letter as soon as I return— As soon as I return for I am going to N. York in a day or two with your Mother and Elizabeth— I shall stay a week.

I think I shall be much refreshed by new thoughts and new objects on which to muse this winter in the *icy* seclusion of Groton! But do not anticipate much *pleasure*. E. too feels very cold about the change she has wished so long.— I have been much engrossed of late by her plans and preparations— I am allowed to tell you in greatest confidence that William P. has offered himself—that is to say he has expressed ardent attachment, regret for the past, and a hope that if he can place himself in a proper situation to claim her hand she may favor his suit. This she is willing you should [k]now as you have been made acquainted with those particulars of their connexion so unfavorable to William P.

I do not know whether to be glad or sorry— On the one hand this cancels the bitter part of his experience in some measure. She has no longer the misery of remembering the person she has loved heartless or ungrateful— She does not now feel that her young affections have watered but the desert though they have produced but "weeds of rank luxuriance, tares of haste" She need not feel herself utterly powerless and gets rid in short of the victim—the Mrs Hemans part of her troubles—[1] On the other hand he is not worthy of her and could never keep her good and happy and if he were so and could so, her father will never consent to her marrying him— And I fear she will now be infinitely less likely to forget him— He talked of going to Louisville to see *you* (I cant imagine for what purpose) if he should you will be discreet.

I passed last eveg at Mr Everett's.— All the dramatis personae changed from last autumn except Mr and Mrs E[,] M. Soley and myself—and!! Mr Osgood in Mr Angier's place—at least so it seemed on a slight survey.[2] Pray has this youth dignity or independence of feeling? I only ask for information—

Mr Robbins has had a call to Mr *Emerson's* I went all Sunday with Sarah to Brattle St to hear Mr Channing preach.[3] I was deeply interested in the morning sermon which was upon the text— Work out your salvation with fear and trembling— That of the afternoon on the omnipresence of the Deity was very beautifully written but did not come so home to my previously unfinished trains of thought— He does not read the hymns well. His emphasis is faulty, cadences governed by no rule and manner much too rapid, indeed very conversational. I hope you read the hymns well— I think you do for I always thought your manner of reciting poetry showed that sensibility which commands attention and sympathy even where exception is taken to the taste and emphasis in detail.

What fault do you find with Goethe's lyrics— Each one gives a mood of the mind with marked expression and intense and beautiful language— Does not the perusal of them rouse your imagination and make you think or in some cases rouse you to unexpected passion— What would you have? If you want sympathy read Schiller. I have been quaffing more Martineau sherbet of late with much satisfaction. I believe I told you in my last of her letter to Mr Ware.

Do you study now or are you so happy as to be obliged to write and act all the time. Let me know the texts of some of your sermons I wish to write some in the style of Saturday evening.[4] By the way you have never answered what I said about that book. Always answer my questions if possible— I cannot forget a question till I get it answered.

I wish to study ten-thousand, thousand things this winter— Every day I become more sensible to the defects in my education— I feel so ignorant and superficial. Every day hundreds of questions occur to me to which I can get no answer and do not know what books to consult. Today at the Navy yard!— I did so wish I had had some person of sense with me to explain sundry things— I must study Architecture at all events. That is part of my plan this winter I *will* know the minutiae of *that*— I am tired of these general ideas. They did well enough for conversation but cannot satisfy me when I am alone. I hope I shall greet you with some new ideas when you return. Whatever I learned at Groton makes a very defined impression upon me because I cannot talk it out and draw my inferences.—

Here is a man talking to Bill about Frankenstein— After getting the *story* from her he says "a very good outline but where is the moral?— Tieck would have been delighted— Moral of Frankenstein forsooth?—

I would fain say some thing very fine before I close, but I cannot— I cannot— Adieu worse written than ever I grieve to say.—

P S. I am now on very pleasant terms with Sarah She talks to me plentifully.

(MH: bMS Am 1569.7 [464])

1. Felicia Dorothea Hemans (1793–1835), a poet best known for "Casabianca," which has the line "The boy stood on the burning deck."
2. M. Soley is Mary Soley (1807–81), Fuller's friend from her schooldays at Miss Prescott's; Joseph Angier (1808–71) was Clarke's classmate and good friend who also became a Unitarian clergyman.
3. William Henry Channing, who was seeking a pulpit.
4. Isaac Taylor published his *Saturday Evening* (1832) anonymously.

14. To James F. Clarke

Novr 26th 1833.

My dear Friend,

I thought four days ago when I received your letter that I would not write to you any more. But Sarah tempted me tonight to write "a note only a note by Clinton" She seemed to wish so much to pour out wealth of letters from Clinton's pockets that I could not resist.[1] I shall not answer your letter now— I do not clearly comprehend the tone of it— However as you say, though coldly, that you are "mine as ever" I shall address you as my dear, kind friend always; if not perfectly sympathizing with my feelings yet almost always comprehending my thoughts, and oh *so* different from the apparently ossified human beings whom I meet— You see I have the grace to say *appar*ently.

And yet I will answer one part of your letter though I will not tell you much that I have thought about it— Do not fear being so "terribly outward" Is it not what you have so long asked— and for the want of quick sensibility tell me how should it be otherwise. Must not our feelings sink down deep— *deep* when the bark which bore the rich freight is stripped of all its sails by a rough gale from the seeming beauteous coast on which we were seeking to land them. But trust the prophecy of one who has as good a title as any Sybil to utter oracles to other hearts; some reflux of the tide will cast them on some shore of palms and fragrance where no breath can tell of the black waves which once closed over them. So much for the Souvenir style!— I had a very fine time in New York— It was to me a "moon-lit *"ocean""* I saw Elizabeth beginning to be happier— and felt sure that change was doing and would do her good. I saw many pretty things; the prettiest Titian's Bella Donna (about whom I shall write a novel) and Anna B—[2] I went through the second chapter of my acquaintance with this "fairy-like musick" very happily. I made some amusing acquaintance, heard wealth of good stories, and collected quantities of those most desirable articles new ideas. But I shall not tell you about it, for in comparison with your new world this slight interlude in my ancient and honorable existence would seem flat and unprofitable.

I went this afternoon with Sarah and Eugene to see Medora—[3] I am too sorry that you are not here on her account.— I was not however affected as many are— I was first awed by the spiritual presence and then enchanted by beauty. I have no pathetick associations with death. No link rivetted in my heart chains me to that afterworld which as yet I have sighed for more in mind than heart.

Sarah said to me in a low voice "She looks like one whose heart would break at once, she could not wait to suffer much" I answered by some of Byron's lines about the "pure porcelain" but I believe she did not recognize them—[4] Probably Don Juan has been omitted in her Education

I shall send you the description of some other pictures I saw in N York if you wish.— One trait struck me— A young gentleman who went to hear Mr Eastburn with us—[5] (There was the loveliest church musick it wideoped Elizabeth's heart) said to me when we came out "I always like to hear sermons on this subject. We cannot be too frequently reminded of the danger of merging the past and future in the present. Here is indeed our greatest danger." When I said that mine and that of most persons whom I knew was the opposite he thought I spoke in irony and seemed to have been as much troubled by his selfunconsciousness as some of us have been by our selfconsciousness— Your cousin J. M'Kesson made me his confidante— I was about to be flattered but next day he paid the same compliment to E— I like him however.

Bennett Forbes is engaged to Rose Smith.[6]

I was at Cambridge some days since. Mrs Farrar was writing to you she told me. Mr Elliott was there but I did not enjoy seeing him at all. I seemed to exercise a petrifying influence. Mrs. F. complained that he was not half so agreeable in my society— This I thought ungrateful in your disciple inasmuch as I was the means of establishing him there. George Davis is in town and has paid me several visits. He came one evening with Harriet R.— They talked much about you [ ] of course.— She was rather empressée toward me w[ ] I thought capricious— N'importe. I am going ho[me] tomorrow—

Home—

James— What should you think of my coming to th[e] West and teaching a school—I wish to earn money to go to Italy— Not quite yet— My children want me at present— But by and by would this be a feasible plan?

I shall not give Ellen your George Davis message. Her head is giddy enough already— She has g[ot] one admirer of the name of Clarke which at the impulsive age of 13 is quite enough to impede her progress in French more than is like to prove agreeable or convenient to her governess.

I am very silly to send you all this *stuff* in return for your unfriendly good-for-nothing letter. Adieu— tis eleven P. M. and I've a novel to finish— Village Belles—[7] much superior to Goethe— O much I assure you— "As ever yours"

M.

(MHi)

1. George Clinton McKesson (1809–51) was Clarke's cousin.
2. Anna Barker, who later married Samuel G. Ward.
3. Horatio Greenough had finished a sculpture, his first nude, inspired by the dead Medora of Byron's "The Corsair."
4. Fuller quotes Byron's *Don Juan,* "Thrice fortunate! who of that fragile mould, / The precious porcelain of human clay / Break with the first fall."
5. Manton Eastburn (1801–72) was the rector of the Episcopal Church of the Ascension in New York City.
6. Robert Bennett Forbes (1804–89), later a China merchant and ship owner, married Rose Green Smith.
7. *Village Belles* was the first of Anne Manning's many novels.

15. To Frederic H. Hedge

Groton 30th Novr 1834.

My dear Friend,

A severe indisposition has prevented my thanking you sooner for your prompt and kind reply to my note. For the same reason I have not been to ask Mr Robinson whether he can supply me with such of the books as I think I shall want.[1] In a day or two I hope to be able to go out and shall then see him— I will write to you again in a few days by Eugene who will pass a day or two in Boston on his way to Virginia and ask you for such as I cannot have from him; Eichhorn I do not believe he has—[2] I will send also the Tieck which I shall not use as I intended. I have your Uhland and three vols. of Richter which shall be faithfully returned as any other books you have the kindness to lend me.[3] These have been in my possession some months but I have had no quiet time for reading or study— Now I hope to be more free.

My object is to examine thoroughly as far as my time and abilities permit the evidences of the Christian religion— I have endeavored to get rid of this task as much and as long as possible to content myself with superficial notions and knowledge—and, if I may so express it, to adopt the religion as a matter of taste— But I meet with Infidels very often, two or three of my particular friends are Deists—their arguments and several distressing skeptical notions of my own are haunting me for ever— I *must* satisfy myself and having once begun I shall go as far as I can.

With regard to Mr Emerson, I had two *reasons* (if they may deserve to be so called) for wishing him to see my Tasso.[4] It gratified me that a mind which had affected mine so powerfully should be dwelling on something of mine even though 'twere only new dress for the thoughts of another— And I thought he might express something which would be useful to me. I should like very much his corrections as well as yours if it be not too much trouble. I think I may revise it as an exercise. I did wish very much to have it published when I first wrote it, because I expected for it some money which I would much have liked to have at my command. But there was so much difficulty made that I am now tired of the thought.

Mr Robinson brought me your article on Phrenology as "capital—[5] logical, pungent, beautiful style and what not! He said you "were becoming one of the first writers of the day" and borrowed your Election Sermon. In Mrs Farrar's last letter she says "I admire Mr Hedge's article on Phrenoy very much; it is spirited yet perfectly good natured" and other remarks in the same strain— I am much pleased with it myself and have read it twice— It confirms my first opinion that the pen is your true engine of power. I know little of the world which you inhabit while I am here and can ill report its suffrage— *This* has nothing in common with it and letters are poor things at best, though far, far better than nothing.

I rejoice that you and my friend James have taken to writing to one another. Few have appreciated you more fully than he even while you were personally unknown to him. I hope you will be friends. You will always find him *genuine* as far as he goes.— I got a volume of Frazer's Mag and read all the Sartors I could find— Also Memoirs of Count Cagliostro in two Flights which pleased me mightily—[6] I cannot but wonder however he is willing to write in that odious vulgar magazine. Poor Bulwer is shamefully abused there and without the slightest knowledge of his true faults either. I happened today on B's little critique on Scott which I like very much—though his objections to Scott's want of mannerism, *want of style* as he calls it amused me and I think he would find it difficult to support his assertion that all great prose writers have had style, if by style is meant what might be travestied in the "rejected addresses" as Scott's poetical manner was— Have you read his Pompeii or dont you read his works now?—[7]

No! I have *not* seen Coleridge's Epitaph and I wish you would copy it for me if not too long.[8] I see Mr Hillard's speech about the pirates considerably lauded in newspaper style—[9] Perhaps he may be a distinguished man yet, but I have not much faith in it—he has not health enough, nor what is worse independence enough. Some things about Mr Dewey remind me of H.[10]

I hope you will accept Mr Emerson's invitation and come here at the same time— It would be pleasanter for you in summer and you could see me with more satisfaction but when the "green and bowery summer" comes— I may not be here and you may be in Bangor— But do not go without reason good I beg— With your habits of mind I think you will regret leaving the vicinity of Boston much and more—

Remember me to your friends and believe me most truly yours

M. F.

(MH: fMS Am 1086 [10:98])

1. Charles Robinson (1793–1862) was the Unitarian minister in Groton.

2. Johann Gottfried Eichhorn (1752–1827), who had been professor of theology at Göttingen, was known for his literary and historical analysis of the Bible. Hedge had suggested that she read his *Einleitung ins alte Testament* (1780–83).

3. Ludwig Tieck (1773–1853) was a prolific fiction writer and editor. Which volume Fuller means here is unclear, though she was familiar with his *Phantasus* (1812–17), a collection of his shorter prose. Ludwig Uhland (1787–1862) wrote verse tragedies, poems, and ballads.

4. Fuller had translated Goethe's *Torquato Tasso*, but she never published the work.

5 "Pretensions of Phrenology Examined," *Christian Examiner* 17 (1834): 249–69, was a review of Johann Kaspar Spurzheim's *Phrenology, or The Doctrine of the Mental Phenomena.*

6. Thomas Carlyle, whose *Sartor Resartus* had begun in the November issue of *Fraser's Magazine,* and whose "Count Cagliostro: In Two Flights," appeared in the July and August issues.

7. Edward George Bulwer-Lytton had been "abused" by William Maginn, a founder of *Fraser's,* in the June issue; Bulwer-Lytton's "Death of Sir Walter Scott" appeared in the *New Monthly Magazine and Literary Journal* for October 1832; his *Last Days of Pompeii* was published in 1834. Fuller reviewed it for James Clarke's *Western Messenger,* August 1835.

8. Coleridge had composed his epitaph shortly before he died, on 25 July of that year.

9. George S. Hillard (1808–79) had defended twelve men who had captured the brig *Mexican* in 1832.

10. Orville Dewey (1794–1882) had been the Unitarian minister at New Bedford until he had a breakdown in 1833. He later resumed his career in New York City and became prominent as a preacher and writer.

16.   To James F. Clarke

Groton 1st Feb 1835.

Dear James,

My mind has been so strongly turned towards you these several days that though I owe you no letter I must write. Often in reading or meditating, thoughts strike which I think I wish so much I could communicate to my friend James— If he could only come in this evening as he used to do at Cambridge I would pour forth such a flood. And he—he would gravely listen and then—rise abruptly and go out as if he were disgusted with all I had said but—a month or more after he would come out with an answer which showed that he had thought about it and if he did not agree at least had not been disgusted— Ah well a day this delightful cornerwise contact of character is over for ever. The thought makes me melancholy the best thing I can do since I cannot assail your mind is to assail your pocket and take thence a half-a-dollar for the service of the nation—

So—where was I?— Oh about Reinhard's memoirs—did you, dear "Minister" ever read them for I am going to quote from them for some time—[1] So if you have not read them do so and particy Letter IX and noting what is said therein of the method we should take in examining revelation give me your opinion thereon— *Do it in form*— I want it— Observe the valuable results of his six years patient industry, admire that truly German spirit which produces fruits of such perfect ripeness, those habits of patient investigation, that freedom of spirit joined with candour and humility— See how beautifully his life passed, spirit constantly victorious over the rebellion of matter, every hour employed in pursuits as useful as elegant, that genuine charity, that consistent sweetness and humility— He gave away the fruits of his own soul to the poor; How delightful his domestick life— Oh my friend how lovely is the picture of a good man!— I *hope* it is not flattered— Read it and see if it does not affect you as it does me— I think you will find passages which may be useful to you partiy on the way in which he made general literature and great love of philosophy aid to form the practical part of his religious character. Similar thoughts have occupied your own mind. He seems to have performed what you could conceive and wish therefore are capable of performing. You will not agree with his *doctrine* but that is nothing— And tell me how goes your Unitarianism— Before you went to the west I remember you were grafting sundry notions of your own on that most rational system. Have you decided yet how regeneration is to be accomplished—

Have I ever asked you whether you had read Manzoni's Lucia and which of his two priests you prefer.[2] Surely never did writer invest the clerical character with such grace and dignity— Borromeo is my favourite I dont think any thing can be finer than the scene in which Borromeo rebukes the curate— I have become rather intimate with Manzoni and am marvellously taken with his elevated morality, his tender piety, his various and accurate knowledge and his pictorial power. If you were here I should persecute you with extracts from his writings.

My life has lately been embellished by the establishment of an

Atheneum in G. which enables me to read the Foreign and Quarterly reviews— Ever since we have lived here I have had to study when at home because I could get nothing to read and then to suffocate myself with light reading when in Boston that I might keep up with the gallop of the age— *Now* I shall fare better And there is a fine article on Coleridge which I daresay you have read, if you have not—*do* for my sake and if you have sympathize with me.[3] There is some ignorance and much partial judgement but also many brilliant, feeling remarks and interesting particulars— Note the parallel between Coleridges conversational powers and those of Sir J. Mackintosh Also Coleridge's one sided critique on Faust and *above* all a piece new to me entitled "The Pang more sharp than all"—[4] by which I was reminded of some lines of yours which I saw lately *not* where I *should* have seen them first! to wit in print "thus goes the old / Or if it stays, its flower and freshness gone Fetters the limb weighs down the heart like *stone*—[5]

By the way these lines have quite obliterated the impression your yawning account of Niagara made upon me last summer.

And speaking of Niagara I see your friend Dr Lieber's book much abused in the last N. E. Mag— Literary coxcomb is the best name they can afford him.—[6]

Now let me ask you some questions for I feel impertinent to night— How many hours a day do you study and *what*, any thing except sermon writing. Do you feel more or less alone than when with us— Is the promised freedom *joyous* or joyless? Which do you learn most from the book of Nature, Goethe or St Paul— and are you going to stay in the West always?— How are your friends, the Poles?— My desire to go to the West is revived by the doings at Lane Seminary—[7] That sounds from afar so like the conflict of keen life— There is the greatest fuss about slavery in *this* little nook An idle gentleman weary of his ease has taken to philanthropy as a profession and here are incessant lectures. I rarely go but I attended to hear the English emissary Thomson whom you must have read about in the papers I wish you or any of my friends who need forming as speakers had been there.[8]

A voice of uncommon compass and beauty never sharp in its highest or rough and husky in its lowest tones— A perfect enunciation; every syllable round and energetick though his manner was the one I love best very rapid and full of eager climaxes. Earnestness in every part sometimes impassioned earnestness a sort of "dear friends believe, *pray* believe—I love you and you *must* believe as I do" expression Even in the argumentative parts— I felt as I have so often done before if I were a man decidedly the gift I would choose should be that of eloquence— That power of forcing the vital currents of thousands of human hearts into *one* current by the constraining power of that most delicate instrument the voice is *so* intense— Yes I would prefer it to a more extensive fame, a more permanent influence—

Did I describe to you my feelings on hearing Mr Everett's eulogy—on la Fayette[9] No I did not for that was when we had quarrelled and while I was staying at Mrs Farrar's with Anna Barker and Mr Dewey— singular constellation. That was exquisite— The old hack-neyed story— not a new anecdote, not a single reflection of any value— but the manner, the manner— the delicate inflections of voice, the elegant and appropriate gestures the sense of beauty produced by the whole which thrilled alike the most gentle Anna and the most ungentle Margaret to tears flowing from a deeper and a purer source than that which answers to Pathos.— This was fine but I prefer the Thompson manner. Then there is Mr Webster's unlike either simple grandeur, nobler, more impressive less captivating—[10] I have heard few fine speakers— I wish I could hear a thousand I never have heard you say what sort you liked best will you tell me? I think I admire or rather *feel* Mr Taylor's style of eloquence less than most persons.[11] I suppose because I have less simplicity and less tenderness.

Are you vexed by my keeping the six vols of your Goethe— I read him very little either I have so little time— many things to do at home my three children and three pupils besides whom I instruct for hire Yes James, I am beginning to serve my apprenticeship to the world in good earnest— We shall see how it will end yet Earning *money*— think of that.— Tis but a little but 'tis a beginning. I shall be a professional character yet— But my children come on finely verily I think I have done them much good if some future gardener do not root it all up— I do not believe you will ever get three human beings at a time into better order than I have them— By the way— I have always thought all that was said about the anti religious tendency of a classical education all nonsense and old wives' tales— But their puzzles about Virgil's notions of heaven and virtue and his gracefully described gods and goddesses have led me to alter my opinion and I suspect from reminiscences of my own mental history that if all governors dont think the same tis from want of that intimate knowledge of their pupils minds which I naturally possess— I really find it difficult to keep their *morale* steady and am inclined to think many of my own skeptical suffering[s] are traceable to this source. I well remember what reflections arose in my childish mind from a comparison of the Hebrew history where every moral obliquity is shown out with such naiveté and the Greek history full of sparkling deeds and brilliant sayings and their gods and goddesses, the types of beauty and power with the dazzling veil of flowery language and poetical imagery cast over their vices and failings But to return to Goethe What do you consider to have been his religious opinions?— I speak seriously— give me a definite answer which I may compare with my own ideas— I am deeply interested in the Old testament— I have read Jahn's histy of the Hebrew commonwealth that I may be able to connect and understand all the disjointed parts— I am now reading the O.T. in my old German copy. (thinking it would seem more fresh in a foreign tongue) with the assistance of Eichhorn and Jahn's archaeology—[12] whether I shall persevere no one knows— Life grows scantier, employments accumulate I feel less and less confidence in my powers. You, dear James, speak of "catching my onward spirit" and I know this from you is not meant ironically but I think your progress is vast compared with mine— Sometimes I doubt whether I make any, whether I am not merely giving up one thing for another— Certainly I do not learn or think so fast as I once did But I *must* stop; this is the thirteenth page I have written this evening— If you do not think my letter worth half a dollar you must sell it at auction for what you can get. But if you do— think it worth the half-dollar I have a proposal to make I will if you please write to you the *first* of every month if you will write on the *16th* beginning with this— We shall thus have time to receive one another's letters and write once a month which is more than we have done of late— Eugene and I write to one another once a fortnight on stated days and like it— I used to hate regular arrangements but I have become quite a creature of routine— If you agree write this coming 16th— I feel as if only *begun* to write to you— Shall not sign the letter lest you should decide to *sell* it.

(MH: bMS Am 1569.7 [466]; MHi)

1. Franz Volkmar Reinhard's *Geständnisse seine Predigten und seine Bildung zum Prediger betreffend* (1810) had been translated by Oliver Taylor and published in Boston in 1832.

2. Alessandro Manzoni's novel *I promessi sposi* was published in 1827.

3. "The Poetical Works of S. T. Coleridge," *Quarterly Review* (August 1834).

4. Sir James Mackintosh (1765–1832) had answered Edmund Burke's *Reflections on the French Revolution*. Fuller wrote an article on Mackintosh in 1836. The *Quarterly Review* writer remarked on Coleridge's idea that *Faust* was a failure and then quoted from Coleridge's "The Pang more sharp than all."

5. Fuller quotes from Clarke's unpublished poem "Niagara."

6. Francis Lieber, *Letters to a Gentleman in Germany* (1834).

7. The Presbyterian Lane Seminary had been founded in Cincinnati in 1829. In 1834 several students formed an antislavery society, which both the trustees and faculty denounced. Thereupon, half the students at Lane resigned and moved to Oberlin.

8. George Thompson (1804–78), the English abolitionist, spoke in Groton on 15 January.

9. Everett delivered the eulogy at Faneuil Hall on 6 September 1834.

10. Daniel Webster (1782–1852), United States senator from Massachusetts, was the most compelling New England political orator of his day.

11. Edward Thompson Taylor (1793–1871), the minister at Boston's Seaman's Bethel, was later a model for Melville's Father Mapple.

12. Johann Jahn, *History of the Hebrew Commonwealth*, trans. Calvin Stowe (1828), and, probably, *Jahn's Biblical Archaeology* (1823), Thomas Upham's translation of the original Latin *Archaeoligia biblica* (1814).

17.   To Frederic H. Hedge

Groton 1st Feby 1835;

My dear Friend,

I confess I am disappointed that you should come as far as Concord and not accept my invitation to visit us also for a few days. But I think you must have had some particularly good reason for I would not lightly believe you indifferent to seeing me.

Indeed I do not like the idea of your going to that not wild but *meagre* domain of Maine at all and I do think the Christian Examiner would be just the thing for you— But ah! this money this money it has fettered me always and is like to more and more, what then must it one who does not stand alone but has three other living beings dependant on his care. In sooth it is not "hesitating "between the profitable and the excellent" so much as between the necessary and the excellent. Can you live near Boston on eight hundred a year?— And yet this going into mental solitude is desperately trying. I can appreciate it now-a days— I often try to solace my self by repeating when alone Carlyle's beautiful rhapsodies on the almost miraculous benefits of silence—[1] or by saying Goethe remarked aye even he "We all talk constantly a great deal too much[;] talking is the very worst way of expressing thought, best mature it into action by a silent process as the tree puts forth its fruit"— But to me the expression of thought and feeling is to the mind what respiration is to the lungs and much suffering and probable injury will ensue from living in a thick or harsh atmosphere.— But I *have* nothing "wise" to say no conclusion, the result of nicely balanced arguments, therefore after requesting that you will let me know your decision when it is made, I shall be silent on the subject and "the workman within your own mind will quietly clear away all rubbish as soon as is necessary."

You were quite right about Eichhorn— I have passed over that part of the first volume which discusses the state of the text, different manuscripts &c. It is nonsense for one without learning to read it. I could only follow the wise author blindfold.— I do not get on fast. I dont know how I should like to hear any one else say it but I have long thought my mind must be as shallow as it is rapid and am now convinced of it by the difficulty I find in pursuing this study connectedly. I want to take a general survey of the subject to comprehend the relation which the parts bear to one another, *then* to meditate but the habits of my undisciplined immaterial flutterer are constantly tormenting me— I wish to think before I have proper materials to think upon and at all the picturesque places I have a restless desire to write stories or rather fragments of stories which have nothing to do with my present purpose— I wish, if possible, to be a Christian and to become so not in sickness and adversity but in health and in the full possession of my reasoning powers— I have felt myself a Christian but it was at times of excitement, skepticism returns besides, a religion should not be adopted from taste but conviction. I remember you talked to me once of your friend Mrs Ripley's doubts.[2] I wish you would tell me about this again. I was not interested in the subject then as I should be now but if I mistake not you said she had not perfect faith in the immortality of the soul— I have never been troubled on that score but it so often seems to me that we are ruled by an iron destiny— I have no confidence in God as a Father, if I could believe in Revelation and consequently in an over-ruling Providence many things which seem dark and hateful to me now would be made clear or I could wait— My mind often burns with thoughts on these subjects and I long to pour out my soul to some person of superior calmness and strength and fortunate in more accurate knowledge. I should feel such a quieting reaction. But generally I think it is best I should go through these conflicts alone. The process will be slower, more irksome, more distressing, but the result will be all my own and I shall feel greater confidence in it— Will you write me a short account as to what school of philosophy Eichhorn belonged.— I cannot get at a Conversations Lexicon as I so often wish. And give me an exact definition of the phrase "die hohere Kritik"—[3] I am flattered that Mr Emerson should wish to know me. I fear it will never be but 'tis pleasant to know that he wished it— I cannot think I should be disappointed in him as I have been in others to whom I had hoped to look up, the sensation one experiences in the atmosphere of his thoughts is too decided and peculiar. I forget to tell you that Dr Channing, maugre all my prejudice against Channing women, made me feel as if I might love and reverence him much—[4] Fortunately perhaps, I did not see enough of him to get much P-ized Please write to me as soon and often as is consistent with your engagements— I never felt so much genuine confidence towards you as I do now— in faith yours

M. F.

Is there a 4th vol of Eichhorn?

(MH: fMS Am 1086 [10:99])

1. "Well might the Ancients make Silence a god; for it is the element of all godhood," which Fuller would have found in his essay "Characteristics," in the 1831 *Edinburgh Review*.

2. Sarah Alden Bradford (1793–1867) married Rev. Samuel Ripley, with whom she kept a school at Waltham. Mrs. Ripley was a distinguished intellectual, a close friend of Hedge and later of Fuller.

3. Hedge replied that the term is "a criticism of the inward spirit rather than the letter[,] of the matter rather than the form, a judgment of the opinions of the author & their truth on genuineness & authenticity[,] on the age, country & authorship of a doubtful production;— in poetry— of the degree in which the higher qualifications & true essence of the art have been attained— of the inward & deeper meaning of a work."

4. William Ellery Channing (1780–1842), the leading liberal minister of the time, was the man most responsible for the shift from orthodox Congregationalism to Unitarianism in New England.

18.   To Frederic H. Hedge

Groton 6th March 1835—

Dear Henry

Your letter was doubly kind, being written under such circumstances: I fear this unpleasant suspense is wearing you out but must hope this blessed spring season will bring some favorable omen to turn the scale on the right side. Do you love Spring?— I have for years dreaded it but now that my farewell to the Ideal is in one sense completed my feelings are becoming natural and I can welcome the time when "old" enchantments stir the blood,

Like vernal airs that curl the flood.—

I have heard much of Miss Jackson and should think her every-way calculated to make Mr Emerson happy even on his own principle that it is not the *quantity* but the *quality* of happiness that is to be taken into consideration.[1] How is it that men who marry a second time usually select a wife of character and manners entirely unlike their first. This seems the case with Mr E— and I have just heard a similar instance a gentleman in N York married a young girl of my acquaintance, a gentle, fanciful golden-haired blue-eyed maid— Two years she was "crown to his cap and garnish to his dish." She died at the age of 19— two more years pass and here he is engaged to a woman of six and twenty, as ugly, as ungraceful and as simply devoted to duty as possible with a mind, very substantial, indeed, but from which the elegant imaginings de sa premiere could never have elicited a single spark.— This must be on the principle of reaction, or natural desire for balance of character.

Your periodical plan charms me: I think you will do good and what is next best gain fame. Though I have been somewhat jostled in this working-day world I have still a great partiality for the goddess who

vires acquirit eundo
parva metu primō; mox sese attollit in auras,
et caput inter nubilia condit.[2]

I shall feel myself honoured if I am deemed worthy of lending a hand albeit I fear I am merely "Germanico" and not "transcendental"— I go by
fits and starts: there is no knowing what I should wish to write upon next
January: at present the subject I should select would be the character of
King David aesthetically considered (is this English).

I take the satisfaction I expected in the study of the Old Testament. I
am gradually creating a new world out of the chaos of old, confused and
inaccurate impressions— Soon I shall have finished these vols of
Eichhorn and trouble you for more.

You advised me to read Swedenborgian writings by way of counterpoise
to Eichhorn,— Which—? perhaps I could procure them— I lately happened on five sermons by one of that sect which pleased me much though
the writer as such was no great things—[3] Did I mention to you an avatar of
that great man Dr Grigg on these barbarous demesnes. Verily much did
he pour into mine ears on the subject of Skullology and very sentimental
was he on the subject of certain expressions in your Article which he took
à pied de lettre. "What" says he "does Mr H. really think *I* think when
holding in my hands the brain of the lamented Spurzheim that I am lay-
ing them on the image of the Deity?— Ah *could* I, *did* I"?!!&c—

Your ci-devant tutor Mr Bancroft has been delivering a *curious* address
at Deerfield. If I thought you would care for it I would send you the account in Cousin George's paper— My father requested me to write a little
piece in answer to Mr B's attack on Brutus in the N.A. Review which he
published in the Daily Advertiser some time since— It was responded to
(I flatter myself by some big-wig as *we* say in Groton) from Salem. He detected some ignorance in me nevertheless as he remarked that I wrote
with "ability" and seemed to *consider me* as an elderly gentleman *I considered* the affair as highly flattering and beg you will keep it in mind and furnish it for my memoirs as such after I am dead.

I want to know the facts about Goethe and Lili, can you give them me?
This somewhat passée affair troubles me; I want to know did he give her
up from merely interested (ie selfish) motives.[4]

Tell Mary I recd her note with pleasure and shall write to her when I
send you your books. As ever your friend

M. F.

(MH: fMS Am 1086 [10:100])

1. Lydia Jackson (1802–92) of Plymouth married Emerson on 14 September.
2. Vergil, *Aeneid*, referring to the goddess Fama. C. Day Lewis translates the lines:

> gathering strength as it goes; at the start
> A small and cowardly thing, it soon puffs itself up,
> And walking upon the ground, buries its head in the cloud-base.

3. The ideas of Emanuel Swedenborg had been popularized by Sampson Reed in the 1820s and deeply affected Emerson and Hedge much more than Fuller.
4. Goethe had fallen in love in 1775 with Anne Elisabeth Schönemann, the daughter of a Frankfurt patrician family.

19. To James F. Clarke

Groton 28th April 1835.

My dear James, I am glad you are so punctual since it enables me to be so too— your letter found me last Sunday confined to my bed with a severe indisposition and it was the only Sabba-day thing I had.

I fear you are doing too much just now— Beware, lest by and by when the power of mental effort is very important to yourself and others you should find it exhausted— I should not like to see you with lead in your head like poor Mr Dewey— just when every body was wide awake for you.— If you like my pieces I will write one on Coleridge's Table talk when it comes out—[1] I might be equal to that, though not one of his philosophic works— Why you call me "transcendental" I dont know. I am sure if I am on[e] it is after the fashion of le Bourgeois Gentilhomme.[2] As far as I know myself I am at present "all no how" except on matters of taste— "View of Goethe"—[3] Why dont you write a *Life* of Goethe in 2 vols octo accompanied by criticisms on his works— This vision swims often before mine own eyes, but I know too many are swimming there of the kind and would gladly see this one realized by a friend— If *I* do it— there shall be less eloquence perhaps but more insight than a De Stael.[4]

As to the Hebrew tales I have written the first but cannot now think it worthy your eye— After the agony of so miserably failing to my Ideal is calmed I shall read it and see whether there is sufficient hope of success to encourage my continuing the series— Since you encourage me I would ask—would translations from the modern French novelists take with your reading public— would any Cincinnati publishers buy one of a very clever little fiction called "Cinq-Mars."[5] It would make a thin duodecimo— and, if it took, the healthy might be culled from the incessant productions of that literature and added to ours. My aim is *money*— I want an independent income very much, but I could not venture any thing in which my own pride and feelings are engaged for lucre. But to translating in four modern languages I know myself equal and if I could set some scheme of this kind going it would suit me very well. But with all my aspirations after independence I do not possess sufficient at present to walk into the Boston establishments and ask them to buy my work and I have no friend at once efficient and sympathizing— If I cannot make my pen avail me I must ere long take other means—

You have undoubtedly heard of William Channing's engagement—[6] but perhaps you have long been in his confidence— I was surprised, as I had for more than two years supposed him secretly attached to my friend Miss Barker, and his manner last autumn when he visited us both in Cambridge confirmed that idea. I admired much at that time the cheerfulness with which he spoke of life and its different probations, but my admiration is somewhat diminished now I know that he was at that time so happy in his affections; even the disappointments of a lawful and honorable ambition may be borne when there is this sweetness in the cup— You probably know the lady. I should think her heart must be a fresh fountain; her expression and manner are peculiarly sweet and artless.— And you, dear James, is there no Julia Allen for you, young, innocent, refined, [ ] enough to gratify your tastes and able to appreciate your heart— If that heart had such an home, we should hear no more of "ill regulated feelings" happiness would be the regulator— But I am trespassing on my limits as I am not the amica del cuore— I will talk to you of one who is so to me— Anna Barker— have I ever told you how much I love her?— you know my magnetic power over young women— well! some ten or twelve have been drawn into my sphere since you knew me— to all I have given sympathy and time (more than was agreeable) to her alone— love, confidence warm as if I still knew Disappointment only by name or dark presentiment. The ground we have in common is not extensive, but full of fragrant flowers and wet with gentle dews.— Never could fancy create a being of greater purity grace and softness— Sarah proposed to me to write a novel and make myself a heroine— Whether I might not, with some aid of poetical embellishment, figure in real bloody tragedy I wot not— but if I write a novel I shall take Anna for my heroine.

I am going to Boston tomorrow, yet direct your next here— I shall probably return in time to receive it— Mrs Farrar has been much out of health and "towering" to Washington &c on that account.

Did you ever hear of Henri Heine?—[7] I have seen some extracts from a work of his on modern German belles lettres which are highly amusing. Have been fascinated into reading Richter's Flegel Jahre—[8] and cannot resist the *original* mind when I am with it though not of the kind I naturally like— Hard to get into the stream and harder to get out as somebody in Blackwood said about Rabelais.

(MHi)

1. Coleridge's *Table Talk* was published that year, but Fuller did not review it.
2. In Molière's *Le Bourgeois Gentilhomme* (1670), M. Jourdain, the bourgeois, hires a philosophy master to teach him spelling and the almanac.
3. To urge her to write, Clarke had playfully said he wanted to see "your '*View of Goethe*, 2 vols. 800, Philadelphia, Carey Lea & Co.—' Send me a copy of it, will you?"
4. Fuller early knew the work of Anne Louise Germaine, baronne de Staël-Holstein, especially *Delphine* (1802) and *Corinne* (1807). She was in many ways an intellectual model for Fuller.
5. Alfred de Vigny, *Cinq-Mars* (1826).
6. The following year Channing married Julia Allen.
7. Fuller had read excerpts from Heine's *Zur Geschichte der neueren schönen Literatur in Deutschland* (1833), which she discussed in her "Present State of German Literature" in the July 1836 issue of *The American Monthly Magazine.*
8. Jean Paul's unfinished novel was published in 1804–5.

20.   To Timothy and Margarett C. Fuller

Boston June 2d 1835.

Dearest Father,

I was very glad to receive your letter although 'twas but brief. You have of late omitted to write to me when I was absent and I have felt as if you thought of me less than I wished you should.

I have been passing ten days at Cambridge with Mrs Farrar and indeed they were most happy— Every-body so kind—the country beautiful, and my own spirits so light— We made little excursions almost every day— Last Saturday I rode twenty two miles on horseback without any fatigue— Mrs F. had a most agreeable party the day before I came away. But of all these things Ellen will give you the particulars if you are interested to hear them. The Higginsons say Eugene's pupils love him extremely and that Col Storrow too seems much pleased with him—[1] I think we ought to feel satisfied that he should secure so much love and esteem after five or six months close scrutiny. W. H. is still very good and as well disposed as ever— They seem much pleased with him at Avon-place. He passed yesterday with us: he was excused from the store as it was Marsylvia's wedding day— I believe it is the first amusement time he has allowed himself since he left us—

I saw a good deal of your former ward Thornton Davis while in Cambridge but propose giving you the account viva voce.[2]

And now I have something to tell you which I hope— Oh I *hope*— will give you as much pleasure as it does me.— Mr and Mrs Farrar propose taking me with several other delightful persons to Trenton Falls this summer. The plan is to set out about the 20th July— go on to N York, then up the North River to West point, pass a day there— then to Catskill, pass a day there then on to Trenton and devote a week to that beautiful scenery— I said I had scarcely a doubt of your consent as you had said several times this winter you should like to have me take a pleasant journey this summer. Oh I cannot describe the positive extacy with which I think of this journey— To see the North River at last and in such society! Oh do sympathize with me— do feel about it as I do— The positive expences of the journey we have computed at forty seven dollars— I shall want ten more for spending money— but you will not think of the money— *will* you? I had rather you would take *two hundred* dollars from my portion than feel even the least unwilling. *Will* you not write to me immediately and say you love me and are very glad I am to be so happy???

It was very unkind in Mr Robinson to have Mr Emerson during my absence. I think I shall join Richard and Arthur in attending Mr Kittredge's— I must write a few words to mother so adieu from your most affectionate daughter

M.

Beloved Mother,

I passed a day while in Cambridge with Aunt Kuhn who is much better and full of love for you— Mrs Story, I understood, was not at all well; I did not see her— Louisa Selfridge tells me she has sent you those seeds: I am very glad— I should not have liked her if she had not— But of our visits to her, Marsylvia's wedding &c Ellen must give you the particulars. I am so full of the North River I can write of nothing else O dear, *dear* Mother— will you not be as glad as I am? Oh I am so delighted, so filled with it that I cannot but dread disappointment. My spirits have been in such an exalted state for some time past, I fear something dreadful must be to happen and nothing seems to me so likely as your making yourself sick— Oh do not I entreat you, think how unhappy you would make me in a moment— Sarah Clarke is to return with me a week from Thursday and then you can set off for Canton at once if you please. I shall not mind having every thing to do— if I can but go to Trenton. Much sewing will be needful but Ellen says she will do every thing she can to help me— do not be vexed with Ellen for staying— she has been a very good girl and would have gone with a good grace at any moment if I had said the word. She is resolved to try not to be selfish but help you all she can. She will tell you about the Danas. I enclose a letter from Eugene which you can read aloud except a passage which I have put in brackets as it relates to another person's affairs. Then please put it away in my drawer. With love to my boys and Rebecca please burn this letter from your *transported* daughter.

M.

(MH: fMS Am 1086 [9:35])

1. Eugene was teaching school in Culpeper County, Virginia, and staying in the home of Col. Samuel Appleton Storrow (1787–1837).
2. George Davis's brother, John Thornton Kirkland Davis, who later changed his name to Wendell Thornton Davis.

21.　To Abraham W. Fuller

Groton 6th Novr 1835.—

My dear Uncle,

I am as sorry as you can be and ashamed to boot that I cannot acquaint you more particy with the dates of my Father's public life. But since I am so ignorant I really have no means of becoming less so as we find but few fragments of his journal.

The cow and two large hogs hogs have been killed and the greater part of them prepared for the use of the family. Poor Mother has had a world of trouble with them at their death as she had all their lives; she is but ill repaid for all her toils, in having to take them at the appraisal. Pray, my dear Uncle, make things as easy to Mother as you can; the responsibilitie[s] and cares of her situation are very great. She is quite ill but will write a few lines to you tomorrow, if possible.

We *do* wish to discontinue the Christian Register as, if we take but one paper, we would wish it of a more general character. We have not yet decided what to take.

As Wm told me you had sometimes opportunities to send out to Cambridge, I have taken the liberty to send two notes— I do not feel particy interested about "gay company" and should like to hear news about yourself. I am very sorry Clifford has been so sick, he must have had a sad time and Aunt Sarah too.[1] Wm told me you watched with him several nights. I hope he does not need watchers now.

Let us hear from you as often as convenient Affty your Niece.

S. M. Fuller

(MH: fMS Am 1086 [9:39])

1. Her cousin Clifford Belcher (1819–79) was then a student at Harvard. Her aunt Sarah Fuller (1772–1849) was her father's oldest sister.

22. To James F. Clarke

Groton 29th Jany 1836.

Dearest Friend,

I have been passing five weeks in Boston and Cambridge which have done me a great deal of good; I rccd your Mississippi letter while there but was too much engaged to write. On returning yesterday I found your beautiful Mobile letter which I must answer first of all the file which stares reproachfully at me— Yes my dear friend, there is indeed a higher sympathy between us— I am no longer without God in the world and in my new feelings of peace I value more all the hearts in which my Father has given me a portion— The clouds of distrust and false pride have rolled off from my mind and in my state of protection I can love and trust in simplicity and fearlessness. Would I could tell you more of the present condition of my being for it is blessed. O pray for me, you who are indeed very good that I may be able to perfect my present development by courageous and wise action. My circumstances are very difficult I am called on for a decision of great importance to me— I seem to approach the crisis of my temporal existence— I am near the parting of the Ways. Since you are not near enough to advise pray for me that I may be neither rash nor cowardly but may be guided into that course which will be for my best good. I cannot but think your effectual fervent prayer will avail me much.— No more of this now!

Yes— Anna Barker is lovely and as you say she loves me much; it is rather sad that so much space should lie between us. Pray tell me in your next with feminine minuteness all you saw and heard of her for I am deeply interested and can get little information. I am quite satisfied about *"friend of the Mind"* now by what you say— I know very well I used to be the friend of the Heart; but you have so often called me by this other name the past year and the tone of your letters has been so cold and repressing that I thought you meant to depose me from my ancient niche. It is all right I see— Yes if you can indeed learn to love any love but that of imagination you will be beloved, fear not— The maiden you describe is not such a phoenix but she may be found and make you happy when found— More of this another time.— Thanks for the Goethe and what you say of what I should do. I will lay it to heart— Write any thing which occurs to you on the subject I dare say I shall fructify thereupon. It is a great work. I hope nobody will steal it from me— I took a dose of Fichte while in C— but it did not do— I could not understand.— Can you recommend me a *good Hist of Philosophy.* Nobody could, so I have brought home two which are not at all what I want— Tennyman's and Buhle's— both in German. I want something lucid and compendious— I have been reading today the Western Messenger.[1] Your tribute to your grandfather is truly eloquent— and the eloquence is that of both heart and mind.[2] It is a warm and warming outpouring from a most hallowed fount. It gave me much delight— But you must let me scold you for your translations of Goethe I suppose they are just as you first wrote them out and certainly very bad— What vexes me is that as your bits of Schiller are good people will suppose these are equally so. It is a shame to degrade such a very transparent and flexible style into English whose literalness makes it unfaithful. Surely we should consult the idiom of our own language if we want to do justice to a writer who valued form so highly. Then why is it not that Epithalamium better done? How many beautiful ideas marred for want of a proper finish— You *can* do it— those verses you gave me when you were here were done as they ought to be. The Genuine Portrait, though imperfect, is much less so— Do not let living in the West lower your literary while it elevates your moral standard— You cannot be a poet of the first order but your ideas well deserve that you should pay more attention to their *expression*

I have had many happy hours with Miss Martineau. I trust we shall now be dear friends forever— My only fear is that she overrates me as is her wont where she loves. *I* shall not be disappointed in *her*

I have thought so much about her, perhaps I shall write you a letter on the subject one of these days— I have said only the least bit of what I meant. I have so much to tell that would be interesting to you. I meant to have told you about Wm Channing's Swiss journal which I read and Mr Alston's new picture[3] but there is no room now so farewell from yours affectionately

M. F.

Has Abraham quite recovered?

(MHi)

1. Clarke had begun to publish his journal, *The Western Messenger,* to which Fuller contributed.

2. "Character of James Freeman, D.D.," *Western Messenger* 1 (January 1836): 478–87.

3. Washington Allston (1779–1843) was living in Cambridgeport. Fuller probably refers to his *Rosalie,* which was completed in 1835 and about which she wrote a poem.

23. To George T. Davis

Groton, 1st Feby, 1836—

My dear Cousin,

I received your letter sometime since but was staying in Cambridge at the time and could not conveniently answer it. Since I returned I have read the life of Sir James Mackintosh with great interest. I think few things have ever been written more discriminating or more beautiful than his strictures on the Hindoo character, his portrait of Fox and his second letter to Robert Hall after his recovery from derangement. Do you remember what he says of the want of *brilliancy* in Priestley's moral sentiments:— those remarks, though slight, seem to me to mark the character of his mind more decidedly than any thing in the book. That so much learning, benevolence, and almost unparalleled fairness of mind should be in a great measure lost to the world for want of earnestness of purpose might impel us to attach to the latter attribute as much importance as does the wise uncle in Wilhelm Meister.[1]

As to the trifle I sent you on *the* great question I thought I perceived while in Boston that the time for polishing it was already gone by. It is however valuable to me to have written it, slight as it was, for the interest thus excited has led me to acquire more information from various quarters and I am already considerably enlightened on the subject. No effort is ever utterly lost! I doubt there is nothing in it worthy of reproduction but about this should like your opinion. Perhaps I may solicit your aid on some other occasion since you boast such power over the press!—

I have recd two letters from James lately. One from N. Orleans and one from Mobile!— The latter contains some beautiful passages: if you were here I would read them to you. Have you seen what he has written about his grandfather?— It is a fine tribute.

Your brother I was glad, a few days since, to hear has recovered. Perhaps he is with you now— he seemed to wish it— I saw less of your mother than I had intended.

I am obliged by your and Harriet's invitations to Greenfield.— If it be possible I will fix a time for you to meet me and pass a week or two with you as you propose. But my plans are all painfully undecided. That of my going to Europe is again revived among my friends. If I go it will be in August with Mr and Mrs Farrar and Miss Martineau— and to be with Miss M. while in London, an arrangement equally delightful and profitable to me— All that I could do and see would seem to open up many prospects to me— but then, on the other hand, the moment I return I must maintain myself and you know we women have no profession except marriage,

mantua-making and school-keeping. If I can make up my mind that it is
[ ] for myself to go, I think matters can be so arranged that it will not
eventually be a loss to my Mother and family. I intend to be very wise and
deliberate til the last moment; and I rather think I shall not go; staying behind will be such a pretty trial to my fortitude and quite finish my moral
education— Indeed at the expense of my intellectual but this last is quite
a secondary affair— 'tis said. Oblige me by not speaking of all this— such
plans are best never known except by their fulfilment!— I only wish to say
that if I do not go to Europe, I may come to Greenfield as this last is somewhat less difficult— Meanwhile, with remembrances to Harriet yours truly

M. F.

(MCR-S)

1. Either Natalia's uncle in Goethe's *Wilhelm Meisters Lehrjahre* or the uncle of Hersilia and
Julieta in the sequel, *Wilhelm Meisters Wanderjahre.*

24.   To James F. Clarke

Groton 19th April 1836—

Dear Friend,

Your letter imparted to me a pure satisfaction; the heart seemed to
speak in it without reserve— Sometimes it seems as if you had a feeling of
pride which stood between you and me, or some other feeling!— 'Tis but
a film— yet sufficient to prevent you from radiating much heat upon my
earth-bound state.

Who is the imaginative love. Give name and date!— I am shocked to
perceive you think I am *writing* the life of Goethe— No! indeed! I shall
need a great deal of preparation before I can have it clear in my head.— I
have taken a great many notes but I shall not begin to write it till it all lies
mapped out before me. I have no materials for ten years of his life— from
the time he went to Weimar up to the Italn journey— Besides! I wish to
see the books that have been written about him in Germany by friend or
foe— I wish to look at the matter from all sides— New lights are constantly dawning upon me and I think it possible I shall come out far
enough from the Carlyle view perhaps from yours and will distaste you
which will trouble me.

In a brief, but seemingly, calm and authentic notice of Goethe's life
which I met with in an English publication the other day I find it stated
that his son was illegitimate, that he lived out of wedlock with the mother

for twenty years and only married her on acct of the son as late as 1806—
I confess this has greatly pained and troubled me— I had no idea that the
mighty "Indifferentist" went so far with his experimentalizing in *real life*. I
had not supposed he *"was"* all he *"writ,"* and have always maintained that
stories which have been told me as coming from Dr Follen[1] which represented him as a man of licentious life could not be true because he was living at a court whose outward morality, at least, must be pure under the
auspices of a princess like the Grand duchess Amelia.— In the same publication many, not agreeable, hints are thrown out respecting those very
ten years which I know so little about.

How am I to get the information I want unless I go to Europe— To
whom should I write to choose my materials— I have thought of Mr
Carlyle but still more of Goethe's friend Von Muller—[2] I dare say he would
be pleased at the idea of a life of G. written in this hemisphere and be very
willing to help me. If you have any-thing to tell me you will and not mince
matters— Of course my impressions of Goethe's works cannot be influenced by information I get about his *life* but as to this latter I suspect I must
have been hasty in my inferences— I apply to you without scruple— These
are subjects on which *gentlemen* and *ladies* usually talk a great deal but apart
from one another— you, however, are well aware that I am very destitute
of what is commonly called modesty. With regard to this, how fine is the remark of our present subject. "Courage and modesty are virtues which every
sort of society reveres because they are virtues which cannot be counter-
feited, also they are known by the *same hue*"—[3] When that blush does not
come naturally into my face I do not drop a veil to make people think it is
there All this may be very *"unlovely"* but it is *I*. As to sending the 40 vols, do
not, till you know [cer]tainly that I shall not go to Europe— That will be
decided the first of June and I will write and tell you— When I wrote for
the Goethe I thought it *was* decided but it is not. My mind is much harassed by anxiety and suspense— add to this that my health has been most
miserable for two or three months back. So I do not accomplish much— If
I thought my constitution was really broken and that I must never again
know my natural energy of body and mind I should be almost overcome,
but the physician says it is only the extreme cold winter acting on a frame
debilitated by a severe illness and all the painful emotion which came after
and that the summer will probably restore me.

What subjects do you wish me to write upon for your mag. and how can
I send if I *do* write. It seems to me I have but little to give the West. I have
left myself no room for critiques on your writing but by and by I will do
what you desire— Would you not like me to wait till I have read your N.
American piece.[4] Be assured you have heart and mind sympathy from
me.— I should like to come to the West very much perhaps if I do not go

abroad, I might for a time if I could do something to pay my way. Perhaps you do not know that I am to have scarce any money.— I suppose if I have health I can earn it as others do— I have a protege that I wish you could get a place for. She is a farmer's daughter, far from elegant or pretty but with a sterling heart and mind and really good education. She knows Latin, French and Italian and could teach the common English branches and something of Mathematics I have taken some pains with her and feel a desire that her earnest wish to go and teach at the South or West should be gratified.— She is persuaded it would do her good and I know enough of the misery of being baffled and hemmed in on every side by seemingly insignificant barriers to feel an interest in giving her a chance to try her experiment too. She would make a good governess or assistant— if any thing of the sort falls in your way think of *her* an thou lovest *me*.

I know you must hate these crossed letters—

M. F.

I have been reading, with delight, Herschell's discourse on Nat. Philosophy— Do you know it?[5]

(MHi)

1. Charles Follen (1796–1840), a German émigré, was the first professor of German at Harvard.
2. Friedrich von Müller (1779–1849) became chancellor of Sachsen-Weimar in 1815.
3. Fuller quotes from Goethe's "Maximen und Reflexionen," from *Wilhelm Meisters Wanderjahre.*
4. Clarke reviewed books by Mann Butler and James Hall in the July *North American Review.*
5. Sir John Frederick William Herschel's *Preliminary Discourse on the Study of Natural Philosophy* (1830) was a commentary on Bacon.

25.   To Ellen K. Fuller

Groton 21st April 1836.

My dear Ellen,

I think I observe notwithstanding all the kind interest you take in my affairs an affectation of coldness in your letter— Why is this?— because I did not write to you as long a letter as to others. I was very weary and knew you would learn my little news from my letter to Mother. Besides I do not think you ought to dwell on every instance where I may seemingly fail to meet your feelings when you have such reason to be sure my heart is always right toward you.

I wish much to have you happy and I think you will be so. Belinda tells me you make persevering efforts to subdue your temper and I feel satisfied with what I hear of you generally. I do not speak perhaps as warmly as you think I ought and it is because I have so often been deceived in judging from hearsay and should like to see with my own eyes and hear with my own ears before I speak very decidedly.

Yes I do think you have been, for you, pretty deliberate about Miss Dwight. I am glad she loves you and that you take pleasure in loving her— As to your making her a present, your generous feelings I dislike to check, but, really, I know nobody less able to make presents than yourself— Where are you to get money for all the necessaries you want? Summer is coming and many things must be bought. We shall not know for many months how much or how little we have to spend. Nevertheless consult Mother and if she thinks you can spare the money I should like to have you gratified.

You can give 75 cents or a dollar for my buckle. I do not know what sort would be best as I have not looked at any— Use your judgment, only let it be strong.

Give my best love to mother. Say that I recd her letter to-day and was much relieved by so doing. Nothing of importance has happened. Rebecca is still pretty well but misses her medicine. Mr Park has been here and says all is going on right. Reuben has been ploughing for two days.— I am much better and stronger in body this week. Lloyd is my chief trouble, but for him I could do a great deal and as it is I have not been idle. I do not wish her to trouble about my gown: if it is tolerably pretty I shall be content. It is not worthwhile for me to write to her again since you wished me to write to *you* but she knows I am always thinking of her.

I suppose Miss Martineau says just whatever she thinks of the Bostonians as she does of all things and persons without regard to effects. She has reason to think ill of them in some respects I daresay she adhered to justice in whatever she said. Little importance should be attached to on dits about a person like her.

I saw S. Woodbury to day: she desired her love to you and expressed impatience for your return.

Now my dear Ellen I am tired and have nothing further of consequence to say. Write to me b[y] Mother give my love to E and B. and believe me always with sincere affection your Sister

M.

I am very familiar with Retsch's illustrations of Faust and admire them much. See as many good pictures and engravings as you can.[1]

(MH: fMS Am 1086 [9:40])

1. In 1816 Goethe suggested to Moritz Retzsch that he illustrate *Faust*, and he did so that year.

Ellen Kilshaw Fuller. Courtesy of Willard P. Fuller, Jr.

26.   To A. Bronson Alcott

Groton 25th August 1836—

Dear Sir,

I am not quite sure that I understood your last words at Mr Emerson's. *As* I understood, you had applied to some other person to assist you in your school before you thought of me and would write to me after receiving an answer from that person. A letter since received from Miss Peabody leads me to think that you may on your side be expecting to hear from me and, as I find it necessary to come to some decision about my employment for the winter, I think it best to write to you at any rate.

Will you have the kindness to answer this letter as soon as possible informing me whether you are desirous I should take Miss Peabody's place; whether, if I do take it, you expect me to reside in your family as she did; and whether any-thing would be expected from me beyond the instruction in Latin or other languages which you mentioned to me, with any other circumstances which you may think proper for me to know in order to my decision. Also whether you could (if you wish me to come and I decide on doing so) dispense with my assistance till the 29th of September or the 1st of October. I could, if necessary, begin my lessons earlier, but my family affairs are so situated that it will be much more convenient to me to devote the coming month to their arrangement.

Every thing about me is in a state of uncertainty but I suppose, if I do not hear from you before Friday of next week, that I shall on that day set out on a journey which will occupy ten days or a fortnight. I should, however, leave directions for any letter from you to be forwarded to me.

My acquaintance with your views and character is not sufficiently thorough to give me a confidence that I could satisfy you. But I think as far as I understand your plan I might carry it into execution as successfully as most persons, and I should like to become more conversant with your method of teaching. It would be but an experiment on both sides, for, as I have never yet been subordinate to any one, I cannot tell how I should please or be pleased. But your proposal has attracted me more than any which has as yet been made to me.

If I was right in my first supposition and you did *not* make me any direct proposal but only spoke of the possibility of doing so, do not let this letter embarrass you. You have only to say how it was.—

With much regard yours

S. M. FULLER.

I am sorry that I have forgotten your first name and have no present means of ascertaining it so as to direct my letter properly. I am not usually so inaccurate; but I hope that, being directed to the street where you live, my letter will not fail to reach you.

(MH: 59m-312 [120])

27.   To Ellen K. Fuller

26th August [1836]
[Groton]

De[ar] Sister

I never meant that you misspelt from ignorance. What I *said* was that you were in the habit of leaving out both letters and syllables from writing in too much hurry which is the truth and which produces the effect of bad orthography. I do not remember what I said about Eliza Tenny[?] I was in jest I believe; I was not unkind, I am sure. You must not be hasty to suspect unkindness, least of all should you from me who have shown you so sincere affection,— I do *not* expect as much from you as from M. Salisbury who is several years older. If you cultivate habits of industry and a cheerful, hopeful temper, I shall be well satisfied. I *am* well satisfied with you as far as I can judge from what I hear. I do not expect you to make *progress* in your Italn. If you do not lose what you have learned it is all I expect from you this summer, and I depend on your persevering in learning a little lesson every day. Do not be concerned about your faded frocks; if you are neat and lady-like in your manners they will not injure you with any person whose good opinion is worth having. Now that every one knows our circumstances it is no disgrace to us not to wear fine clothes, but a credit. I wore a "faded calico frock" in the presence of much company while at Concord, and it did not prevent my exciting respect and interest. You must, my sister, pray to our Heavenly Father to strengthen you to rise above the opinion of this world as far as vanity is concerned and only to regard it from motives of kindness and modesty. It is very difficult for young persons to do so; the lesson is long and often severe, but the acquisition is worth it all. From this source I get the little strength I have and the same will be given you if you seek it. [ ] do not suspect I think you particularly inclined to vanity. I do not by any means, but we are all in beginning life deficient in separating things of real importance from those which are not so.

Mother gives her consent to your inviting the twins, but does not think Mrs R. will let them come. She sends much love to you. Give mine to grandmother Aunt and cousin Ellen. Aunt's visit was pleasant to us and I should have liked to have had it prolonged. Mother recd yesterday a very pleasant letter from Ellen's Mr Hill. Affectionately yours

M. F.

(MH: fMS Am 1086 [9:43])

28. To Ralph Waldo Emerson

Boston 21st Sept 1836—

My dear friend,

I may venture to begin so since you have subscribed yourself my friend— I have just received your letter. While I was with you you very justly corrected me for using too strong expressions on some subjects. But there is no exaggeration in saying— I *must* be allowed to say that I *detest* Mr Robinson at this moment. The last thing I did was to beg that he would not invite you to preach at Groton without ascertaining that I should be there, and, if I had not, said any thing now knowing how great my disappointment was on the former occasion common good nature should have prevented his doing the same thing again. Do not go, dear Sir, I intreat you, if it is possible to make any other arrangement— Is it not possible to postpone it till the third or second Sunday from this next? I fear it is not possible, but if it is I think you will do it for my sake, for I would do twenty times as much for yours. If that must not be and if I can come to Concord Saturday afternoon will you take me with you to Groton— It would be merely to spend Sunday; I should be obliged to re-turn to Concord and come here again for I have not half-finished what I came to do— I am not sure that this would be agreeable to you, nor that I could do it at any rate, but I might try to arrange it. I should like to baffle the malice of my pastor, and hear better preaching than his own if I could.— If you were to see me just now, dear Sir, you would not like me at all for I am very far from calm and have quite forfited my placid brow but I flatter myself that my vexation will seem nothing worse than earnestness on paper.

I thank you much for "Nature." I hear much conversation about it that amuses me.[1] I have it already. I gave a copy to Miss Barker and she in re-turn gave me one accompanied by Philip van Artevelde. I would not de-cline it lest I should not receive a copy from yourself though I confess I hoped I should be so honored. I should indeed be too happy to pass a day at Concord with Miss Barker and she would have been very glad to come, but she goes to-day. Her father is with her and wishes her to go and I feel that I ought not to expect her to stay; for a brother whom she loves more than all her kin, except her parents, is to leave New York in a few days for Antwerp where he is to remain as Consul and she may not see him again for years. It has been both painful and gratifying to me to see her. I find her true to herself as yet, and lovely as ever but so many people have beset both of us that we have had little chance for any profitable conversation. The peace and seclusion of Concord would have been just what we wanted. But I doubt whether we could have gone even if I had received Mrs Emerson's kind invitation earlier.— Mrs Emerson does not love me more than I love her; but I am not sure how successfully our visit might have ministered to her well-being— It is all over now but it is very annoying to know that you were so near us on Sunday and that nothing but my unfortunate want of eye-sight prevented my having a chance of at least showing Anna to you— If you think this ebullition worthy an answer please direct to the care of James Dana, Charlestown. I am going there to stay two or three days.

respectfully and affectionately Mrs Emerson's and your friend

S. M. FULLER.

You must not make a joke of my anxiety about next Sunday, but take it seriously as I am feeling. It is a great gain to be able to address yourself directly, instead of intriguing as I did last year.

(MH: bMS Am 1280 [2335])

1. Emerson's *Nature* was published on 9 September.

29.   To Frederic H. Hedge

Boston 6th April 1837.

Dear Henry,

I have been wishing and wishing, trying and trying to write to you this past month and after all can get no hour for the fulfilment of so good a purpose unless at the fag end of a busy eveg itself the flavorless postact to a bustling day. So please take my letter kindly and marvel not if there should be nothing in it worthy of you—or *me*!

Firstly I would scold that you are not coming here till May. Here I have been living six months and you would not come and now you must needs be planning to come just as I am going away.[1] You manage very ill, to take no thought of me in any of your plans. The end of it will be that we shall not be able to talk when we do meet and that will, I think, be very grievous. For, upon the whole, I have had as satisfactory talks with you as I shall or can have in this world. And why must they end?— Just because you will not come where I am.

Secondly why is it that I hear you are writing a piece to "cut up Mr Alcott?"[2] I do not believe you are going to cut up Mr Alcott. There are plenty of fish in the net created solely for markets &c no need to try your knife on a dolphin like him.— I should be charmed if I thought you were writing a long, beautiful, wise like article showing the elevated aim and at the same time the practical defects of his system. You would do a great service to him as well as the publick and I know no one so well qualified as yourself to act as a mediator between the two and set both sides of the question in a proper light. But the phrase "cutting up" alarms me. If you were here I am sure that you would feel as I do and that your wit would never lend its patronage to the ugly blinking owls who are now hooting from their snug tenements, overgown rather with nettles than with ivy, at this star of purest ray serene.[3] But you are not here, more's the pity, and perhaps do not know exactly what you are doing, do write to me and reassure me.

3dly, is it not naughty in you to throw your Bangor ice water on all the Goethero-American lyrics that were swelling into bud?— Translations, as somebody printed the other day, are no better at best than an asylum for the destitute but that asylum must be provided. I dare say the public know nothing about *lyrics*. They will read the things as *verses* and be content. I hope you are not so romantic as to think of raising people up to the level of your own tastes.

4thly Why did you not send me your lecture? Have not I a claim as a *literary friend*? I was obliged to *steal* it, which did not look well in me, a schoolmistress!

—These are all my questions.— As to my biography, much of it cannot be given on a piece of paper like this. I have learned much and thought little, an assertion which seems paradoxical and *is* true. I faint with desire to think and surely shall, the first oppory, but some outward requisition is ever knocking at the door of my mind and I am as ill placed as regards a chance to think as a haberdasher's prentice or the President of Harvard University— As to study my attention has been concentrated on the subjects about which I teach. There was a time when my dearest books became detestable to me on account of the duty work I did upon them. But that bad time is passed and I think I could do what I would if I staid here.

As to reading I have read only two books, Coleridge's Literary remains and Eckermann's Conversations with Goethe, both very good!—[4]

I see many people and some of them are very pleasant but you know the best of them.

I have been very unwell all winter and am now rather worse. If May flowers and June breezes do no good I must prepare either to leave this scene or become "that extremely common character, a confirmed invalid." But I intend to get perfectly well, if possible, for Mr Carlyle says "it is wicked to be sick."— When you write tell me how you like his Mirabeau.[5] Farewell. Remember me to your wife and present my respects to your children. I am sorry to hear that Mr Bradford is going to leave you, but glad you can hold converse with Mr Woods.—[6] I daresay I shall not write again, or if I do, no better a letter than this—for I write very bad letters now.

As ever your friend

S. M. FULLER.

(MH-AH)

1. After Fuller left Alcott's school, because he did not pay her, she accepted an offer to teach in Providence at Hiram Fuller's Greene-Street School.

2. The editor of the *Christian Examiner* not only asked Hedge to review Alcott's *Conversations with Children on the Gospels* but demanded a negative review. Hedge declined.

3. Fuller alludes to images in Thomas Gray's "Elegy Written in a Country Church Yard."

4. Johann Peter Eckermann (1792–1854) was Goethe's companion and unpaid secretary. He had just published *Gespräche mit Goethe,* which Fuller later translated. *The Literary Remains of Samuel Taylor Coleridge* was published in 1836.

5. In a recent letter to Emerson, Carlyle had said, "It is a dreadful thing sickness; really a thing which I begin frequently to think *criminal*—at least in myself." His "Memoirs of Mirabeau" appeared in the January issue of the *London and Westminster Review.*

6. George Partridge Bradford (1807–90), Hedge's classmate at Harvard, was a teacher who later joined George Ripley at Brook Farm.

30.   To Ralph Waldo Emerson

Boston.
11th April 1837.

"Revd and dear Sir,"

I recd yesterday morng your letter in which you ask for the Necklace, and was troubling myself much to devise how I could give back what had never been in my possession, when the desired article was brought me from the Post Office where your emissary had deposited it. I was able to read it through yesty afternoon and so return it with many thanks. It is good—but not, to my mind, half *as* good as the Mirabeau.

I think it is somewhat ungracious in you to resume your gift of the proof sheet which I was about to lay in lavender by the side of that first most appropriate token of your regard, with which you honored me during my first visit to Concord, to wit the autograph of Jeremy Bentham. To me, as a lady of enthusiasm and taste, such twigs from the tree of genius, however dry, are of course inexpressibly valuable. I shall expect from you, in lieu of the proof sheet (if you *will* give it to Mrs Ripley) an autograph of Bonaparte, or Metternich, or at the very least of Grandison, Cromwell La Fayette.[1]

I send you a note from Mr R[ipley] on the subject of Eckermann as I showed him yours, thinking that the shortest way of telling the story.[2] You see how it is. Unless he himself proposed my making an arrangement to translate it for some other publishers than his, I can do nothing. And I dare say it is quite as well. I have yet to see whether I shall have strength to chase butterflies, let alone edible animals, this summer. Please send me his note if you send me any thing done up in paper; if not keep it for me till that good day which shall see me at Concord.

My friend and charming pupil Jane Tuckerman is going to England the first of May and if you wished to send any thing to Mr Carlyle she would like to take it, I am sure.[3]

I take the liberty to send Merck and the two first vols of Zelter.[4] Do not trouble yourself to send them back. All the miseries which encompass the fag end of a sojurn in a city are thick upon me. What with milliners, mantuamakers, shopkeepers, notes that must be written, and calls that must be made, now or never, under penalty of general odium, (to say nothing of parting talks with sundry people I do really like) the Hand of the mind has almost lost its power to grasp and the Eye of the mind is not permitted to rest in peace upon the moon or stars. But I look to Concord as my Lethe and Eunoi after this purgatory of distracting, petty tasks. I am sure you will purify and strengthen me to enter the Paradise of thought once more.

Last night I took my boldest peep into the Gigman world of Boston. I have not been to a large party before and only seen said world in half-boots, so I thought as it was an occasion in which I felt real interest, to wit, a fete given by Mrs Thorndike for my beautiful Susan, I would look at it for once in satin slippers. Dr Channing meant to go but was too weary when the hour came. I spent the early part of the eveg in reading bits of Dante with him and talking about the material sublime till half past nine, when I went with Mrs C. and graceful Mary.[5] It was very pretty to look at. So many fair maidens dressed as if they had stepped out of their Grandmothers' picture frames, and youths, with their long locks, suitable to represent pages, if not nobles. Signor Figaro was there also in propria— Sa et la.— And Daniel the Great, not however, when I saw him, engaged in an operation peculiarly favorable to his style of beauty, to wit eating oysters.[6] Theodore Parker was there and introduced to me.[7] I had some pleasant talk with him but before I could get to Spinoza, somebody seized on me and carried me off to quite another S.—to Supper.— On the whole it all pleased my eye; my fashionable fellow creatures were very civil to me and I went home glad to have looked at this slide in the magic lantern also.

I prattle on to you as if you liked prattling and as if I had time. Forgive and Farewell. If it is really "wicked to be sick" I should think you might teach your own son better at so early an age.[8] Bid him get quite well and strong that I may see him play *Peep* with all the vivacity which is, I hear, so much admired. Dear love to the sainted Lidian—

—yours as ever

S. M. FULLER

Miss Tuckerman's voyage is postponed in consequence of the illness of a relation. I shall know when I come to C. when she will go, if she does go.

Wednesday—

An accident prevented this packet from going today as I intended it should, but, as Thursday is the day mentioned in your note, I hope it will arrive in time.

(MH: bMS Am 1280 [1236])

1. Carlyle's "Diamond Necklace" appeared in the January–February issue of *Fraser's Magazine*. He had sent Emerson bound copies of it, the Mirabeau essay, and a proof sheet from his forthcoming *French Revolution*. In the "Mirabeau," Carlyle names "Grandison-Cromwell Lafayette" as one of Mirabeau's nicknames.

2. Fuller had begun to negotiate for her translation of Eckermann with George Ripley (1802–80), the minister at Boston's Purchase Street Church, who was publishing a series of translations in Specimens of Foreign Standard Literature. One of the best scholars of his generation, Ripley left the church in 1841 to found Brook Farm.

3. Jane Francis Tuckerman (1821?–56) had been Fuller's student and was later her assistant on the *Dial*. In 1843 she married John Gallison King, with whom she lived unhappily.

4. Johann Heinrich Merck (1741–91) was a Darmstadt literary figure. His *Briefe an Johann Heinrich Merck von Goethe, Herder, Wieland . . .* (1835) deeply impressed Emerson, who told Fuller that it is "inestimable to the biography of Goethe." Karl Friedrich Zelter (1758–1832) was a composer whose six-volume *Briefwechsel zwischen Goethe und Zelter* was published in Berlin, 1833–34.

5. Dr. Channing's wife, Ruth Gibbs Channing (1778–1870), and their daughter, Mary (1818–91).

6. Daniel Webster.

7. Theodore Parker (1810–60) graduated from the Divinity School in 1836 and settled at West Roxbury in 1837. A central figure among the Transcendentalists, Parker remained within the church as a learned, combative scholar and minister. He contributed many times to the *Dial* during Fuller's editorship.

8. Emerson's son Waldo (1836–42), whose death deeply grieved Fuller.

31. To James F. Clarke

Groton 13th May 1837.

My dear friend James,

A letter recd this aftn from Sarah, though about as barren and careless as mine to you by Miss Goddard's friends, brings you two so forcibly to my mind that I can no longer defer my promise of writing you a long letter from this place.

I have now been at home ten days and am still quite unwell, yet, I think, better and growing better. I suppose I shall never entirely recover from the shock my constitution received at the time of my Father's death. The fatigue and excitement of that period came upon me at a time when I was so ill able to bear it, and all my pursuits and propensities have a tendency to make my head worse. It is but a bad head; as bad as if I were a great man. I know I am not entitled to so bad a head by any thing I have done; but I flatter myself it is very interesting of me to suffer so much and a good excuse for not writing pretty letters and saying to my friends the good things I think about them. Indeed it is not exaggeration to say that what with my engagements and what with my head I could barely live from day to day and that there was no time when I *could* write any letter.

I was so new to a public position and so desirous to do all I could that I took a great deal more upon myself than I was able to bear. Yet now the twenty five weeks of incessant toil are over I rejoice in it all and would not have done an iota less. I have fulfilled all my engagements faithfully. I have acquired more power of attention, self-command and fortitud[e] I have acted in life as I thought I would in my lonely bower. I have acquired some kn[ow]ledge of means, and, blessed be the fat[ ] of our spirits! my aims are the same as they were in the happiest flight of youthful fancy.

I have learnt too at last to rejoice in all past pain. I have now found its practical benefit. I see that my spirit has been so judiciously tempered for its work— In future I may sorrow but can I ever despair?—

The beginning of my winter was forlorn. I was always ill. I often thought I might not live. The work but just begun perhaps I must die. The usual disappointments were about me. Those from whom I had expected aid disappointed me. Others who aided did not understand me. My enthusiasm fled about the things I loved best when I seemed to be buying and selling it. I could not get the proper point of view— I could not keep a healthful state of mind. Mysteriously a gulf seemed to have opened between me and my most intimate friends. For the first time for so many years I felt entirely, absolutely alone. My own character and designs lost all romantic interest in my eyes. I felt vulgarized, profaned forsaken, and was obliged to smile so brightly and talk so wisely all the while.

But all these clouds past away. I hope, I trust these were the last agonies of factitious life and that I shall now repose in the arms of nature and destiny, that my heart will now vibrate in unison with the soul of the world. Leben im Ganzen [is] to be my motto— can I be disappointed?—

I will try to tell you what I have done with my classes in the way of study. To one class I taught the Gn language in the way I tried with Sarah and the Randalls. S. will remember. I thought myself very successful; at the end of three months they could read 20 pages of Gn at a lesson and very well. This, class of course, was nothing to me except in the way of observation and analysis of language.

With my more advanced pupils I read in 14 weeks, Schiller's Don Carlos, Schiller's artists and Song of the Bell besides one lesson in wh I gave a sort of lecture on Schiller,— Goethe's Hermann and Dorothea, Goetz of Berlichingen, Iphigenia, First part of Faust (three weeks of thorough study this as valuable to me as to them) and Clavigo, thus comprehending samples of all his efforts in poesy &c bringing forward some of his prominent opinions. Lessing's Nathan, Minna, Emilia Gaelotti, parts of Tieck's Phantasus, and nearly the whole firs[t] vol. of Richter's Titan.—[1] With my Italn class I read parts of Tasso, Petrarch, (whom they came to almost adore) Ariosto, Alfieri, and the whole hundred cantos of the Divina Commedia with the aid of the fine Athenaeum copy and all the best commentaries. This last piece of work was and will be truly valuable to myself.

I had besides three private pupils, Mrs G. Lee, (who became very interesting to me) E. Shattuck, and little E. Bond who had not the use of his eyes I taught him Latin orally and read the Hist of England and Shakespeare's histl plays in connection.[2] I gave this lesson every day for ten weeks; it was very interesting, but very fatiguing to me. Mr Alcott's school wa[s] also very fatiguing. I, however, loved the chi[ ] had many valuable thoughts suggested there. I cannot have room to write about this now, nor about Mr Alcott whose society was much to me. By the way, dear James, I rejoice in the warm interest you have taken for Mr A. It was like you and has not been lost on his heart as I saw from a passage in his journal.

—As you may imagine I have not yet written the Life of Goethe but have studied and thought about it a great deal. It grows in my mind with every thing that does grow there. It is now engaged to Mr Ripley on such terms as I could desire. Three years are given me to write it in and it can be recd as much sooner into the series as I may wish. My friends in Europe have sent me the books I need on the subject I am now beginning to work in good earnest. I see is possible my task may be taken from me [o]r somebody in England that in doing it I may find myself in compe[tition] but I go on in hope, secure at all events [ ] will be the means of the highest culture.

I fear I am injuring you and trespassing on your generosity in keeping your Goethe, but I have not been able to send for it till now. I trust to receive it from Europe in Autumn and shall then return yours with a thousand thanks.

My readings with Dr C. amounted to but little except that this gave me oppory of seeing him a great deal. When I went to bid him good bye he asked my how he could send to you and I told him

I hope correctly. I made many agreeable acquaintances and several dear friends whom I have no time or room to tell about now. Mr and Mrs Ripley I enjoyed delightful hours with. I am very sorry— I did not see this ink on my writing desk till it was too late will you forgive so bad-looking a letter rather than not have any?— I know you will but do, please, burn it—

I have not answered your letter as I meant— perhaps I never shall now till we meet. When will that be? I wish I had room to tell you about Mr Emerson's lectures and the week I have just passed at his house and his beautiful baby—

When Sarah returns she will not find me in Boston, though possibly I may be there next winter I shall be in Providence R. Island. She must stop and see me as she comes— I depend upon it. I know she has a friend lives there and at Revd Mr Hall's she will hear where I am. I do not yet know myself where I shall board but shall go to Providence the first of June. I have been tempted there by the liberal salary offered me and other inducements. I am offered a thousand dollars a year for teaching four hours a day in my own department. But if it does not suit my health or tastes, or interferes with my main project I shall not stay I have only promised to try it. If I find a letter from you there I think I shd answer it soon.

Do not speak to any one but Sarah of my engagement with Mr R. about the Life of G.— it is indeed like the secrets of the stage so many know it, yet I wish to avoid all unnecessary publicity. For often I am ashamed and think I am too, *too* unfit for so great a work.

Lebewohl mein Jungende Freund.—

M. F.

(MHi)

1. Fuller's reading was heavily weighted toward eighteenth-century drama. Not already identified are Schiller's *Don Carlos, Infant von Spanien* (1787); *Die Künstler* (the play, not the poem of the same name) (1789); "Das Lied von der Glocke" (1799); Goethe's *Hermann und Dorothea* (1797), *Götz von Berlichingen* (1773), *Iphigenie auf Tauris* (1787), the first part of *Faust* (1808), and *Clavigo* (1774); and Lessing's *Nathan der Weise* (1779), *Minna von Barnhelm* (1763), and *Emilia Galotti* (1772).

2. Hannah Farnham Sawyer (1780–1865), a writer, married George Gardner Lee; Eleanor Shattuck (1819–42) was the daughter of George Shattuck, a prominent Boston doctor.

32.   To John S. Dwight

Groton 31st May, 1837.

Dear Sir,

Miss Tuckerman writes me that you are desirous to know what I have done in the way of translation. I am truly ashamed when I think of my large promises and small performance.

> "Wie wenig, ach! hat sich entfaltet,
> Diess wenige, wie klein und karg."[1]

There have, indeed, been few hours since my return home that I have felt equal to exertion of any sort, but all which I have spent in attempts at translation have made me painfully sensible of my presumptuosness in undertaking what I did. I hope you will forgive me, for I had no idea of deceiving you, but thought some good daemon would stand my friend when I should attempt to do what I so much desired; but not a breath of inspiration has been vouchsafed. My book of translations is but a sorry sight; and I never rise from it without a strong desire to wash its witness from my hand and, indeed, to wash my incompetent hands of the whole affair— Goethe's unrhimed poems are entirely beyond me. When there is no metre to guide me I can bear no words but his own and could never get beyond the first verse of "Das Göttliche"— I have translated great part of Das Ideal und das Leben, and about half of die Künstler, but I am altogether dispirited by the result and cannot, at present, summon courage to go on.[2] I send you some of the poor things I have done and, I fear, the best— I fancy few so harmonious and delicately finished can have been submitted to you!!—

"Die Worte des Glaubens"— "worte des Wahns," "Spiel des Lebens"— and "Hoffnung" by Schiller "Eins und Alles" and "Sehnsucht" by Goethe I have translated but still worse than what I send.[3] The little piece "To a golden heart" is done, I think, better than any of these, though translated several years ago— That from Schiller "To my friends" is very bad. I merely send it, because copied on the same piece of paper and I have not time to recopy.[4]

I shall be in Boston on Friday and stay till Saty but, as I may not see you, shall leave this parcel with Mrs Ripley.[5] I know you must be disappointed but wish to prove to you that I have, at least, not been entirely unmindful of my promises.— I do not think you will wish me to go on but, if you do, *faute de mieux,* please write to me at Providence, tell me what has been done already by yourself and others and let me know my latest day of grace, if I am to try any more. I shall make no more promises as neither time or capacity *may* be granted me to do any-thing— With best wishes for your success

S. M. FULLER.

Providence June 8th

I did not see Mrs Ripley and forgot to leave this parcel for you— Since I have looked at Dauer im Wechsel again it seems to me too unworthy; and I am inclined if time should permit to try again.[6] But I cannot tell as yet whether time will permit—I have had no moment since I came here.— I send two of Mr Clarke's translations— all which I could find.—

Please say to Miss Tuckerman that I hope to write both to her and Miss Sturgis in a few days—[7]

(MB)

1. From Schiller's "Die Ideale": "Ah, how little has unfolded itself, / that little, how small and mean."

2. Dwight published two translations of Goethe's "Das Göttliche" (1785), his own and one by George Bancroft. Fuller translated it in her essay on Menzel in the January 1841 *Dial.* Dwight also published his own translations of Schiller's "Das Ideal und das Leben" and "Die Künstler" in his *Select Minor Poems, Translated from the German of Goethe and Schiller.*

3. Fuller names Schiller's "Die Worte des Glaubens" (1797), "Die Worte des Wahns" (1799), "Das Spiel des Lebens" (1796), and "Hoffnung" (1797); and Goethe's "Eins und Alles" (1821) and "Sehnsucht" (1793).

4. Dwight published Fuller's translation of "An ein goldenes Herz, das er am Halse trug" (1789) but not that of Schiller's "An die Freunde" (1802).

5. Sophia Dana (1803–61), daughter of Francis and Sophia Dana of Cambridge, married George Ripley in 1827.

6. Her translation of Goethe's "Dauer im Wechsel" (1803) was not published in her lifetime.

7. Caroline Sturgis.

33.   To A. Bronson Alcott

Providence 27th June, 1837.

Dear Sir,

I had flattered myself that you would have been in haste to begin our correspondence since you disappointed me of the expected oppory of conversing with you at the time of the dedication of the school— But since you will neither come nor write my desire to hear from you is so strong that I must do something on my side—

I am sorry you were not here to listen to Mr Emerson's "good words" which fell, if I may judge from the remarks they called forth, on stony soil—[1] Yet there is always comfort in the thought that, if such seed must not fertilize the spot for which it was intended, the fowl of the air may carry it away to some more propitious clime. And I myself—who was much cheered and instructed on the occasion, may be that bird if there should be none other, which I may not think. For here also the Sun speaks, and the Moon smiles, and here also human souls must be alive to their vocation and some must know how truth and knowledge are to be wooed and won—

I am much pleased with my new haunt as far as the eye is concerned— I believe you have never seen the building— it is in excellent taste and all the arrangements speak of comfort quiet and even elegance. Nothing is wanting to make it look the home of thought except more books, a few casts and a picture or two which will be added in due time.— As to the occupants of this fair abode I have not yet seen them through and through but feel now able to form a tolerably fair estimate of the state of the children and from their state can infer that of the families to which they belong. It is low compared with Boston and even with villages in its vicinity, for here is the hostile element of money getting with but little counterpoise— Yet there is an affectionate, if not an intelligent sympathy in this community with Mr Fuller and his undertaking which will not, I trust, be felt in vain.[2] Mr Fuller is in many respects particularly suited to this business. His ready sympathy, his active eye, and pious, tender turn of thought are so adapted to all the practical part; The danger arising from that sort of education which has unfolded there is that he may not be sufficiently systematic and not observe due gradation and completeness in his plans. However all is tentative that is doing yet and those Powers who have so [favored] him will now, it is to be hoped, turn a [fairer] side to the light— I often think, dear Sir, with pleasure on the roundness (as Mr Emerson perhaps would express it) of your world— There were details in which I thought your plan imperfect, but it only needs to compare pupils who have been treated as many of these have with those who have been under your care to sympathize with your creed that those who would reform the world should begin with the beginning of life— Particularly do I feel the importance of your attempts to teach the uses of language and cultivate the imagination in dealing with young persons who have had no faculties exercised except the memory and the common, practical understanding. In *your* children I found an impatience of labor but a liveliness of mind, in many of *these* with well-disposed hearts, [the] mind has been absolutely torpid. Those who have been under Mr F's care are in far better state than the rest.—

I hope you will write soon and let me know as much of your thoughts and affairs as you can. Please give my regards to Mrs Alcott and believe me always sincerely your friend.

S. M. FULLER.

(MH: 59m-312 [122])

1. Matt. 13:5.

2. Hiram Fuller (1814–80), who was not her relative, moved to Providence in 1836 and began his Greene-Street School. He later moved to New York City, where he wrote for the *New York Mirror* and became sympathetic to the South in the Civil War.

34. To Arthur B. Fuller

Providence 5th July, 1837—

My dear Arthur—

I was glad to get a few lines from you, but I wish you to study the art of saying more in your epistles and saying it well. Nothing [but] practice is necessary for this I know, as you have plenty of thoughts in your mind. Many boys in our school of ten or eleven, inferior to you in natural capacity, write better. They have acquired some power of expression and a neat hand by the practice of keeping a journal for Mr Fuller and some of their intimate friends to read. *All* the scholars in the upper department of our school are now to do this. Each has been provided with a book, neatly bound in morrocco, and lettered on the back "School journal." I, too, have one of these books, but do not write in it as much as my pupils do in theirs— They are very anxious to know if they shall ever be permitted to read mine— I tell them; perhaps so, if I am able to speak well of them in it.— Last week some of theirs were read aloud to the school, though without mentioning the names of the writers. The journal of one boy who spoke of the girls as "sweet sisters" and "fair *as Eden's garden birds*" excited a general *smile*. We are too refined to laugh loud at the Greene St School!!

I will now tell you how I pass my time and give some idea of our school. I am, (bid Mother marvel,) almost always up at 5 and sometimes at half past 4 in the morning. I am completely dressed by 6 and then devote myself to my own studies till half past 7 when we breakfast. My school lessons require no preparation and I have got them nicely arranged now. They are in composition, elocution, histy, three classes in Latin, one of boys, several of whom I am much interested in and will describe them when I write to Richard, two classes in Natural philosophy, and one in Ethics. These are so distributed as not to fatigue me at all. At half past 8 I go to the school. You enter through a wide, gate, a piazza, and a pretty, wide door into a small entry on each side of which is a dressing room, one for the girls and one for the boys. Each dressing room is furnished with looking glasses, pegs for each scholar's hat, or bonnet, and places for overshoes if they wear them. There are two doors into the great hall one for the girls, one for the boys, so they need never and do never romp or interfere. This hall is thickly carpeted, the walls are white, finished with pink, the ceiling arched with a place in the centre for a chandelier, if it should be needed. We talk of having eveg conversations or dances, or musical parties for scholars next winter—but nothing is decided about that. Between the doors stands the piano with a neat French cloak upon it. The principal color of the carpet is orange which harmonizes very well with the black and brown desks and chairs. There are on each side of this hall two rows of boys and girls, *all* neatly dressed, indeed, some people object to us that rather too much ambition about appearance is encouraged, but if they lived there they would like the comfort of dealing with neat well dressed people as well as we do. At the upper end on a platform raised two steps from the floor stand Mr F's chair and study table with shelves and drawers for books and papers. On it stand two vases for flowers wh are filled by the children; (tell Mother we had two blossoms from a tulip tree to day and they are beautiful,) and four glass goblets from wh the children drink water wh is kept for them in a handsome urn before the platform. On the right hand is a sofa for visitors and where I too sit when I am not in one of the recitation rooms. Mrs Nias and Miss Aborn are generally in the morng down stairs where is the schoolroom for the little children, with the washroom &c—[1] I see I shall not have time to describe them particularly as I could wish

All these young people look healthy and *excessively* happy. They seem enchanted with the school. Almost all are docile, many eager in improvement. I have already become attached to individuals. I find all very easy to manage and feel as if they were beginning to understand what I want of them. As I said before I will describe some of my favorites a week or two hence when I write to Richard. I shall write to Mother next. Perhaps, too, I shall tell him about the procession and the fireworks wh I saw yesterday from the roof of the mansion House.

I did not receive the books till day before yesterday and then not without a deal of trouble and vexation. But I deserved it for my carelessness in omitting my direction I suppose I thought I had given it and, being in haste, did not read the letter over. Ellen's roses were mouldy, but I thank her as much as if they were fresh. I generally have bouquets from the school girls every fair day— I see I did not tell what I did with the rest of my day after school. I get home when I do not go to walk, a little before one, dine at half-past, lie down till three, then write or study till tea time. After tea walk or make visits till ten,—to bed about eleven. So I live very rationally—

Dear Mother must not make herself sick, unless she wants to make me miserable.— Love to All the family and Rebecca. If Miss Tilden is with you give my regards to her and say I am glad she is with you for Mother and Ellen's sake. Eugene must write me about his journey to Boston &c— Has John Randall gone? very afftly your Sister

M.

(MH: fMS Am 1086 [9:44])

1. Georgianna Nias, the dancing teacher, was an Englishwoman; Frances Aborn (1816–90), another teacher, was the daughter of Fuller's landlady.

35. To Margarett C. Fuller

Concord 5th Septr 1837—

My very dear Mother,

Do not suffer the remarks of that sordid man to give you any uneasiness—[1] Proceed to act as we agreed when I was with you. It is perfectly clear to my mind that the arrangements we then made are the right ones and I do not fear to hold myself responsible for the consequences.

If Abraham Fuller continues to annoy you in this manner I am decidedly of opinion that the management of our affairs had better be transferred to someother lawyer. I think Hillard and Sumner would give us satisfaction; their reputation stands very fair:[2] They arranged Mr Tuckerman's affairs at the time of his failure; both would be interested in me. If you preferred an older man we can find such an one. We pay Abraham and we could as well pay another man who would confine himself to his proper post of managing the money. You must, my dear Mother, steadily consider yourself as the guardian of the children. You must not let his vulgar insults make you waver as to giving the children advantages to which they would be well entitled if the property were only a third of what it now is. I cannot like you think that feelings of kindness, however narrow the mind of the writer, could induce him to taunt you or Eugene or say things which he knows to be false. Do not suffer yourself to be puzzled or scared by such stuff. No Judge in the world will ever interfere with your management of the minor children unless we who are of age request it, as you are well aware we never shall.

Fit out the children for school, and let not Lloyd be forgotten. You incur an awful responsibility by letting him go so neglected any longer. I shall get Ellen a place at Mrs Urquhart's, if possible; if not, I may take her to Providence, for I hear of no better place. She shall not be treated in this shameful way, bereft of proper advantages and plagued and cramped in the May of life. If I stay at Providence and Abraham manages to trouble you about money before we can get other arrangements made I will pay her bills, if I do not stay there, I will put the affair into the hands of a lawyer: we will see if she is not to have "a year's schooling from twelve to eighteen. I am not angry but I am determined. I am sure that my Father, if he could see me, would approve the view I take. If means are wanting I am sure I could find them. If I stay in Providence and more is wanting than can otherwise be furnished I will take a private class which is ready for me and by which, even if I reduced my terms to suit the place, I can earn the four hundred dollars that Ellen will need. If I do not stay I will let her have my portion of our income with her own, or even capital which I have a right to take up and come into this or some economical place and live at the cheapest rate. It will not even be a sacrifice to me to do so for I am sated and weary of society; and long for the oppory for solitary concentration of thought for my book. I know what I say— if I live you may rely on me.

Nothing will grieve me so as to know that you have given up the plans we arranged. My only regret is that you are to give that sum of eighty dollars to a member of our family whom it will in nowise benefit. I advise you to sell as much of the stock as you can and use the money for fitting out the children and paying up your house bills. The school bills may be sent to A. W. So soon as I receive money at P and have a safe oppory I will send you some. Be firm, and pay no attention to the thoughts of your low-minded brother in law.

Ellen must take great care not to take cold, now that she has the eruption on her. I should be very sad, if any ill should come to my good little sister. Write to me on Saturday, direct to Providence let me know how she is and how Frances Shattuck is. God be with you, my dear Mother, be sure he will prosper the doings of so excellent a woman if you will only keep your mind calm, and be firm. Trust your daughter too— I feel increasing trust in mine own good mind; we will take good care of the children and, one another. My best love to Eugene, love to the boys and Rebecca. Never fear to trouble me with your perplexities I can never be situated so that I do not earnestly wish to know them. Besides things do

The Fuller family. Daguerreotype, early 1850s. From the Left: Arthur, Eugene, Ellen, Margarett Crane, and Richard. Courtesy of Elizabeth Channing Fuller and Willard P. Fuller, Jr.

not trouble me as they did for I feel within myself the power to aid—to serve. Mention the Tildens when you write. I do hope the journey will benefit poor Maria.

Most afftly your

S. M. F.

Wednesday morng— I feel so anxious about Ellen that I wish you would write directly you receive this— direct to Boston instead of Providence, care of H. H. Fuller, post paid—

I will take Eugene's letter from the P. Office in Boston and send it to Groton. He will probably get it Saturday or Sunday.

(MH: fMS Am 1086 [9:45])

1. Abraham Fuller had been appointed executor of Timothy's estate.
2. George Hillard (1808–79) and Charles Sumner (1811–74) were law partners in Boston. Hillard, a close friend of Hawthorne, was interested in literature; Sumner later became the most prominent abolitionist in the U.S. Senate.

36. To Caroline Sturgis

Providence Rhode Island
16th Novr 1837—

My dear Caroline,

When I saw your Father in September I felt a natural delicacy about interfering in your affairs, (although conscious of very pure and kind motives) and apologized, to which he replied by begging me not, and saying that he must always consider any manifestation of interest from me in your behalf as a *kindness and a favor*—[1]

When I spoke of your coming here and asked if it would be agreeable to him, he replied *it would extremely so;* that *he could have no objection except from the fear that I might be taking too much care upon myself.*— When I asked if he would *object to your boarding at the City Hotel* with me, and gave some reasons for fearing he might, he said that he had *perfect confidence in your discretion,* and that any *arrangement I might think proper for myself he should also esteem proper for you,* and left me, requesting *to hear from me on the subject as soon as I should decidedly know what arrangements I could make.*

Remembering all this distinctly (for I was much pleased by your father's manner and spoke of it to several of our mutual friends and by repetition even his words were impressed on my memory,) I cannot but feel strong indignation at the statements contained in your letter, at the levity and discourtesy with which I *seem* to be treated, and at the unnecessary trouble which has been given me.

I have nothing to say as to what you shall do. My feelings towards you are unchanged. They are those of warm affection and interest for your welfare. I know not of another young person of whom, under my present circumstances, I would have taken similar charge. I have avoided taking one into the house who would have given me very little trouble, and whose friends were earnestly desirous of having her under my influence— I may venture to say that my motives with regard to you were those of dis- interested, and uncommon kindness, and ought to have been met in a very different manner.

The question as to whether you shall come rests with yourself and your family. Here or any-where I shall be glad to receive you. I might cease *to visit you* but should always be happy to have you v[is]it me. I live at Mrs Susan Aborn's, Aborn St.— Any hackman when you leave the cars would know where it is. I should not wish to receive you before Tuesday unless you can mail a letter so that I can get it on Saty to tell me that you can come on Monday. We have no Sunday mail, I believe. And this much cer- emony, at least, is due me and quite necessary as I must inform my hostess about your coming.—

As to transcendentalism and the nonsense which is talked by so many about it— I do not know what is meant. For myself I should say that if it is meant that I have an active mind frequently busy with large topics I hope it is so— If it is meant that I am honored by the friendship of such men as Mr Emerson, Mr Ripley, or Mr Alcott, I hope it is so— *But* if it is meant that I cherish any opinions which interfere with domestic duties, cheerful courage and judgement in the practical affairs of life, I challenge any or all in the little world which knows me to prove such deficiency from any acts of mine since I came to woman's estate.—

You are at liberty to show this letter if you please to your parents. I per- mit but do not *require* it, because I think as your letter was written in haste some expressions may have given me exaggerated notions— You are on the spot, and can judge; do as you think proper.

Let me once more, before I close, repeat to you the assurances of my af- fection. If you have dallied with me, I know it is not your fault— You would never wilfully interfere with my comfort or feelings in any way and are in- capable of treating me in an indelicate manner. But at the same time, if you do not come, I shall not write again. I do not wish to be needlessly agi- tated by exchanging another letter on this topic— I will let you know when I am in Boston and see you there at least once— Sincerely your friend

S. M. FULLER.

(MH: bMS Am 1221 [209])

1. William Sturgis (1782–1863) was a wealthy merchant, who undoubtedly disapproved of Fuller's literary circle.

37.   To Margarett C. Fuller

Providence 18th Novr 1837.

My dear Mother,

As I am just this moment at leisure, I think I will begin a letter to you although uncertain whether I shall be able to finish it.

I am sorry Ellen's reports should have occasioned you so much alarm about my health. As to what I said about the probability of never being perfectly well again; it is, you know, my disposition always to prefer being prepared for the worst— I do not trouble myself about it or look gloomily forward to a future which lies in the hand of God. I am cheerful, steadfast; if I should never be well I yet trust to do well. The only part of it I regret is that nothing but dissipation agrees with me. You need not be afraid of my exerting my mind too much. It is no longer in my power to write or study much. I cannot bear it and do not attempt it. Heaven, I believe, had no will that I should accomplish any-thing great or beautiful. Yet I do not dispair, daily I do a little and leave the result to a higher power. As to my writing constant bulletins of my health; it is impossible— I cannot; it would be too irksome; even disgusting to me, and quite like our old acquaintances the Misses Williams; besides my feelings vary so much from day to day that I should probably be feeling well and bright by the time you had my letter and were mourning over my ill health. If I am seriously unwell I will certainly let you know— I do not wish to write a minute account of my circumstances, but I shall see you in Boston in about three weeks, and then, if I am not better, you can talk with a physician and I will take tonics— I feel much better these last few days, Ellen fixes eggs with wine and they do me a great deal of good.

I think Ellen very much improved both in mind and manners. I take pleasure in her society and should like to have her remain with me, if it were best for her, but I am satisfied it would not be. She has, I believe, enjoyed herself here very much. All her things are nicely made up and she looks very pretty in them. She has been about here a good deal and seen some of the best people who are pleased with her. Mr Fowler the phrenologist, has been here, and examined both our heads. His sketch of her was excellent.[1] She will tell it you when you meet.

Mr Hastings, (Fanny's father) has been here this afternoon. He is a droll man.

My love to Eugene— Tell him I hav[e] had two letters from Thesta, the last of which I have not yet answered. She wishes to come here awhile, and board this winter. Said "she was very triste at Kingston, she scarce knew why" but I do— she is too fond of the excitement of society.

I believe, when I wrote, we had not seen Ellen Tree.[2] She passed a day in Providence with some parishioners of Mr Farley's and Mr F. took Ellen and myself, with Elizh Channing, to see her. We had a very agreeable eveg. She is very pleasing in her manners, talks very intelligently and read to us some of the last scenes in Ion.[3] I forgot to ask her how she liked Uncle Abraham!

I shall write to Richard next time. Do not urge me to write more frequently; once a fortnight is as much as I can. I pay like attention to no one else. Nothing disagrees with me so much as writing, and I avoid it when possible. Letters from those in whom I am most interested, from Mr Emerson, M. Channing, S. Ward have been lying for many weeks unanswered in my desk.

I hope you have of late been undisturbed and that every thing goes on smoothly. Love to the boys and Rebecca. I am so glad Lloyd is fairly at school, a weight is lifted from my conscience. Heaven bless you, dearest Mother, your and Eugene's affectionate letter was very grateful to me.

In all love and duty yours

S. M. FULLER.

Tell Eugene I am charmed with Ernest Maltravers and think it Bulwer's best.[4]

(MH: fMS Am 1086 [9:56])

1. Orson Fowler (1809–87), who, with his brother Lorenzo, lectured frequently on phrenology, a topic in which Fuller had a lifelong interest.
2. Ellen Tree (1805–80) was an English actress then touring the United States.
3. Thomas Noon Talfourd, *Ion* (1835).
4. Edward Bulwer-Lytton, *Ernest Maltravers* (1837).

38. To Anna Jameson

Providence Rhode Island
22d Decr 1837

Dear Madam

The enclosed is a copy of a letter which I addressed to you some weeks since, supposing you to have returned to England.

How great was my mortification on a late visit to Boston to find that you had just left that city, and that, as you had passed much of your time with persons whom I know well, I too should have enjoyed your society if I had gone thither a little earlier.

But all this pain was increased when I was told by Dr Channing that you had lived so long in the family of Goethe's daughter in law and were consequently the very person in the world who could best aid me.[1] He added that you seemed to feel a natural delicacy about any new disclosures. But oh! if I could but see you I am persuaded that you would tell me all I wish to know— Is it quite impossible for me to see you? How I wish I was famous or could paint beautiful pictures and then you would not be willing to go without seeing me. But now— I know not how to interest you,—the miserable frigid letter within will not interest you— Yet I am worthy to know you, and be known by you, and if you could see me you would soon believe it, and now I need you so very much. I would come to New York and see you if it were possible, but I fear it is not. I have no days to myself except Saturday and Sunday. I teach in the mornings in a school the other five days in the week— You must not get an ugly picture of me because I am a schoolmistress. I have not yet acquired that "strong mental odour" that Coleridge speaks of.[2] I am only teaching for a little while and I want to *learn* of you.

I had quite given you up, for Mr Dwight told me you were to sail in a few days and I saw no means of getting at you, but Mr Thompson, an artist, who was here today, tells me you are still expected in New York and that he hopes to see you there.[3] May I request th[at] you will write me a line and say [how] long you shall be there although I fear, I fear I cannot come. And when a few hours talk with you would do me so much good— *are* there not hard things to bear in life?—

Be so good as not to speak of my intended work— it is known only to a few persons. Precarious health, the pressure of many ties make me fearful of promising what I will do.— I may die soon—you may never more hear my name. But the earnest aspiration, the sympathy with greatness never dies— Es lebt im Asche—[4]

Respectfully

S. M. FULLER.

(CtY)

1. Ottilie von Pogwisch (1796–1872) married Julius August von Goethe in 1817.   Mrs. Jameson recorded her impressions of the Goethe family in her *Visits and Sketches at Home and Abroad.*

2. About teachers, Coleridge said in a letter, "with respect to females, do they not all possess a sort of *mental* odour?"

3. Cephas Giovanni Thompson (1809–88) was a portrait painter.

4. "It lives in ashes."

39.   To Arthur B. Fuller

Providence 31st Decr 1837,—

My dear Arthur,

I wish I were near enough to send you some new year's gift tomorrow, but, since I am not, you shall, at least, have a letter.

I thought you would like to have a picture of the house where I pass so many hours and have, therefore, taken one of the bills to write upon. I sent one to Richard and intend writing to Lloyd in the same way by and by.

I was very glad to get your letter, but very sorry it was so short. I want my brother, who can talk so fluently, and who has many thoughts which *I* should think worth knowing to learn to express them in writing. It is the more important to me as I may, probably, be very little with you the remainder of my life, and, if you do not learn to write, you and I, who have been such good friends, may become as strangers to one another. It is more desirable that you should write than I, both because you are changing more than I shall change, and because I have many occupations and many claims on my feelings and attention; you, comparatively, few. I wish you would begin a letter to me as soon as you receive this, write in it from time to time as things occur worth telling and whenever the sheet is full send it me. I will not fail to answer it as soon as I can. You need not pay postage when you write to me, but I will pay when I write to you as I suppose you want all your pocket money.

You express gratitude for what I have taught you. It is in your power to repay me a hundred fold by making every exertion now to improve. I did not teach you as I would, yet I think the confinement and care I took of you children, at a time when my mind was much excited by many painful feelings, have had a very bad effect upon my health. I do not say this to pain you or make you more grateful to me, (for, probably if I had been aware at the time what I was doing, I might not have sacrificed myself so,) but I say it that you may feel it your duty to fill my place and do what I may never be permitted to do. Three precious years at the best period of life I gave all my best hours to you children— let me not see you idle away time which I have always valued so, let me not find you unworthy of the love I felt for you. Those three years would have enabled me to make great attainments which now I never may. Do you make them in my stead that I may not remember that time with sadness.—

I hope you are fully aware of the great importance of your conduct this year. It will decide your fate. You are now fifteen and if, at the end of the year, we have not reason to be satisfied that you have a decided taste for study and ambition to make a figure in one of the professions, you will be consigned to some other walk in life. For you are aware that there is no money to be wasted on any one of us, though, if I live and thrive, and you deserve my sympathy, you shall not want means and teaching to follow out any honorable path—

With your sister Ellen's improvement and desire to do right and perseverance in overcoming obstacles I am well satisfied. I feel pretty sure Richard will do well, but I feel greater anxiety about you, my dear Arthur. I know you have both heart and head, but you have always been deficient in earnestness and forethought May God bless you, may I assist you to conquer these faults and make this coming year a prelude to many honorable years!

If Mr Haven is still at Leicester I wish you to present my compliments to him and say that I much regret never having had an opportunity to thank him for his kind care of you when you were there before[1] Next time I write, I will not fill the whole sheet with advice. Advice, generally, does little good, but I will not believe I shall speak in vain to my dear Arthur.—

Very affectionately your sister

S. M. FULLER.

(MH: fMS Am 1086 [9:46])

1. Luther Haven (1806–66) of Framingham was the assistant preceptor at the Leicester Academy until he went to Chicago to become superintendent of schools.

40.   To Ralph Waldo Emerson

Providence 1st March 1838—

My dear friend,

Many a Zelterian epistle have I mentally addressed to you full of sprightly scraps about the books I have read, the spectacles I have seen, and the attempts at men and women with whom I have come in contact. But I have not been able to put them on paper, for even when I have attempted it, you have seemed so busy and noble, and I so poor and dissipated that I have not felt worthy to address you.

At present I am not at all Zelterian in my mood but very sombre and sullen. I have shut the door for a few days and tried to do something— You have *really* been doing something! And that is why I write— I want to see you and still more to hear you. I must kindle my torch again. Why have I not heard you this winter?[1] I feel very humble just now yet I dare to say that being lives not who would have received from your lectures as much as I should. There are noble books but one wants the breath of life sometimes. And I see no divine person. I myself am more divine than any I see— I think that is enough to say about them— I know Dr Wayland now, but I shall not care for him.[2] He would never understand me, and, if I met him, it must be by those means of suppression and accommodation which I at present hate to my hearts core. I hate every-thing that is reasonable just now, "wise limitations" and all. I have behaved much too well for some time past; it has spoiled my peace. What grieves me too is to find or fear my theory a cheat— I cannot serve two masters, and I fear all the hope of being a worldling and a literary existence also must be resigned— Isolation is necessary to me as to others. Yet I keep on "fulfilling all my duties" as the technical phrase is except to myself.— But why do I write thus to you who like nothing but what is good i e cheerfulness and fortitude? It is partly because yours is an image of my oratory. I suppose you will not know what this means. and if I do not jest when I write to you I must *pray*. And partly as a preliminary to asking you, unsympathizing, unhelpful, wise good man that you are to do several things for me. I hear you are to deliver one of your lectures again in Boston. I would have you do it while I am there. I shall come on Wednesday next and stay till the following Monday Perhaps you will come to see me, fo[r] though I am not as good as I was, yet as I said before, I am better than most persons *I* see and, I dare say, better than most persons *you* see. But perhaps you do not need to see anybody, for you are acting and nobly— If so you need not come yourself, but send me your two lectures on Holiness and Heroism to read while in Boston. Let me have these two lectures to read *at any rate,* whether you come or no. Do not disappoint me. I will treat them well and return them safe. I shall be at Mr Sturgis's all the time. I shall come out on Thursday to hear you at Cambridge, but they wrote me that lecture would be on the Heart and not so fine as some of yours.[3]

I have not read any books except what every body reads, Gardiner on Music (thank *you* for that; it was a great deal to me.) Carlyle as noble as I hoped, absorbing me quite for a fortnight, Lamb's letters, Whately's Rhetoric.[4]

Lately I have been amusing myself with looking at you through two pair of spectacles of very dissimilar construction in Brownson's review and the Democratic.[5] I have a disciple of yours in my German class—a very lovely young man. He has never seen you but gets regular bulletins of you from some friend in Boston— I suppose I could get them animated into inviting you to speak to the Larvae here if you would come. Several gentlemen promised me their aid, if there was a chance of getting you. Adieu Sanctissime. Tell Lidian that the thought of her holiness is very fragrant to me. Tell your son that if he has grown less like Raphael's cherubs I will never forgive him. Tell my dear Elizabeth that I love her just as I did last August, but shall probably never write to her—[6]

Devoutly if not worthily yours

S. M. FULLER.

(MH: bMS Am 1280 [2341])

1. Emerson had a busy lecture season. Between November and March he gave his Human Culture series in Lowell, Boston, Framingham, and Cambridge.

2. Francis Wayland (1796–1865) was president of Brown from 1827 to 1855.

3. Emerson delivered his lecture "War" on 12 March in Boston; "Heart" opened his Cambridge series on 8 March. "Heroism" and "Holiness" were the eighth and ninth lectures.

4. William Gardiner, *Music of Nature* (1832); Thomas Carlyle, *The French Revolution* (1837); Thomas Noon Talfourd, ed. *The Letters of Charles Lamb* (1837); Richard Whately, *Elements of Rhetoric* (1828).

5. Orestes Brownson (1803–76) had a long religious and writing career, moving from Universalism to Roman Catholicism. He founded *The Boston Quarterly Review,* in which Fuller read his review of Emerson's Phi Beta Kappa address. *The United States Magazine and Democratic Review,* founded and edited by John Louis O'Sullivan, published Elizabeth Peabody's review of Emerson's *Nature* in the February issue.

6. Elizabeth Sherman Hoar.

41.   To Caroline Sturgis

Providence—[24?] July 1838—

Your letter, my dear Cary, deserved an immediate answer, but I can hardly prevail on myself to write even at this late date. In that cool place where you have been so fortunate as to pass this excessively hot weather you can have no idea how I have suffered. The thermometer has been at ninety and ninety three many days when I have walked a mile and a half from my school home. And I walk in same distance in morng Repeatedly I have been wrought up almost to frenzy by the heat— I have been obliged to sit down and cry a long while after I got there to relieve myself and repeat the process on returning home.

Home! Oh Cary, my extreme weakness has made me feet so homeless, so forlorn! at such times I have felt so much the need of somebody to bring me strengthening drinks, or to bathe my head. However I shall drag through somehow, I suppose.— In many respects I am more fortunate than heretofore. I suffer no violent pain, I have an appetite— the country is very lovely round me and though I rarely feel able to take walks, I look out of my window with great satisfaction and watch the afternoon lights and shades. I do not attempt to do any thing unless I am obliged. I know what a terrible weight of business must come on me by and by to pay for all this inertia, but I cannot help it. This is the first time I have really felt so utterly incompetent to do any thing. I do wish I could yield entirely to this languour. I wish I could lean on some friendly arm for a while It cannot be. I cannot even neglect my friends with impunity, for, if I do they will not write to me.— You have not written again, though you have nothing to do, and are in a cool atmosphere. I had, some fortnight since a long letter from Mr Emerson I will show it you sometime. He says he had some two hours or more of good talk with you "*which is much.*" The address is to be printed— I did not go down to hear.[1] I could not have made such an exertion at any rate, but Mrs Cumming was with me then. She plays with as much genius as ever. I will take you to hear her if I have an oppory. But shall you not stay in your fairy home through August. I do not think I shall go to Newbury with you, though I often long to see that river. But I do not need beauty so much now for I have had it this summer. And I may have no more days at Groton. W. Channing (Revd) is staying at Mother's now but I suppose he will be gone long before I return.

There is a seat on the top of this house and I was very happy there last moon. I used to go up there and watch the sunset, and the moon till twelve o'clock It lights up the distant river here and there. One night was magnifique thunder clouds in the west rent every moment by the most Pandemonic lightning I ever saw, and the moon riding opposite on her car of clouds, with the full look of peace and love. Then sailed immense black clouds, fishshaped, portentous, slowly over to her, but she quenched their ill intent and made them pearly and lustrous by her glance.—

I wish you had been here. I wish you were here to night. I could talk. But you see I cannot write letters. Thank me for this nothing and write to me dear Cary. O—if you knew how I have been perplexed worldly ways. I sometimes think I will not kill myself in Providence at any rate— does not Mr Morrison want somebody to help him "do good" at N. B. I should like to do good and stay at Nashon too. Or if I had one friend here to me like what I suppose Mr Swain is to Mr M. it were well for me.[2] Write soon again, thy last letter was good. S. W. has returned to Boston. I do not like to write even to him; think how indolent I must be.

M.

(MH: bMS Am 1221 [212])

1. Emerson's address to the senior class at the Divinity School on the evening of 15 July was published in August.

2. John Hopkins Morison (1808–96), who had tutored Robert Swain (1819–44) in New Bedford, had become the Unitarian minister there in May.

42.   To Richard F. Fuller

Providence, 30th [27?] Octr 1838—

My dear Richard,

Your letter was duly received and I was pleased both by the manliness of thought it showed and by the care with which it was written. There are some mistakes and one or two slight improprieties which I shall point out to you when I see you. These are in the style and handwriting.

As to the subject of your letter, it has not changed my opinion except in this respect. I think that Lloyd had best go to Stoughton the first Decr. Will you say to our Mother that I think he will in many respects be more favorably situated there than at home. If he does not learn much in lessons the influence on his character and manners is better. And peace at home is all important to me. I earnestly hope she will send him.

I am equally clear that you had best remain at home till we leave Groton. I know that Mother wishes it strongly, and her wish should be law, not only to your conduct but your feelings. There is no hurry about you. You can undoubtedly go away to school by the first of May and in May you will only be fifteen. After that time you will be able to pursue your education uninterruptedly as our dear Mother will no longer need that aid, which you have been so fortunate as to render, and I believe so far with truly dutiful good will. It is extravagant to send every boy from home while we still have a home. I admit that you have a better claim than others, but Arthur is too old to wait, and Lloyd unfortunately is unfit to take your place. Rely upon me, your faithful friend, that, if you make up your mind to pass this winter at home and do every thing in your power to assist, you shall not in after life have the least occasion to regret it.

With regard to your studies I am no longer situated as I was when I devoted all my mornings to you, Ellen and Arthur. My time is very valuable, even in a pecuniary point of view. While at Groton I must devote to writing all the time that I am well and bright, and after two years incessant teaching should prefer an absolute respite from that occupation. But I have engaged to give your sister lessons in German twice a week and will give you lessons in Latin and composition the same days. That is I will hear all the Latin you can prepare between whiles, and your sister Ellen will give you daily lessons in French. If your brother Eugene will do the same for you in Greek and writing I shall be very glad. The other branches you name I think you had best defer till you go to school. Mr Haven is fond of mathematics and offered to give Arthur extra lessons, if he should take such interest in you, I think you would be grateful

I do not wish you to make me any compensation in money. I receive from private pupils at the rate of half a dollar for a quarter of an hour lesson. But you cannot pay me at that rate, nor would I take a private pupil this winter for *any money*. Compensate me by willingness to take my advice and by that neatness in your dress, politeness in your manners, and devotion to the wishes of our Mother which will tend to make my home happy this winter.

I trust you will acquiese in my opinion. I think you must feel that your honor and happiness is one of my chief objects in life and that I would not sacrifice your good to my own convenience With love to the family and to Fanny I am your affectionate sister

S. M. FULLER.

Tell Fanny that her father made us a short visit a day or two since.

Tell Eugene I shall send the paper to Uncle A. today, but that no newspaper came with it. Ellen has a bad cold, but seems stronger and in better spirits.

(MH: fMS Am 1086 [9:51])

13. To William H. Channing

Providence, 9th Decr 1838—

My dear Mr Channing

or may I just rather begin with My dear friend,

Mary Channing gave me some message from you which I could not understand about writing to you at Cincinnati— Although I do not know *what* was desired yet I may suppose that, if you wished a letter, it was in the hope of getting from it entertainment or other good cheer. As nothing of that kind will be afforded by this document, I will not make the imperfectly understood invitation my excuse but beg you to kindly receive a letter written about my own plans, written to you because you can give me light—for mercy's sake.

I am on the point of leaving Providence, and I do so with unfeigned delight, not only because I am weary and want rest, because my mind has so long been turned outward and long[s] for concentration and leisure for tranquil thought, but because I have here been always in a false position and my energies been consequently much repressed. To common observers I seem well placed here, but I know that it is not so, and that I have had more than average difficulties to encounter, some of them insurmountable. But from these difficulties I have learned so much that I cannot but suppose my experience is to be of further use.

I do not wish to teach again at all. If I consult my own wishes I shall employ the remainder of my life in quite a different manner. But I forsee circumstances that may make it wrong for me to obey my wishes.

Mother has sold her place at Groton, and as she is to leave it in April, I shall go home and stay three months with her. These three months at least I dream of Elysian peace, of quiet growth and other benefits no doubt well known to your imagination

Then I hope to prevail on her to board with Ellen and me, and send the boys to school for some months. But after that we must find a sure foothold on the earth somewhere and plan anew a home.

But this leaves me nearly a year for my own inventions. If at the end of that time, it should seem necessary for the good of all concerned that I should teach again I wish to do it, and by the success I have already attained and by the confidence I now feel in my powers both of arrangement of a whole and action on parts feel myself justified in thinking I may do it to much greater pecuniary advantage and with much more extensive good results to others than I have yet done.

I am not without my dreams and hopes as to the education of women. They are not at all of the Martineau class, but, though brilliant, such, I think, as you, or any spiritual thinker however sober-minded would sympathize in. I have not space for any detail, but, should this prove at last my vocation, I do believe you would think them entitled to your aid.

Several lures have been already held out to me in case I should return to an occupation in which few persons of ability are at present engaged. But each of these plans seems to me in some respect ineligible for my family if not for myself.

Two years since Mr J. Walker was in Boston and left this message, (as I understood it) with a friend for me "that such a school as I could keep is much wanted in Cincinnati and that if I could make up my mind to be transplanted thither, I need only write to him, and he could make arrangements."[1]

I have always had some desire to be meddling with the West, and have only been checked in my tendencies thitherward by the mode[s]t fancy that the East was not at a sufficiently advanced step of culture for my plans, how then should her younger sister be!!!

This message turned my thoughts towards Cincinnati. I have made many enquiries about the place and the result is that I think that place would, on the whole, suit me better than any other I have in view.

It would be an excellent starting point for my brothers, and I could, I suppose, be more independent of *aristocratic patrona[ge]* than in any of the great Eastern cities.

If you should remain there it would be a very strong additional inducement to come. Mother, as you saw, is both naturally and professionally a *parishioner.* She would want a clergyman whom she could respect, aid, and love. You so completely won her heart and Ellen's that I think your pastoral care would make them contented with any decent fold. To me your sympathy and the cooperation to which you would, I believe, be inclined would be most valuable.

I should be *near?* my friend's James, and Mr Eliot or at least within sympathizing distance which I am not now. James says somewhat of Louisville, but I do not think I should like that place except for his friendly and intelligent aid.

Do not think I should not expect many dangers and difficulties. I should so, and have confidence in my own energy and *external* patience. As to *patience of the spirit,* I have laid to heart your wise reproof and I hope, not without some profit.

But, as my plan would be for an expensive establishment of which I should have the sole responsibility, because I should want absolute power, as it would be a very important move for my family, and as, if I again undertake any plan, it will be laid for years that I may not only sow but reap, I wish to have it long under consideration, and that I may also have all proper means for this you, who are on the spot, can be of the greatest advantage to me, if you will not esteem it a trouble and I think you will not.

You may not stay and I may never be obliged to teach again but if you should and if I should I only want you to keep the project in your eye. See whether you think I could have sixty girls on the same terms as in Boston or Philadelphia. Whether I can have some three or four intelligent men and as many as even one woman who will steadily and understandingly aid and abet me. Whether the influences around you are such as would suit Mother and improve my sister and brothers. The rest you know.—

If I do something of this kind it will not be before Jany 1840— What hostile or friendly star may not take the ascendant before that time? But you will be at Cincinnati till spring at all events.— A letter will reach me at Groton any time from Jany to April.

James will convey to you much gas and some small drop of essential fragrance from Boston. I have had some pleasant hours [ ]

(MB)

1. James Barr Walker (1805–87) was a Presbyterian minister who soon moved to Cincinnati.

44.   To James F. Clarke

Groton 8th Jany 1839—

My dear James,

I believe I am not too tired tonight to write you my second letter.

Let me tell you first a little about Emma.— The acquaintance between us never grew after the letter I showed you, but we were on a pleasanter footing than before; I left her with little regret, for I could do little for her, and I want a softer and more genial atmosphere round me. The public ways of life present rough inaccessible places in plenty without bringing them so near home.

Natheless I had a great esteem for her I hope she is as well placed now as she can be.— I fear they may be a little too fussy for her, but I think she cannot fail to get some advantage from that position.

Little Ellen grew much upon me the latter part of the time, so arch and winning were her ways. Very soon I shall write both fathers.

You asked me if you might copy any verses you liked from my journal and I gave you an over hasty assent. When it was returned I found a pencil mark (which I supposed might be yours) against one or two which I cannot be willing to know in the possession of another. If you have those beginning "In this sad world &c or those beginning "The brilliant day draws to a brilliant close[,] I must ask you, as you love me and value my feelings to destroy the copies immediately.

And this reminds me to ask whether any lines by me on the promise "I will not leave you comfortless" were ever published in the W. Messenger.[1] Mother is positive they have been and with my signature. I cannot believe it, but wish to ask you and do not forget to answer me.

And I wish now as far as I can to give my reasons for what you consider absurd squeamishness in me. You may not acquiesce in my view, but I think you will respect it *as* mine, and be willing to act upon it as far as I am concerned.

Genius seems to me excusable in taking the public for a confidant. Genius is universal and can appeal to the common heart of man; But even here I would not have it too direct— I prefer to see the thought or feeling made universal. How different the confidence of Goethe, for instance from that of Byron.—

But for us lesser people who write verses merely as vents for the overflowings of a personal experience, which in every life of any value craves occasionally the accompaniment of the lyre, it seems to m[e] that all the value of this utterance is destroyed by a hasty or indiscriminate publicity. The moment I lay open my heart and tell the fresh feeling to any one who chooses to hear— I feel as much profaned as if I were to go into the midst of a Providence party and talk as I did to you one night about my want of Christian humility— When it has passed into experience, when the flower has has gone to seed, I dont care who knows it, whither they wander.— I am no longer it— I stand on it.— I do not know whether this is peculiar to me or no, but I am sure the moment I cease to have any reserve or delicacy about a feeling; it is on the wane.

About putting beautiful verses in your maga— I have no feeling except what I shd about furnishing a room— I should not put a dressing case into a parlor, or a bookcase into a dressing room, because however good things in their place, they were[?] not in place there— And this not in consideration of the public, but of my own sense of fitness and harmony. I do not undervalue your pet, but its whole character is popular. I would use for it such a poet as Milne rather than Tennyson and Bryant rather than R. W. E.— Yet, for this latter, as his view is entirely opposed to mine, and he assumes in theory at least that there is no need of adaptation and gradation, my feeling was simply that I had scarce ever known him show his verses and I had no right to give them away without his leave—

Dear friend truly yours

S M. F.

(MHi)

1. "Jesus, the Comforter," *Western Messenger* 4 (September 1837): 20–21.

45. To Caroline Sturgis

Thursday eveg 7th Feby [1839]—
[Groton]

Dearest Cary,

I was grieved to send such a paltry answer to your last letter. I do not like to do those hurried things, but it could not be helped.— It seemed there was some superfluity in my advices, but I think they will do no harm.

What I have thought about W. S. in relation to you is too linked with other matters to be told here. I must reserve it for a personal interview.

I hope and believe that none of my comments will prevent your writing to me as freely as you have done.

Cary—I was much moved by what you say of Jesus— He will yet be your best-beloved friend;— with all the blurs, that a factitious, canting world places between us and him, with all the love for liberty of the speculative mind, we cannot at last dispense with, we cannot get away from the divine character, the profound sympathies, the exalted ethics of that Man of Sorrows.[1]

I partook of the communion last Sunday for the third time, and had beautiful thoughts about the bread and wine which some day I may tell you.

If I do not now respond to your letter in words, I do with my heart.— I *do* consider you worthy to be my friend. You are yet to be tried, there is nothing tested in you yet, except your taste for Truth and your apprehension of what is high. I do not think your fortitude is cheerful enough to be respected as a virtue, but it is enough to give your character consistency

I have great faith in you.— And I do not wish to urge myself on you as a heroic or a holy friend. I believe it is best to receive me principally through the intellect.

Yet love me as much as you can.—

I cannot find any of Anna's letters which seem suitable to show. Indeed they are so sacred to me that I dont know as I could have brought myself to send them away. When the "beautiful story of her life" as she calls it, is brought to a denouement I may then *read* you some of the letters with a running commentary. But clouds still hang about my star of stars, and none of her history is so completely past as to have become a part of Poetry.

I think I will not send you any more of Jane's letters. You have the most beautiful why should you wish to weaken the impression

Tasso you have.

I send your drawing books, but wish to look them over with you sometime.— You will find in one of the books some pencillings by J. F. C. Please give them to Sarah, and tell her James said he had sent her some things that he would like me to look at, and ask her if she can give me a copy of the verses to E. Keats and the two sets on the *ring* and give her my dear love.

I recommend to your perusal two articles in the last No. of the Westminster Review on Heloise and Rahel von Ense.[2] Two remarkable women indeed! In Rahel I think you may recognize well known lineaments.— Observe what she says (quoted by Goethe) about being *born only to live;* and what the Reviewer says of "feeling about feeling." The Westminster indeed is petri de talent of late— There is Miss M's crack article too, vigorous eloquent stained with credulity, exaggeration, and man deification as ever.[3] She has placed her abolitionist friends in the most ludicrous light, by her fine portraits; but I suppose they wont mind it. Amern Abolitionists have as little leisure to think of *good taste* as Clarkson had of *the salvation of his soul.*

I shall not write to you again, unless it be a short note for several weeks.

I write a great deal too much, and at this rate shall never get well. Thirty six letters, all long ones, I have dispatched beside all the other writing I have done. Tomorrow I shall write two more and that closes my letter list. After that I shall not write one which is not absolutely necessary, till my translation is off my hands. Your ferns are up and their presence is cheering. I trust you will be generous and write to me, perhaps often. Do not send this parcel to Jane till you have a perfectly safe opportunity Affectionately

MARGARET F.

Lloyd is too much fascinated with Eleanor to give her up yet.

(MH: bMS Am 1221 [219])

1. Isa. 53:3. "He is despised and rejected of men; a man of sorrows, and acquainted with grief," read by Christians as a prophecy of Christ.

2. One article reviewed *Lettres d'Abailard et Héloise;* the second reviewed nine books by and about Rahel von Ense (1771–1833), who was the hostess of a literary salon in Berlin.

3. Harriet Martineau, "The Martyr Age of the United States," *London and Westminster Review* 32 (1838): 1–59.

46. To George Ripley

Groton 21st Feby [1839]

Dear Sir,

The proofs can be sent by the mail as well as any way, though I send them back by the "virtuous man," that I may also get rid of all the M.S. which I have finished.[1] Here are a hundred and fifty sheets. I shall send, in a few days, perhaps twenty more including my preface and the few pages of the book which remain to be translated.

As I find that two pages of my handwriting (in which the greater part of the book lies) make one of your print, I think the volume will contain about fourhundred pages. I think I have already cut out all I ought, but may, in the proofs, see some passages that could be dispensed with. You will not praise my M.S. any more, but we are so soon to remove and so much is to be done, that neither my brother nor myself have time to copy. I am desirous to get this off my hands as fast as I can, without slighting it.

As to the proofs the expression "some title" corresponds with Eckermann's meaning I believe. "Habe zu betrachten *gewissermassen* als den Schmuck" is the phase Tranquil *hour* will do, standing for any period of time. The title Counsellor is wrong; the word Justiz,-beamt I had confounded with Justizrath. It should be officer of justice, strictly; if you think it of any consequence please substitute the right phrase. I expect the chief trouble throughout will be with titles of men and books as, when I could not translate them to my mind, I have left them in German. Perhaps it would have been better not, but such combinations as Upper-forest-counsellor look very formidable in English.

As to the use of capitals— I have been so desirous of avoiding that copious sprinkling of great As and Bs and Cs that seems to mark the pages of every body who has learned a little German that, perhaps, I have fallen into the opposite extreme. But is it not equally correct to write— I met at the coffee house an officer of the marines, as I met at the Coffee house an Officer of the Marines—

Please mark every thing you see amiss; as I am desirous of making the publication of this book the means of drilling myself in details which, naturally, have not before attracted my attention.

Please give my love to my friend, Mrs Ripley, and ask her if she will not welcome me to the neighborhood of Boston. I shall be only five miles out, and shall see you often; that is, if you do not pass all your summers on *lakes.*— Truly yours

S. M. FULLER.

Will you do me the favor to send the other parcel to Mr Sturgis's?—

"In the year ninety" was the way the good Dr had it, and I retained it with other imperfect phrases of his, because they give, at least to me, the feeling of an almost quaint simplicity. 1790— is, of course, the date

(VtMiM)

1. Fuller was completing her translation of Eckermann's *Gespräche mit Goethe.*

47.   To Charles K. Newcomb

Groton 4th March 1839—

My dear Charles,

No doubt you wonder that, after taking so much pains to get a letter from you, I should so long delay to answer it.— But, alas, it came like a summer bird, when old Winter has begun to seal the streams, and unclothe the trees; or a wedding guest the day after the joyful rite.— The eight weeks of tranquil reading, writing, and walking were over. I had enjoyed a holiday longer than any I have known for some years; I had quitted that element of meditation, and free communion with Nature which you and I both love so truly and passed into a condition as busy, as wearisome, though, surely, not as annoying, as I ever knew at Providence.

It was by no means a *ruse;* that saying of mine that I had many things to say to you. I have often in my walks along the banks of the now silent little stream, which I am about to leave, or through the solemn evergreen woods, whose silence, colder, if not deeper than that of summer noon, gave verge enough for reverie, addressed many remarks to you, some good, some not, but all such as you would have liked!! For Charles likes whatever rises naturally from the mind of a friend, whether it ascend till it be beautified by the Sun into a Lamb of Heaven, or curl away gray and feeble. He likes it, though it be but vapor, for, however evanescent, it tells a story of intercourse between earth and the golden lamps above.

But all my tales of sudden bursts of light, tearing apart the violet curtains and casting them aside upon the distant hills who raise their gentle heads to woo the veil, all my solemn brooding twilights, less beautiful, but more poetic, and all the tales the Spirits of the trees told me by the glimpses of the moon, thoughts of books too which we had both been interested in. All is—weggeschnitten—as the Germans say—and behold me—here.[1] Every thing in such confusion— I can say nothing now except, dear Charles, I was very glad to get your letter. Do not regret writing it, because you cannot have a very good one in reply. I wanted it so much, because our last conversation had left an anxiety about you in my mind. I was fain to know whether you were tranquil in mind or only outwardly, and it pained me to have all *real* intercourse between us so suddenly checked.

Now write again or not, as you feel disposed I shall feel tranquil about you, after what you have said. As to all the good things I will say them next time I walk with you.

The task which now so engrosses me is fatiguing and melancholy, yet so interesting that I cannot think of any thing else. It is the arrangement of my father's papers. My poor father!— If I were disposed to draw a hackneyed moral, surely there never was a fitter occasion. These papers had been accumulating for forty years. College journals themes, law minutes, minutes of the most interesting debates in the Mass and U S legislature, a voluminous correspondence on almost all subjects; he had never all those years had time to examine these papers, he had just prepared the study, (at the end of the garden for we had not room in the house) in which he meant, after finally settling his professional affairs to look them over when he died. He was in that building only twenty four hours before his death.

How well he was prepared to meet the fiat which went forth so suddenly, I find abundant evidence in these papers. Well as I knew my father, I know him hourly better and respect him more, as I look more closely into those secrets of his life which the sudden event left open in a way he never foresaw. Were I but so just, so tender, so candid towards man so devout towards a higher Power.—

I cannot think of any thing else, my dear Charles, and though I have been engaged with them many days there is work for many more, since well as I knew his affairs, as many documents are to be burnt I am obliged to look at each one separately. I have many many other things to do, before we remove. When I am undisturbed once more, you shall hear what I think of Carlyle &c— Meanwhile this comes only to say, that I am, as I was, yours affectionately

S. M. F.—

Please remember me to your mother and Lizzy, and say that I am much obliged by your mothers full response to my queries. I will see Charlotte as soon as I can after we go to Willow Brook.

(MH: fMS Am 1086 [10:127])
1. "Cut away."

48.   To Caroline Sturgis

Groton 4th March
1839—

Dearest Cary,

As this is the last day I suppose that I shall have a half hour's leisure to write to any one, I heartily wish it were in my power to write you a good letter in return for yours which always have some good thought in them. But as it is not I think I will at least tell you *why* it is not.

Last night as I was lying awake and thinking in most painful restlessness of all possible things, and among others of your designs for my poems, I thought— Thinks I to myself,— Cary supposes, I daresay that I do not love her much. She always excused my writing her such miserable letters while I was at work with my school, but now, she thinks I am in solitude and at leisure, and, if I thought of her as I ought, would write her many letters full of pictures, thoughts and sentiments.

Then thinks I to myself I'll tell her how I have passed the time since I came home. It will give her some idea of the way in which my life is drained off, and she will never be surprised at my omissions, and, perhaps, it may make her own leisure seem more valuable to her.

When I came home I was determined to take every precaution to ensure my having the whole time for myself.— I had it mentioned to all the neighbors, that I was worn out, and should not go out. I declined their invites so as not to offend them, five or six of those who knew me best, made me short calls which I have not yet returned. I have never been to any house and to church only once. I have not spent two hours in the society of any person out of our own family. I stay in my own room always till about nine in the eveg; when *very* busy, I do not go down then or to meals. I have not seen half as much even of the family, as I wishcd.

I had several loose robes fixed to wear this winter that I might lie down, whenever I have severe pain, and apply friction, when necessary. This has, really, done good, and as I have only had the trouble of keeping myself *neat* without any *fixing*, dressing has taken not a quarter the time it usually does.

Mother and Ellen have mended my clothes, when necessary. I have had no duties of the worky sort except taking care of my own room, paying some attention to Mother and Ellen when sick and teaching Ellen and Richard two afternoons in the week.

Out of this whole time I have not been confined to the bed above four or five days in all. I have had no amusement to take up my time, except that I have walked a mile or two those days when the weather permitted and five or six times have played on the piano.

For seven years I have never been able to pass two months so much as I pleased and never expect it again, and I have been as industrious as any beaver. Why then will you say—no more or better letters?

I have had the curiosity to keep a list of my letters and I have written just 50 before this, since the 3d Jany, when I came home— *more to you* than any one else.

As soon as I came home I arranged the first two days my books and clothes. Then my papers, which I had not been able to for more than three years. I burnt a great many, and I sent you those I selected for you.

I settled up the accts of my two little girls, wrote to them and their parents.[1]

I wrote about twenty letters then. This took about ten days, at the end of that time I was sick from fatigue. As soon as I was able to sit up, Mother and Ellen were sick While they were so and I getting better, I studied over parts of Goethe; and read two of Plato's dialogues, and a no of the London and Westminster As soon as I was able I begun on my trans. Revised what had been written and compared it with the orig and wrote out the remainder All the other writing I have done has been the other letters and a very little in my journal. All the reading I did was occasionally when lying down in day time Mr Very's sonnets and pieces, Jane's letters, the Stirlings in two Blackwoods and little bits of Plato, Coleridge, Goethe and Ben Jonson. After I went to bed I would read myself to sleep with chapters out of Vivian Grey, and Maryatt's novels, and I read the debates in Congress.[2] I also had talks with Mother about our future arrangements.

This took up all my time till last Monday when before two o'clock, I finished my translation. In afternoon, I begun my next piece of work on which I have been engaged ever since all day and all the eveg, till to day, I felt so wearied I thought I must take a holiday.

This is the arrangement of my father's papers, the accumulation of forty years from the time he entered College till now. He brought them all here hoping to arrange them himself.

I had no idea till I began what a labor it would prove, but, though I have been at work a week, and examined more than a thousand letters, I seem scarcely to have made an impression on the great heaps of paper. It is a very interesting, though very fatiguing work, and teaches me a great deal.

As soon as I can get through with it, I shall pack the books which we are to take and select those we are to sell, and make many other arrangements for the auction which is to take place on the 19th. After that I shall have much to settle, before I escape to Concord where I shall pass a day or two, then to Boston, where I shall see you for some hours. Then we will talk of Poetry and Personality!— But I see I cannot write again, unless it be some short note.

Perhaps you think I might as well have written something on such subjects as all these details, but I never can speculate when I am in my practical trim.

Still planning when and where, and how the business can be done,"[3] I have read of men who could write on such subjects in all the stir of every day life and yet play well their parts, but I confess tis beyond me.

On the whole I feel with some sadness that I can hardly be a real friend to any one more. The claims upon me are now too many. I am always sacrificing myself more than is for my health or fame, yet I can do very little for any one person.

I know that you, my dear Cary, *ask* nothing, but I cannot help feeling you must and have a right to expect it. So I think I will now say Dear Cary, Though you are much younger than I, yet I have that degree of respect for your mind and character that I can look on you as an equal friend. I also love you, and, probably, no other person you know could be so much to you as I, notwithstanding all my shortcomings— Can you be contented, in consideration of your greater freedom and leisure, to do much for, receive little from me. Above all, can you be contented to write to me often and sometimes receive no reply, generally a meagre one. When I see you I shall always, I suppose, be able to talk. But writing is too fatiguing to my body, let alone the constant occupation of my mind. Yet not to hear from you often would grieve me. Indeed the week is darker hued in which I do not receive a letter. Yet they make me feel as if I ought to answer. If I am sure you do not expect it, and that you feel always that my mind answers,

I shall write no letter unless I am able and then they will be good, though perhaps few.

I am ashamed when I think what letters I have written you, and I wish you would burn all the worthless business scrawls. You deserve different treatment. I think I shall like the designs very much. They are complicated, but not more so than many of the best things in ancient and modern Art. Please do them, and I will read you passages from Goethe's Propylea out at Willow Brook, as a fit expression of my gratitude

I will not tell you now wh I like best for what I think good reasons till I see them in pencil I did not ask Mrs Jameson for any thing except some local particulars, and still think her conduct ungenerous, but not so much so, since I now think her knowledge more scanty than I had supposed. And the book seems to be addressed to Mrs Austen.[4] I do not wonder she thought it impertinent in an obscure stranger to propose doing what Mrs A, whom she seems so much to admire, did not feel competent to undertake. I have learnt some matters of fact from her book wh will be of use.

I send you my favorite Prince, as I believe you do not own him, and I thot you might like to read about his pictures, castles &c again.[5] If not, only let him lie in your room till I come, he is too refined to be an intruder any where, though his coat is not in the best condition.

Will you do me the favor to send the other as directed.

Do write, if you can feel like it to yrs afftely

S. M. F.

(MH: bMS Am 1221 [220])

1. James Clarke had arranged for the daughters of two families in his Louisville congregation to go to Providence to study with Fuller. Emma Keats (1823–83), the poet's niece, and Ellen Clark, daughter of L. B. Clark, followed Fuller to Boston.

2. Jones Very (1813–80) had been a tutor of Greek at Harvard before he became deranged. John Sterling (1806–44), a member of a literary circle that included Carlyle, Mill, and Tennyson, wrote under the pen name Archaeus. *Vivian Grey* (1826) was Benjamin Disraeli's first novel; Frederick Marryat (1792–1848) was a British naval officer and novelist.

3. Fuller quotes George Herbert's "The Church-Porch."

4. Sarah Taylor Austin (1793–1867) was an English translator of German works.

5. Hermann Pückler-Muskau, *Tutti-Frutti* (1834).

49. To Eugene Fuller

Saturday eveg June 8th 1839—

My dear Eugene,

As your shirts have been returned today and Mother proposes sending them on Monday, I will give you our journal up to this time. I think you left us overshadowed by clouds of surpassing blackness, which did not dissipate till the following Tuesday. At Cambridge Port you heard the history of poor Ellen Messenger. This made me really sad, though I did not know her, and did it not bring up in your mind a thought of Mary T.?

I do not know that any thing occurred that would interest you till Monday. Sunday eveg J. Balch and Gardiner Weld called here to invite Ellen and myself to go out in their boat the following eveg. They also wished me to invite all my former pupils from Miss T.'s. I did so and her manner of refusing to let them come was such as to bring on the eclaircissement, which, however, as I was otherwise engaged and could not see her did not take place till the following Wednesday.

We went in the boat with the Welds, Balchs and a Miss Jarvis to whom Dr Weld is *engaged*.[1] The engagement came out this week. She is said to be a good girl, and, though far from pretty will, as you know, be a suitable pendant in that respect to her fiancé—

The row was pleasant enough, but the walk to and fro the pond so long, and, to me, so stupid that I shall rarely, if ever, tempt the wave with them, though the Dr was really most assiduous in pointing out the beauties of the margin,—or marginal beauties.

On Tuesday we were blest at last with a sunny day, and I did joy in it. I thought we had had enough of the weather you found so propitious to reflection. C. Sturgis came out in the aftn, we took a delightful walk and she staid all night. That night, too, Mrs Newcomb, from whom I had recd a letter to announce her advent, came.[2] She was desirous to have some conversation with Miss T. about Charlotte and Miss T. coming here for that purpose and opening a conversation with me We were led to discuss the past in presence of Ellen.

She was disposed to impute the chief blame to you and says you treated her very sadly when you went there last winter. She owned, however, to her desire to prevent our getting the house, and even to asking Mr Green to get the refusal for that purpose! But she gives as a reason her unwillingness to have Mary disquieted.— She was exceedingly shocked that I could suppose she would be unwilling to have the girls influenced by me, or intimate with Ellen, (towards whom however she showed in my opinion a decided dislike and hostility.) She had expected so high-souled a person as I to understand her better!! She loves Mother now, did love Ellen once, admires me and supposes she should love me if she knew me!!

I cannot, of course, give the particulars of a conversation that lasted more than three hours, and surely never lady talked more nimbly or with more force of epithet than she. The result of it was that I thought better of her inasmuch as I thought she had been able to justify her conduct to herself all through, but considered it according to my notions, unhandsome, indirect, and bespeaking a sort of character I do not like. I told her as gently and courteously as I could what I thought, but said that I regretted the pain I gave and would not, if I could avoid it, give any in future. She was quite overwhelmed at last, though thinking herself much aggrieved by these *base suspicions*. I told her I would not agree with her as I considered there had been cause enough to warrant or suggest them. Mother also stood her ground manfully considering that tears were shed. We patched up a hollow peace, and I trust there will in future be little or no intercourse. I feel much relieved that all has been said, at least on our part. I think I shall take back Emma and Charlotte the next winter.

Wednesday, Thursday. Rain but Caroline Kuhn came here on Thursday and staid all night Friday, (yesterday) it was fair. I went to Boston in the morng and went first to the Allston gallery. There I saw the Misses Ward from N York of whom I have heard so much. They were accompanied by their tutor, Mr Cogswell, and Miss Hall who paints miniatures so beautifully and their cousin and brother, so cried up for talent.[3] The eldest of these swains was frightfully ugly, both walked as if their backs were out of joint (which I take to be the present fashion) and wore their hair very long and curled at the edges, whether by the hand of Nature or Art I know not. The second Miss W. is not to be compared with Ellen for beauty, and if I could judge from the little I saw of the well known Julie she is inferior to E. in mind and as affected as she can be. I was inclined to be more worldly and low-minded than is my wont, and to murmur at the attention these wealthy damsels attracted when if poor Ellen had been there nobody would have noticed her, despite her beautiful face. I was introduced to Miss Julie, and Miss Hall, but went no farther. Mr Dana and Charlotte were there and the fair Anna Shaw— I dined at Mr Ward's (S's father) with whom the dames and knights of the N. York exchange returned that P. M. Mrs Ward brought me home in aftn and went in to see Mother. Charles Newcomb passed the night here. To day had been very fine and I have been very happy with my books. Rebecca Tillinghast is engaged to Dr Willing of Phila, large fortune, first connections, age 25, further the deponents say not as yet.

Revd H. Bellows is engaged to some lady in N. York.

Richard and Lloyd have both made short visits to Chelsea, and returned much edified. R. recd from Mr T. a silver pencil case "as a mark of estcem"! Jane is very unwell.

Mother is pretty well and in good spirits. Ellen's eyes are no better and she has a great deal of headach.

I have not seen the Ripleys yet and do not know how my book sells. In Providence all the copies sold immedy, and the people like it very much. I have recd a letter of praise from Mr Emerson which I value more than I should a voucher from any other quarter. S. Ward says his father is reading it with great devotion and likes it much. I should think if he did, most would. When I write again I shall, probably, know more.

I will add a few lines tomorrow eveg—

Sunday eveg—

Nothing particular has transpired— I send the London and Westminster, wishing you to read and send it back in the course of a week if poss. It may be left with Belinda or I will go there for it.

I should also like you to write me whether you should have time or money to go to Niagara, if I wished it. I have only the slightest notion of it and do not really think I can go, but shd like you to tell me whether it would be poss for you, if for me. I shd also like you to ascertain what would be the exact expense for each of us, and answer me on this subject *by Saty next.*— Very afftly yr sister

M.

A letter from Wm to Uncle A. more plausible than ever. He will be home in a week or two.

(MH: fMS Am 1086 [9:172])

1. Joseph Williams Balch (1819–91); Christopher M. Weld (1812–78), a homeopathic doctor; and Mary Ann Jarvis (1815–98).

2. Rhoda Mardenbrough Newcomb (1791–1865), Charles's mother, was a strong-willed woman who was part of the intellectual circle that Fuller knew in Providence.

3. The members of the New York Ward family (not to be confused with the unrelated Boston family of Samuel Gray Ward) whom Fuller met were Julia Ward, later Howe (1819–1910); Louisa Cutler (1823–97); Ann Eliza (1824–95); and Francis Marion (1820–47). The cousin is Henry Hall Ward (1820–72); the others are Ann Hall (1792–1863) and Joseph Green Cogswell (1796–1871). Despite her slighting comments about Julia Ward, Fuller later became her good friend.

50. To Sarah Helen Whitman

Jamaica Plains
10th June 1839—

The very magnificent sunset of tonight—a violet curtain drawn aside to display a golden city with its citadel built up into the very central heaven, and the slight shower which came to melt all these gorgeous fabrics into one glistening canopy reminded me of a sunset we saw at Stetsons last summer and impels me to write to you, my dear Mrs Whitman. And speaking of sunsets, Have you read the Onyx Ring in Blackwood and do you remember the "violent and resplendent hour" there described. Mr Emerson thought it too theatrical. I liked it. This author, Sterling, who wrote also the Crystals from a Cavern and the fine poetical pieces signed Archaeus is a great encouragement to me.[1] I see that the force of the human intellect is not all turned yet to tact and accomplishment, but that meditation broods and Genius flashes still. In the Onyx Ring there is an admirable side view of Goethe in the character of Walsingham. It shows a degree of refinement and insight beyond any thing I know on the same subject.— I am much pleased by your remarks on the Helena— pray give me your impressions whenever you can, in reading these works; they are just and delicate and will revive my interest. I hope you have read my translation of Eckermann, as there you will find several of your questions about Faust answered. I shd like also to know what you think of Goethe at eighty after having seen him (in Werther) at twenty three.

Your description of P. virtu amused me much. If you will come to Boston you shall see a genuine "Rambert" or what Mr Allston vouches for as such. It is at the Atheneum Gallery and is called the Shipmaster of Amsterdam. There are also better copies than we are wont to see from Salvator, Poussin, Ruysdael, Claude Lorraine and Vandyke, and one very sweet picture, a copy from one of Raphael.

I am nowise inclined to *faint* when I go to the Allston gallery, being always much exhilarated to see that any man has been able in our society to live true to such a standard. But I staid there too long one day, got one of my nervous spasms in the head and was obliged to send for a physician while on a visit. This I suppose gave rise to the story, which, however, do not contradict as I think it makes me appear very interesting, something like the Chevalier Mozart or—Amanda Fitzal [ ] Child of an Abby! But you really owe it to yourself to come to Boston and see Mr Allston's pictures. It is a bath of roses, potent enough to perfume one's earth for days and years of after life.

You wish to know my condition. I am as happy as I can be. My health is much improved. I have beautiful Nature, beautiful books, beautiful pictures, beautiful engravings, and retirement and leisure to enjoy and use them. My mind flows on its natural current and I feel that I have earned this beautiful episode in my Crusade. Nevertheless I doubt not that you, my dear Mrs Whitman are wise enough to enjoy the summer more than I do. The description of your unbought pleasures, was to me inexpressibly pathetic. O how equal is Nature, is Fortune, could we but see, rather could we *feel* it— I *see* it well enough. But, for me, my desires dilate with my horizon! However I feel myself blest now in living at harmony with myself which I never did in your city. Your city however I think of with affection.

I hear the fair Rebecca T. is to be married, pray present her my affectionate congratulations and please tell me about it when you write If you visit
Boston, you must come and see me. I will show you my wild rocky walk, my
grove of whispering pine, my little waterfall and answer all your questions.
How is Susan? She does not send me any message? Afftly yours

S. M. Fuller.

(ViU)

1. Among Sterling's several contributions to *Blackwood's Edinburgh Magazine* at this time
were "Crystals from a Cavern" (March 1838) and "The Onyx Ring" (November–January
1838–39).

51.   To Caroline Sturgis

[28? June 1839]

Friday—

Your letter goes to my heart. Yet let me not answer it hastily. For reflections have passed in my mind which do make it doubtful to me whether
we can continue *intimate; friends* we shall always be, I hope, after all we
have known of one another.

It is not because I shrink from the pain or trouble, or because I am not
willing to say the whole truth that I do not come out with all that has
passed in my mind. It is because I have so much pride that I am always in
danger of being unjust. And I have always wished to be not merely generous and tender but scrupulously just to you, Caroline. I feel that you have
character enough to claim that I should think about you, and judge you
by your own nature. In order to this I must put time and other objects between you and me. You, too, will know the state of your own mind better
by and by. Let us wait. And meanwhile why should we avoid seeing one another? We cannot be, more estranged than we were at Nahant. And as I
have asked Marianne, I hope you will come. So much as we have to control ourselves in life a lesson never comes amiss. We need not be false, nor
need we be cold, and it is not desirable to attract the attention of others to
any misunderstanding.

May heaven be with you and your soul be wise duly to appreciate its own
position!

(MH: bMS Am 1221 [213])

52. To Elizabeth Hoar

Jamaica Plain—
17th August 1839—

Dearest Elizabeth,

I intended writing you a letter to be enclosed in the pacquet I have been making up for Mr E. when it occurred to me that I had better write by post and ask you to tell him that it shall be found as well as the Brentano vols. at Mr Adams Thursday by 10, morning.[1]

What I wished to say to you is this— I hear you are very unwell, and that, though you have had leisure this summer, it has done you no good. So I want you to go to the sea-side. I believe you have never been there, and you ought to try it, in the expectation that it may make an era for your mind. But when there is a chance that it may brace you again to strength and healthy sensation, and when you may combine the delight of renewed bodily health with that of new thought— O do try it—if only for the chance.

When my head is oppressed and a dry feverish heat irritates my skin and blood so that each touch and sound is scorpions and trumpets to me, take me, kind fairies, if ye can find a flower bell sufficiently large to hold me and carry me in my sleep to where the tall rock casts its grotesque shadow on the yellow sand. There let the plash of the waves and the fanning of the sea-breeze awake me. That breeze is healing and cheer, mild and earnest it cools my brow, it soothes my brain, and new strings every sense. I can open my eyes for the lids are no longer heavy; I can gaze where brightest light loves to linger on the swelling waters, those streams of gold, those myriad diamonds are not too much for me who blinked but now at a sunbeam. You would feel so too, I think. And there how happy you will be when first embraced by the very arms of nature, your ear and mind filled, needing no thought but of the solemn harmonies of sky and sea, you will feel as if the mighty Mother had always before kept you like a little child studying the hornbook at her knee and that never till now had you been near enough to feel the beating of her heart. And then, when the first raptures are over and you are no longer entranced but only wide awake in soul and eye what happiness to sit upon the rocks and see the beautiful poetic shapes, the phantoms of your hope advancing on the distant surge to greet you. It seems that they will be borne to your very feet, but no, not so shall Beauty be given us, but you shall see with your eyes Venus, sea born, of whom before you have only dreamed and love ever after foam and sea weed better than the reddest roses—which celebrate the loss of Adonis.

Will you not go, dear Elizabeth, and feel and see these things and others of which I know not yet. Could I give you any feeling what the Sea has been to me you would go. But go before it is cold, or you will not be happy.

I rejoice Jane is to visit you.

But do not have her while Mr E is gone I want him to know her.

I shall not come to C. till Mr E's return as Mr Alcott has been so lately, and it is not convenient to me.

Mr E can show you my Bristol journal if he think it worth your reading. But it does not tell the marvels of the sea, for there you do not get at it.

The Basilikum is in great glory; I have not worn any of it yet; reserving it for some fair hour, but have put a sprig as a book-mark into the Life of Raphael.[2] Will you not come to see it? I want to see you very much. Love to Lidian, to dear Mamma, and dear little Waldo. Is he lovely still? I almost fear to ask, for it is time for his human nature to be showing its ugliness.

Your faithful friend

MARGARET F.

(ViU)

1. Fuller sent Emerson an essay on modern French literature, her journal of her trip to Bristol, Rhode Island, some journal sheets on art and music, and Bettina Brentano von Arnim's *Goethes Briefwechsel mit einem Kinde* (1835).

2. Antoine Quatremère de Quincy, *Histoire de la vie et des ouvrages de Raphaël* (1824).

53. To Caroline Sturgis

Jamaica Plains
7th Octr 1839.

My dear Caroline,

Your letter, for which I had often wished in calmer days, arrived nearly a week ago in the very first days of Anna. At that time I could not even read it.— I could not think of our relation, so filled was I so intoxicated, so uplifted by that eldest and divinest love.

Yesterday she went away to stay two or three days, and I was obliged to take immedy to my bed, and am not yet really well enough to be up. The nights of talk and days of agitation, the tides of feeling which have been poured upon and from my soul have been too much for my strength of body or mind.— Even yet I cannot think of you, my Caroline. I cannot tell what I shall think or feel.

I write now because else you would not know why I was silent.

I do not know whether any time soon I shall recover from all the fatigue and various excitements of the past six weeks. I know not when I can free my thoughts from the poems which have oermastered them of late, but of this be sure, the first hour when I can meet you in a way worthy of us I will.

I loved you, Caroline, with truth and nobleness. I counted to love you much more. I thought there was a firm foundation for future years. In this hour when my being is more filled and answered than ever before, when my beloved has returned to transcend in every way not only my hope, but my imagination, I will tell you that I once looked forward to the time when you might hold as high a place in my life as she. I thought of all women but you two as my children, my pupils, my play things or my acquaintance. You two alone I would have held by the hand. And with Mr E for the representative of religious aspiration and one other of Earth's beauty I thought my circle would be as complete as friendship could make it.

How this hope was turned sickly, how deeply it was wounded you know not yet, you do not fully understand what you did or what passed in my mind.— I will own that in no sacred solitary wood walk, in no hour of moonlight love had I been able to feel that that hope could recover from its wound. My feelings had not changed since you went away. I had not been able, much as I desired it, to take a different view of the past or future. But your letter has changed it. Your vow is registered in heaven.— I know not yet whether I can avail myself of it, but, oh, my Caroline, for mine you must ever be in memory of your first hours of real youth, blessed the Great Spirit, that it has been offered, that you have not been permitted to quench a flame upon so lonely, so ill sustained an altar.

Whatever is done shall be noble, be true. Only for a moment did I cease to love you. I wept at the loss you were to sustain in me. I would have given all but self-respect to save you. I said, World-wise, at least I can always be her friend in the spirit realm I will wait for her. O may it be that on earth I can walk with you.

—Write again and tell me when you will return and if it is not to be soon I will write to you when the good hour comes though I would much rather talk, there is so much to be told—

Margaret F.

About the class it is of no consequence *to* decide. If after your return and knowing *from me* all the circumstances you wish it, I will receive you then. Mr E. has not asked why you did not write to him. He asked me of you, but I merely told him we were silent now by mutual consent.

(MH: bMS Am 1221 [224])

54. To Ralph Waldo Emerson

Jamaica Plain,
24th Novr 1839—

My dear friend,

Your letter brought me joy;— Mr Alcott was here when I recd it. He came out to pass three or four hours and it would have been a very pleasant interview but that I was under the influence of the concluding headach of a three weeks course. I have not now been troubled with one for nearly a week so that I feel both happy and wise, and could bring the Finite much more resolutely in face of the Infinite than on that day! I had thought of going into town tonight to hear Mr A. discourse on *Genius,* but it rains and I will talk with you, instead of hearing him.

I send you the canto in the poem of Caroline which I half promised. I have had many doubts about it, but finally I see so much beauty here that I cannot be willing not to share it with you, especially as I cannot hope to share it with any other person. I have given her last letter of the winter that you may better appreciate the flux and reflux of mind. Next to this read the two passages in my journal where I have turned the leaf, they were read by her and to the conversations which sprung from them several passages in her letter refer. To make the whole complete you should see a letter of mine upon the wind; but neither C. nor I has that now. The little poem of Drachenfels in the marble paper book also had much effect on her thoughts, it is to that she refers about the dragon voice!

I thought this chapter out of my poetical journal might interest you now all the the verses, even the translns bear some reference to Anna, W. and myself.

Those on Beethoven &c are very bad, but not without glimmers of my thoughts. If you wish to read the rest of the Winter Clouds, you must remember that it was a cloudy time; my sufferings last winter were almost constant and I see the journal is very sickly in its tone. Now I am a perfect Phenix compared with what I was then and it all seems Past to me.

I hesitated about sending you any papers now because you are busy writing, but then I reflected that you would not wish your mind strained up to your subject all the day, but might like some grove of private life, into which you might step aside to refresh yourself from the broad highway of philosophy. All these papers I commend to your most sacred safekeeping wherein they may continue for three or four weeks.—

I have not prepared Rakemann's programme as I intended.[1] He is coming here again and I will then send you *two*! I shall not tell Caroline that I have shown you the letters till by and by when all is as past to her as to me.

I am sorry you read the wrong Sands first though in André there is a vein of the best in the two others is seen her worst. Mauprat is at the shop now; it is worth your reading, but not your buying and they let them out by the week. I shall get for you Les Sept Cordes de la Lyre, if ever it is in my power[2]

What is the Harleyan Miscellany; an account of a library?—[3]

Mille mercis for the tickets. I am too happy to think it will probably be in my power to use mine this year the others were delivered according to direction! You have really cheated me to send no notes on the pictures I shall expect very good lectures to make up for it

Will you not send me my friend Mr Sterling's letter. I will return it promptly!

M. F.

I thought to send Tennyson this time, but I cannot part with him, it must be for next pacquet. I have been reading Milnes; he is rich in fine thoughts, but not in fine poetry, and his Christianity is often forced in till it becomes what Mr Alcott calls noxious.[4]

(MH: bMS Am 1280 [2345])

1. Ludwig Rackemann was a German violinist and piano player who gave concerts in Boston and in private homes. He and his brother, Frederic William, who came to the United States in 1842, played often in New England.

2. Fuller, who was impressed with the novels of George Sand (Aurore Lucie Dupin, baronne Dudevant) (1804–76), had encouraged Emerson to read *André* (1835), *Leone Leoni* (1835), and *Indiana* (1832), but he could not find *Mauprat* (1837), which she also recommended. Fuller had read *Les Sept Cordes de la lyre* when it appeared in the *Revue des Deux Mondes* the previous summer.

3. The *Miscellany* was a reprint of tracts from the library of Edward Harley, second earl of Oxford.

4. Richard Monckton Milnes, later first baron Houghton (1809–85), had published *Memorials of a Tour in Some Parts of Greece, Chiefly Poetical* (1834), *Memorials of a Residence on the Continent, and Historical Poems* (1838), and *Poems of Many Years* (1838).

II

Nature Has Seemed an Ever Open Secret

1840–1844

Nature has seemed an ever open secret, the Divine
a sheltering love, Truth an always spraying fountain.

———————

Fuller had begun as early as 1835 to write critical essays and reviews for James Clarke's *Western Messenger* and for *The American Monthly Magazine*. For them she wrote essays on German and British literature, and she reviewed several biographies. When she and Emerson and a group of like-minded friends decided to found their own journal, she was a logical choice to be the editor. The first issue of the *Dial* appeared in July 1840. For the next two years, the magazine dominated her life. She did all the expected work—she solicited manuscripts; she edited the material (sometimes severely, as young Henry Thoreau found out when she rejected an essay of his); and, inevitably, she filled its pages when she fell short of suitable matter. The journal was both a blessing and a burden, for though it provided a ready outlet for her ideas, it consumed her time and energy. Fuller had a clear vision of the magazine as an open forum. Though she wanted the contributions to be well written, she was open to a range of ideas—more open than Emerson, who was more interested in brilliance than in breadth. The *Dial* established Fuller as a critic of major importance. She never completed a planned biography of Goethe, but she did write a long, thorough essay on him as well as on lesser-known writers, such as Philip James Bailey, whose *Festus* impressed her. During her two-year editorship Fuller wrote at least thirty-three pieces, from notices to elaborate essays on topics ranging over contemporary Anglo-American and European topics.

The journal brought her closer to Emerson, with whom she had already developed a friendship. She corresponded frequently with him about *Dial* matters; she visited his home in Concord, and she probably fell in love with him. At least she became so fond of him that she chastised him for being aloof, prompting both a defensive letter in October 1840 and an entire essay on friendship in his first volume of essays. Theirs was a close, productive relationship, for he was a luminous presence, not only to Fuller but to all who knew him. On her side, Fuller helped draw Emerson out; she challenged him as no one else did.

During those years Fuller deepened her friendship with Caroline Sturgis, the daughter of a wealthy Boston merchant, who had some artistic talent and an interest in many of the ideas about the spiritual life that animated Emerson and Fuller. The three of them carried on an intense correspondence, and she and Fuller vacationed together, sometimes quarreling, sometimes intensely enjoying each other's company. Fuller consistently attracted younger women to her, but the friendship with Sturgis was her longest and most consistent with a woman. Earlier women friends, such as Almira Penniman, Anna Barker, and Elizabeth Randall, married and grew distant, but Carrie Sturgis remained constant in Fuller's affections.

Along with the *Dial*, Fuller kept up her Conversations in the early 1840s, and she took part in Boston's intellectual life: she attended plays and concerts, saw the art exhibits at the Athenaeum, held private parties for artists and performers, and kept in touch with a wide circle of correspondents. But the *Dial* was taking its toll. Finally, in March 1842, she told Emerson that she could not continue, for the magazine never grew; she had received no pay for her editorial labors, and it was time for a change. Reluctantly he agreed, assumed the editorship, and freed her.

Thanks to her successful Conversations and a few private pupils, Fuller now felt free to travel. On May 1843 she and Sarah Clarke, James's sister, went to Niagara Falls on the first leg of a long trip. From there they went to Chicago, to the Illinois prairie, to Wisconsin, and then to Mackinac, Michigan, where Fuller saw the annual gathering of Indian tribes. The trip gave her opportunities to talk to immigrant farmers, to observe how women lived in new circumstances, how Chicago was becoming a metropolis, and how reduced the Indians were under the supposedly benevolent care of the federal government. It was, Fuller found, material for a book, which became *Summer on the Lakes, in 1843*.

The work was Fuller's first attempt at a book-length narrative, and it won the attention of Horace Greeley, the founder and editor of the *New-York Tribune*, the Whig daily and weekly newspaper that had become the largest and liveliest in New York City. Greeley, whose wife had been a participant in Fuller's Conversations, offered her a substantial salary to move to New York late in 1844 and become the head of his "literary department." This opening gave Fuller the chance to expand her readership instantly, but it required the decision to leave New England for a stranger world in New York. But before reporting to Greeley she set off with Sturgis for a vacation in the Catskills, where she revised a long essay on women she had written for the *Dial*. Fuller spent the early autumn of 1844 in seclusion rewriting the essay into her most famous work, *Woman in the Nineteenth Century,* which Greeley published in February 1845.

The move from Boston to New York City was symbolic, for it ended one distinct part of Fuller's life and began another. The letters in this section show Fuller at the height of her critical abilities: she not only edits the *Dial* and makes it an important literary voice, she writes some of her best criticism for it. The letters show the daily life of an editor, but they also show Fuller's emotional life in her friendships with Carrie Sturgis and Emerson. Many of the letters are detailed travel essays that document her responses to the West. Finally, her letters show her at the center of her family, the source not only of income but of direction for her siblings and support for her mother.

55. To Caroline Sturgis

Monday eveg, [1840?]

Dear Caroline,

I think what is poetical in your verses is of the purest tone. And even where most unmusical and unfinished they have the great beauty of being written to the dictation of Nature. The most irregular pulses beat with the mighty heart.

I hope you will be induced to perfect yourself in this mode of expression for the degree to which you have succeeded surprizes me. Your verse is almost as good as your best prose; with practice I think you would be most free in rhythm. Self-adopted chains well suit ambitious natures.

Some of these strains are to me of ineffable pathos. To live in your life is soothing and mystical to me even as the pine forest.— Show me whenever you can what you write, what you do. I shall not often answer it directly, for such is not my way, but each drop will swell the wave of thought, of life,—till you hear the rebound.

One thing I admire at in you is your steadiness of nature, how I am often and not least tonight tired to death of the earnestness of my life. I long to do something frivolous to go on a journey or plunge into externals somehow. I never can, my wheel whirls round again.

I build on our friendship now with trust, for I think it is redeemed from "the search after Eros"[1] We may commune without exacting too much one from the other.— Intercourse may be suspended at times, but not eventually broken off. Believe me worthy to know your nature as I believe you worthy to know mine. Believe as I do that our stars will culminate at the same point.

But think not, my Caroline, that thought can save thee from the grand mistake of sometime fancying that you love a mortal. Only *that* fire can burn away some useless parts of your being and leave the pure gold free! But it shall not beggar, nay it shall not impoverish you, for to a soul which has been true so long its horoscope stands sure.

I write hastily. I know not what daemon hurries my pen and makes me feel as if I stole time now when I write to my companions. I will not often write to you—directly, but will at times show you leaves from my journal. Of Ellery's verse I think not much;[2] I am ill at appreciating a nature so noble, yet with no constructiveness and no force of will. Yet I take no vulgar view of him either. If clear thoughts come I will write them to himself. In hope that this night is a happy one to you, yours—(*how* you know.)

M. F.

(MH: bMS Am 1221 [235])

1. Probably a reference to the poet Klingsohr's tale of Eros and his foster sister, Fabel, in Novalis's *Heinrich von Ofterdingen.*

2. William Ellery Channing (1817–1903), called Ellery to distinguish him from his famous uncle, for whom he was named, was a prolific poet. At one time he had been in love with Sturgis before he met and married Ellen Fuller. Channing was long championed by his close friend Samuel G. Ward and later by Emerson. He was mercurial, moody, sometimes brilliant, and always capricious. Channing had a gift for conversation and became Thoreau's most frequent companion in walks through the countryside.

56.   To Frederic H. Hedge

Jamaica plain
1st Jany 1840.

My dear Henry,

I write this new years day to wish you all happiness and to say that there is reason to expect the new journal (in such dim prospect when you were here) may see the light next April. And we depend on you for the first No. and for solid bullion too. Mr Emerson will write every number and so will you if you are good and politic, for it is the best way to be heard from your sentry box there in Bangor.—[1] My friend, I really hope you will make this the occasion for assailing the public ear with such a succession of melodies that all the stones will advance to form a city of refuge for the just. I think with the greatest pleasure of working in company with you. But what will it be? will you give us poems or philosophy or criticism, and how much, for we are planning out our first No. by the yard. Let me hear from you directly.

Except one scrap of a letter to Mr Ripley I have seen no word from you since you left us. But in the journal you will write to us constantly and of your best life.— I have little taste, myself, for this epistolary medium. It does not refresh like conversation, it does not stimulate, like good serious study or writing.

Were we near I should have a vast deal to tell you, but my life is rather a subject for a metaphysical romance than a gazette. I waste much time in sickness and am now again under medical care. Also I have a good deal of domestic care which I like quite as little. I have three young ladies with me to be carved into roses "with flowers and foliage overwrought." My class in town succeeds very well I think, but it breaks up my time a good deal.[2] They talk as much as I could expect and seem deeply interested in the subjects. I think also of giving readings in Boston from Goethe's Miscellanies, if they collect a circle large enough to make it worth my while.— When I am at home I write all I can, to what purpose time will show!

Mr Emerson is lecturing well; his introductory was noble.[3] He makes statements much nearer completeness than ever before; this all the audience feel.

The world is somewhat occupied with Mr Norton and Mr Ripley.[4] The seeming mildness of Mr N's late rejoinder gives him at present the advantage, but Mr R. comes out again this week.

I write in haste pray you write at leisure and forth with. With best wishes of the new year to Lucy, believe me in hope, trust, and love always your friend

MARGARET F.

(MH: fMS Am 1086 [10:103])

1. Hedge at first abruptly rejected her request but then relented enough to publish "The Art of Life,— The Scholar's Calling" in the October issue. The first issue of the *Dial* appeared in July.

2. Her "Conversations."

3. Emerson began his "Present Age" lecture series in Boston on 4 December. Fuller heard the fourth, "Politics," the evening after she wrote this letter.

4. George Ripley had quarreled with Andrews Norton in print for over three years. Most recently Norton published his own address to the Divinity School students (*A Discourse on the Latest Form of Infidelity*), an attack on Emerson. Ripley published his *Reply to Norton's Remarks on Spinoza.*

57. To Sarah Helen Whitman

Jamaica plain
21st Jany 1840.

My dear Mrs Whitman,

It has always seemed to me unnatural to write to more than one person at a time. Either I am quite engrossed in a correspondence or good for nothing in it. I am not excited by the thought as by the face of a companion. I pray you forgive my being a bad correspondent in consideration of my being a ready talker.

Your article looks very fair in print and is, I am told, much commended, but I fear Orestes B. pays in nought more solid than praise.[1] Such was the case and, on beginning this year when he applied to several persons to aid him, I know he offered no more glittering bait. But I will inquire.

There are few German books for sale in Boston, now Burdett has given up his shop. You will be more likely to find them at Behr's in New York. The vol of Tieck could not I presume, be bought, you might get it from the library of Harvard university, if you have a friend there. I send you a book of mine, one of Richter's finest works. I think its fancy, humor, and sweet humanity will delight you. You can keep it till April, you will find it quite a study, for Richter loves to coin words, and seeks his thought even in the most distant mint.

You joke about my Gods and Goddesses but really my class in Boston is very pleasant. There I have real society, which I have not before looked for out of the pale of intimacy. We have time, patience, mutual reverence and fearlessness eno' to get at one another's thoughts. Of course our treatment of topics is superficial but good, I think as far as it goes. I took up the Grecian mythology as a good means of opening a vista to the plain I sought and the topics were pursued thus.

Jupiter—	Creative Energy, Will.
Apollo—	Genius.
Bacchus,	Geniality
Venus Urania—	Ideal Beauty.
Cupid and Psyche,	Redemption of the soul by human experience.
Venus again	on which they wrote as well as talked.
Pallas.	very inadequately treated.

I then availed myself of a good oppory to drop the Mythology, and begin again by dividing the universe into Poesy, Philosophy, Prose then Poesy (following Coleridge's classification) into Poetry, Music, Painting, Sculpture, architecture and the histrionic art. We then took up Poetry and, after some consideration of its different forms, are taking up the poets. Shakspeare and Burns next time This in reference to some discussion of the words satire wit and humor called up by the question given out for last time, Whether there be any such thing as satirical poetry? I wish you would write and send me *your* definitions of poesy, poetry, wit and humor, fancy and imagination.

I wish you could come to town and be present at one of these conversations.

As soon as Mr Emerson's lectures are over I am to take that eveg to give readings from Goethe's works on the Fine Arts to a small circle.

These sort of things suit me very well. I also read some fine books, have now and then some thoughts and see some good people. So I am more good-natured than when you knew me, for then I had less leisure, less sympathy and less congenial pursuits. I still intend to come to P. in order to show myself in this more favorable light, in April or May, probably. You must invite Lorenzo [Da Ponte] to meet me.— By the way Belshazzar tarried on his way— did he see any fresh script of Upharsin— where is he!.[2]

I am sorry to hear such reports of my friend Miss —— I trow it is no part of Xty to deny your neighbor's claim to be religious his own way. But I dare say she does herself injustice as was the case in the days of my acquaintance with her. She was inclined to insist, persist, and dogmatize too much in conversation, but in her heart I thought very desirous to do justice and find truth. Your circle at P. is too narrow and you are too close together and jostle too often to see one another fairly. I used to be much annoyed while there by habits of minute scrutiny unknown in wider circles and, meseems, very injurious to fairness of view.

I have now written all day and my poor fingers are sadly tired. This is a longer, if not a better letter than you ever before recd from me. I hope you will not be ungrateful but write soon to yours truly

MARGARET F.—

(RHi)

1. Whitman reviewed Fuller's *Conversations with Goethe* in the January issue of Brownson's *Boston Quarterly Review*.

2. Lorenzo Da Ponte (1803–40), son of Mozart's librettist, taught Italian literature at the University of the City of New York. In the fifth chapter of Daniel, King Belshazzar saw a hand writing on a wall, "Mene, Mene, Tekel, Upharsin."

58.   To William H. Channing

Jamaica Plain,
22d March, 1840—

My dear friend,

This eveg is not a very good time to answer your letter, but I must take it, *faute de mieux,* because I want to say to you. Though your plan be a brave one, and I would wish to become acquainted with Ernest as speedily as possible, yet if you be not ready at once to commence your pilgrimage with him, send some short pieces. I do not ask as James was wont for "bundles" of fine original compositions but make use of the modester words *some* or *several* and I pray you heed my request, for with this first number we want room for choice. I have myself a great deal written but as I read it over scarce a word seems pertinent to the place or time. When I meet people I can adapt myself to them, but when I write, it is into another world, not a better one perhaps, but one with very dissimilar habits of thought to this where I am domesticated. How much those of us who have been much formed by the European mind have to unlearn and lay aside, if we would act here. I would fain do something worthily that belonged to the country where I was born, but most times I fear it may not be.

What others can do, whether all that has been said is the mere restlessness of discontent, or there are thoughts really struggling for utterance will I think be tested now. A perfectly free organ is to be offered for the expression of individual thought and character. There are no party measures to be carried, no particular standard to be set up. A fair calm tone, a recognition of universal principles will, I hope pervade the essays in every form I hope there will neither be a spirit of dogmatism nor of compromise. That this periodical will not aim at leading public opinion, but at stimulating each man to think for himself, to think more deeply and more nobly by letting them see how some minds are kept alive by a wise self-trust. I am not sanguine as to the amount of talent which will be brought to bear on this publication. I find all concerned rather indifferent, and see no great promise for the present. I am sure we cannot show high culture, and I doubt about vigorous thought. But I hope we shall show free action as far as it goes and a high aim. It were much if a periodical could be kept open to accomplish no outward object, but merely to afford an avenue for what of free and calm thought might be originated among us by the wants of individual minds.

James promises nothing but if I can get him here I shall expect some sound rough fruit of American growth. From Mr Emerson we may hope good literary criticisms, but his best thoughts must, I suppose take the form of lectures for the present.

But you will see I wish you were here that I might talk with you once. I cannot write well to any one to whom I do not write constantly. But we shall write constantly to our friends in print now. When I have finished "Ernest" I will seal and send a letter I writ you last summer provided it seems fit for an appendix to the record of your search.

My dear friend, you speak of your sense of "unemployed force."— I feel the same. I never, never in life have had the happy feeling of really doing any thing. I can only console myself for these semblances of actions by seeing that others seem to be in some degree aided by them. But Oh! really to feel the glow of action, without its weariness, what heaven it must be! I cannot think, can you, that all men in all ages have suffered thus from an unattained Ideal. The race must have been worn out ere now by such corrosion. May you be freed from it! for me, my constant ill-health makes me daily more inadequate to my desires and my life now seems but a fragment. At such hours we take refuge in the All, we know that somewhere in Nature this vitality stifled here is manifesting itself. But individuality is so dear we would fain sit beneath our own vines and fig trees.

Farewell, pray write to me again if it suits you so to do. I should answer all the letters, a compliment I do not always pay. My respects to Miss Channing.[1] Mother and sister are not near me now, but they think of you ever with respect and love.

Yours

S. MARGARET FULLER.

(MB)

1. Probably Channing's sister, Lucy Ellery Channing (1809–77).

59. To William H. Channing

Jamaica Plain
19th April 1840

My dear friend,

I received and read a day or two since your folio sheet with great delight. I am very glad you have begun at once on your new plan instead of sending last year's fallen leaves; I am much pleased with the first chapter and hope you will keep Constant in Rome some time. I want to send you some notes of my own on the Sybil and Prophet you speak of, but there is not room on this little sheet. When I can afford to buy one of those large ones, perhaps I will, unless indeed I publish them with a string of other Americanisms upon Michel; I will not promise to correct well for you myself, for I am ignorant and careless in these details, but you may be sure Mr R. will be miserable if there is a comma amiss, and he is to be the corrective as I the [*illegible*] element in this new organization. I do not expect to be of much use except to urge on the laggards, and scold the lukewarm, and act Helen Mac Gregor to those who love compromise, by doing my little best to sink them in the waters of Oblivion!![1]

Things go on pretty well, but I dare say people will be disappointed, for they seem to be looking for the gospel of transcendentalism. It may prove as your Jouffroy says it is with the French ministry; the public wants something positive, and finding such and such persons excellent at fault finding raises them to be the rulers, when lo! they have no noble and full Yea, to match their shrill and bold Nay, and are hurled down again—[2] Mr Emerson knows best what he wants but he has already said it in various ways.— Yet I deem the experiment is well worth trying; hearts beat so high, they must be full of something, and here is a way to breathe it out quite freely.— It is for dear New England that I wanted this review; for myself, if I had wished to write a few pages now and then, I had ways and means of disposing of them. But in truth I have not much to say, for since I have had leisure to look at myself I find that, so far from being a great original genius, I have not yet learned to think to any depth, and that the utmost I have done in life has been to form my character to a certain consistency, cultivate my tastes, and learn to tell the truth with a little better grace than I did at first. For this the world will not care much, so I shall only hazard a few critical remarks, or an un[pre]tending chalk sketch now and then, till I have learned to do something. There will be some beautiful *poesies* about prose I know not yet so well. We shall be the means of publishing the little Charles Emerson left as a mark of his noble course, and though it lies in fragments you will think yourself a gainer by it I am sure.[3]

Please when you write to James tell him he must write me a better letter before I write to him, for that I thought when I opened his last some one had sent me a leaf from a copy book, the lines were so far apart, also that I sit here at my window waiting for his poem. I hope James will come here and live, albeit he must leave you to do it.

I suppose you hear all that would interest you that is doing here, for I know you have excellent correspondents, so I have egotized quite at my ease. Your dear mother I did see *often* and had hoped to see *much*, but though I was with her so often, yet, on those evegs when I gave the readings at her room I never once was well enough to talk with her after. But it is a pleasure to me even to see her face which lights up with the same noble, youthful earnestness—as in former days when there is any good thought living near her. But she rather slandered you, I think, for she spoke of you as a man of more plan than performance. I shall go and tell her what admirable promptitude you have shown. My dear Mr Channing, you must not write to me again unless you wish, for I remember you told me you did not like to write letters, but, if you do, I hope you will tell me about yourself and your various relations. You will not now misunderstand me or think I live in a mere intellectual curiosity surely, yet ah! how many

Fuller's letter to William H. Channing, 19 April 1840. Boston Public Library/Rare Books Department. Courtesy of the Trustees.

more times you must misunderstand before ever you know me, I felt when last we met. But I shall have your true friendship sometime, I am sure, in faith and hope yours

M F

(MB)

1. In Scott's *Rob Roy,* Helen MacGregor is a fierce woman who threatens destruction to any who oppose her.

2. Channing was translating Théodore Jouffroy's *Introduction to Ethics, Including a Critical Survey of Moral Systems* as volumes 5 and 6 of Ripley's Specimens of Foreign Standard Literature. W. D. Wilson reviewed it in the first issue of the *Dial.*

3. Charles Chauncy Emerson (1808–36) was Waldo's younger brother. Fuller published his "Notes from the Journal of a Scholar" in the first issue of the *Dial.*

60.   To Ralph Waldo Emerson

Jamaica plain,
May 31st 1840.

My dear friend,

I take this large sheet without being sure I shall fill it. This weather makes me, too, very impatient of the artificial life of reading and writing, though I dont think that "weeding onions" would be the way I should take of linking myself to Nature in this her liebersvollste Tag.—[1] You did wrong not to come here. I had a great deal to say to you which I shall not write. However I dont wonder you economize your time if you are to have your house full of company all the beautiful, solitary summer. I will try not to wish to see you.

I cannot write down what the Southern gales have whispered.— I shall talk mere gossip to you now.— Of Providence, you have really got up a re-vival there, though they do not know it.[2] Daily they grow more vehement in their determination to become acquainted with God. If they pursue the chase with such fury a month or two longer I think they will get some thoughts about—themselves. I was much pleased by the correctness of their impressions about you and about Mr Ripley. Charles gave as good a sketch of you as I could draw myself— Mr Greene said some piquant things Mrs Burges had expanded like a flower in your light. She has re-ceived at last just the impulse she needed. I sympathized in her happiness on my celestial side, and, on the demonical, I amused myself with annihi-lating Mr Pabodie who offered himself as a prey to the spoiler.[3] I wish you had been there I think you would not have been too sweet to be amused; he provoked it from such a low vanity.— Susan, the Recluse, was absent on a journey, and she goes to the theatre now in the costume I formerly described to you.[4] She will be the founder of an order of lay nuns!— I was much pleased with the way in which some of my girls received the lectures. They understood at once.

I had a (to me) very pleasant visit from Mr Alcott. I saw him by the light of his own eyes. With me alone he is never the Messiah but one beautiful individuality and faithful soul. Then he seems really high and not merely a person of high pretensions. I think his "Sayings" are quite grand, though ofttimes too grandiloquent.[5] I thought he bore my strictures with great sweetness for they must have seemed petty to him.— Tell him that Mr Ripley verified at once my prophecy and said what I told him would be said about the Prometheus.

Mr Ripley is most happy in the step he has taken. He seems new-born.[6] The day you went to town with me as we were talking about it, I told him what is thought of him as a preacher, and expressed doubts as to his being able to build up a church here. I told him I had hoped when he broke away he would enter on some business and leave preaching. But he said he could not without a trial; that he knew as well as any body that he never had preached, but that was because he had never been on his true ground, that he had much he longed to say and was sure that in suitable relations he should be able to breathe out what was so living in him. He showed himself a fine, genial, manly person that day. I feel that he has many steps to take before he arrives at his proper position. There is to me a manifest inconsistency in his views. But this will be a valuable experiment to him. He will yet be free and fair, I hope *complete* in his way.

There are only thirty names on the Boston subscription list to the "Dial"; I hope you will let me have your papers by next Friday or Saty. Send Ellen Hooper's too if you have done with them.[7] And will you not send me Carlyle's letter containing the sketches of Landor and Heraud.[8] And tell me a little what you said to Milnes of his review.[9] I thought you might like to see this letter from Miss Martineau Mr Sumner says she is not likely to live, but I suppose she knows the exact truth.[10] No one would be willing to deceive one who looks on death with such a bright and rational calmness. Do not show it to any unless Lidian or Elizabeth, for though I believe every one here now knows what her illness is, I would regard her wishes as far as I am concerned.

Farewell, dear friend, yours always,

M F.

You do not speak of "Man in the Ages." Have you looked at it, and will you send it with yours.[11]

Did I not leave at your house my copy of Chartism you gave me, and, if so, will you send it me? when the proofs come.[12]

Looking at your letter again I am reminded to say a few words of Shelley. You disappoint me a little. How can you, who so admire beautiful persons when you see them in life, fail to be interested in this picture of so beautiful person. I do not look at Shelley's journals &c for me, but for him He inspires tenderness. I do not care whether I knew the thought before or not. I am interested to know what *he* thought. But even from your point of view the Defence of Poetry seems to me excellent It seems to me not "stiff" but dignified, and no otherwise "academical" than as showing a high degree of culture. If there are many statements as good I do not know them. But I am afraid you will abide by your say. tell me if by and by you look my way.

I send you a few slight notes I made on the Life of Michel, if you look at them when you read it, it will be as if I read it with you.—[13] I send you a leaf of James Clarke. What he says of me is akin to what I expressed to you while at Concord. What he says of Landor is good, I think. I send you a leaf from my journal to give Mr Alcott. Tell him it was written long ago, but will give him some idea of the feeling he has always excited in me For he would have it the other day that "there was nothing but a veil of words between us. Will you send me André by Cary, And tell me if you like Mr Briggs.[14]

(MH: bMS Am 1280 [2348; 2383])

1. "Most charming day."
2. Emerson read six lectures of his "Human Life" series in Providence in March and the first of April.
3. Albert Gorton Greene (1802–68), a writer; Eleanor Burrill Burges (1803–65), the aunt of George Curtis; and William Jewett Pabodie (1813–70), a Providence poet.
4. Susan Anna Power (1813–77), Sarah Helen Whitman's sister.
5. Alcott's "Orphic Sayings" were, however, often mocked by unsympathetic *Dial* readers.
6. George Ripley had decided to resign his pulpit at Purchase Street Church. He announced his decision to his parishioners in October and left in January 1841.
7. Ellen Sturgis (1812–48), Caroline's sister, married Robert Hooper in 1837. Fuller and Emerson published eleven of her poems in the *Dial.*
8. In a letter to Emerson, Carlyle had described John Heraud (1799–1887), the editor of the *Monthly Magazine,* as "a loquacious scribacious little man." Carlyle characterized the poet Walter Savage Landor (1775–1864) as "a soul ever promising to take wing into the Aether, yet never doing it, ever splashing webfooted in the terrene mud."
9. Milnes reviewed Emerson in the March *London and Westminster.* Emerson told him that he aspired to win Milnes's approval of "far broader & bolder generalizations" than those to which Milnes objected.
10. Harriet Martineau was confined to her room with an illness from 1839 to 1844.
11. Thomas Treadwell Stone, "Man in the Ages," which Fuller published in the first issue of the *Dial.*
12. Emerson had given Fuller a copy of Carlyle's *Chartism* (1839), the American edition of which he had arranged.
13. The notes of her reading of Quatremère de Quincy's biography of Michelangelo.
14. George Ware Briggs (1810–95), the associate pastor at the First Church, Plymouth, who, with George P. Bradford, had been visiting Emerson in Concord.

61.   To Ralph Waldo Emerson

Jamaica plain,
5th July, 1840.

My dear friend,

I wrote you a long letter on Friday after receiving yours, but on reading it over could not resolve to send it, so you will go to the letter box once again in vain. I am very sorry to be inattentive, but I have felt entirely unlike writing. I have moods of sadness unknown I suppose to those of your temperament, when it seems a mockery and mummery to write of lite and the affairs of my acquaintance. Then I plunge into occupation, and this fortnight past have been no moment idle. I do hope that in the next stage of our existence whatever be our pains and difficulties we may not have these terrible seasons of faintness and discouragement. I ought not to have them now for I will never yield to them or live in their spirit a moment. But when I do not write to you it is always either that I feel so, or am so busy I cannot.

Until I shall have seen Mr R. I cannot answer all your questions. Mais à present, you can have as many numbers as you want for yourself or your friends of this first no, but our contract with them was that twelve numbers should be given to Mr R. each quarter for the use of contributors. Of these I receive two.— Mr Thoreau will have it of course as we hope his frequent aid. But I did not expect to furnish it to all who may give a piece occasionally. I have not sent it to E. H. or C. S. or W.— I sent a list to W. and J. of those to whom I wished this no. sent.[1] I did not give Mr Stone's name, but doubtless Mr R. did. I will see about it, however. I presume Mr Cranch is a subscriber as is J. F. Clarke and others who will write, but I will look at the list when in town next Wednesday.

I desired Mr Thoreau's Persius to be sent him, as I was going away to Cohasset at the time it came out and I understood from Mr R. that it was sent and he did not correct it I do not know how this was, the errors are most unhappy. I will not go away again when it is in press.[2]

I like the poetry better in small type myself and thought the title page neat and unpretending, but have no such positive feeling about such things that I would defer entirely to your taste. But now we have begun so I should think it undesirable to make changes this year, as the first vol should be uniform. I wish I had consulted you at first, but did not know you attached great importance to externals in such matters, as you do so little in others. The marks shall be made and the spaces left as you desire however after our respected poems!

I am glad you are not quite dissatisfied with the first no. I feel myself how far it is from that eaglet motion I wanted. I suffered in looking it over now. Did you observe the absurdity of the last two pages. These are things they had to fill up blanks and which thinking twas pity such beautiful thoughts should be lost put in for climax. Admire the winding up, the concluding sentence!! I agree Mr Alcott's sayings read well.

I thought to write about the expostulation in your last letter, but finally I think I would rather talk with you.

The next number we will do far better. I want to open it with your Article.[3] You said you might wish to make some alterations if we kept it— do you wish to have it sent you, the first part is left in type; they had printed a good deal before finding it would be too long. E. H's "poet," some of Cary's best, Ellery, and "the bard born out of time"! we must have for that

I suppose you did not see Ellery at all or you would have mentioned it, and that you have heard news of W from himself. I had a very good time at Cohasset with Cary, and when we meet will show you a few verses she wrote there. But I am reminded to say a few words apropos to her. C. told me you had spoken to her of my friends. This made me think you could not have fully understood the feeling which led A— to trust you with a tale which was not hers only. A— though frank is not communicative, she has perfect power of keeping a secret. I do not think she would have spoken on this subject to any other than yourself. You gave her the feeling of the holy man, the confessor who should enlighten her at this moment to act in conformity with her purest and highest nature. She felt at once that she was spiritually in relation with you, and spoke as she would in the confessional. Do not think because persons are intimate with me that they know this or any of my other friends' affairs. I know how to keep relations sacredly separate. I should never have let *you* know any thing about this if we had been intimate forever unless A. had. I never told C. till the other day as she knew so much I could not bear she should put the vulgar construction on the matter and told her enough to show how true and noble he had been. But I shall speak to none other. And whatever people may surmise they do and should know nothing. The monument should be made of the purest marble alone.

When you see Mr E. G. Loring I wish he may show you some letters from Jane he brought me the other day.[4] I think you would feel their beauty. That to him about the Carlyles is very good, but not so charming as one to Miss King which I fear you will not see.

Charles Newcomb has been passing three or four days with me. He is wretchedly ill. I think he may die, and perhaps it would be well, for I doubt if he has strength to rise above his doubts and fears. Oh how I thank Heaven that I am made of firmer fibre and more resolute mind. No sharp pain can debilitate like this vacillation of mind.

I hear Rakemann play frequently. I have regretted much that you do not live nearer that I might have you at two or three musical entertainments. Especially one eveg when Knight was here and sang Beethoven's

Rosalie.[5] Life ripples in in various ways, but I know that that it brings any thing *positive* fit for the Concord mart George Simmons has been to see me.[6] S. Clarke has passed a night with me. I am going to pass next Wednesday morng with her at the Hall of Sculpture. I wish you were to be in town also. It is very pleasant to be there, the hall is full and not too full.

Affectionately yours,

S. M. FULLER.

Carlyle's letter shall go next time I send by stage.

(MH: bMS Am 1280 [2349])

1. Weeks and Jordan of Boston published the *Dial.*
2. "Aulus Persius Flaccus."
3. The opening article in the next *Dial* was Emerson's "Thoughts on Modern Literature."
4. Ellis Gray Loring was a Boston lawyer and a founder of the New England Anti-Slavery Society.
5. Joseph Philip Knight (1812–87), an English singer and composer, toured the United States from 1839 to 1841. "Rosalie" was adapted from Beethoven's "Adelaida."
6. George Frederick Simmons (1814–55) had graduated from the Divinity School in 1838 and was then the Unitarian minister in Mobile, Alabama, where his antislavery sermons were not welcome.

62. To Ralph Waldo Emerson

19th July 1840.

I suppose it is too warm for my dear friend to write at least to so dull a correspondent, or perhaps it is that I have asked so many things. I am sorry you did not send the verses, for I wanted to take one or two for filling the gaps, and now have been obliged to take some not so good. Have you not some distiches to bestow? I have two or three little things of yours which I wished very much to use but thought I must not without your leave.

When I wrote the first line of this letter I thought I should fill it up with some notes I wished to make on the hall of sculpture. But I was obliged to stop by a violent attack of headach, and now I am not fit to write any thing good and will only scribble a few lines to send with your proof which Mr R. left with me. He is much distressed at what he thinks a falling off in the end of your paragraph about the majestic Artist, and I think when you look again you will think you have not said what you meant to say. The "eloquence" and "wealth", thus grouped, have rather l'air bourgeoise— "Saddens and gladdens" is good. Mr R. hates prettinesses, as the mistress of a boarding house hates flower vases.[1]

"Dreadful melody" does not suit me. The dreadful has become vulgarized since its natal day.

So much for impertinence! I am very glad I am to own these remarks about the Meister. As to the genius of Goethe the statement, though so much better than others, is too imperfect to be true. He requires to be minutely painted in his own style of hard finish. As he never gave his soul in a glance, so he cannot be painted at a glance. I wish this "Kosmos Beauty" was not here ever again, one does not like their friend to have any *way*, any thing peculiar, he must be too individual to be known by a cough or a phrase.— And is this *costly* true to the sense of kostiliche; that means worthy a high price, the other obtained at a high price, n'est ce pas? I cannot like that illustration of the humors of the eye.— I wish the word *whipped* was never used at all and here it is twice in nearest neighborhood

At this place I was obliged to take to my bed,— my poor head reminding me that I was in no state for criticism. I have marked the parts I admire in the piece. It is really grand. I am sure you will be delighted with my approbation!

Are not you coming hither soon? I begin to want very much to know more about you. How is Lidian? that worthless Elizh I see is behaving just as I told her she would about her visit to me. What does Waldo say, and what has Ellen learnt? Be good to me, by and by I will be good so as to deserve it.

Meanwhile

> Accept a miracle instead of wit,
> All these dull lines by Spenser's pencil writ![2]

I let S. W. see Carlyle's letter, as I thought you would be willing and desired him to return it to you.

Cannot you send a distich to fit in here at the end of your piece.

(MH: bMS Am 1280 [2350])

1. Ripley and Fuller are commenting on "Thoughts on Modern Literature."
2. Fuller modifies Hazlitt's quip " 'Accept a miracle, instead of wit: / See two dull lines with Stanhope's pencil writ.' "

63.   To Caroline Sturgis

Thursday,
Oct 22d 1840.

dear Caroline,

Love goes forth towards you as I read your truest words. I would fain bless you for your recognition. I would sound a trumpet note clear as light now that you are ready for the Genesis. You will go forth, you will leave your heaven, you will not only make the lights, the night, the day, and the great sea but in the least creeping thing will harmonize love and express faith in the revolutions of being. Amen— now may be looked for the Sabbath when a divine consciousness shall proclaim *it is very good.* Life and peace bloom at once and the One divides itself to win the last divinest birth of Love.

But I can say very little now, scarce a word that is not absolutely drawn from me at the moment. I cannot plunge into myself enough. I cannot dedicate myself sufficiently. The life that flows in upon me from so many quarters is too beautiful to be checked. I would not check a single pulsation. It all ought to be;— if caused by any apparition of the Divine in me I could bless myself like the holy Mother. But like her I long to be virgin. I would fly from the land of my birth. I would hide myself in night and poverty. Does a star point out the spot. The gifts I must receive, yet for my child, not me. I have no words, wait till he is of age, then hear *him.*

Oh Caroline, my soul swells with the future. The past, I know it not. I have just written a letter to our dear Waldo which gives me pain. It was all into the past. His call bids me return, I know not how, yet full of tender renunciation, know not how to refuse. All the souls I ever loved are holy to me, their voices sound more and more sweet yet oh for an hour of absolute silence, dedicated, enshrined in the bosom of the One.

Yet the cross, the symbol you have chosen seems indeed the one. Daily, hourly it is laid upon me. Tremulously I feel that a wound is yet to be given. Separation! to be severed for ages from my rapture and the angel forms through which it shone, must not that be so? Oh, because I dread it, because my courage is not yet so perfect as my submission, because I might say, Father, if it be thy will let this cup pass, shall I not be forced to drink it? Oh the prophetic dread and hope and pain and joy. My Caroline, I am not yet purified. Let the lonely Vestal watch the fire till it draws her to itself and consumes this mortal part. Truly you say I have not been what I am now yet it is only transformation, not alteration. The leaf became a stem, a bud, is now in flower. Winds of heaven, dews of night, circles of time, already ye make haste to convert this flower into dead-seeming seed— yet Caroline far fairer shall it bloom again

Was it as you say that I wished too much to make a virtue bloom in my particular garden. If so I dare to say it was not for me, but for the Universe. I loved the realizing of ideas, and this was easiest in the nearness of mine own persons but it seems to me that they were always recognized with utmost joy elsewhere.

Still I perceive this love of realizing is here in the desire I feel for nun like dedication in these months to come. All that I have ever known comes up in my thoughts on the other side from what it did. I was stern and fearless. I am soft and of most delicate tenderness. I rushed into the melee an Amazon of breast undefended save by its inward glow. Shrouded in a white veil I would now kneel at the secretest shrines and pace the dimmest cloisters— I rushed out like the great sea, burst against all rocks, strewed with weeds and shells all matted and forlorn the loveliest shores, welcome alike the graceful nymph and the slimiest monster to a refuge or a death[.] in my deep mysterious grottoes I feared no rebuff, I shrunk from no publicity, I could not pause yet ever I sobbed and wailed over my endless motion and foamed angrily to meet the storm-winds which kept me pure— I would now steal away over golden sands, through silent flowery meadows farther still through darkest forests "full of heavenly vows" into the very heart of the untrodden mountain where the carbuncle has lit the way to veins of yet undreamed of diamond.

One day that I once lived at Groton rises on my thoughts with charm unspeakable. I had passed the night in the sick chamber of a wretched girl in the last stage of a consumption. It was said she had profaned her maiden state, and that the means she took to evade the consequences of her stain had destroyed her health and placed her on this bed of death. The room was full of poverty, base thoughts, and fragments of destiny. As I raised her dying head it rested against my bosom like a clod that should never have been taken from the valley. On my soul brooded a sadness of deepest calm. I looked ay I *gazed* into that abyss lowest in humanity of crime for the sake of sensual pleasure, my eye was steadfast, yet above me shone a star, pale, tearful, still it shone, it was mirrored from the very blackness of the yawning gulf. Through the shadows of that night ghost-like with step unlistened for, unheard assurance came to me. O, it has ever been thus, from the darkest comes my brightness, from Chaos depths my love. I returned with the morning star. No one was with me in the house. I unlocked the door went into the silent room where but late before my human father dwelt. It was the first winter of my suffering health the musings and vigils of the night had exhausted while exalting me. The cold rosy winter dawn and then the sun. I had forgotten to wind up the clock the day marked itself. I lay there, I could not resolve to give myself food The day was unintentionally a fast. Sacredest thoughts were upon it, and I comprehended the meaning of an ascetic life. The Angel that meets the pious monk beside the bed of pestilence and low vice, that dwells with him in the ruined hut of his macerated body, hovered sweet though distant before me also. At times I read the Bible at times Wordsworth I dwelt in the thoughtful solitudes of his Excursion I wandered like his white doe.[1] The change from my usual thoughts and feelings was as if a man should leave the perfumed, wildly grand oft times poisonous wildernesses of the tropics the crocodiles and lion hunts and haughty palms, for the snowy shroud, intent unpromising silence, and statuesque moons of the Northern winter from which Phenix like rises the soul into the tenderest Spring. The sunset of that day was the same which will shine on my last hour here below.— Winter is coming now. I rejoice in her bareness, her pure shroud, her judgment-announcing winds. These will help me to dedicate myself, all these Winter spirits will cradle my childhood with strange and mystic song. Oh Child who would'st deem thee mine canst thou read what I cannot write. No only one soul is there that can lead me up to womanhood and baptize me to gentlest May. Is it not ready? I have strength to wait as a smooth bare tree forever, but ask no more my friends for leaves and flowers or a bird haunted bower.

(MH: bMS Am 1221 [242])

1. "The Excursion" (1814) and "The White Doe of Rylston" (1815). In the latter, Emily Norton, the last of her family, returns to her ancestral home and is joined by a white doe, which becomes her companion. After her death, the doe watches over her grave.

64.   To Caroline Sturgis

[ca. 25 October 1840]

I have read over these letters twice.— At Newbury I was disappointed in them, for then my soul, all bathed in rosy light, floated away from this cold blue.

But now I am in a less glowing atmosphere and looking this way see the rising stars. May thy voice call many forth. May I be pure of sight to discern the whole galaxy.

Yet Waldo is still only a small and secluded part of Nature, secluded by a doubt, secluded by a sneer. I am ashamed of him for the letter he wrote about our meeting.— It is equally unworthy of him and of what he professes for you. He calls you his sister and his saint yet cannot trust your sight. There are many beings who have reached a height of generosity and freedom far above him.

But none is truer, purer, and he is already profound.

What is all this talk about the positive degree? Still this same dull distrust of life! When the sun paints the cloud, when the tree clusters its leaves, when the bird dwells more sweetly and fully on a note than is necessary just to let his mate know he is wanted, the comparative and superlative degrees are used— The fact on which Waldo ever dwells in the world of thought, that whatever is excellent supersedes the whole world and commands us entirely for the moment, is expressed in the world of feeling by use of the superlative. Do we say dearest, wisest, virtuosest, best,— we make no vow, but express that the object is able to supersede all calculation

O these tedious, tedious attempts to learn the universe by thought alone. Love, Love, my Father, thou hast given me.— I thank thee for its pains.

I cannot read these letters without a great renewal of my desire to teach this sage all he wants to make him the full-formed Angel. But that task is not for me. The gulf which separates us is too wide. May thou be his friend, it would be a glorious office. But you are not so yet.

(MH: bMS Am 1221 [225])

65. To Bettina Brentano von Arnim

Boston, U S.—
2d Novr 1840.

Dear Bettine,

For how can I address you by any title less near than that by which you have become so familiar to our thoughts. I write to you in the name of many men and many women of my country for whom you have wrought wonders. How many have read the records of your beautiful youth and ceased to distrust the promptings of their own young hearts! How many have looked back from maturer years and wondered that they also did not dare to *live*! How many have counted each pulse of your heart of love, how many more been kindled into flame at the touch of your genius!

We want to know more of you, Bettine. In your youthful ideal we see such promise! Your childhood was so prodigal a May-time, we want to know that you have bloomed into an eternal youth. Since you have trusted us with the secret of your love, will you not trust us farther? We have read again and again the manifold records of those early years of inspiration. We drink deep of the nectar cup, and yet long for more. We ask all men who come from your land, Have you seen Bettine?— What know you of the Child?— Is she weeping beside the monument of Goethe, or has she ascended a pedestal of her own?— But they do not speak intelligently of thee! They do not tell us what we want to hear. Thou art dear to us, thou art the friend of our inmost mood. We do not wish to hear street gossip about thee. We will not hear it. Speak to us thyself.

Give thyself to us still farther. There lives none perhaps now who could speak fitly of thee but many who would listen intelligently.

I do not believe you will refuse to gratify our desire. Though expressed by an obscure individual it is the desire of many hearts. I would say of a new world,— but all worlds are new to ardent natures like yours. Writ[e] to me or print it in a book. Tell us how the years have flown, what brought on their wings. There is one question above all we would fain ask. You will divine and, I trust, answer it. I give my name, though it will be a word without significance, in hope that you will address yourself to me and thus enable me to give the great pleasure to others of hearing more from their friend. We have written here no book worthy to send you; should any printed leaves accompany this, it will be merely as a token of respect.[1] But you are wise, you have the spiritual sight, the breath of our love will be wafted to you and you will see whether we are yours. The bearer of this will tell you how to direct if you are disposed to fulfil the hope of yours in faith

S. MARGARET FULLER.

My messenger may miss you. Address to care of Hilliard, Gray and company and I shall receive the letter. Or to that of Rev George Ripley Boston.

(Goethe- und Schiller-Archiv)

1. She sent copies of Dwight's *Select Minor Poems* and the *Dial.*

66. To William H. Channing

Sunday 8th Novr [1840]

It has been a great disappointment not to hear from you this week. Your mother let me know of your safe arrival, but I had expected you would write to me almost immediately, so hard is it to cure some people of vanity!

Most beautiful was my meeting with our friends the first day of this month, the first of our new alliance. The moon came in so stilly. We sat together all the evening, with but few words, all three meeting in one joy.

I cannot think about it or write about it except of

"a fair luminous cloud
Enveloping the earth"[1]

and

"When the little halcyon builds her nest the waters wait and the storms too till she be ready to leave it, even if they wait fourteen days."

Yet, strange to tell, my first thought when they had gone was 'I would not be so happy.'

Is it that whatever seems complete sinks at once into the finite?

Anna's strongest expression of pleasure and which she repeated again and again was "I feel as if I had been married twenty years." Tuesday Cary spent with me, and we read all Mr. E's letters to both of us this summer. They make a volume, and passages are finer than any thing he has published.

Wednesday I opened with my class. It was a noble meeting. I told them the great changes in my mind, and that I could not be sure they would be satisfied with me now, as they were when I was in deliberate possession of myself. I tried to convey the truth, and though I did not arrive at any full expression of it, they all with glistening eyes seemed melted into one love.— Our relation is now perfectly true and I do not think they will ever interrupt me.

Anna sat beside me, all glowing, and the moment I had finished she began to speak. She told me afterwards she was all kindled, and none there could be strangers to her more.

I was really delighted by the enthusiasm of Mrs Farrar. I did not expect it; all her best self seemed called up, and she feels that these meetings will be her highest pleasure.

Ellen Hooper too was most beautiful. I went home with Mrs Farrar and had a long attack of nervous headach. She attended anxiously on me, and asked would it be so all winter. I said if it were I did not care, and truly I feel now such an entire separation from pain and illness, such a calm consciousness of another life while suffering most in the body, that pain has no effect except to steal some of my time. And I believe it compensates by purifying me. I do not regret it in the least.

Mrs F. told me some very interesting traits from her visit to Butternuts, if I have time I shall write them out for you. The first story of Melissa will remind you of a beautiful passage in De Maistre's Soirees de St Petersbourg if you have ever read them.[2]

The second of *Edith* the schoolmistress I am not sure I can do justice to. Did you not choose the name of Edith because it gives an idea of such purity. Sometimes the stars drop a name on the person to whom it belongs as in the case of the Edith of Butternuts.

I have been writing the companion to the Yuca, the Magnolia, for the Dial. I hope you will like it.[3] All the suggestion was that he said its odour was so exquisite and unlike that of any other Magnolia. If you like it, I will draw the soul also from the Yuca and put it into words.

Sophia Ripley has been here all day. Mr R. this eveg, and since they went our landlord to whom I have been preaching that the life is better than meat, for the things he said grieved me for his soul. He seemed moved, and even if he did not hear me, the boys did and were struck with the contrast betwixt Living and "getting a living." [ ]

(MB)

1. Coleridge, "Dejection: An Ode."
2. Joseph de Maistre's *Les Soirées de Saint-Pétersbourg* (1821) is a dialogue whose topics are evil, suffering, and the efficacy of prayer.
3. Fuller published her "Magnolia of Lake Pontchartrain" in the January *Dial*, but she did not publish "Yuca Filamentosa" until January 1842.

67.   To Henry D. Thoreau

1st Decr. [1840]

I am to blame for so long detaining your manuscript.[1] But my thoughts have been so engaged that I have not found a suitable hour to reread it as I wished till last night. This second reading only confirms my impression from the first. The essay is rich in thoughts, and I should be *pained* not to meet it again. But then the thoughts seem to me so out of their natural order, that I cannot read it through without *pain*. I never once feel myself in a stream of thought, but seem to hear the grating of tools on the mosaic. It is true as Mr E. says, that essays not to be compared with this have found their way into the Dial. But then those are more unassuming in their tone, and have an air of quiet good-breeding which induces us to permit their presence. Yours is so rugged that it ought to be commanding. Yet I hope you will give it me again, and if you see no force in my objections disregard them.

S. M. FULLER.

(NNPM)

1. "The Service," which Thoreau never published.

68.   To Ralph Waldo Emerson

Jamaica plain
6th Decr 1840.

Dear Waldo,

W. Story's piece cannot be admitted into this number of the Dial, if only on account of its length.—[1] Even if you did not give your essay on Art there would not be room for this, as the number is nearly full with what I have promised to receive, and this would occupy at least thirty pages of print.

I am well pleased by the remarks on works of art. And like the spirit of the whole, though it does not enable to form a sure estimate of the author's mind, as I seem to hear Page talking all through it.[2]

If these are your pencil-marks you did not, I think, read it through, the latter part is so full of bad faults in style and imagery which you have not marked. I mention this because if W. S. is inclined to take the pains (which would do him a world of good) to sift and write it over I would insert it in the April number.

He might take some other subject than the Gallery (the Night and Day for instance) and yet interweave what he has said of all the statues as illustrations of his opinions.[3] I wish too he would compress his article; it is too long for us, and would also be improved there by. And take heed of such expressions as "hung for hours on the head" (of Augustus) &c

If he will do this he must let us know by the 1st Jany, for I have already a good deal on hand for the April number.

I shall depend on your Essay and hope to receive it certainly on Wednesday, for we are harried now. Shall have the proofs of "Orphic sayings" sent to Mr A. but wish him to be sure and return them next day. He will not get them for a week or more.

Will you forgive me if I do not publish Ellery's verses now? I have others which I prefer for this no. and there are reasons not worth stating here, but which I can tell when we meet.

These sonnets have the fault of seeming imitated from Tennyson, and, though they have some merit, it is not *poetical* merit. If I publish them, I cannot all together. I will take the last for this no, if he is willing it should go alone, and lets me know in time. Though I have many short poems in my drawer I like better, yet I do not wish to discourage these volunteers who are much wanted to vary the manoeuvres of the regular platoon.

As to the Mythological evegs, let that pass for the present, for my life is as yet all too crowded, and I do not want any new call quite yet. But I will bear your promise in mind, supposing I feel ready for such meetings presently.

Nothing but business letters till this Dial be out. And then my family, all absent, compel me to over much letter writing. So bear with dulness from your affte

M.

(MH: bMS Am 1280 [2352])

1. William Wetmore Story (1819–95), son of Justice Joseph Story, initially repelled Fuller; she disliked his circle of friends, who included James Lowell. Story became a lawyer and a

distinguished writer on law but gave it up to become a sculptor in Italy, where Fuller became his close friend. The essay she here discusses was not published in the *Dial.*

2. William Page (1811–85) studied with Samuel F. B. Morse and became a successful painter. Like Story, he was friendly with Lowell.

3. Horatio Greenough made casts of "Day" and "Night," monuments on Michelangelo's tomb of Giuliano de' Medici in Florence. The casts were deposited in the Boston Athenaeum in 1834.

69.   To Maria Weston Chapman

Jamaica plain,
26th Decr 1840.

My dear Mrs Chapman,

I received your note but a short time before I went to the conversation party. There was no time for me to think what I should do or even ascertain the objects of the Fair.[1] Had I known them I could not by any slight suggestion have conveyed my view of such movements. And a conversation on the subject would interrupt the course adopted by my class. I therefore, merely requested Miss Peabody to show the papers and your note to me before I began on the subject before us.

The Abolition cause commands my respect as do all efforts to relieve and raise suffering human nature. The faults of the party are such as, it seems to me, must always be incident to the partizan spirit. All that was noble and pure in their zeal has helped us all. For the disinterestedness and constancy of many individuals among you I have a high respect. Yet my own path leads a different course and often leaves me quite ignorant what you are doing, as in the present instance of your Fair.

Very probably to one whose heart is so engaged as yours in particular measures this indifference will seem incredible or even culpable. But if indifferent I have not been intolerant; I have wronged none of you by a a hasty judgment or careless words, and, where I have not investigated a case so as to be sure of my own opinion, have, at least, never chimed in with the popular hue and cry. I have always wished that efforts originating in a generous sympathy, or a sense of right should have fair play, have had firm faith that they must, in some way, produce eventual good.

The late movements in your party have interested me more than those which had for their object the enfranchisement of the African only. Yet I presume I should still feel sympathy with your aims only not with your measures. Yet I should like to be more fully acquainted with both. The late Convention I attended hoping to hear some clear account of your wishes as to religious institutions and the social position of woman. But not only I heard nothing that pleased me, but no clear statement from any one. Have you in print what you consider an able exposition of the views of yourself and friends?— Or if not, should you like yourself to give me some account of how these subjects stand in your mind? As far as I know you seem to me quite wrong as to what is to be done for woman! She needs new helps I think, but not such as you propose. But I should like to know your view and your grounds more clearly than I do.

With respect

S. M. FULLER.

(MB)

1. The annual Massachusetts Anti-Slavery Fair, a fund-raising activity, opened on 22 December.

70.   To Caroline Sturgis

Sunday eveg
Jany 24th 1841.

dear Caroline, Can you do any thing about tickets to Mr E's lecture in case he should not send us any.[1] I shall come to your house tomorrow aftn as I said I would. If you have prepared your mother I intend talking with her about Spring St.

I have read no Dante, nor thought about any lesson to you, but hope the inspiration will come with the hour—truly—I have had no appetite for his banquet.

Hercules I fancy when *in* the fire which so pleased his father Jove, could not have touched the cup, though filled with nectar by Hebe his bride.

Dante,— thou didst not describe in all thy apartments of Inferno, this tremendous repression of an existence half unfolded, this swoon as the soul was ready to be born. Thy Lucifer upholds the earth, but bears not on his heart the weight of future heavens *known not felt,* pressing, yet still of incalculable dimensions.

Poets of the lesser orders suffer not thus To them "some God gives to tell what they suffer"

"Still day and Night alternate in their bosoms"

But in the intervals of life they write what they have lived, saying what they have felt.

But they who are but the hieroglyphics of their future being. Souls which must be all before they can speak one word, Destinies strangely mismatched with the ungrateful Hermes, travel to the mount of life through fields of graves, and nothing is heard but the slow tread of their footsteps.

My wings were just budded; they are pushed back upon my heart, but they are no longer tender with the plumage of the nest, they will not fold back over it and keep it warm again. So the breast must ache.

Silent lies the pool, all nature crowded around in the prayer of conscious mutilation. Yet will it move no more till the true Angel descend.

The ruined city lies beneath the moon, cold and barren falls her light, on palaces, richly sculptured, but without a roof or a hearth stone, on temples of purest marble, but bereft of their gods. The lion and the dragon have gone forth into the desert, the owl hoots her dull comment, the young Eagles are not yet strong enough to cry till they are heard by their far distant sire!

Oh I could write it into endless images, all, all of lead. But hoard thy life, faithful Aloes! Shroud thy love, unwearied snow, yield not a single violet, to this warm but black rain. There is no spring to pierce to thy heart, say nothing if thou canst not tell thy heart. Yet even to day a bird sang.

To *stand* and wait, I cannot.[2] I will lie down on the earth and look up at the sky. My Star has hid its beam, but many others are there, cold to me yet bright. I cannot love them, yet will bless Eternity that gives them their turn. Probably they were lost in night while mine was in the ascendant. Pray for me, radiant friends, I bless, I do not envy ye. I bide my time God's time.

(MH: bMS Am 1221 [243])

1. "Man the Reformer," which Emerson read on 25 January and published in the April *Dial*.
2. From Milton's Sonnet 19: "They also serve who only stand and waite."

71. To Richard F. Fuller

Concord,
25th May, 1841.

My dear Richard,

I enclose this letter from Mother, probably the last I can receive from her. I took away the last leaf by Eugene as it contained something I thought he might not like to have me send about. It is written with sweetness and self-possession; he seems to feel as if he knew very well what he is about. Let us give him the most affectionate reception. You will see what Mother wishes to have done about her plants. I need not, I know, commend them to your care.— I want you Saturday eveg or Sunday to go to C. Port to Mrs Gannett's and tell her I think they may arrive next week, yet I cannot be sure as they may stay longer either in Louisville or Cincin than I now suppose. If they receive my letter on their way they will probably all three, Mother, F. and W. H. go out directly to Mrs Gannett's and if she has not two rooms vacant then, Mother can go to Aunt K's till Mr Brodhead's family leave Mrs G.— You had better read aloud what I say that Mrs G. may distinctly understand. And give her my best respects.

I am living here the quiet country life you would enjoy. Here are hens, cows, pigs! and what I like better wildflowers and a host of singing birds. By the way, I dont think you could gratify Mrs Ward more than on the Sunday you go to Jamaica to get her a bouquet of wild flowers. Borrow a tin pail or box and wet them when you put them in; they may thus be brought to town perfectly fresh. Mr. Emerson works five or six hours a day in his garden and his health which was in a very low state this spring improves day by day. He has a friend with him of the name of Henry Thoreau who has come to live with him and be his working-man this year. H. T. is three and twenty, has been through college and kept a school, is very fond of classic studies, and an earnest thinker yet intends being a farmer. He has a great deal of practical sense, and as he has bodily strength to boot, he may look to be a successful and happy man. He has a boat which he made himself, and rows me out on the pond. Last night I went out quite late and staid til the moon was almost gone, heard the whip-poor-will for the first time this year. There was a sweet breeze full of appleblossom fragrance which made the pond swell almost into waves. I had great pleasure. I think of you in these scenes, because I know you love them too. By and by when the duties are done, we may expect to pass summer days together

I have had a letter from Lloyd, stating that "he did not like the Community as he expected, for he has to work when he does not wish to"!![1]

My love to Arthur. I wrote to him before I recd his letter. Probably I may not write again as I expect to be in Cambridge by Monday eveg next. very affectionately your sister

M.

(MH: fMS Am 1086 [9:71])

1. Lloyd was staying at Brook Farm.

72. To Ralph Waldo Emerson

Brookline.
Monday evening 21st June. [1841]

Dearest Waldo,

By the light of this new moon I see very clearly that you were quite in the right and I in the wrong.[1] I dont know how I could persist so in my own way of viewing the matter in the face of your assuring me that myself had fixed a later day and of your exertions to keep your engagement and bring your poesies. I think I was very ill-natured, perverse, and unreasonable, but I am punished when I think of you riding home alone and thinking it all over as I know you must for I have been able to get into your way of viewing it now. Whatever I may have said in my pet this afternoon be sure I can never be long ignorant what is due to you and that I am more happy to find you right than to be so myself because in many respects I value you more than I do myself. In truth today there was a background to my thoughts which you could not see, and I might have known you could not but which altered the color and position of every object. Now will you not as soon as you sincerely can write to say that you will bear no thought of this unless I behave again in this ungracious way and then you must tell me what I said this time and check my impetuous ways. I wanted this afternoon as soon as you were really out of the house to run after you and call as little children do kiss and be friends; that would not be decorous for two Editors, but it shall be so in thought shall it not? If you dont answer me well I will not be vexed to make up for so much crossness today.

Your affectionate

MAGDALEN

I have changed my name for tonight because Cary says this is such a Magdalen letter.

(MH: bMS Am 1280 [2554])

1. Apparently the two had had words over Emerson's poem "Woodnotes," which he had just completed and thought to publish in the forthcoming issue of the *Dial*. Fuller had already sent the issue to the printer, however, so the poem had to wait for the October issue. In reply, Emerson said, "I shall never dare quarrel with you, if you are so just, mitigable, & bounteous."

73. To Margarett C. Fuller

Cambridge
20th July, 1841.

Dearest Mother,

I today recd a letter from Mrs D'Wolf, expressing a warm desire that you should visit her. I know it will give her daily pleasure for you to stay as long as you can feel inclined.[1] She wants me to let you know how very retired they live lest you should find it dull, but says if you can enjoy it she shall much, and thinks you will love her little Willie, of whom she seems very fond.[2] Mr D. W. has been very ill, and the children have had the whooping cough severely, but they are all recovering now. When you are ready to go write three days beforehand and direct Mrs M. D. Wolf Care W. B D Wolf, Esq. Bristol R. I. and say just when you will come that they may meet you with the carriage at the landing. The best way is for you to go to Providence in the morng cars, go to Mrs Newcomb's or Mr Grinnell's and take the boat for Bristol in the afternoon. I hope you have made arrangements with Mrs G. so that you will not be paying for your room all this time, for I know M[ary] would delight to have you stay there as long as you choose and you could not be more agreeably situated. There is nothing that I know of to bring you back here at present, for both Arthur and I are going away in a few days, so dont waste your money for want of clear plan.

I have a letter from dear Eugene who seems quite confident that Wm will help him, and therefore did not expect to return. Also one from Ellen in a much more cheerful strain and still expecting to set out in August. She had not recd yours. Also one from Richard whose heart seems fixed on going to College. W. H. has been to see me: he is much depressed, by not getting more business while at N. Bedford. I confess I feel very weary of them all; there is not one except Arthur on which my mind can rest, and I long to fix it on my own plans where I am clear and sure and strong, and might find repose if not happiness. But we must both be patient. Although I am not in favor at all so far as I see yet of your going to Canton, yet now you are on the spot. I wish you to look steadily and fully at that also. See how it would suit you and whom else of your family it could avail. My friend W. is as much at sea as ourselves.[3] I have talked with him of the plan we mentioned and his heart inclined towards it, but new circumstances have come up in his lot the past week, and I cannot tell at all how he will incline at last. Beside here is Richard steering in an opposite direction.

I had a very happy time at Spring St, health and spirits and sunshine were ours. Now I am very busy preparing the next Dial and have so much writing to do that it is very fatiguing to write this or any letter in addition.[4] I want you to write me this week, direct care Prof. Farrar Cambridge.

I went to see Grandmother on Saty; she was pretty well. Remember me with affection to my Aunts and please mention in your letter how Aunt A[bigail] is— very afftly yours

MARGARET F.

Write neatly and elegantly I pray to the elegant M[ary].

(MH: fMS Am 1086 [9:58])

1. Mary Soley DeWolfe (1807–81), Fuller's friend from schooldays, married William Bradford DeWolfe (1810–62).
2. "Willie" is William Bradford DeWolfe, Jr. (1840–1902).
3. William Henry Channing, who had considered leaving the ministry.
4. In the next *Dial,* Fuller published two long essays, "Lives of the Great Composers," and a review of Philip Bailey's poem *Festus.*

74. To Margarett C. Fuller

The Glen, R. I.
22d August, 1841

Dearest Mother,

The reason you have not heard from me sooner is that the glare from the rocks and water affected my eyes so much that I have been afraid to use them. I have suffered, too, in my head considerably from too much exposure to the sun. That cool elastic air from the sea is very delusive: I used to get all scorched and not know it till I came into the house.— I left the Paradise farm house about a week ago and came here to my ancient haunt; the soft green of the Glen and the thick gloom of Dr Channing's beautiful shrubberies are most soothing after the bright blue sea. This is my last day here; tomorrow we return to Cambridge.

Dr C's family are kind as ever. I go there every day. William C. is staying there now, and will remain till Thursday. He asks after you with much affection. His lot seems finally decided. He will not go back to the West, but take a farm next spring, and his Mother will accompany him. He is going next week to look at one in Stockbridge, which, if large enough, they would like, as many of their friends live there. These prospects make him happy at last. From him I learn that Ellen is in Cincinnati, and they are trying to get a school for her there, though without much prospect of success, so she changed her intentions after writing to Richard. Have you letters from her, or from Eugene? I have none now for near a month, and am very desirous to hear. But place children, and goods and a' steadily in the Divine guard, dear Mother. Do not poison your benign spirit with anxiety. The time is come when the younger members of the family must run those risks which are to form their characters, and develope their powers; Mother and sister must now "stand and wait" rather than counsel or cherish.

From Frances I have a letter, dated Nantucket written apparently in excellent spirits. She says she returns to Cambridge 1st Septr but does not say what arrangements she has made for her confinement, nor where she expects to be at that time.[1]

From Richard I have a very manly and considerate letter about the Wilson place. It certainly seems a chance of securing a home where we *might* live if we wished that is a pity to let slip. But I can get no clear light to buy it. I agree with you that I do not see how we could live there just at present without more expense and difficulty than is wise to encounter. Yet it might prove a better investment of part of the money than the present mortgage, even if we bought it to let. Dare you trust me, if time should press, and I could get the advice of friends learned in the law (of purchase) to take any step I may think best on returning to C I do not think I should think best [to] buy it, yet if it could be got for 18–oo it might be a real bargain. Write to me immedy on this subject, as also, when you expect to be in Cambridge. I shall not remain there long. Yet do not hurry your present visit. But when you are ready to come, Aunt K. for a day or two when you and I can meet, or the Randalls for *the* visit where I can see you equally well, would be very glad to have you.

My best love to Mary. I wish it had been in my power to see her and hers But I feel now that I have had play enough and want to return to work, and to plan the future. Keep up your courage dearest Mother. This is a trying time in your life, but none better than yourself can feel there is a justice which cannot fail those who are innocent and strive to be just

Most affectionately your daughter

M.

Mrs Brown has a son three weeks, Mrs Harrison one ten days old.

(MH: fMS Am 1086 [9:74])

1. William Henry Fuller's wife, Frances Hastings Fuller (1819?–87).

75. To Ralph Waldo Emerson

[October, 1841?]

How true and majestical it reads; Surely you must have said it this time. The page flows too, and we have no remembrance of "Mosaic or Medal."

Dear Waldo, I know you do not regard our foolish critiques, except in the true way to see whether you have yet got the best *form* of expression. What do we know of when you should stop writing or how you should live? In these pages I seem to hear the music rising I so long have wished to hear, and am made sensible to the truth of the passage in one of your letters "Life, like the nimble Tartar &c[1]

I like to be in your library when you are out of it. It seems a sacred place. I came here to find a book, that I might feel more life and be worthy to sleep, but there is so much soul here I do not need a book. When I come to yourself, I cannot receive you, and you cannot give yourself; it does not profit. But when I cannot find you the the beauty and permanence of your life come to me.

"She (Poesie) has ascended from the depths of a nature, and only by a similar depth, shall she be apprehended!"— I want to say while I am feeling it, what I have often (not always) great pleasure in feeling— how long it must be, before I am able to meet you.— I see you— and fancied it nearer than it was, you were right in knowing the contrary.

How much, much more I would fain say and cannot. I am too powerfully drawn while with you, and cannot advance a step, but when away I have learned something. Not yet to be patient and faithful and holy however, but only have taken off the shoes, to tread the holy ground. I shall often depart through the ranges of manifold being, but as often return to where I am tonight

(MII: bMS Am 1280 [2357])

1. Responding to Fuller's claim that she needed a deeper friendship, Emerson replied he was always open to change: "Whoever lives must rise & grow. Life like the nimble Tartar still overleaps the Chinese wall of distinctions that had made an eternal boundary in our geography."

76. To Ralph Waldo Emerson

[October, 1841?]

My dear friend, We shall never meet on these subjects while one atom of our proper indidividualities remains. Yet let me say a few words more on my side. The true love has no need of illusion: it is too deeply prophetic in its nature to be baffled or chilled, much less changed by the accidents of time. We are sure that what we love is living, though the ruins of old age have fallen upon the shrine. The "blank gray" upon the hallowed locks, the dimmed eye, the wasted cheek cannot deceive us. Neither can the dimunition of vital fire and force, the scantiness of thought, the loss of grace, wit, fancy and springing enthusiasm, for it was none of these we loved, but the true self, that particular emanation from God which was made to correspond with that which we are, to teach it, to learn from it, to torture it, to enchant it, to deepen and at last to satisfy our wants. You go upon the idea that we must love most the most beauteous, but this is not so. We love most that which by working most powerfully on our peculiar nature awakens most deeply and constantly in us the idea of beauty. Where we have once seen clearly what is fit for us, if only in a glance of the eye we cannot forget it, nor can any change in the form where we have seen it deceive us. We know that it will appear again and clothe the scene with new and greater beauty.

For the past year or two I begin to see a change in the forms of these my contemporaries who have filled my eye. It is a sight that makes me pensive, but awakens, I think, a deeper tenderness and even a higher hope than did these forms in the greatest perfection they ever attained. For they still only promised beauty not gave it, and now seeing the swift changes of time I feel what an illusion all ill, all imperfection is. As they fail to justify my expectation, it only rises the higher and they become dearer as the heralds of a great fulfilment. The princely crest is lowered, the proud glow of youth, its haughty smile and gleaming sweetness are fled, every languid motion assures me that this life will not complete the picture I had sketched, but I only postpone it for ages, and expect it on the same canvass yet.

The fact you repel of the mother and the child as seen in other nature does not repel, why should it in human Nature? It is beautiful to see the red berry, the just blown rose and the rose bud on the same stalk as we sometimes do; nor are we displeased with the young blossoming scion that it grows up beside the aged tree; it borrows rather a charm from the neighborhood of that which it must sometimes resemble. But I might write a volume, and then should not have done. I seem to myself to say all when I say that the chivalric idea of love through disease, dungeons and death, mutilation on the battle field, and the odious changes effected by the enchanter's hate answers my idea far better than the stoical appreciation of the object beloved for what it positively presents. I would love in faith that could not change and face the inevitable shadows of old age happy in some occasion for fidelity.

Nevertheless I will not send the letter to Ellery, for he may feel more like you than me about it though I think not, for what I have known of him is that he is tender and ever fond, and takes peculiar pleasure in the natural relations. He admired my mother just as William C. does, and I felt as if his feelings would be the same. But since I have been led to question I will keep this and write another letter.

Waldo has brought me your page, and he looked so lovely as if he were the living word which should yet reveal to the world all that you do not feel ready to say.— I really did not mean to show you the letter to Cary but merely to gratify my fancy by having all the letters to these interesting persons under your seal. Do not regret having read it, for I do not care, since

I can tell you I did not intend it; the only feeling was that what I had to say to you I should wish to say to yourself direct, and not to another, letting you see it. But just as I should not care for C. to show you the letter, so I do not now, for your having seen it Do not fancy that I complain or grieve. I understand matters now, and always want you to withdraw when you feel like it; indeed, there is nothing I wish more than to be able to live with you, without disturbing you. This is the main stream of my feeling. I am satisfied and also feel that our friendship will grow But I am of a more lively and affectionate temper or rather more household and daily in my affection than you and have a thousand evanescent feelings and ebullitions like that in the letter. Cary has made a picture of the rock and the wave; if she had made the rock a noble enough figure it might stand for frontispiece to the chapter of my deepest life. For the moment the rock dashes back with a murmur, but it always returns. It is not now a murmur of sorrow but only the voice of a more flexible life. *I would not have it otherwise.* The genial flow of my desire may be checked for the moment, but it cannot long. I shall always burst out soon and burn up all the rubbish between you and me, and I shall always find you there true to yourself and deeply rooted as ever.

My impatience is but the bubble on the stream; you know I want to be alone myself.— It is all right. As to the shadow I do not know myself what it is, but it rests on your aspect, and brings me near the second-sight as I look on you. Perhaps if we have Scotch trists enough I shall really see the tapestry of the coming time start into life, but, if I do, I shall not tell you, but with wise economy keep it for a poem which shall make ever sacred and illustrious the name of yours

MARGARET.

(MH: bMS Am 1280 [2358])

77. To Margarett C. Fuller

Christmas eve.
[24 December 1841]

Dearest Mother,

I want very much now to hear from you again, whether you continue to improve, and how you bear this cold weather. I hope you will have a full letter for me ready to send back by Mr Cleverly.

Will you also let me see this letter from Eugene, if you can, and send me back this letter of dear Richard's without letting any see it. Can you not write a few lines to R. I talked with Mr E. of your anxiety about him; Mr E says he looks blooming, but fears he does not take exercise enough. H. Thoreau reports him to have done a great deal in his studies.

Lloyd I suppose will be with you this week.

I am in a state of extreme fatigue; this is the last week of the Dial and as often happens, the "copy" did not hold out, and I have had to write in every gap of time. Marianne J. and Jane have been writing for me extracts and &c, but I have barely scrambled through, and am now quite unfit to hold a pen. Tomorrow I mean to spend all the morning at the bath and in the open air, and see if I cannot get revived.

I have had some great pleasures lately. I believe I wrote you of my happiness in hearing the Creation. Last Sunday night I heard the Messiah, and then for the first time truly recognized the might of Braham. On Tuesday I heard him again at his concert. Of all these I shall write a particular account to Eugene and will send you the letter before I send it him that you may see in detail what I think of this truly great singer.

I very much regret you should not have heard him; there is hope of his return in the spring, if so, you must not forego it on any account.

I also have heard at the Odeon one of Beethoven's grand symphonies of itself worth living for.

Every body is running to the Anti-Slavery fair, said to be full of beautiful things from England. I wish I could go and buy pretty new years gifts for you and those I love, but I must not so avoid temptation. I had myself a beautiful present from there yesterday.

Mrs Farrar desires much love to you. She has not got out yet. Have not seen the Randalls for several days but both E. and B. heard Braham on Tuesday. The Channings spent an eveg here, are much delighted to hear of Ellery's getting the place, send much love to you.

W. H. C. asks much of you; he was here on Sunday and went with us to hear the Messiah. You can think of him now as in better health and spirits.

Mrs Clarke is taken suddenly very ill, but the medicines seem to relieve her.

I send you a book which must have back by a week from next Monday. Say whether you like it, and want the rest; whether you can get books there; how much time you have for reading &c &c &c

Best love to F. and kiss to pretty baby. Is there any thing else I can do for you, dearest Mother your much fatigued but cheerful daughter

MARGARET.

Saturday morng
Half past one.

I feel much better this morng for exercise, and will scribble a few words more. This morning I recd from Anna Ward a Xmas box of a sweet pretty collar, a sweet pretty note and a cake frosted by her own hands with Christmas on it in blue letters. This was a kind little attention.

How I wish I had twenty dollars to lay out in presents for my friends! One is sorry to be poor these festal days, as well as in those of famine.

I gave two dollars a yard for your bombazine; that at nine shillings or ten and six was a great deal too coarse and would just have spoiled the garment. I suppose you would have done differently, but dont believe you will be sorry in the end. Velvet was two dollars and a half a yard, this is the same as I got for my bonnet and cheap I believe as any that is good.— The black gloves are my Xmas present to you. The other pair please give to Aunt Abba with my love. I thought they would be nice to slip on when she is doing the "cold things" she spoke of in her letter to N. Kuhn.

Elizabeth and Maria have just been here. E. said she was feeling pretty well. Before I got talking with them Mr Eustis and M Channing came in so I cant tell you much about them.

Mrs Clarke continues very ill; they fear she will have a lung fever. I shant feel easy till I hear from you

MARGARET.

I send also a pair of my woolen hose. I do not wear them in town and they will be of use to you in that cold pl[ace.] I have kept a pair to wear when I ride

(MH: fMS Am 1086 [9:79]; bMS Am 1610 [51])

78. To Margarett C. Fuller

Boston, 15th
Jany. [1842]

Dear Mother,

I do hope this lovely day finds you better, but notwithstanding all you say I know very well you cannot have comforts where you are, good food and quiet at home, exercise and pleasant objects abroad such as your now delicate health requires. I intreat you to take every care of yourself for my sake and that of the children, if for nothing else.

Sam Ward recommended the Life Assurance company, as a perfectly safe place where to invest your money, and one where at his request they would probably receive it, though, he said, they did not like the care of small sums. I think I had better not invest it till the other is recd also which you said would be due about this time. Worcester rail-road stock pays higher interest, but is not so certain. N England bank stock about the same, write, if you have any preference among these three.—

Have you heard of the death of Eleanor Shattuck, of Russell Freeman —and of Mr Bussey.[1] —It is said that the beautiful place at J. P. is bequeathed to Mrs Motley during her life. I hope she will allow as free entrance to the beautiful wood as her grandfathers did.

All our friends are well. Mary Channing said she should bring here a letter for you, if recd in time I shall inclose it. I send one from me to Eugene which, having read, please put into the post-office next time you send. Return Richard's.— The Channings had a letter from Ellen this week; no news of importance, I believe.

I could not but sympathize with your tender feeling about poor Fanny yet I feel that it would have been much better for Wm as well as herself, if she could have seen clearly the right, and persisted in her own view. He would have seen with her by and by. However I do not wish to say any more. I suppose she will go.

I expect to come to Canton the first week in Feby, probably the latter part of the week, but will write again about it.

I am very much grieved to hear of your ague, pray take all possible care against cold.

I will give you my diary since F. was here.

Tuesday p. m. Lesson from half-past three till five, S. Howes, a fine generous English sort of girl who interests me much.— Half-past five tea at Mrs Bancroft's. Sir John Caldwell there an elderly Engh Baronet who has become much interested in the Science of the Soul.[2] To Mr Walker's lecture with them. Immense crowd up to the very roof of the Odeon. Lecture in a truly large noble and gentle spirit. Finished little before 9.   Home to Mrs B's Mr Eames of N. York there, a showy but also really "talent-full" young man who is lecturing here.[3]

Wednesday. Walk after breakfast; Lesson M. Ward from ten to half-past eleven. Dress— class from twelve till two— pretty good time. P. M. wrote awhile then lay down. Mr Eames's lecture, went with Bancrofts and Baronet, like himself showy but brilliant. To Peabody's where Mr and Mrs Grattun were to meet me.[4] Charles Sumner tells me his far famed stories of Prince Metternich Mr and Mrs Grattun.— Mr a jocose bon vivant— Mrs a sweet and kind woman who has read a great deal and thought somewhat— Home *too* tired.

Thursday— walk, lessons from ten till one, very tired, walk and go see Mrs Farrar a moment. P. M.— Mrs Cleverly, now recovered, puts all the obstacles she can in the way of my reception evening. Left Aunt M and Sarah C. to Mary and went to give a lesson half past three till five. Lay down a short time, Mrs Symonds made me tea in my room got dressed in time for lecture After lecture a large and brilliant circle, Wards, Shaws, Greenoughs Sturgiss many pleasant men Eames the lecturer, Eames the painter,[5] Sir John flying about with busy delight James Clarke concocting bon mots in a corner. Mr E. enjoyed it

(MH: fMS Am 1086 [9:99])

1. Benjamin Bussey (1757–1842), a Revolutionary War soldier, was a wealthy horticulturist who developed Woodland Hill, a 300-acre tract in Roxbury. Mrs. Motley is his granddaughter, Maria Antoinette Davis (1814–94), who married Thomas Motley, Jr., in 1834.

2. Mrs. Bancroft is Elizabeth Davis Bancroft, who attended Fuller's Conversations. Sir John Caldwell (1775–1842) was a Canadian lawyer.

3. Charles Eames (1812–67) graduated from Harvard in 1831 and became a lecturer. He later was a diplomat.

4. Thomas Colley Grattan (1792–1864), an Irish writer, was British consul in Massachusetts. His wife was Eliza O'Donnel.

5. Joseph Alexander Ames (1816–72) was a self-taught painter from Roxbury.

79.   To Ralph Waldo Emerson

Boston, March 8th, 1842.

Dearest Waldo,

My letter comes along tardily, but I have been ill much of the time, and the better days so full in consequence of the enforced indolence of the bad days that thoughts and feelings have had no chance to grow for the absent; Yet that is not all, there has been a sort of incubus on me when I looked your way, it disappears when we meet, but it returns to prevent my writing. Your letter (of 1st March, but not received till today) drives it away for the present. I have thought of you many times, indeed in all my walks, and in the night, with unspeakable tenderness, in the same way as I see you in your letter and of that time when you were in N York, two years ago, so much that I have been trying to go to Cambridge and get your letter in which after seeing the ships go by, you turn to the little dead flowers of the year before that grew upon the wall— But I suppose you have forgotten all about it.— I will not follow this path;

I have to day a dear letter from dear Elizabeth. It came with yours. She says the right words as always when she speaks, the words which meet my heart, and I felt very grateful to her for writing when I could not to her.—

Mr Alcott came last Sunday and spent some hours in talking with me His need seemed to be to make "a clean breast on't." He told me that he looked with less approval on the past year than on any former of his life, how he had pined for sympathy, had vainly sought it in the society of crude reformers, found them limited as the men they opposed, had sunk into moody musing and then "found himself on the borders of frenzy"— But, said he, perhaps it has not been in vain. I have learned to know my limitations,— the need man has of a gradual education through circumstances and intercourse with other men; And "I have gained the greatest gain of my life in the magnanimity of a friend" And then, as he spoke of what you had done and "above all the manner of doing it" he wept a plenteous shower of gracious tears.

I must say, I envied your faith in him, your fidelity to him, as I saw his calm face watered by those tears. Indeed I have always prized them even when I could not sympathize and wished you valued sight less and character more. But we are always elevated when we see any fidelity, any love that suffereth long and is kind.

He then spoke of me, how he had often distrusted me from the very first, and, at times, did so still. I told him that was nothing peculiar to him; it seemed the friends I loved best and had supposed my vowed fellow-pilgrims did the same, but the fault, in his case, was, he never showed distrust to me, but spoke of it to others,— now that he had spoken of it to myself, all was well.

This interview did not increase my confidence in him, nor did I feel that I could respond to his expressions of wish for sympathy. I still saw the same man, seeing states in the intellect which he will not humbly realize in heart and life. He had been to see W. Channing, he was going to West Roxbury, and I felt that after he had talked out this ne[w] phase to a dozen people, it would have done its work, and truth be left unembodied as far as depends on him. Yet I see, too, he is sincere in his own way, and that it is very hard for me to be just to him. I will try to be more gentle and reverent in my thoughts of him, if only because he has felt you at this moment.

Caroline, Sam, and I, all have letters from Ellery, theirs full of verses, mine of whimsies. I liked mine. My Mother now expects to go to Cincini and live with the two children a year.

Anna W. is confined to her bed; she has over-exerted herself and the physician says she must lie there a fortnight. I have been able to go to see her only a few minutes— Sam passes the evegs in her chamber painting. Each eveg he conceives and executes some little sketch, which may, I fear, prove less for the good of his eyes than of his mind.

Cary is well. I see her but little, yet this last week more than usual and in much sweetness. She, too, seemed to find difficulty in writing to you and for the same reason, to one loved it is needful to give all the life, or else the best.— Charles was here and we had the divine musical evening together. He had been fostered by your sympathy into yet more courage and will give Dolen for the Dial— I finished the 1st no Günderode last night, it will be out early next week. The two vols are to be translated in four numbers.[1] I have just got into the spirit of writing to you as the paper ends, perhaps I will write again tomorrow if I do not it will be because I have not time

Always yours

MARGARET.

Tell me more about those dim New Yorkers.

(MH: bMS Am 1280 [2362])

1. Elizabeth Peabody published the translation. Only one of the four planned numbers appeared.

80. To Ralph Waldo Emerson

[17? March 1842]

My dear Waldo,

I requested Miss P to write to you, but, after looking over her letter, I want to add some lines myself. I hoped they would get at these particulars before you returned from N. York, that you might hear them on your way and not be teazed as soon as you arrived at your quiet home, but you came earlier than I had expected. Yesterday I found myself so unwell, and really exhausted, letters recd from the family made my stay here so uncertain that I wrote the little notice with regard to the possibility of suspending the Dial for a time, feeling that I must draw back from my promise that I would see to the summer no.— But this morng after J. Clarke and Miss P. had at last the means of almost entirely examining the accounts, they give me the result you find in her letter to you, which makes it impossible for me to go on at all.[1]

I could not do it, in future, if I have the same burden on me as I have had before, even as well as I have done. There is a perceptible diminution of my strength, and this winter which has been one of so severe labor I shall not recover fully from for two or three months. Then if I must take up a similar course next winter and have this tie upon me for the summer I think I should sink under it entirely.

I grieve to disappoint you after all the trouble you have taken. I am also sorry myself, for if I could have received a maintenance from this Dial, I could have done my duties to it well, which I never have all this time, and my time might have been given to my pen, while now for more than three months I have been able to write no line except letters. But it cannot be helped. It has been a sad business.

I think perhaps Mr Parker would like to carry it on even under these circumstances. For him, or for you it would be much easier than for me, for you have quiet homes, and better health. Of course if you do carry it on, I should like to do any thing I can to aid you.[2]

There must be prompt answer as the press will wait.

Your affectionate

MARGARET.

(MH: bMS Am 1280 [2361])

1. James Clarke and Elizabeth Peabody examined the accounts of Weeks & Jordan, the previous publishers of the *Dial,* and found that the firm had overstated the paying subscribers, so Fuller could expect no payment for past or future work on the magazine.

2. Despite his reluctance, Emerson edited the journal for its final two years.

81.   To Elizabeth Hoar

March 20th. 1842,
Sunday eveg

My dear Elizabeth,

I have wanted to write to you this day a good letter, in reply to yours which was so dear to me Sunday is my only day of peace, and how often, as in Providence, have I blest again and again the "sweet day of sacred rest."— My Sundays have been golden, only all too short, but unfortunately to day I am not well. I am tired out now so that there is constant irritation in my head which I can only soothe by keeping it wet with cold water, and pain, such as formerly, in the spine and side, though not so acute. I have also a great languor on my spirits, so that the grasshopper is a burden, and though as each task comes I borrow a readiness from its aspect as I always do brightness for the moment from the face of a friend, yet as soon as the hour is past I am quite exhausted, feel as if I could not go a step further, and the day, as a whole, has no joyous energy.— I do not suffer keen pains and spasms as I used to do, but on the other hand have not half the energy in the intervals I supposed *then* in fact I never used to get well, but be always in a state of tension of nerves, while now I am not.— Then I constantly looked forward to death; now I feel there has been a crisis in my constitution. It is a subject of great interest to me as connected with my mental life, for I feel this change dates from the era of illumination in my mental life. If I live I shall write a full account of all I have observed. Now that my mind is so calm and sweet, there seems to be no fire in me to resist or to consume, and I can neither bear nor do what I could while much more sick, but am very weak. No doubt this finds its parallel in what we know of the great bodily strength of the insane.

This word reminds me of a little thing I wished to tell you. Mother passed the afternoon at the insane asylum at South Boston and there she saw a black woman who was in a high state of mind. She told Mother "there was no church but the body, if men went into built churches with any purpose except to learn better how they might keep the body an undefiled temple, they only burnt chaff and stubble before the Lord."— "When I lived in the world," said she, "I had not much time to go to churches and worship; as my family was large and poor, but we kept a cow, and when we could spare any milk, I gave it to the hungry; that was my act of worship."— One other incident Mother told which pleased me, but it is too long to be written down here.

I saw yesterday in a book a story of an insane priest which reminded me of Mr Alcott I will show it to you sometime.[ ]

(MHarF)

82.   To Ralph Waldo Emerson

Boston,
9th April, 1842.

Dear Waldo,

I understand you have given notice to the Public, that, the Dial is to be under your care in future, and I am very glad of this for several reasons, though I did not like to express my feeling as you seemed reluctant to bind yourself in any way. But a year is short time enough for a fair trial.

Since it is now understood that you are Pilot, it is not needful for me to make the observations I had in view. The work cannot but change its character a good deal, but it will now be understood there is a change of director, too. The only way in which this is of importance to me is that I think you will sometimes reject pieces that I should not. For you have always had in view to make a good periodical and represent your own tastes, while I have had in view to let all kinds of people have freedom to say their say, for better, for worse.

Should time and my mood be propitious, I should like to write some pages on the amusements here this past winter, and a notice at some length of Hawthorne's Twice told tales. I was much interested by the Gipsey book, but dont incline to write about it— Longfellow sent us his poems, and if you have toleration for them, it would be well to have a short notice written by some one (*not* me)— I will have them sent to you and the little prayer book also.[1] If you do not receive the latter, it will be because I could not get it, not because I have forgotten your wish. Please mention in your next, whether you did not find "Napoleon." I do not see it among my papers, and think I must have given it you.[2]

As to pecuniary matters, Miss Peabody I have found more exact and judicious than I expected, but she is variable in her attention, because she has so many private affairs.[3] She will do very well under your supervision, but a connection with her offers no advantages for the spread of your work whatever it may be. But you have always thought the Dial required nothing of this kind. Much, much do I wish for myself I could find a publisher who is honest, and has also business talents. Such a connexion ought to be permanent. But I can hear of no person in Boston or elsewhere that it is desireable to be connected with, so I suppose I must still jog on as before, this dubious pace. But if ever you get any light in this quarter, pray impart.

I should think the Dial affairs were now in such a state that you could see clear into the coming year, and might economize about it considerably.

Well! I believe this is all I have to say, not much truly.

I leave town Monday eveg and go to Cambridge for a few days. On Friday or Saturday I go to Canton to board with an Aunt of mine for four or five weeks. I think I shall be there perfectly retired and quiet; it suits my convenience in many respects to go. I wish I could feel as if the Muse would favor me there and then, but I feel at present so sad and languid, as if I should not know an hour of bright life again. It will be pity if this hangs about me just at the time when I might obey inspirations, if we had them, but these things are beyond control, and the demon no more forgets us than the angel. I will make myself no more promises *in time.* If you have any thing to say to me I should receive a letter here as late as Friday morng, if directed to Miss Peabody's care. Afterward direct to me at Canton. Care Charles Crane.

I thank you and Lidian for your invitation and know well your untiring hospitality. Should it seem well so to do, I will come. I cannot now tell how I shall feel. After Canton I shall go to Providence, for a few days, then to N. Bedford to pass a week with Aunt Mary Rotch. Farewell, dear Waldo, yours as ever,

MARGARET.

I still have thoughts of going to the West, but shall not know about it for some weeks.

(MH: bMS Am 1280 [2363])

1. Fuller reviewed Hawthorne's volume in the July issue; Emerson reviewed George Borrow's *The Zincali*. They did not review Longfellow's *Ballads and Other Poems* or Dorothea Dix's *Meditations for Private Hours*, the "prayer book" Fuller mentions.

2. A poem by Benjamin Franklin Presbury (1810–68), which did not appear in the *Dial*.

3. Elizabeth Peabody was now publishing the *Dial.*

83. To Caroline Sturgis

3d June [1842]

Dear Caroline, I have Hoffmann's works belonging to W. Story; it is a great heavy book with only a paper cover, and I have broken the back all to pieces.[1] I thought you might like to read it, as though many of the stories are ill-wrought and fantastic, others are beautiful, and contain interesting passages on the arts, especially music. And it is a good book to read now and then when you are tired, for the wild humorousness stirs the blood and would while away an hour else wasted. Now after you have done with it, (if you please take it with you for the summer.) and if not *now*, will you have a new back pasted on and return it to W. S.— Tis of no use, for no doubt he will have it bound and not try to read it in this clumsy form, but I cant return it in this condition. I enclose a demi-dollar having had such jobs done for less, they will see to it from any booksellery. I shall send the book to Miss Peabody for you.

Of late I have been able to bear the heat of noon out doors and I think of you every day in the fields spangled with their myriad golden flowers, and where wild geranium and even the aster are already seen, or lying beneath the pines and junipers so ambrosial in the heat of noon. You often told me how beautiful noon was, but I had not felt it; the sun then seemed to me merciless and cruel, and the aching temples longed for the cool shadows and breezes. But now I have enjoyed it, it seems the best, cruel things seem beautiful when we can suddenly bear them.

Yesterday, I took with me all your poems and read them often in the day, it is the first time for long. I felt you near and dear. The harmony of the world sounded again within, and the destinies of those I love seemed clustered round, not too near, but gracefully, and decorously grouped full of life and silent love like the trees. My friends are certainly real existences to me, and immortal for when I look on them again after a separation I know them better as I do the trees. Yesterday I knew you better than ever before. Reconcile dear Waldo to me, if he is vexed with me, interpret to him since you know his language, and my thought has not been veiled from you. I do not mean, tell him what he does not know, but let him understand Some demon urged me to a sally of haughty impatience towards him; it was that. The wave plunging deeply rises to assault the pure serene, to challenge its distance, its vague, and ask if it be really blue. Returning from the thicket, thorny and tangled but where grows the *healing plant* let them receive me into their houses, for I am weary. I could not knock a great while, I would have all love and promise now like the June day. How many flowers there are, how fearless they look. I am not fearless enough yet to put out a flower, else I would give it you. Even the oaks this spring put forth too soon, and one day I found them black with frost. Adieu, dear Cary, how do you bear the absence of the angel child?[2] It has seemed to me I could not bear to see his vacant seat. These flowers grow on his grave. I think of it very often, yet still his life seems with me like the others.—

                                                                          M.

(MB)

1. Probably E. T. A. Hoffmann's *Sämtliche Werke in Einem Bande,* which had 1,157 pages.
2. Fuller deeply mourned the loss of Waldo Emerson, the poet's first child, who died on 27 January of that year.

84.   To Sophia Peabody

Saturday June 4th. [1842]

My dear Sophia,

After reading your letter I wanted to write a few lines, as we met in such a hasty, interrupted fashion. Yet not much have I to say, for great occasions of bliss, of bane,— tell their own story, and we would not, by unnecessary words, come limping after the true sense.[1] If ever mortal was secure of a pure and rational happiness which shall grow and extend into immortal life, I think it is you, for the love that binds you to him you love is wise and pure and religious, it is a love given not chosen, and the growth not of wants and wishes, but of the demands of character. Its whole scope and promise is very fair in my eyes. And for daily life, as well as in the long account, I think there will be great happiness, for if ever I saw a man who combined delicate tenderness to understand the heart of a woman, with quiet depth and manliness enough to satisfy her, it is Mr Hawthorne. How simple and rational, too, seems your plan of life. You will be separated only by your several pursuits and just enough daily to freshen the founts of thought and feeling; to one who cannot think of love merely in the heart, or even in the common destiny of two souls, but as necessarily comprehending intellectual friendship, too, it seems the happiest lot imaginable that lies before you. But, if it should not be so, if unexpected griefs or perils should arise, I know that mutual love and heavenly trust will gleam brightly through the dark. I do not *demand* the earnest of a future happiness to all believing souls. I wish to temper the mind to believe, without prematurely craving *sight,* but it is sweet when here and there some little spots of garden ground reveal the flowers that deck our natural Eden,— sweet when some characters can bear fruit without the aid of the knife, and the first scene of that age-long drama in which each child of God must act to find himself is plainly to be deciphered, and its cadences harmonious to the ear.

I wish you could have begun your new life so as to have had these glorious June days in Concord. The whole earth is decked for a bridal. I see not a spot on her full and gold bespangled drapery. All her perfumes breathe, and her eye glows with joy. I saw a *rose* this morning, and I fear the beautiful white and Provence roses will bloom and wither before you are ready to gather them.

My affectionate remembrance to your friend. You rightly felt how glad I should be to be thought of in the happy hour and plan for the future. As far as bearing an intelligent heart I think I deserve to be esteemed a friend. And thus in affection and prayer dear Sophia yours

MARGARET F.

(NN-B)

1. On 9 July, Sophia Peabody married Nathaniel Hawthorne (1804–64). James Clarke performed the ceremony, and the couple moved immediately to Concord, where they lived in the Old Manse.

85. To James F. Clarke

Cambridge, 31st July
1842.

My dear James,

When I told Sarah how far I had gone in my communications to you, she expressed pleasure at your knowing these things, but some anxiety as to your discretion. This has troubled me since, and the more on account of some words said by me to you that might put you off your guard, therefore permit a few lines addenda

I said "I was happy in having no secret". It is my nature, and has been the tendency of my life to wish that all my thoughts and deeds might lie, as the "open secrets" of nature free to all who are able to understand them. I have no reserves, except intellectual reserves, for to speak of things to those who cannot receive them is stupidity rather than frankness. But, in this case, I alone am not concerned, but one whose nature is unfolded in the solitudes of reserve, whose delicate feelings, so different from mine, I ought to fear to violate. There is, also, another whose peace might be disturbed by the disclosure of facts which few, I fear, have hearts to understand. My own peace for the remainder of my days might be deeply wounded by any carelessness here. Therefore, dear James, give heed to the subject. You have received a key to what was before unknown of your friend, you have made use of it, now let it be buried with the past, over whose passages, profound and sad, yet touched with heaven-born beauty, "let Silence stand sentinel."

I reflect with satisfaction on the intercourse we have had on this journey. You will better know how to pardon the probable wreck of my life's health and purposes, and the non-fulfilment of its earthy promise. You will not refuse for inscription to my funeral stone, She hath done what she could.

I have been happy in the sight of your pure design, of the sweetness and serenity of your mind.[1] In the inner sanctuary we met— But shall I say a few blunt words such as were frequent in the days of intimacy and, if they are needless you will let them fall to the ground. youth is passed, with its passionate joys and griefs, its restlessness, its vague desires. You have chosen your path, you have sounded out your lot, your duties are before you. *now* beware the mediocrity that threatens middle age, its limitation of thought and interest, its dulness of fancy, its too external life, and mental thinness. Remember the limitations that threaten every professional man, only to be guarded against by great earnestness and watchfulness.— Your parish is not composed of minds that will call on you for your best mentally, though for a sincere, and reverent temper worthy your desire.— You have lost Mr Keats, and I see not that you have any other friend who will call on you for your best, and feed the mind languid with continual exertion.[2] So take care of yourself, and let not the the intellect more than the spirit be quenched.— I am obliged unwillingly to hurry to a close. Your faithful friend

MARGARET.

(MHi)

1. In February 1841, Clarke organized the Church of the Disciples in Boston. He was its minister until his death.
2. George Keats (1797–1842), brother of the poet, lived in Louisville.

86.   To Richard F. Fuller

Cambridge
11th August, 1842.

Dear Richard,

I dont see any way I can do about your money, unless to inclose it in a letter. I am sorry to do this, as you will have to pay double postage, probably, next time you must take enough to secure you against emergencies. If this sum is not enough, (I could not judge from your letter,) you might borrow a small sum from Mr Lawrence, and send it to him on your return, but I hope this will not be necessary.

Your letter was very pleasant to me, and as to the journal I shall be glad to read, ay, and correct it, too! You do not speak of Groton. That place is very beautiful in its way, but I never admired it much, both because the scenery is too tamely smiling and sleepy, and because it jarred my mood. My associations with the place are painful. The first passage of our lives there was Arthur's misfortune, my first weeks there were passed in Arthur's chambers.[1] These darkened round as the consequences of our father's ill-judged exchange, ill-judged at least as regarded himself, your Mother, and myself. The younger ones were not violently rent from all their former life and cast on toils for which they were unprepared. There your Mother's health was injured and mine destroyed; there your father died, but not till the cares of a narrowed income, and collisions with his elder sons which would not have ended there had so embittered his life and made him so over anxious that I have never regretted that he did not stay longer to watch the turning of the tide, for his life up to 1830 had been one of well-earned prosperity, which, after that time, was rapidly ebbing from him, and I do not think adversity would have done him good, he could not reconcile himself to it, his feeling was that after thirty years labor and self-denial he was entitled to peace and he would not have had it.

You were too young to feel how trying are the disorders of a house which has lost its head, the miserable perplexities which arose in our affairs, the wounds your mother underwent in that time of deep dejection from the unfeeling and insolent conduct of many who had been kept in check by respect for your father, her loneliness and sense of unfitness for the new and heavy burden of care. It will be many years yet, before you can appreciate the conflicts of my mind, as I doubted whether to give up all which my heart desired for a path for which I had no skill, and no call, except that *some one* must tread it, and none else was ready. The Peterborough hills, and the Wachusetts are associated in my mind with many hours of anguish, as great I think as I am capable of feeling. I used to look at them, towering to the sky, and feel that I, too, from my birth had longed to rise, but I felt crushed to earth, yet again a nobler spirit said *that* could never be. The good knight may come forth scarred and maimed from the unequal contest, shorn of his strength and unsightly to the careless eye, but the same fire burns within and deeper ever, he may be conquered but *never subdued.* But if these beautiful hills, and wide, rich fields saw this sad lore well learned they also saw some precious lessons given too, of faith, of fortitude, of self-command, and a less selfish love. There too in solitude the mind acquired more power of concentration and discerned the beauty of a stricter method. There the heart was awakened to sympathize with the ignorant, to pity the vulgar, and hope for the seemingly worthless, for a need was felt of realizing the only reality, the divine soul of this visible creation, which cannot err and will not sleep, which cannot permit evil to be permanent or its aim of beauty to be eventually frustrated in the smallest particular.—

Ellery is gone to Concord to stay, and you can see him there at any time. He now expects to pass the winter there in writing. Mother and Ellen will return by the middle of Septr. If you defer your visit till the end of the week, or till you are on your way back to Cambridge, you may see me too. I shall probably be there next week. I am glad you like your books. I have been reading Herodotus. I find these Greeks, though I can only read them in translations the most healthful and satisfactory companions. I keep one of them by me always now. You should not have tried Cousin on Locke but his Introduction[2] Affectionately your sister

M.

Ought I not to say that my younger brothers too laid here the foundations of more robust enterprizing and at the same time self denying character than the elder had been led to by more indulgent nurture.

(MH: fMS Am 1086 [9:83])

1. A servant accidentally hit Arthur in the eye with a piece of wood in April 1833.

2. Victor Cousin discussed Locke in his *Cours de l'histoire de la philosophie* (1829); Caleb Sprague Henry published a translation, *Elements of Psychology* (1834). Henning Gotfried Linberg published a translation of *Cours de philosophie . . . Introduction à l'histoire de philosophie* (1828) as *Introduction to the History of Philosophy* (1832).

87.   To Samuel G. Ward

Concord[1]

August 21st 1842

The Sunday came with its usual contracts of sunlight, coolness, and pleasure. But you came not with it, at which I did not grieve, for I have nothing to offer you, or any one, in society, though God knows I do bear you with me in my heart. I am under a painful weight of debt to you for large store of kindnesses in the past, and in the present, and am glad to find my faith does not diminish in your bounty, or my affection grow cold in absence. I think you stand well among the figures on my canvass,— a reasonable man, whom the demon of vanity has not led into idleness or contempt for his kind. I am free to carry you as a recollection which I am past doing for many, and only wonder you have escaped all the nonsense of our day so well and stand steadily drudging at your broker's shop, like many another son of Adam. Whence came that broad prudence which has made its nest in your brain, unless from Minerva herself?

I shall never pay off even the interest of this large debt I owe you, of fine thoughts, of noble deeds, now running on so many years, but if there is any God who meets men face to face, and knows their merits, I believe your goodness to me will not go unbalanced. I was born to a fortune, though not of pence, for which last, truly, I cannot bow. I came in, to meet the splendid hearts of friends, who have matched their earliest gifts, every day down to this present; I have been conquered out of my desperate monodies, by the sounds of their cheerful speech. Yet, though I love them more, I am every day more careless of them, being but a poor creature at the best, and my only mercy with any at the nib of the pen. My speech to men has failed to pay its dividends, yet my capital stock is not withdrawn.

I will confess, once for all, I had longed to see you a painter, and not a merchant out of the intolerable stupidity of my nature, which still owns a treacherous inkling for pictures and poems, and I have not even so far cured this miserable vanity, as not now and then to scribble some paltry line. I used to gaze on you, and say to myself, this man must needs be the painter of our country, and as one in the serried ranks of his friends, I shall witness his victories over the immortal beauty, with some little satisfaction, as high as my nature will go in that line, which I do confess is not lofty. The very mould of this man's face was built for the life of statues, buildings, and splendid landscapes. He will set the century on fire, with the beauty of his conceptions, and burn up the stubble of our degeneracy in a flame which shall lick away the stars. Once in five hundred years, God sends some pitiful figure to convince us that we are only dead bones in his presence, and life springs into charming, from the touch of his finger, as if he did create.

I had linked these silly thoughts with you, and many times, in imagination, have I sat in your studio, and wept over my inadequate strength to grasp the greatness of your landscapes or statues in my eye, and played some comic part among your creations which went nigh to lunacy. Yet, it was not without a touch of ravishment, when I saw you spring on shore after your Italian voyage, as light as some creature of the element, and the translation of all the beauty of many centuries. I felt it was a glad hour for art, and that our Prometheus still held the divine fire on the point of his pencil. Of course, it was that you must be the Painter of the time, redeem our souls from their Lethean slumber, and waft us into the upper airs of felicity. Such were the silly tricks, my fatuous imagination played with the honest domain of common sense, for even then I had a pitiful snickering after verse, and already had made some wretched rhymes.

When I learned you were to become a merchant, to sit at the dead wood of the desk, and calculate figures, I was betrayed into some unbelief, as if this information was the lusus of a report, the shadow of the chimney's smoke. Yet it came true, as many another unbelief of mine has.

I would you had starved yourself lean, for two-score years, over a few shavings in some garret, and therein fixed an iron spear in the hard breast of Art, and forced it to yield its elixir. I would that Art had crushed you in its bronze vice, until your life ran out a rich wine of beauty. Had only a great despair passed its stained fingers across your temples, and drawn therein ten perpetual furrows. Had want showered early over your classic form its grey mantle of cloud, had you wept bitter tears, over five hundred failures of your pencil stung your palm, as though it had carried an asp to its handle

So wretched a mendicant am I, at the great gate of riches, and so low are my conceptions of that ripe prudence which tarries in your intellect, as if fourscore years had unladen their mighty freights of experience in your mind, I feel assured, both by the honor I bear your deeds, and by the respect I feel that the path you now creep in is the best.

I do but paint the shadows which intrude momentarily in my being and pass forever more over the fathomless lake of my existence. Yet I have been fortunate, and plucked some sunny spring-flowers, which shake their blue bells over this ruin that I was. It matters not, in this brief and flying moment, which we call life, after all, what we accomplish. Unresting nature bathes each infant as he rises out of the visionless sea with these fair, gentle influences, and does not demand back even the husks of our joys. Ever swings at th'other end, the melancholy portal at which we exit, a line of shadow between two worlds of spotless beauty.

> Who paints not here,
> Paints in that other sphere,
> And bends his line
> With forms divine.

By the stroke of the clock, I see the meridian hour sits full upon the fields. Yon stately elm, with its central shadow, else sheeted in this crown of sunlight, which ever day wears for the full noon hour, emblems again the picturesqueness of our fate. I see the tasselled corn ripening in the glorious warmth; I do note the green turf of the bank below me, and the blue of the peaceful sky. So infinitely genial may also fall the noon-hour of your life, and the gratitude of your poor friend be like some little birds' song in the grand meridian concert. With which I also conclude myself, yours in love

(MH: fMS Am 1086 [9:91])

1. The letter probably is a copy that Fuller made of the letter she actually sent to Ward.

88.   To Caroline Sturgis

Concord, August 30th 1842.

Cary dear your letter did not come till it had often been wished for. Though you seem now always near and dear, joined by invincible bonds to my life, long silences are somewhat sad, and I am always glad when they are broken.

We are having, I think, a pleasant time. W. and E. and I all scribble or pretend to scribble in our several apartments all the morning. I generally see one or the other of them some part of the day. Waldo is very lovely, though in a subdued tone of spirits, and rather passive in thought, he softly shines upon the day. He thinks of you with his unbroken affection. I think he does not feel towards any one so strongly as he has sometimes. Perhaps the loss of his boy makes all ties seem less real to him, perhaps it is only a long still time.— Ellery is very fond of him, is with him in the most easy, familiar way, and occupies his thoughts agreeably. I see much of Ellery; often he charms me. I love his face, the feeling in his cheek, and the wild light of his eyes. But there is a touch of the goblin in his beauty. I like the demon better, black chasms and crater fires, rather than wild ignes fatui of the swamp. He is fresh every day. While the moon lasted, we used to sit on the east door step till quite late evenings. E. talked all the time and sometimes said the finest things. Since then, it has not been so good;— I must always take the tone of his mind, not bring him to mine, sometimes I like this much, entirely to be taken from myself, but at deeper times I should like to bring him to me rather. Yesterday was a day sacred to me. E. asked me to walk in the afternoon and I went with him, but great part of the time it seemed to hurt my day, but the last hour was good. It was a calm golden afternoon and one of the solemn refulgent sunsets. E. was inspired by it,— when I came home I was glad I went with him. I often wish the things he says to me were written into poems instead. The more they charm me, the less I can keep them in mind, the flowers fade in an instant. But his presence has led me to many thoughts.— You are much in his mind, he wrote to you a week ago Sunday. I dont know why he did not send the letter, it must have been good, for every thing else he wrote that day was. As to his doing any thing, his plan is to write a few months for the magazines and see if he can get engagements to write for money; I dont know whether he will do any thing of it; he is so changeable. It is terrifying to a more snail-like nature, (I mean as to some house always at hand) to see any one so sensitive, moody, and plastic to every change. I suppose there are defences I do not see, else such an one could not live from day to day. I think he really loves Ellen, and that this connection is one that ought to come in the course of his experience. He says she is never out of his thoughts a moment. He does not over rate her, I believe, but he likes her action upon him. She accommodates herself to all his fancies[?], yet, having so much will, she stimulates him. He says he always feels when she comes in or goes out of the house.— His thoughts of S. W. are beautiful, far better he expresses the truth than it has ever been expressed. He loves to dwell on the thought of him, but slighted him now in Boston, just as heretofore.— Of William, too, he says fine things, discussing the genius of his life, though not seeing him wholly.

Of Charles I hear that he is getting well. W Story's lecture on music at Commencement was much admired. I mean to borrow and see if I like it.[1]

Farewell, I hope you will write again. Your first summer's letters from your island are dear to memory as angel visits in dark days. I love to think of you there. Now you write from the beech tree and not the grape vine, though you say you prefer grapes to beech nuts.— I have a verse of yours here, which is sublime, it paints the situation with a firm grasp, on the reality no preaching, no O be loyal, or be lofty &c— it begins "Bound in the prison of my own sad soul."

I should be peacefully happy, here, but I cannot forget little Waldo, yet I am peaceful, and in far better health than before, this summer. May the days be sweet to you!

MARGARET.

(MB)

1. Story lectured before the Harvard Musical Society on 24 August.

89.   To Ralph Waldo Emerson

Sunday 16th Oct [1842]

Dear Waldo—

I can hardly believe that it is a month this day since I passed a true Sabbath in reading your journals and Ellery's book, and talking with you in the study.[1] I have not felt separated from you yet.— It is not yet time for me to have my dwelling near you. I get, after a while, even *intoxicated* with your mind, and do not live enough in myself. Now dont screw up your lip to an ungracious pettiness, but hear the words of frank affection as they deserve "mente cordis" Let no cold breath paralyze my hope that there will yet be a noble and profound understanding between us. We have gone so far, and yet so little way. I understand the leadings of your thought better and better, and I feel a conviction that I shall be worthy of this friendship, that I shall be led day by day to purify, to harmonize my being, to enlarge my experiences, and clear the eye of intelligence till after long long patient waiting yourself shall claim a thousand years interview at least. You need not be terrified at this prophecy nor look about for the keys of your cell.— *I* shall never claim an hour I begin to understand where I am, and feel more and more unfit to be with any body. I shall no more be so ruled by the affectionate expansions of my heart but hope is great, though my daily life must be pallid and narrow.

I must not try to say to you much that has passed in my mind which I should like you to know. I find no adequate expression for it.

I do not know whether it is owing to this feeling of your mind being too near me that I have not yet been able to finish the ragged rhymes I meant for you. I got along well enough till the point of division came, where I wanted to show that the permanent marriage cannot interfere with the soul's destiny, when lo! this future which has seemed so clear, vanished and left me without a word, yet unconvinced of your way of thinking. There lies the paper, and I expect the hour may yet come when I can make out my case, if so, it will be sent

Will you have the rhymes I gave Lidian copied and sent me by Ellery, that is, if she wishes to retain the original. Dont think this request silly! I want to put them in my journal of that week, they interest me from their connection And will you send my little picture and all the papers you have of mine E. Hooper's and Caroline's letters &c

Penknife and key were touching symbols for me to leave, how can L. wish to send them back?— My love to her. I hoped she had had her share of nervous fever. To be sick and lose this weather of Paradise is sad. I have lost it well nigh as much amid my affairs. And yet not wholly for though shut up in the house, I have had the loveliest view from my window the same as from the window where I used to read the Italian poets, in young days. The thoughts of that time come back like an old familiar music at sight of the river and gentle hills; they are fair to me still. Heaven be praised it is the same cadence that I love best now, though then less rich, less deep—

Apropos to the Italians, I am inclined to suspect H. T. of a grave joke upon my views, with his "dauntless *infamy.*"— There is also *abstraction* for *obstruction,* which one would have thought such hacknied Shakespeare might have avoided.— I *am a little* vexed, having hoped my notice might meet the eye of the poet.[2] Henry's verses read well, but meseems he has spoiled his "Rumors" &c by substituting

> And simple truth on every tongue

for

> All the poems are unsung,

or some such line which was the one that gave most character to the original and yet I admire the

> tread of high souled men.[3]

The Dirge is more and more beautiful, and others feel it no less than I.[4] S. Ward no less.— I like Parkers piece much; it is excellent in its way, the sneer is mild, almost courtly.[5]

Your essay I have read with delight, but it is true the passage about fate is weak; Seek a better.[6] Why cannot the fate behind fate be brought out somehow? Saadi I have read many times.[7] As to my own piece every one praises the few Rhine ballads, none the Romaic.[8] If you could get me vouchers of interest for the Romaics, I should be encouraged to make a rosary of all the rest.— If any thing occurs to me I shall write for your Dial. I think now I should like to write my impressions of Dr Channing.[9] If you go away I should *rather* you would leave the *Record of the Months* to me than to any one else, allowing sixteen or twenty pages for it, but if you are here will give any thing I may have to your discretion.— The new Essays, come and read to me, if not to Boston, I pray.

Alas! here I am at the end of my paper, and have told you nothing of my stay at Brook Farm, where I gave *conversations* on alternate evenings with the husking parties. But you will come to see me in my new home, and then I will tell you. My first visitor last Sunday was S. Ward. My second next day W. Channing. The following day I expected *you,* and since you were not so kind as to come, observe with pleasure that your letter dates from that day. Adieu, dear friend, be good to me, think of me, and write to me. The days of toil and care are coming when I shall need your ray, mellow if distant. I owe to the protection of your roof, to the soothing influence of your neighborhood, and to the gentle beauty of the Concord woods, some weeks of health and peace which have revived my courage so unusually dulled last summer. To Lidians unfailing and generous kindness also I owe much. But you must be the better to me for my thanks

"Most welcome they who need him most."[10]

Love to Mamma and Lidian, and salute for me sweet Edith of the dewy eyes[11]

Richter is as you say. I will send you a little notice of the book from my journal.

(MH: bMS Am 1280 [2367])

1. Channing's *Poems* (1843).
2. Thoreau had read proofs in Emerson's absence. Several errors marred Fuller's review of Tennyson in the October *Dial.*
3. Thoreau's "Rumors from an Aeolian Harp."
4. Ellery Channing's poem.
5. Parker had defended the Rev. John Pierpont, who had incensed his Hollis Street congregation by preaching against rum.
6. "The Conservative."
7. Emerson's poem "Saadi."
8. Fuller's essay "Romaic and Rhine Ballads" opened the October issue.
9. Emerson, not Fuller, wrote the tribute to Dr. Channing for the January *Dial.*
10. From "Saadi."
11. Edith Emerson (1841–1929), third of Emerson's children.

90. To James F. Clarke

Tuesday eveg 14th Feby 1843

My dear James, To have mislaid my best pen seems to warn that I shall postpone writing you a few lines that I had in my mind, but I perversely decline listening to the Daemon, friendly though he might be so perhaps I shall be let from expressing myself.

As to what we were saying *of forms,* I am reminded of the description of the constantly changing abodes of the peasant at the mouth of the Indian river. As its great sweep casts up fresh islands, the peasant goes higher in his boat, plants his grain, builds his light hut, and garlands it speedily with the large-leaved vines of that climate. A season or two he rejoices in the verdure and fruit of his garden when lo; he discerns the river which gave is taking it away again. He obeys the hest of the bounteous stream, enters his boat and seeks out another island. Thus, says the observer, if the benefits of his care be often taken from him, he is, on the other hand, constantly presented with a virgin soil. And if he does not sigh for the forests and cities of the mainland, but uses the peculiar advantages of his own position, he is a happy man.

Just so with us at present, we are in the stress of a great stream of change which gives on one side but takes away on the other. Let us keep ready then our light boats, and our bag of seed-grain well protected from the water, that is furniture enough for life at present We will not sigh for the sacred depths of the slow growing forests, for its secret springs and glades, and wild-flowers. Those are beauteous, but *not ours* and have not this quick springing verdure and these strange wild fowl and fish, and the loud rushing music of the stream enough to tell for one day?

But let us be wholly in the spirit of the stream since we are in it. Let us not stiffen in our innovations! It was not, as you said "to pick to pieces your form." that we thought the other day. Neither to demand from it *"perfection, as a form"* But that a pliant medium should be presented for the ever present spirit, not *brittle* but *plastic*

Tiresome is our life at times, perhaps forlorn, when we would lean on a pillar of strong marble seeking the heavens, and find nothing but a reed. But the wiser mind rejoices that it can noway be excused from constant thought, from an ever springing life, and must in this day stand beneath a naked heaven whose light no dome built by the energy of man is able to intercept.

I never wrote you the letter I meant on the little door and its inscription which is indeed the one yourself does realize. The substance would have been this. Having once read it (the inscription) through, we must again begin to read, understanding the better to *be bold,* that we have now learnt not to be *too bold.* Is it not so? that when we begin to be bold under God we will not again be over-bold as man.

Farewell, dear James. I will hope a letter from the great Babel, a letter of good tidings from your hand.

MARGARET.

(MHi)

91. To Ralph Waldo Emerson

9th May. [1843]—

Dear friend,

I am trying to write as hard as these odious east winds will let me. I rise in the morning and feel as happy as the birds and then about eleven comes one of these tormentors, and makes my head ache and spoils the day. But if I get ready to print, as I think will be the case by the middle of next week, I wish to be sure of the first place, because I wish to go away quite free and not be followed by proof sheets to Niagara![1]

We shall go the last week in this month or the first of June, and I think I shall go to Chicago and the Lakes, and be absent some weeks. The Eastern girls are as bad as the East winds only in a different way, one *will* come and the other wont. Anne thinks they will come tomorrow. I cant tell, but sigh about Lidian a doleful Ach, with each sunset that they are not here yet.

S. W's child is named Lydia because his mother in the flesh bears that name. Had it been a son it would have been named Jacob Barker! Why is not the advent of a daughter as "sacred" a fact as that of a son. I do believe, O Waldo, most unteachable of men, that you are at heart a sinner on this point. I entreat you to seek light in prayer upon it.[2]

I have read a shallow book Howitt's Germany, shallow, but with items not to be found elsewhere.[3] I have a really good book Die Seherin von Prevorst.—[4] However I am tired now of books and pens and thought no less, and shall be glad when I take wing for an idle outdoors life, mere sight and emotion. Ever your

M.

Can you send me the vol on Philosophical Necessity giving an acct of the St Simonians &c.[5]

I hope you are getting time for your chapter.

(MH: bMS Am 1280 [2365])

1. Fuller was writing "The Great Lawsuit. Man *versus* Men. Woman *versus* Women," for the July *Dial.*

2. Sam and Anna Ward's second child was Lydia Gray Ward. Emerson had said in a letter to Fuller, "Though no son, yet a sacred event."

3. William Howitt, *The Rural and Domestic Life of Germany* (1842).

4. Justinus Kerner, *Die Seherin von Prevorst* (1829), about which Fuller gave an expansive account in her *Summer on the Lakes, in 1843.*

5. Probably she means Pierre Leroux's *De l'humanité, de son principe, et de son avenir* (1840), which Emerson was reading and which Brownson had reviewed. Claude-Henri de Rouvroy, comte de Saint-Simon (1760–1825), was the founder of French socialism; his work focused on class conflict and historical necessity.

Ralph Waldo Emerson. Steel engraving by Stephen Alonzo Schoff, after Samuel Worcester Rowse. National Portrait Gallery, Smithsonian Institution.

92.   To Ralph Waldo Emerson

Chicago, 16th June
43.

Your letter, dear friend, was the first I received and most welcome. I stand rather forlorn on these bustling piers. I put a good face on it, but, though I believe I shall yet draw some music from the stream of sound, I cannot vibrate with it yet. In this thoroughfare scarce better thoughts come than at the corner of two busy streets.

The dissipation of thought and feeling is less painful than in the eastern cities in this that it is at least for *material* realities. The men are all at work for money and to develope the resources of the soil, the women belong to the men. They do not ape fashions, talk jargon or burn out life as a tallow candle for a tawdry show. Their energy is real, though its objects are not invested with a poetic dignity

It does not seem half so unpleasant to see them really *at it,* as it did coming along to hear the talk of the emigrants from the East, so wholly for what *they could get* It did not please to think that the nation was to be built up from such materials as teemed in the steam-boats, or crowded the landings. At one of the latter I selected from the tobacco chewing, sharp, yet sensual looking crowd, (and it was, they said, the entire male population that was out to stare at the steamboat.) one man that looked more clean and intellectual than the rest, and was told he was a famous Land-Shark.

Here I am interested in those who have a mixture of Indian blood. With one lady I may become well acquainted as she is to travel with us. Her melancholy eyes, slow graceful utterance, and delicate feeling of what she has seen attract me. She is married here and wears our dress, but her family retain the dress and habits of their race. Through her I hope to make other acquaintance that may please me

Next week we are going into the country to explore the neighborhood of Fox and Rock rivers. We are going in regular western style, to travel in a wagon, and stay with the farmers. Then I shall see the West to better advantage than I have as yet.

We are going to stay with one family, the mother of which had what they call a "claim fight." Some desperadoes laid claim to her property which is large they were supposed to belong to the band who lately have been broken up by an exertion of Lynch law. She built shanties in the different parts, she and her three daughters each took one to defend it. They showed such bravery that the foe retreated.

Then there is an Irish gentleman who owns a large property there. He was married to the daughter of an Irish earl, his son, a boy who inherits the her fortune he has left in Europe, and since the death of his wife lives alone on the Rock River; he has invited us to stay at his house, and the scenery there is said to be most beauti[ful.][1]

I hear too of a Hungarian count who has a large tract of land in Wisconsin. He has removed thither with all his tenantry several hundred persons they say. He comes to market at Milwaukie, they call him there the Count; they do not seem to know his name. We are to stay at Milwaukie and I shall inquire all about him I should like to know how he has modified his life from the feudal lord to the brotherly landlord. I should think he must be a good and resolute man to carry out such a scheme successfully.

I want to see some emigrant with worthy aims using all his gifts and knowledge to some purpose honorable to the land; instead of lowering themselves to the requisitions of the moment as so many of them do.

Niagara and the great lakes, seen for the most part under lowering skies with few fitful gleams of light, have left on my mind rather the impression of a vast and solemn vision than of a reality. I got quite tired at last of seeing so much water in all ways and forms. Yet am glad I have had it and just so. I got so familiar that I might have been tempted to address even the British fall with the easy impertinence of the Yankee visitor "I wonder how many years you've been aroaring at this rate. I wonder if all you've been pouring could be ciphered on a slate." I shall be very willing to go inland and ford shallow streams However the lake voyage *is* very fine. You stop often to wood for hours, and can then escape into the woods We did at the Manitou islands and saw real old monarch trees. And though I want now to get out of sight of the water for a while I cant forbear going to walk on the narrow shore of Lake Michigan. There is almost always a strong breeze and real billows tumbling in with a wild gray expanse and steamboats fire winged cleaving the distance. It is grand too to take a walk which might be extended with scarce a variation of feature for hundreds of miles.

Write again, for I dont know when I shall return certainly not till August— Mention the Christian name of Mr Wms and I will try to see him on my way back.[2] I shall stay a day or two in Buffalo with an old friend.[3] Love to your Mother and Lidian. I am relieved to hear the Kennebecker proved true at last. I have thought of it many times.

Your ever affectionate

MARGARET.

direct your next letter here too. I shall return here before going to Mackinaw.

(MH: bMS Am 1280 [2369])

1. She met Alexander Charters (b. 1800) from Belfast, who settled in Dixon, Illinois, and married Ellen Boomer (d. 1832), also of Belfast.

2. Isaiah Thornton Williams (1819–86) was educated at the Exeter Academy in New

Hampshire. Williams stayed for a time in Concord, where he formed a friendship with Emerson and Thoreau. He studied law in Buffalo in the office of Millard Fillmore. After practicing law in Buffalo, he moved to New York City in 1854.   In 1849 he married Ellen E. White, daughter of Ferdinand Elliot White of Boston, who died in 1877.

3. Albert Haller Tracy.

93.   To James F. Clarke

Milwaukie, 28th July 1843.

Dear James,

Your letter came to me one morning with most sweet influence. I warmly thank your affectionate thoughtfulness of me, and will avail myself of it, should it be necessary to enable me to see all I wish to see, and I suppose it will so far as I can judge.[1] I am desirous to remain till the payment of the tribes at Mackinaw this takes place early in Septr; there are then four or five thousand Indians assembled and I should have an opportunity to see this remnant of a great past, such as may never occur again.[2] We wish to go previously to the Sault, Green Bay &c on the Indiana which makes a trip there the 14th August, for, as to the canoe voyage to the pictured rocks, that appears to be quite given up, and your brother S. speaks coldly of going even to the Sault, and William, I suppose, cannot go away again, as he was absent so long at Rock River.[3] But to Mackinaw if not to the Sault Sarah and I can go by ourselves, be there at the time of the Indians are and pass some days in enjoying the natural beauties of the place. Thence I shall set my face homeward.

Tomorrow, I *hope,* for there is much changing of plans from day to day, as must be when ladies depend on men of business we go into the country as far as Madison and shall see something of Wisconsin.

This place is beautifully situated, there are many fine walks, and one close at hand upon the bluff, on the edge of the lake. The light house too is at our will to ascend and lock the door on the rest of the world. There Sarah and I watched the progress of a thunder-shower over this magnificent lake, the Buffalo was coming in and the scene much alive with other craft; it was a glorious scene— I much enjoy the lake now, and shall leave it with grief. I love to go each day and watch the changes of color upon it, for each day it wears a new face.

Dear James, you cannot think how much I enjoyed receiving your beautiful verses, seeing you inspired once more. The daily track of theological life, I love not to tread, but on the green and flowery field beneath this mellow July moon, how sweet to find my friend of many years. Yes! it was such a moon, so mellow in its glorious brightness as this last, which has kept me awake many successive nights, that shines in your verse, none of a colder narrower beam. You have never written better, so finely, yet simply is the image kept up, the versification full and free, the feeling soft and manly. They came just at the right moment. Sarah and William and I enjoyed them in full, and then came a letter from your Anna, saying how she had just received them.

I have become a friend to your brother William, too. I always thought I should and now I am. I do not know whether he is most engaging as a companion, or most to be loved as a man; he is so open and free and sprightly, yet large and noble in all his feelings.

With Sarah I enjoy being the same as ever. Your mother too is the kindest, most affective, and amusing companion. She puzzled a great deal about your verses. Whom can they be about, who has *the whitest forehead?* &c &c like Goethe's friends finding out the innumerable Lottchens.

She bids me to tell you to write the moment you have any thing to tell about selling her place, as this will affect all her plans, if it is sold, she wishes to go to Meadville and thence home in September, if not to return to Chicago and stay there till late (I do hope the Wards will buy it, I should like to see them there) Also to charge you to go to the sea shore and scold you violently for not having gone already.— Sarah has been greatly moved by Mr Allston's departure.[4] Nothing could have been so sad for her. Send any particulars you can about him. Adieu, my friend.— I have no letter from Arthur but hear he is surely coming. Affectionately yours

S. M. FULLER.

(MHi)

1. Clarke sent Fuller $50, "so that you may not be hurried by want of means."

2. Fuller visited Mackinac Island in August, when almost 2,000 Indians had arrived for the annual event.

3. Clarke's brothers, Samuel C. (1806–97) and William Hull (1812–78), who lived in Chicago.

4. Washington Allston (1779–1843), the painter with whom Sarah Clarke had studied, died in Cambridge on 9 July.

94.   To Samuel G. Ward

Milwaukie,
3d August, 1843.

My dear Sam,

I have let a longer interval than I intended pass between my letters, but first I waited for yours, and then, I thought I would postpone writing till after my journey in Wisconsin, from which I returned last night. It has been pleasant, but I saw nothing like the Rock River Edens. We passed one day in the neighborhood of a chain of lakes, where there was fine fishing for the gentlemen; they fished from sunrise to sunset while we rode about, hunting the picturesque, in charge of our host, a native Kentuckian, a mixture of the boy, the hunter and chivalrous gentleman very agreeable in brief companionship. He knows no less than forty of these lakes, and, from one high point, thirteen can be seen at once. They are clear as you described Chrystal Lake, and with beautifully wooded sloping banks, sometimes rich with oaks, sometimes more wild with the tamarack. In the afternoon we saw at a distance on the banks of the Silver or Nepossa Lake, an encampment of Indians. A poor remnant of the tribe that used to inhabit these regions have returned, driven back, it is said, by the Pawnees, perhaps, *drawn* back rather by invincible homesickness. The farm of our host had once been the beautiful site of one of the largest Indian villages, and lying among the long grass the other day he saw one of them standing on the brow of the hill, with folded arms, surveying the old home, over whose soil the tent poles are still scattered. "I was," said he, "*somewhat* moved by the melancholy of his look, and kept still, observing him, when at last I did move, he started, snorted out an angry *hui*, turned on his heel, and stalked away."

They have been in Milwaukie since we were here, the poorer sort highly painted, dancing before the stores and taverns to get whiskey and food, the grandee strolling about, sullenly observing every thing. One was a noble Roman figure; he had a very large red blanket, with a purple rim, falling from his shoulders to the ground, which he wore with great grace and dignity he was the finest looking Indian by far I have seen.— In this encampment there were not more than thirty or forty; we got out and went to the encampment, and just as we got there a violent thunder storm came on, during which we had to take refuge under their tents, too low to stand upright in and too small for more than three or four to get in together. Their grave and graceful courtesy, near us as they were, prevented even the dirt, though that was *as* great as I expected, from being offensive. The kettles were boiling over fires in the open air, which the rain could not put out. Their horses much excited by the thunder were careening wildly around among the trees, one theatrical looking old Indian stood gazing up to the heavens, while the rain poured and the thunder crashed there could not be a finer scene. The first object we saw on arriving crouching at the mouth of a tent was a family groupe, the foremost member of which, a beautiful looking, wild-eyed boy, perfectly naked, except a large gold bracelet on one arm was the foremost member. We compared him with the South Sea Island king who considered the cocked hat presented him by the Europeans as a full court dress.

Next day we visited some Swedes, established on the bank of Pine Lake.

It is surprizing what numbers of Swedes, Danes, and Norwegians are here in Wisconsin, and still arriving in great numbers. But the sight of these we visited today made my heart ache. They were a young couple of elegant and cultivated persons who came out here as soon as they were married with golden dreams no doubt of a life of mutual love, and rural freedom and money enough to have secured at least some share of *comfort* in the hard life to which the circumstances of these regions compel, had not the husband, Colonel Schneider injured his foot on the passage. Since he has been here, near a year now, he has scarcely been able to use it, and it has constantly grown worse, so that he has not been able to superintend his work people, and they have been imposed upon in every way, so that now they feel too poor to be willing to go to a city for medical attendance and the new physician here threatens amputation Their first child is dead: it lies on the point that juts into the lake; the mother raised with her own hands the pile that marks the spot. She has gone through all the hardships that women do here; they have not marred her beauty yet but only left a shadow in the rich dark eyes. But his expression touched me still more, as he sat so disabled with his books and papers round him and obliged to see his wife exert herself in the way she must even to attend on him. It was a pretty picture for the log cabin; he had such a handsome *storied* face, with his dog at his feet, his guitar in the corner, and his little purple cap on his brown locks; she looked like some Italian lady he had persuaded to run away with him for love. He seemed dignified and calm as if he would not waste time on useless regrets and if he ever gets well, they may be happy yet if not in Wisconsin.

—Well! I must come to a close, dear Anna, I am *very* sorry you dont get strong.— I am wonderfully the gainer in strength and spirits for my summer.— Will you write, Sam, once more and direct to Chicago, and they will forward me the letter. Yours, though brief, have been a great pleasure to me.

MARGARET.

(MH: bMS Am 1465 [922])

95. To William H. Channing

Chicago, 16 August 43.

As I am going in the boat as far as Mackinaw with a party for N. York, I will send you a few lines by them,— for a post-office letter it seems I have not materials of worth.

Ever since I have been here, I have been unwilling to utter the hasty impressions of my mind. It has seemed they might balance and correct one another till something of wisdom resulted. But that time is not yet come.

When I have been in the country, its beauty has filled me with rapture, but among *men* oh, how lonely! If it is my fault that I have met with so little congenial, it has not been for want of good will. I have earnestly wished to see things as they are, and to appreciate the great influences which are at work here at their just value. But they seem to me to tend so exclusively to bring the riches out of the earth; should that task ever have a long period *exclusively to itself?*— I have now seen a good range of character, both in country and in town, and it has been a cause of true grief to me, dear William, that I could do nothing in aid of your purposes, simply for this reason, that I have had no intercourse with any one, with whom I should naturally introduce a mention of objects such as your periodical is intended to pursue.[1] Always it has been that I should hear from them accounts of the state of the country, in politics or agriculture, or their domestic affairs, or hunting stories. Of me, none asked a question. Like Mr Es lonely poet

What she has, nobody wants[2]

I have not been led to express one thought of my mind with warmth and freedom since I have been here, and all I have ever learnt or been is useless as regards others in the relations in which I meet them as a traveler or visitor. I dare say it might not be so, if I lived here, and had quiet tasks of my own. Then I should meet people, only as natural affinity brought us together, and gradually it would be seen that whatever is truly human in one must be of consequence to what is truly human in another, and that the same ether animates the lives of all. But now, it is as I tell you, for, if I have formed one or two ties, it is merely from community of sentiment and taste, some natural sympathy of organization.

My friend, I am deeply homesick, yet where is that home?— If not on earth, why should we look to heaven. I would fain truly live wherever I must abide, but[?] with full energy on my lot, whatever it is. He who alone knoweth will affirm that I have tried to work whole hearted, from an earnest faith. Yet my hand is often languid, and my heart is slow.— I must be gone, I feel, but whither?— I know not, if I cannot make this plot of ground yield me corn and roses, famine must be my lot forever and ever surely.

If the first number of your periodical is sent out here, and has due chance to get read, this people will take it, if it has anything for them that suits their needs; and otherwise it is not desirable they should. I hope to

be of some use in this way. When the first number is issued, send me as
many as you can spare at Cambridge. I expect to be at home by the 20th
or 25th Septr and I have seen enough now to know of some persons to
whom it *may* be of use to send them I believe my stay here may have been
useful, in opening a path for some of my family but as this is not quite decided, I will not write you about it yet.

I stay at Mackinaw a fortnight till after the payment of the tribes and
then home, stopping a day or two at Buffalo. I hope to pass down the
North River which I have not seen for some years, and through your city,
but do not expect to stop there.

Farewell.

(MB)
1. On 15 September, Channing began to publish his new journal, *The Present.*
2. A modification of Emerson's "Woodnotes, I."

96.   To Ralph Waldo Emerson

Chicago, 17th August 43.

I must write to you this evening, my friend, as a solace, though that is a
way you do not like to love or be loved

O what can be so forlorn in its forlorn parts as this travelling? the cease-
less packing and unpacking, the heartless, uncongenial intercourses, the
cheerless hotel, the many hours when you are too tired and your feelings
too much dissipated to settle to any pursuit, yet you either have nothing to
look at or are weary of looking.

This is my last evening in Chicago, (*the place of onions,* is the interpretation of the Indian name, and I can attest there is some quality here fitted
to draw tears and so can two or three infants that are screaming in the
gallery at this instant) I have just done packing Sarah is quite unwell, and
nobody comes in to claim my vacant hour. But there are two of them (the
hours c'est à dire) yet before bed time, probably there will be some leave-
takings.

But I shall scarce leave friends behind me though, perhaps, no foes. I
have not reached forth the hand, neither has it been offered to me. I am
silenced by these people, they are so all life and no thought, any thing
that might fall from my lips would seem an impertinence I move about
silently and look at them unnoticed

Truly there is no place for me to live, I mean as regards being with men.

I like not the petty intellectualities, cant, and bloodless theory there at home, but this merely instinctive existence, to those who live it so "first rate" "off hand" and "go ahead," pleases me no better

The country ah! that is another thing in these wide plains, with their endless flowering treasures one could breathe a breath, free as rapture, over these smooth green hills could stray no more burthened than the deer. But I have not been there all the time. You say, (for I have received your letter this afternoon,) that I did not write you of Rock River, but I had written of it to others who, I thought would show you the letters, and I dont like to write circulars. There were fair days, grand sights, worth coming all this way and paying all this time for. But of details that must wait now till we meet.

At Milwaukie too I had an eye full, every day. From the lighthouse to look out over the lake, to see the thunder clouds gathering, reflected in that vast mirror, and the huge steamers looming up was very fine. Or to follow the margin of the lake beneath the tall bluff whose crumb[ling] soil changed almost daily its bold and picturesque juts, to watch the color on the lake various as the prism with the varying depths lying in strata, an immense pallette, emerald, sapphire, amethyst Or along the smiling river with its many ravines, there grow the most twisted old arbor vitae trees that ever were seen, and the waterfall— but I have not room to describe!

Here at Chicago every thing is flat as Holland. The place is made for trade, and used as such, let us be glad of any thing that fulfils its destiny— Not without sadness even here have I taken my last drive over the prairie, my last walk along the shore, goodbye is always sad; we know we have not taken from the places, from the persons all they were capable to give

I have received your letter and I thank you for all its news.— Who are "the children of the Tunic"?[1] have I lost some hieroglyphic key to the home dialect already. And what is that about "laurels and myrtles," I have seen no such plants here; "red, red roses" grow amid the oaks, but they are not without thorns and their perfume is transient they do not bear gathering

How could I fail in answering your last to speak of the translations of Dante and their paraphrase.[2] I am impatient to see these leaves. Where there is a will, there is a way *surely*. I go to Mackinaw tomorrow to pass a fortnight and then back to Massachusetts, probably to be there by the middle of September. The Dial you sent came safe and though another had been sent I was glad of it, for the first was worn and soiled, though by use of only a few hands. In hope of a meeting ere long, (it is just a year ago today that I went to Concord to pass a pleasant tranquil month) your friend

MARGARET.

(MH: bMS Am 1280 [2371])

1. Emerson's fanciful reference to the Brook Farm residents.
2. Emerson and Ellery Channing had made a joint translation of Dante's *Vita Nuova*.

97.   To Albert H. Tracy

Cambridge 6th Novr 1843.

I cannot forbear, my dear friend, to thank you for your compliance with my request; it was such as I love, frank and full, and yet not so full as I could have wished. I could have wished that you had freely given two hours and two sheets instead of one, then you would not have clipped or compressed the narrative in any part.

I am too grateful for what has been given, and too much afraid of entrapping the "indolent" man i e the man not easily acted upon by common motives! into a continued correspondence against his will, not to be timid in asking for more, yet I will say, should there ever be a time when you incline to write out the train of reasoning which made the crisis in your youth and decided to the change of profession, let me have that leaf also and add it as appendix to what I now possess.

In an English book I read last year, by Capel Lofft, which, under the somewhat oldmaidish title of *Self-Formation*, contains free and accurate descriptions of mental life, are indicated with a good deal of skill those sharp turns of fate or character when, after preparation of unknown length beneath the soil, an unexpected plant springs up and shadows all the remaining scene.[1] With him these seed, though they throve vigorously seemed not native to the soil, and with you there seem to be many signs that medicine rather than law would have suited you. The physician may be so mild, so reflective, so close in his observation of facts, so patient and clear-eyed in inferring laws.

I do not know why you seem so sure that I had some ideal picture in my mind rather than a portrait of you. Perhaps from some recollection of what I was when you were with us, and yet it seems to me that I avowed to you very little of what was in my mind. Yet so keen an observer may have seen that mine was an ardent and onward-looking spirit, and more occupied with its visions than with the actual world around. Still though both from constitution and a premature and excessive culture in the thoughts of Europe, which I have had slowly to undo or transmute to live in my own place and with my own people, idealist enough in that young day my relation to you and the feelings you inspired were strictly real. A girl, such as I was, with a head full of Hamlet, and Rousseau, and the ballads of chivalry, is not inclined to idealize lawyers and members of Congress and *fath friends;* the impression you made on me *was* from *your* nature, not min and such as I then felt, and have since supposed you to be I find you in your own outline.

When I have thought of you, I have felt these very things, that your life might be outwardly common-place, because you were clear-sighted and there would be no straining or effort in parts. I supposed the common day, the common light would suffice to this clear vision. I did not think you needed the embellishments of fancy, or the ardors of temperament. But I have felt that there was no limitation on you to prevent your comprehending anything that might be set before you, and this, in the same sense and degree, I have thought of none other.

If you knew me now, I feel confident that you would think I was not deficient in justness of perception, that life had been a good schoolmaster to me, and had only left enough of the native glow for heart and intellect to warm themselves at on frosty days. I think you would feel that I understood you well, and that I should be inclined to say much to you. Let me then flatter myself with the hope that this may be, and, even if I should not come to you in fact, I shall be led by the thought of meeting sometimes mentally to address you.

Intimacies with persons make no figure in your history, and yet, apart from your brothers, you must have had friendships. Yet if they had been important in unfolding the life, been connections not only of pleasure and esteem, but a bearing of one nature on the other, I think you would have mentioned them.

I was deeply interested in what you say of what the children are to you.[2] How you evade your prevoyance there I do not know, but it is what they are meant to be to us, to renew life in its simplicity, a passionless happiness. I suppose none can enter fully into these feelings, can perfectly know how "very good" is this "new creation" without being really a parent, but I have loved one little boy so long and so well, that I have some idea of what that second life may be. He is dead now and though it is some time since he left us, my thoughts still rest on the remembrance of his looks and words and little ways that seem fraught with such a world of meaning, as they do on nothing else, and I often wonder that the sun can shine upon his grave.

I am glad that yours are boys; men are much wanted in this country and till there have been some nobler men, women cannot have so fair a chance as I wish them. The next generation I trust may not like this be exhausted by a premature excitement of the intellect and may have a wider path to walk in and to as noble a goal.

Farewell, my dear friend, surely in your heart you know it is not fancy

t knowledge that permits me thus to address you. Mother desires her af-
:ctionate remembrance,— yours—

MARGARET F.

(NNC-B)

1. Capel Lofft the younger, *Self-Formation* (1837).
2. Tracy's sons were Albert Haller, Jr. (1834–74), and Francis Walsingham (b. 1839).

98.   To Ralph Waldo Emerson

Cambridge 12th Novr 1843.

Thy letter, o best Waldo, displays the wanted glorious inconsistency, beginning as a hymn in praise of indolence, and ending with demands of
work.— It was a good idea to send me the other plays. I will bring in Taylor's and Coleridge's too, and make an olla, where Stirling will figure to
more advantage than he would alone.[1] Some leaves are written of my
record of the West out of which I hope to make a little book.— It is for
this I want back Triformis, intending to make a chapter at Chicago.[2] I
shall bring in with brief criticisms of books read there, a kind of letter
box, where I shall put a part of one of S. Ward's letters, one of Ellery's and
apropos to that July moon beneath whose influences I received it, a letter
containing Triformis. So delay not to send it back, for when I have once
concocted any such little plan, I am in a fever till I get it arranged, and
you are almost as bad about keeping things as myself, and till I get the paper, I feel as if I never should see it again.

Dont expect any thing from the book about the West. I cant bear to be
thus disappointing you all the time. No lives of Goethe, no romances.—
My power of work is quite external. I can give lessons or do errands while
there are minutes in the day, but I cannot think a thought, or write a line
except under certain conditions. To have you in the world, doing something yourself, and ready to be pleased if I do any thing, I like—but dont
expect. I cannot promise any thing. Often and long I am without any real
energy.—

Yet I hope to write your piece about Strafford, for I have thought it out
in some measure, and I mean to do it soon, while I am reading the books
in the College library about the West, the old travellers I am reading. I
like now to go over the ground with them and shall not continue my own
little experiences till I have done with theirs.

I must scold you about that little translation on these grounds.[3]

When I had the care of the Dial, I put in what those connected with me liked, even when it did not well please myself, on this principle that I considered a magazine was meant to suit more than one class of minds. As I should like to have writings from you, Mr Ripley, Mr Parker &c so I should like to have writings recommended by each of you. I thought it less important that everything in it should be excellent, than that it should represent with some fidelity the state of mind among us as the name of Dial said was its intent.

So I did not regard your contempt for the long prosa on Transcendentalism, Progress &c any more than Parker's disgust at Henry Thoreau's pieces.[4]

You go on a different principle; you would have every thing in it good according to your taste, which is in my opinion, though admirable as far as it goes, far too narrow in its range. This is *your* principle; very well! I acquiese, just as in our intercourse I do not expect you to do what I consider justice to many things I prize. So if I offered you anything for your Dial and you yourself did not like it, I am willing you should reject it.

But if you are going to take any other person's judgment, beside your own, why should you not take mine? Why do you set some other person to read and judge that which pleases *me*, which you know I should have put into the book?

I said I would scold you, however I do not mean to, but simply state how discourteous this act seems to me. It is good to catch sight of such a fact as this now and then; we balance it against his fine speeches and get the average of his view better than else his sweet smiles might let us.

I do not care for your *not liking* the piece, because when you wrote in your journal that I cared for talent as well as genius I accepted the words, written in dispraise, as praise. I wish my tastes and sympathies still more expansive than they are, instead of more severe. Here we differ. I know it, and am prepared for consequences, but this setting some other person to read and judge is quite another thing.

Now I have begun on the chapter of adjustments, let me tell you a little thing about E. Hoar, who hates to have things left out of order. When at Brook Farm I wrote you about E. that she would not stay there because of some little scruple, I supposed about annoying her sister and added it on to her old account. I was vexed at the time because I thought I could have been the means of her having a good time, and I like to have her enjoy herself, and get pictures and materials for thought. Since, it turns out that it was my rude impetuous conduct that made it difficult for her to stay and not little scruples of her own.

Will Lidian be present at my first Conversation? It will be next Thursday 16th eleven oclock morng at Miss Peabody's. I shall then expound certain thoughts, that have interested me during the summer. I fear I shall have but a small class this winter and am sorry for various reasons. But there is no persuading people to be interested in one always or long even.

How is little Edith, she was unwell when last I heard. Dear friend yours ever

MARGARET.

Write word that you will certainly stay here when you come to lecture and when that will be. I want to look forward to a meeting. Please let Ellen have the parcel Tuesday *morng.*

(MH: bMS Am 1280 [2372])

1. Emerson had sent Fuller copies of William Henry Smith's *Athelwold* (1842), J. W. Marston's *Patrician's Daughter* (1841), and Longfellow's *Spanish Student* (1843), to which she added John Sterling's *Strafford* and Henry Taylor's *Philip Van Artevelde* (1834) for an essay on modern drama in the January *Dial.*

2. While Fuller was in the West, James Clarke sent her a copy of his poem "Triformis."

3. Fuller sent a translation of a French work to Emerson, who solicited the opinions of Thoreau and Channing, both of whom said it should not be published.

4. Jonathan Ashley Saxton, "Prophecy—Transcendentalism—Progress," in an earlier *Dial.*

99.   To Anna Barker Ward

Cambridge 26th Dec

43

My sweet Anna,

I would not have you count me among those upon whom gentle cares are thrown away. I treasure them all every movement of pure love and faith in my direction or any other. When I remember how much of this elixir I have already detected amid the bitter waters of life, I feel that I should always greet my friends, nay all men, with smiles.

It is melancholy to me that an interview should, through me, be polluted with sadness, which my pillow would always bring counsels wise enough to remove— It is, indeed, inevitable that I should suffer a good deal of sadness. My wiser mind, my steadfast convictions disown it. I do never doubt the music of the universe amid seeming death or discord. But my spirits get tired out, and my mind refuses to sustain me at times. I suffer extremely now from a lack of vital energy. At twenty I had already lavished more of this on inward conflict than suffices to sustain many mortals through their three-score and ten years, and though I was endowed by nature with a larger share than almost any one, yet so many years of forced exertions and complex cares under almost constant bodily suffering have taken almost all the rest, so that I have scarcely enough now to serve me day by day. Add to this a powerful imagination, which, at the first glimpse, embraces all the dangers of a plan looming up in the future, and, at the least touch of an old wound, retraces and concentres into a moment of perception the long scene of strife and pain where it was made, and I cannot expect to rise entirely above childishness, till I am translated either into a sphere or into a body, better fitted for free and mature existence.

. Let not such apparitions, however, make much impression on you. Believe that I always know I have no more than my share of the tragedy of life, and am sure the time will come when from all tragedy must be reaped due harvests of prayer and praise.

It was even a relief to me to find, after you were gone, that Mother had such real cause for fresh sadness. I never blame her, if mere solitude and thought bring it. She is a widow a mother, separated from several of her children, without the cheering consciousness that they are well, happy, or like to be what old age needs, a sure support, or figures of hope. They all, in various ways, deserve her tenderness, and this must often be a cause of painful thought. Add that she has a disease of the heart always preying upon her. She tries all she can to be cheerful, but sewing which it is needful for her to do to aid us, is bad for the spirits as a steady employment. Do what I can, I am not much of a companion for her. I cannot talk a great deal, or read aloud, if I did, I should not have strength for indispensable duties. Those who should have filled that place and who did fill it well, are absent. Thus, do what I can, I can but fill a gap to keep the coldest wind away, while my heart whispers that I was born to fill the atmosphere around me with light and glow in which all things should bud and leave out and cheer my soul with promise.

This is the ugly side. There are many others and much more often before me, but this will come up in turn. Then I feel as if "I could lie down like a tired child" &c but presently I return to "Hold on in courage of soul" &c &c[1] Who that is mortal does not know these *and so forths.* Who that has turned them once to due profit does not know that the tree born to lift its head into pure air, and rejoice in opulent existence, like Henry here before me, will yet bless with many a blossom the struggles of its root to establish itself in the cold dark earth. It is hardly worth speaking about, we know it all so well, only tears seem to belie our convictions.

Mother had just heard of the death of her only brother. Thirty six years ago the boy left the little farm-house home, without the consent of his parents. He knew they would not give it, if asked, and he was sure that, in some distant Eldorado, he could do more and be happier than in the narrow path marked out for him at home. He and my mother were the flower of the family, sweet-tempered, generous, gay and handsome; they were very dear to one another and to their parents, who were only consoled for the rashness of Peter, by the fortunate marriage of Peggy. This was the only piece of good fortune that ever did befal them, during his life-time my father upheld the house and supplied the place of the wandering son. For a time this last did well, he often sent money to his parents, and sisters; "when he had made *a little more,* he would return, and see the brook, and the old orchard and climb Mount Eros, with his sisters." Then news came that he was married, could not come yet. Then longer and longer gaps in correspondence, for many months, at last for years, they would not know where he was, what doing?— My father once, while at Washington, went into Virginia and found him, but pride made him very reserved. He had gone out without a blessing, and he had not gained what he thought would excuse it, he said he would not return till he had. Then his father died, and it was in one respect too late. So it went on and on, he never came, his aged mother could not forget her only son, nor wish to see him the less, because she at last ascertained that his hair was white, his health broken down, and his fortunes, too. He was intreated to return, and he longed to, wife and children were all dead, and he had no other ties, but he could not bear to come back thus, old, sad, and poor to lift the latch again of the door from which he had stolen by night in presumptuous youth.— It was he, of whom I spoke in the morning at breakfast, to whom I sent by post a letter and inclosure which were never received. A letter had come to mother from him, during her absence; it moved me greatly. He had *never* asked any aid from here, nor did he now, unless we were rich and able. I saw that his spirits were broken, his health declining, but the tone of the letter showed a mind whose pride and delicacy could not be destroyed while fibres of life were left. I wrote him a letter I thought adapt[ed] to move him to further trust, and sent him the same sum he sent mother from the first fruits of his labors, and out of which she bought her first white gown. Poor man! he never received it, and strangers, probably, furnished the last white robe for him. He has been dead some months, but no one near him took an interest to inform his family, and they have only just heard of it in answer to a letter of inquiry.

Oh these long sad tales of ineffectual lives; these are what move me deeply. It *is* sad when a man lays down the burden of life frustrated in every purpose, learning only the lesson Man was made to mourn, but not *why?* Happy the prodigal son who *returns!*

Farewell, my dear Anna. I thank Sam for his letter; it gave me great pleasure May life ever be as fruitful to you both as now, and amid all its changes may there be granted you the solace of mutual tenderness and an ennobling sympathy! Your friend

MARGARET.

(MH: bMS Am 1465 [26])
1. Percy Bysshe Shelley, "On Death."

100.   To Mary Rotch

Cambridge Jan 21st 44.

My dear Aunt Mary
and Miss Gifford,[1]

I am anxious to get a letter telling me how you fare this winter in the cottage. Your neighbors who come this way do not give very favorable accounts of your looks, Aunt Mary, and if you are well enough, I should like to see a few of those prim, well-shaped characters from your own hand, otherwise perhaps Miss Gifford would write and tell me exactly how you are.— Is there no chance of your coming to Boston all this winter?— I had hoped to see you for a few hours, at least— Mrs Farrar tells me that she has urged upon you to consult Dr Wesselhoeft at least once.[2] My own opinion of him, as sagacious and a close observer of constitutions and symptoms, is high, and perhaps this is the best, certainly the rarest part of the physician's art. If your present medical attendant do not succeed in relieving you, I should think it well worth your while to consult Dr W.— *I* cannot follow his advice, wh was that given me by all to encounter no fatigue &c, but *you* could take his prescription and act upon it.

I wrote you one letter while at the West. I know not whether it was ever received; it was sent by a private opportunity one of "those traps to catch the unwary" as they have been called. It was no great loss, if lost; I did not feel like writing letters, while travelling; it took all my strength and mind to keep moving, and receive so many new impressions. Surely I never had so clear an idea before of the capacity to bless of mere Earth, merely the beautiful Earth, when fresh from the original breath of the creative spirit. To have this impression one must see large tracts of wild country where the traces of man's inventions are too few and slight to break the harmony of the first design.— It will not be so long even where I have been now; in three or four years those vast flowery plains will be broken up for tillage, those shapely groves converted into logs and boards. I wished I could have kept on now for two or three years while yet the first spell rested on the scene. But I feel much refreshed even by this brief intimacy with nature in an aspect of large and unbroken lineaments.

I came home with a treasure of bright pictures and suggestions, and seemingly well. But my strength which had been sustained by a free careless life in the open air has yielded to the chills of winter and a very little work with an ease that is not encouraging. However, I have had the Influenza, and that has been almost as bad as fever to every body. *Now* I am pretty well, but much writing does not agree with me.

I wore your black dress at Niagara and many other places where I was very happy and it was always an added pleasure thus to be led to think of you.— I wish, dear Aunt Mary, you were near enough for me to go in and see you now and then. I know that, sick or well, you are always serene and sufficient to yourself, and that you have a most affectionate friend always by your side, but now you are so much shut up, it might animate existence agreeably to hear some things I might have to tell.— The Boston people are eager as usual after this and that, music and Fourier conventions,— lectures excite less interest now; there are such hordes of dullards in that field; it is almost as bad as the church.—[3] Do you remember my friend Mr Lane of "unleavened bread" memory?[4] He has gone to try living with the Shakers. I trust he will thus try out his total abstinence experiment so completely as to give it up. You take "The Present," I suppose, but cannot expect you will be pleased by William's tendency to pledges and plans. I wish you could have heard him speak at the Convention though. The spiritual beauty of his aspect and eloquence melted all hearts.

Well, a few lines in return shall be given, shall they not to yours affecy

MARGARET F.

(MH: fMS Am 1086 [9:115])

1. Mary Gifford (1796–1875), of Dartmouth, Massachusetts, was Mary Rotch's companion.
2. Dr. Robert Wesselhoeft (b. 1796), a German homeopathic physician, later established a hydropathic spa in Brattleboro, Vermont. He and his family lived next to the Fullers in Cambridge.
3. William Henry Channing and several of his friends held a Convention of the Friends of Social Reform in Boston the last week in December and the first in January.
4. Charles Lane (1810–70) was an English reformer who joined with Alcott to establish the communal farm "Fruitlands" at Harvard, Massachusetts. An important part of their regimen was dietary reformation. When Lane left the Alcotts he went to the nearby Shaker community.

101.   To Ralph Waldo Emerson

Cambridge 28th Jany 1844.

Dearest Waldo,

I know you are not a "marker of days" nor do in any way encourage those useless pains which waste the strength needed for our nobler purposes, yet it seems to me this season can never pass without opening anew the deep wound. I do not find myself at all consoled for the loss of that beautiful form which seemed to me the realization of hope more than any other.[1] I miss him when I go to your home, I miss him when I think of you there; you seem to me lonely as if he filled to you a place which no other ever could in any degree. And I cannot wish that any should. He seemed, as every human being ought, a thought fresh, original; no other can occupy the same place. Little Edith has been injured in my affections by being compared with him. She may have the same breath in her, and I should like to love her in the same way, but I do not like to have her put in his place or likened to him; that only makes me feel that she is not the same and do her injustice. I hope you will have another son, for I perceive that men do not feel themselves represented to the next generation by *daughters,* but I hope, if you do, there will be no comparisons made, that Waldo will always be to us your eldest b[o]rn, and have his own niche in our thoughts, and have no image intruded too near him.

I think, too, that by such delicacy, and not substituting in any way what is inferior or at any rate different, we shall best be entitled to see the end of the poem, for I fully expect to know more of what he used to suggest in my mind.— I think of him a great deal and feel at this distance of time that there was no fancy, no exaggeration in the feelings he excited. His beauty was real, was substantial I have all his looks before me now. I have just been reading a note of yours which he brought me in the red room, and I see him just as he looked that day, a messenger of good tidings, an angel.

I wish, if you are willing, I may have a copy of your poem about him, even if it is not finished I will confine it as strictly to myself, as you may desire. Elizabeth would copy it, I know, for me, if you were willing I should have it, and do not like to do it yourself.

I believe you never saw Richard's lines, that they were shown to Lidian, but not to you. At the risk of your having seen, I will copy them, for though rude and simple I think they describe so truly some of the feelings that were inspired.

> Thou fairy child, a gift so sweet
>   So swiftly taken; as if meet
> Ere we may come, for heaven's abode
>   Wast lightly freed from mortal load.
> How fair wast thou! on thy high brow
>   In heavenly lineament—
> Was writ with such significance
>   That they exchanged an asking glance
> Who knew to read the fingering
>   Of heaven

But now, as in Belshazzar's hall
   The Chaldees failed the heavenly call
To tell, so it o'er tasked their powers
   To fathom what in thee was ours.

   Thoughtful and sad, thy earnest eye
Sparkled the question ever— *Why?*
   The many bask in nature's rays,
But in the centre passed thy days,
   Unspeaking, oft thou seemd'st the thought
A sage had into marble wrought;
   Now had concentered here the sage
The fruit of all his thoughtful age.
   Perchance when God thy spirit breathed
And myriad charms about thee wreathed.
   He meant thee for a future race,
Whereto we grow with lazy pace;
   But too soon he gave thee birth
Into the yet unready earth.
   So he has ta'en thee from the scene
Back to the courts of heaven serene &c—

I leave out the words that are less expressive. But several traits are full of expression to me. Especially as the form "fruit of the sage's concentred thought" thus he always seemed to me the child of my friend's mind, born to fulfil his life, for he too always asks the Why though with the same calmness.

I suppose Lidian told you of Miss Parson's reading a letter of yours under Mesmeric influence (of which you make light, so wittily) but as she may not remember all she heard I shall try to write down exactly what James and Sarah told me about it. It was at James's house and only themselves and the Buchanans present.[2] She was tried with five or six autograph letters. On one (of General Wayne's) she passed what they supposed to be a false judgment. On one of Miss Martineau's,—she said "here are so many impressions and so entangled, one coming so quick after the other I cannot feel any thing clearly." They asked her if it was not a good person, she said "the person means well, but would be likely to deceive himself"—

A letter of J. S. Buckminster written when he was a boy being put into her hand, she was averse to hold it and said "it is good for nothing throw it away"[3] On their urging her more and wishing to know of the moral qualities of the person she said "he seemed to her false" and would have no more to do with it. This at first amazed the spectators, but afterwards, considering that the letter was one of those written *to order* about being "schooled by his honored papa" and the like they thought there might be ground for the impressions of the magnetized in this instance, though so contrary to their expectations.

One of Mr Alston's letters affected her at once making her very pale and sick. Buchanan took it from her, saying "it might injure her as the person was recently dead"!! But James observed that, on a previous occasion, she had been very agreeably affected by one of Dr Channing's.

Then was given her one from you to James containing a copy of "The Humble Bee."[4] She expressed pleasure and serenity at once from this contact. "The writer" said she "is holy, true, and brave"

Buchanan,— Brave! how do you mean? Would he fight for the Greeks?—

—He does not fight with such weapons; he has arms of his own.

Buchanan— Arms of reasoning, I suppose.

—Is there not something above reasoning?—

Sarah said that in all she said about you, but especially in her way of putting this question she assumed a tone and emphasis that reminded her of you.

She expressed pleasure in other ways I have forgotten, but then said, He is not perfect, though; there is something wanting.

James urged her to name the "fault"

—It is not fault, it is defect—it is underdevelopment; it puts me in mind of a circle with a dent in it.

They could not get her beyond this for sometime, and at last Buchanan proposed, on her saying she could not *criticize* the person, to magnetize the organ of self esteem that she might overlook him.

—You cannot get me up so high that I can overlook him. I might many, but not him. At last, after much questioning, she said with apparent difficulty "If he could sympathize with himself, he could with every one"— which is, in my opinion, a most refined expression of the truth, whether obtained by clairvoyance or any other means.

Her hand was then placed on the poem. This J. and S. said was to them the most interesting part of the scene, for if they could suppose her to have got from sympathy with what was in the minds of those present what she had said previously, they could not here, for they had nothing in their thoughts but expectations whether she would know it to be a poem and pronounce on its poetical merits.

As she said nothing for some time, J. asked her whether that was something good she had under her hand.

She expressed displeasure. Why did you speak to me, she said. I was not thinking of such things. I was in the country in a sweet place, like the woods at Hingham.— She said it was a place where you would want to lie down on the grass.— not sit down.

They changed the letter for one of Aaron Burr's

She expressed aversion, and for a time would not hold it.— When she did, she made some good remarks, that he was a man all for ambition, yet fond of his family—very fond.

—Would he be successful with ladies, said J.

Too much so, she said.

Then she laughed and said "How he would look down on the last one I was thinking of!

J.— And how would that one regard him

—He is so high above him, that he could not even see him!

On their questioning more, she said, I am only guessing now, the other one I saw, a form seemed before me.

Buchanan Can you not guess whose form?

—It seemed something like Mr Alcott, but not exactly. It might have been Mr Emerson, but I do not know about him well enough to tell.

So much for the clairvoyante, who seems to me a very good and innocent girl.— I am going to see her tried myself, next week, probably. This time I believe I have set down exactly what (not all) that was told me.

This is the first time I have been able to write a word without pain, or read either for four days, during which my head has ached day and night. So today is as good as heaven to me. Yet, you may imagine I accomplish nothing, at least outwardly. These last weeks I have been much happier than in the month of dark December, for I have enjoyed a consciousness of inward ripening and accessions of light. It cannot always be so bitter cold; when it is not, I hope to be able to use my eyes and hands also. Meanwhile expect from me no good works, but write me yourself one letter and think affectionately of your friend

MARGARET.

Is your lecture in town the 7th Feby.[5] What is Mr Lane's address. I shall not write to him now, but should like to be able, when I feel like it. His letter has the true deep tone of his real self, and it is pleasant to see that when he is in his true place, he cannot help seeing *you*

(MH: bMS Am 1280 [2373])

1. The second anniversary of Waldo Emerson's death was 27 January.

2. Anna Quincy Thaxter Parsons (1812?–1906), daughter of Nehemiah and Anna Thaxter Parsons of Haverhill, was active in reform and religious groups. She was a founder of the Boston Women's Associationists Union. Joseph Rodes Buchanan (1814–99), an eccentric author on healing, was from Kentucky, where Clarke probably met him.

3. Joseph Stevens Buckminster (1784–1812), a distant relative of Fuller, had been a powerful, popular minister at the Brattle Street Church.

4. Emerson's poem.

5. Emerson delivered his lecture "The Young American" that evening at the Mercantile Library Association in Boston.

102. To Caroline Sturgis

Cambridge,
May 25th [1844]

dear Caroline,

I dont know whether Ellery will adapt Waldo's plan of notifying his friends severally of such events, but, if not, you will like to know that his child is come and Ellen safe.[1] It is a girl and was born day before yesterday, my birthday. Our youngest brother Edward, who died while I held him, was born on my eighteenth birthday, and given to me.[2] I did not know then I should have such a large family of sons, and mourned for him much, for he was a beautiful child. Ellen has often expressed a wish that hers might be born on that day, and since the event was deferred she began to hope it would. She spoke of it in a letter to me last week.

On Thursday I finished my book just at dinner time and passed the afternoon at Mt Auburn.[3]

I thought much of the time when I, too, should drop this mask of flesh, and who would finish my work. I had a fancy the child was born that day, and hoped it would have been a boy. However my star may be good for a girl, educated with more intelligence than I was. Girls are to have a better chance now I think. She will have my saint's day, and you for a godmother. She will have friends such as I wanted, when a child.

To day is the same day we set out on our journey last year.

Adio

MARGARET

If this child dies, too, her uncle will be grown to about the angelic size in the other world and can take care of her. He had beautiful blue eyes and golden hair as angels, little and great, are described, and perhaps, growing up *there*, his beauty is not tarnished, but only unfolded.

(MH: bMS Am 1221 [246])

1. Margaret Fuller Channing (1844–1932) later married Thacher Loring.
2. Edward Breck Fuller lived from 23 May 1828 to 15 September 1829.
3. *Summer on the Lakes, in 1843*.

103. To Caroline Sturgis

Concord July 25th 1844.

Where art thou, Caroline?— on what black sea art floating now away from me? Black *or* Red?

I am constantly reminded of that game (Rouge *et* Noir I mean) which fascinates the player so, to madness sometimes. Which ever colour they get upon they dont like to leave and try the other, but double their stakes on that.[1]

Yet with me the board has been tri-colored. I began with Rouge, then played a foolish while, and prodigal stakes of thought and feeling and night-watches upon Noir, and now I have got upon Blanche, O Saint, not St Theresa, but Catharine, wedded to the child, please keep me there till I have won back my gold and silver and pearls of price.

What ails this ink? It is Ellery's ink and wont flow from my pen.

Ellery is at Lenox. Ellen is at Cambridge, I am living in their house alone; it is very pleasant. I write and muse and sleep much and study a little and go sit among the trees in Sleepy Hollow and the breeze flows around and the birds sing a few contented notes and the light streams in more and more gently and I feel cradled,— with me the rarest, happiest of feelings. I am borne along on the stream of life I have no weaving to do for myself.

At home here I go sit in the room where Ellery is accustomed to write and enjoy his presence more than ever before. There are old broken pictures against the wall, a dark ladye whose sidelong gaze is somewhat marred by the suppression of part of her nose, a foot alone gleaming from one dingy canvass. Here is Ellery's pipe, breathing through which he orientalizes himself and finds the Sun! Here are the Ledgers betwixt whose dull thick leaves he hides a Poet's Hope.[2]

Ellen has the baby with her, but it is not much loss yet as she had hardly variety enough now. In about a month she will be interesting. She looks like Ellery; her eyes are full of quick sad soul already.

Waldo has been a good playmate singing me long chants of laws and causes and the Metamorphosis. They are the same keys, mostly G. majors, I think, but rich and full strains of Pindaric loftiness if not of Orphic searching stress. Now he is getting up an oration which stammers in its first days and teazes the Father's listening eager ear—[3]

Before I came here I staid with the Hawthornes and enjoyed it much. The river side and the old whispering trees and their wise life of mutual thought and H's all-seeing mellow eyes and stilly growing mind and human heart. And the child worthy the name of Una.[4] She is beautiful and of a calm, harmonious beauty, which will stand. Over her face the smiles beam as light upon the equal heavens. She is tender too, shows as yet no passion, but a full determined nature.—

I would like to hear from you; would you not like to write? Has the cloud opened yet and showed a face of angel or of demon. Have you not written some poems you will send me. Give my love to those ex[c]ellent friends there. Ss whose word we will take for a million to whom we may lend the heart in an uncovered dish. And thou, O maid of deepest Fate hast thou again let the curtain fall between us? If so paint it over with symbolic figures, that looking, I may muse and musing the fire may burn.—

I shall be here till 2d August.

(MB)

1. Rouge et Noir is a solitaire in which the ranks are built in alternate colors.
2. The title of a Channing poem.
3. "Address Delivered in Concord on the Anniversary of the Emancipation of the Negroes in the British West Indies," which he read on 1 August.
4. Una Hawthorne (1844–71) was born on 3 March. Named for Spenser's Una, the type of true religion, Una Hawthorne was the model for Pearl in *The Scarlet Letter.*

104. To Georgiana Bruce

Cambridge 15th August 1844.

Dear Georgiana,

I was greatly entertained and instructed by the Journals. Continue, I beg, to note for me the salient traits of every day. If you really think me capable of writing a Lehrjahre for women, (and I will confess that some such project hovers before me) nothing could aid me so much as the facts you are witnessing

For these women in their degradation express most powerfully the present wants of the sex at large.[1] What blasphemes in them must fret and murmur in the perfumed boudoir, for a society beats with one great heart.

I grieve much that you did not preserve their letters; pray copy if they write you more.

Hope you will stay a year, if circumstances continue as favorable as now. Dully as the days may pass they bring such a scope for observation and thought as can scarcely occur again.

When I can, I will send "The Fairy Queen" to the address you mention, also a set of etchings for "Summer on the Lakes," of which Hecke I believe gave you a copy. They are only in part of the edition, as they make the copies more expensive and I have had some struck off for myself. They are from sketches made by my friend Sarah Clarke on the journey, also etched by her. They can be put into the book as well after binding as before.

I expect soon to publish a more ample version of the Great Lawsuit and if I do, will send you that instead of the number of the Dial which has somehow gone astray to one of the numerous readers who patronized that "noteworthy but unattractive periodical" by borrowing.

I do not attempt to write you a real letter, as I am not well and pressed by various engagements. We break up housekeeping the 20th Septr, there are many affairs to transact.[2] I have something I wish to write and the headach demon is faithful to his prey. But if you write, you will get an answer in some shape, or some time

Meanwhile I shall pay for this sheet as containing only a few lines to thank—

My regards to Mrs Johnson. If I should be on the North River any time in the autumn as is not impossible, I should like to come to Sing Sing. How long could I stay, and what see without disturbing the circle of arrangements?

MARGARET F.

Why dont you write a little narrative of your life on the St Francis. It would not be like writing a journal the Past displays the clear lineaments of objective reality and difficult hills with their tangled forests lie like blue floating islands on the horizon. But perhaps you would rather keep it for a part of your religion

(ViU)

1. Women prisoners at Sing Sing.
2. Fuller soon left for a vacation in New York, where she wrote *Woman in the Nineteenth Century.*

105.   To Sarah Shaw

Sunday 1st Septr 1844.

My dear Sarah,— Sunday is to me in my way a very holy day. If there are words that require to be spoken with the assurance of pure love and calmness, I wait to see if I can speak them on that day. Therefore I have deferred answering your note.

If you can feel towards me as a Mother, after knowing me so long, I should not be afraid to accept the sacred trust, only I should say, my child, my dear daughter, we are all children together. We are all incompetent to perform any duty well except by keeping the heart bowed to receive instruction *every moment* from the only wisdom. I may have seen more, thought more, may be advanced in mental age beyond you, as you beyond your Anna, and she in turn knows more than the flowers, so that she can water them, when they cannot get water for themselves. But though we are not useless to one another, we cannot be very useful to one another either, other than by clearing petty obstructions from the path which leads to our common home, and cheering one another with assurances of a mutual hope.

The Virgin was made worthy to be the mother of Jesus by her purity. We do not suppose she foresaw intellectually all that was needed for his career. But she commended him to the Spirit that had given him to her. With like desire, if not from the same consecrated life, I could wish good to thee who I believe in thy own wishes and a heart uncorrupted, though, perhaps, frail, worthy of great good.

I advise you not to deal too severely with yourself. There is, probably, a morbid tinge in you, though very little compared with others of your family. Treat it, as I do my headach demons, evade, rather than fight with it. Do not spend time in self-blame so much as solicit the communion of noble and beautiful presences.

No doubt you were married too young and have got to bear a great deal in growing to earthly womanhood with your children. But that is nothing either to you or to them compared with the evils of fancying one self really grown up, because a certain number of years are passed. The children may now have fair play, if not the highest advantages.

You do really need some employment that will balance your life and be your serene oratory when you need one. I will talk of this when we meet. Frank asked me to come when we leave this house (the 19th or 20th) and make you a little visit. I should like much to do that and then we will say *the rest.*

I am desirous for Octr and Novr to go to some beautiful and solitary place, where walking about would be pleasure and excitement enough so that I may give myself undisturbed to some writing and study I have in view. I think a good deal of a place on the North River, but if I do not go *there,* of some bold spot on the sea-shore. Will Sarah R. let me know about that place at Manchester where she was. I have thought I might like to go there from what I heard. I suppose it seems public where *you* were. I want a little description of the spot, the money terms and whether I could go if I want to. Cannot one of you ride over to see me by the 10th or 12th and if you cannot will you write. It would give me great pleasure to have the mosses if you continue to wish to give them to me. It is beautiful to have them pass from the sea to the white paper. I *have* thought of you this summer and always with love as your face beamed on me the first thing in the morning or as you held the dear child and her little hand clasped the cross. You and the children must string the Rosary, together.

We will all be Catholics, but we will grow worthy to worship the Mother and Child by not asking too much aid of them. Our Credos shall be resolute endurance of the forlorn hours, our Pater Nosters and Aves acts of faith and love. And so to your father and my father who is "able to keep us from falling," dear Sarah, I commend you—

On reading over my letter I feel as if I assumed age and wisdom more than is natural to me. But you addressed me as Minerva and I easily took the pedestal. Yet I *am* old enough to know surely that if we persist in aspiration He will not leave us comfortless and what more need a Mother in Israel know?

The association of Undine with these ugly books pictures the course of too many lives.[1]

(MH: bMS Am 1417 [176])

1. Friedrich de La Motte-Fouqué, *Undine* (1811), a romantic fairy tale.

106.   To Georgiana Bruce

Fishkill Landing,
20th Octr 1844.

Dear Georgiana,

In consequence of the many changes of place I have made of late your package has only very lately reached me. I have read it with great interest The two characters are such as I have had least opportunity of knowing. Satira's idealizing of herself in the face of cruellest facts belongs to the fairest, most abused part of feminine Nature.

Eliza's account of her strong instinctive development is excellent, as clear and racy as Gil Blas.—[1] I suppose these women have spoken with more spirit and freedom than any whites would; have they not?

You say few of these women have any feeling about chastity. Do you know how they regard that part of the sex, who are reputed chaste? Do they see any reality in it; or look on it merely as a circumstance of condition, like the possession of fine clothes? You know novelists are fond of representing them as if they looked up to their more protected sisters as saints and angels!

I was prevented by attacks of headach from finishing the pamphlet on Women in August. I hope to do it here, as I remain till Decr At present, however, I pass all the fine weather in the open air, and grow strong daily. Meanwhile every hint from you will be of use to my thoughts. And I shall have an oppory to talk with you, for if Mr Channing goes to Sing Sing next Sunday as he expects, I shall go too; if I hear from him that any unforseen cause prevents, I shall still come another day. Caroline Sturgis, who is with me here, will come too.

I am much pleased by your plan of going to Illinois in the spring. You are much more likely to find a fit sphere there than at the South. But of this, too, I will talk when I come, rather than write now, as writing is not good for me, and I am like to have so much to do, that I must avoid all I can.

One thing I wish to say however, lest the time of my seeing you should be delayed. You said you would write an account of your past, if I asked it. I do ask, if you can do it freely. The record, if written with any thing like the force and vivacity you tell it, and with care for arrangement and finish would be in itself of much value, and bring to you the sort of discipline you have desired. And I should think this winter of seclusion, before entering on a new and various life, might be the very, or the only time for it.

I will now say farewell for this time. If I do not come a letter will reach me here by post, or a parcel would addressed to Mr Van Vliet's boarding house. But I shall probably come.

Your friend

S. M. FULLER—

I was at Brook Farm a few hours before I came away, but had no chance to see things fairly. The wheels seemed to turn easily, but there was a good deal of sound to the Machinery; it did not move quite as effortless and sweet as we dream that angel harpings will.

(CSt)

1. Alain-René Lesage, *The Adventures of Gil Blas of Santillane,* a picaresque novel (1715–35).

107. To Richard F. Fuller

Fishkill Landing
23d Novr 1844.

Dear Richard,

I think you may by this time like to hear further notices of your sister's position in these circuits and alternations of our lives. Yet I have not to speak of alternations, only of a portion of pleasing peaceful circuit

The *seven weeks* of proposed abode here draw to a close, and have brought what is rarest, fruition of the sort proposed from them. I have been here all the time except that three weeks since I went down to N. Y. and with W. Channing visited the prison at Sing Sing. This was every way good. I went down on a Friday, seeing the Highland pass in bright hues and purple shadows. A woman on board observed to me that she "had come down by the day boat because she was told there were things here worth seeing." I assured her she had not been misinformed and that she was now on the very spot where these things were. I then pointed her attention to the lofty mountain called "the Crow's Nest" she gazed awhile, and then, with a sigh, admitted "Well! this does beat all!"

On Saturday we went up to Sing Sing in a little way-boat, thus seeing that side of the river to much greater advantage than we can in the mammoth boats. We arrived in resplendent moonlight by which we might have supposed the prisons palaces if we had not known too well what was within.

On Sunday W. C. addressed the male convicts in a strain of the most noble and pathetic eloquence. They listened with earnest attention; many were moved to tears, some, I doubt not, to better life. I never felt such sympathy with an audience, as I looked over that sea of faces marked with the the the traces of every ill, I felt that, at least, heavenly truth would not be kept out by self-complacency and a dependence on good appearances.

I talked with a circle of women and they showed the natural aptitude of the sex for refinement. These women, some black and all from the lowest haunts of vice, showed a sensibility and a sense of propriety which would not have disgraced any place.

When we returned we had a fine storm on the river clearing up with strong wind, and the mountains in their veils. Since then I have finished at leisure *the pamphlet,* and written one or two trifles, also studied much in evenings, Taylor's translations of the old Greek writers, the Confucious, the Desater, and Alkuna, a Scandinavian mythology, have been my best books.[1] I have also read with great delight Landor's Pentameron, rejoicing to find a book of his that is new to me. One of my few regrets at not having money is that I cannot own all his works. I do own most other book[s] of my contemporaries that I prize. H[ow]ever I have him much by heart and own the Pericles and Aspasia.[2] I hope to get his books reprinted here and then *can* own them.

All the fine weather I have passed in the mountain passes, along the mountain brooks or the river. My mind has not been active, but in quiet happiness lived with this fair grand nature. It has been to me just what I wanted and I will not forget to be grateful.

I have seen almost no people, except those who board in this house. With these my relation has been pleasant and afforded amusing incidents and narratives which you, no doubt, will sometime hear.

I am most unusually well, scarce ever a headach, and do not need to lie down all day. I do just enough for my strength and so do it well, in hours unbroken by petty interruptions.

Ellery was here 3 days one of which he passed in the mountains with us; the meeting was very pleasant. He is now in N. Y whither I also go in two or three days I do not begin with the Tribune till 1st Decr

Write to me there, care H. Greeley.[3] Tell more of your new surroundings and your thoughts. I hope the historical studies continue. That will be something noble and solid I expect to give *myself* now for some time to small things except Sundays

I have little news from Boston and none that would interest you. I suppose Mr and Mrs Motte can tell you a good deal. Farewell dear Richard, I shall have little time to write, but will when I can and am ever affecy yr sister

M.

Have you read Mr E's new volume?[4]

(MH: fMS Am 1086 [9:108])

1. Thomas Taylor (1758–1835) was a Neoplatonist. Fuller borrowed Emerson's copy of *The Desâtîr or Sacred Writings of the Ancient Persian Prophets* (1818).

2. Walter Savage Landor, *Pentameron and Pentalogia* (1837) and *Pericles and Aspasia* (1836), a favorite of Fuller's.

3. Horace Greeley (1811–72) was a New Hampshire printer and journalist who founded the *New-York Daily Tribune* in 1841, an important Whig newspaper. He and his wife, Mary, were ardent abolitionists, Fourierists, and Grahamites who supported many social reforms. Fuller lived with them when she first worked on the *Tribune*.

4. Emerson's *Essays: Second Series* had been published in mid-October.

108. To Samuel G. Ward

N. Y. 29th Decr, 1844.

I wish you a happy new year, dear Sam and Anna, and many happy years, and that they may come better and better.

Last year, at this time, we were listening to Rakemann, and some of those strains haunt my memory often. I hope we may hear some music, together, when you come here. That is only one little month from this, and if it be like the last, it will go like lightening.

I have been once to the opera, and once to a concert by the same corps; it is not well worthy the name of music. All Donizetti and such like, poor flimsy melodies, and performed in the common-place Italian manner, vivacity gesticulation, bold clear sonorous singing, but no genius and no passion.

I have been at Ole Bull's concerts, heard his Niagara and Solitude of the Prairie, with both of which I am much pleased. The Philharmonic have not yet given a concert, but will the 11th. Many thanks about Mr Habicht, but, after writing to you, I decided to subscribe with a friend, with whom I shall go regularly.[1]

My life here is a queer one and presents a good many daily obstacles of a petty sort, but I find the way to get along. I like the position; it is so central, and affords a far more various view of life than any I ever before was in. My associates think my pen does not make too fine a mark to be felt, and may be a vigorous and purifying implement. I cannot judge so well of this, but I begin to find the level here. I shall be much employed for some time in visiting public institutions and writing short pieces on such subjects as are thus suggested to me. This will suit me well.

I doubt whether I shall put much outlandish matter into the paper; it is emphatically an American journal. Its readers want to know about our affairs and our future. I shall illustrate from the past, and European life, but shall not dwell much upon them.

I like Mr Greeley much. He is a man of the people, and outwardly unrefined, but he has the refinement of true goodness, and a noble disposition. He has, in his own range, great abilities. We have an excellent mutual understanding.

The people who are brought in my way in his house, are new to me and represent what I have seen least of. I form, for myself, some pleasant acquaintances, whom I shall see mostly at their own houses.

Ellery seems to be going on well. I see him little, as he is engaged all times but Saty, but he writes me funny notes from the office giving me fatherly advice as to my literary course.[2] I gave him the money in a way you would have approved. I saw he needed it, as he probably, as yet, gets none for his work, and I assure you he was touched to the heart. A beautiful light fell across his features.

Ever affectionately your

MARGARET.

(MH: bMS Am 1465 [923])

1. Ole Bornemann Bull (1810–80), a Norwegian violinist, toured the United States in 1844. Fuller reviewed his concerts in the *Tribune*. On the 11th she heard Haydn's Symphony no. 2. Claudius Edward Habicht (d. 1883) worked for a time with Sam Ward at Baring Brothers' bank. He was later the consul in New York City for Norway and Sweden. He had a lively salon of music lovers in New York City.

2. Channing was also working for Greeley at the *Tribune*, though he did not last long.

109.   To William H. Channing

New Year's eve [1844]

I forgot to ask you, dear William, when we shall begin our round of visits to the public institutions I want to make a beginning, as, probably, one a day and once a week will be enough for my time and strength.[1]

Now is the time for me to see and write about these things, as my European stock will not be here till Spring.

Should you like to begin with Blackwell's Island, Monday or Tuesday of next week?

I had much in my mind to say to you this evening, but a visitor has come between. Perhaps it is no matter, I feel as if something new, *and good* was growing. Neither your dark hour nor the pang of sadness that seizes upon me at moments can shake my faith that not only a general, but just now a special good is growing.

I find in my last spring journal these lines of which I had a faint remembrance as you were telling your dream

> Boding Raven of the breast,
> Dost call the Vulture to thy nest?
> Through broken-hearted trusting love
> That Vulture may become a Dove,
> —Yet scare the Vulture from my breast.
> These days have brought too much unrest,
> Let the humble Linnet sing
> Of the assured, if distant, Spring,
> While I baptize in the pure wave,
> Then prepare a deep safe grave.
> Where the plighted hand may bring
> Violets from that other Spring,
> Whence the soul may take its flight
> Lark-like spiral seeking light
> Seeking secure the source of light.

drittissimo calle, I seek said Petrarch but the spiral is the highest form of human ascent."

I have copied exactly from the page. And can I leave thee, my friend, while this wonderful harmony subsists between our minds? Shall words and shadows have power to repel me? Never.

(MB)

1. Fuller wrote of her visits to the penitentiary on Blackwell's Island, the Bellevue Alms House, the Farm School, and the Asylum for the Insane in the 19 March issue of the *Tribune*.

III

---

*The Field Which
Opens Before Me*

1845–1847

I am truly interested in the field which opens before me.

Emerson and other friends thought Fuller had lowered herself by leaving New England and working for a daily newspaper, but she now had 50,000 readers instead of a few hundred (or, with the *Dial,* a few hundred). Equally important, she had new objects of interest. When she was on vacation, she joined William Henry Channing, an old friend who was a reforming minister, on a trip to Sing Sing prison, where Fuller had a Conversation with the women inmates. Immediately after establishing herself at the *Tribune,* she and Channing toured the city institutions—the hospital for the insane, the prison, the hospital for the indigent—and she began to write about the conditions she found. She took an interest in the reformation of former prisoners, and she was deeply involved with the movement to reform prostitutes. Fuller's interests changed markedly in New York: while she retained her interest in literature, the world of social reform became more immediately her concern. Symbolically, she left Emerson behind (and never again was close to him); she left the Transcendental concerns for personal growth in favor of social action that had more immediate results. Greeley and Channing occupied her in ways that Emerson and Hedge had done ten years earlier. In eighteen months she published 250 pieces for Greeley, an output that made her the first woman journalist of note in our literary culture.

In that New York City culture Fuller formed friendships with Parke Godwin, William Cullen Bryant, and Edgar Allan Poe as well as with literary-social hostesses such as Anne Lynch. She renewed her friendship with Lydia Francis Child, whom she had known as a young woman and with whose social reforming she now sympathized. Her work on the *Tribune* called for her to review contemporary literature, and she often met the authors at social gatherings. All in all, her world had expanded.

In February 1845 Fuller met a German businessman, James Nathan. Most of what we know of him is contained in the more than fifty surviving letters she wrote him. It is clear that she fell deeply in love with him and that he manipulated her for his own benefit. From the time of their meeting until well after he left New York, in June 1845, Nathan was at the center of her emotional life. Though the Greeleys and other New York friends knew of him and so did her mother, Fuller kept Nathan walled off from her New England life. She had something close to parallel lives for several months: long, impassioned letters to him coexist with routine letters to her mother and Carrie Sturgis; though she met Nathan often, she never mentioned him in the letters to others. It is clear that she discovered that he kept a mistress, that she accepted his explanation for the relationship, that he made some sort of explicit sexual overture to her, and that he tried to use her position on the *Tribune* to place essays of his own when he was in Europe. It was an intense, finally frustrating and deeply sad experience for Fuller: for the third time she had opened herself to a man, only to be rebuffed.

Fuller's life rose to an intense pitch in 1846, for she got an offer from Marcus and Rebecca Spring, friends from New England who were living in New York, to accompany them to Europe to tutor their son, and at the same time she agreed to publish a selection of her essays in Wiley and Putnam's Library of American Books series. So, in addition to her daily responsibilities for Greeley, Fuller selected her essays, quarreled with Wiley about her choices, and finally saw *Papers on Literature and Art* through the press just as she was preparing to leave for England. Greeley promised to pay her well for travel letters from abroad; she borrowed from Sam Ward, and set off on the trip that had been delayed for a decade.

Fuller and the Springs arrived in Liverpool in mid-August 1846 and then set out for a tour of the north country. On the way she met the aging Wordsworth and renewed her acquaintance with Harriet Martineau. Fuller wrote travel essays for Greeley, one of which detailed a night when she got lost on Ben Lomond and spent the night on the mountainside. In London she missed seeing Elizabeth Barrett, who had recently eloped with Robert Browning, and she met a number of social reformers, such as W. J. Fox, J. J. Garth Wilkinson, and William and Mary Howitt. But her most important new acquaintance was with Giuseppe Mazzini, whom she met at Carlyle's home. Immediately taken with Mazzini (and wearied with Carlyle), Fuller deepened her education in European politics.

After London, the party went to Paris, where Fuller met a full range of liberal writers and thinkers: Pierre-Jean de Béranger, Victor Considérant, Pierre Leroux, and Félicité-Robert de Lamennais. She found that the prestigious *Revue indépendante* had translated and published her essay on American writers (though they got her name wrong), and she finally met George Sand, a writer whom she had championed for several years, despite the novelist's scandalous personal reputation. All of these experiences found their way into her *Tribune* letters. Paris for Fuller was more exciting than London because she met people who were at the center of political controversy and because she met George Sand, who was a major writer and who, like Fuller, was a woman who had fought to establish herself on her own terms. Fuller left Paris with plans to write about Sand and with a clear intention to spend more time there before she returned to the United States.

When Fuller arrived in Italy, in February 1847, the overall political situation looked brighter, for in 1846 Giovanni Maria Mastai-Ferretti became Pope Pius IX, the successor to the harsh Gregory XVI, and embarked on a series of liberal reforms that raised the possibility of lasting change. Italy was then a group of separate states, all of which were under autocratic rule: Austria occupied Lombardia and Venetia; Piedmont was independent but its weak king, Charles Albert, was no liberal; Naples was ruled by the Bourbon Ferdinand. The pope's temporal reign spanned the peninsula through the Papal States. Should Pius succeed in taking the lead, Italy might dream of unification under liberal terms.

Fuller and the Springs saw what tourists came to see: churches, paintings, and sculptures, all of which Fuller wrote about in her *Tribune* dispatches. The party went first to Naples and then began a six-month tour northward. In Rome, Fuller accidentally met a young nobleman, Giovanni Angelo Ossoli, who interested her very much, but she had to leave with the Springs for the rest of their sightseeing. After a stay in Venice, the Springs proposed to go to Switzerland and Germany, but Fuller was determined to stay in Italy—in part, we assume, because of her interest in Ossoli. She parted with her friends, went on to Milan, where she met a group of radical reformers, and made her way back to Rome, despite a severe illness on the way.

The letters of this period show a continuity in Fuller's life, for again she publishes books, again she writes extensively of literary topics, and yet again she is rejected by a man she loves. The James Nathan affair dominated her life for much of 1845, but, as she always did, she continued to grow, even if her hopes were disappointed. Readers will also find her once-dominating interests in literature shifting to social and political issues. Fuller the cosmopolitan met new people easily; she had the curiosity that led her to explore first New York, then London, Paris, and Rome. In these letters readers find her taking stock of a prerevolutionary world, one that seems on the verge of large changes.

1 1 0.   To Mary Rotch

N. Y. 15th Jany, 1845.

Always dear Aunt Mary,

Your letter, with its commission, which shows so much affectionate care for me, comes sweetly. I have not time to think much about being alone here; still, there is enough feeling of it to make such remembrance from my friends doubly grateful.

I do not, at present, take wine, as I can have excellent milk and my head bears it, but in the spring, I may need wine. I shall fulfil your design by keeping your gift, as a little treasure, to which I shall go for indulgences which might be good for me, but which I should otherwise go without. Many things to which I have been accustomed, both for food and medicine, do not come in my way, now; as my hosts are Grahamites and Hydropaths. However, I get along very well; my health has been most unusually good, only, this last fortnight, I have had influenza, but, now, it is almost gone.

This stopped me just as I had begun to visit the Institutions here of a remedial and benevolent kind. So soon as I am quite well, shall resume the survey. Mr G. is desirous I should make it and make what use of it I think best in the paper. I go with William C. it is a great pleasure to us to cooperate in these ways. I do not expect to do much, practically, for the suffering; but having such an organ of expression, any suggestions that are well-grounded may be of use. I have always felt great interest in those women, who are trampled in the mud to gratify the brute appetites of men, and wished I might be brought, naturally, into contact with them. Now I am so; and think I shall have much that is interesting to tell you when we meet.

I go on very moderately, for my strength is not great, and I am now connected with a person who is anxious I should not overtask it. Yet I shall do rather more for the paper by and by. At present, beside the time I spend in looking round and examining my new field, I am publishing a volume of which you will receive a copy, called "Woman in the 19th Century" and part of my available time is spent in attending to it as it goes through the press. For, really, the work seems but half done when your book is *written*. I like being here; the streams of life flow free; and I learn much. I feel so far satisfied as to have laid my plans to stay a year and a half, if not longer, and to have told Mr G. that I probably shall. That is long enough for a mortal to took forward, and not too long, as I must look forward in order to get what I want from Europe.

Mr. Greeley is a man of genuine excellence, honorable, benevolent, of an uncorrupted disposition, and, in his way, of even great abilities. In modes of life and manners he is the man of the people and of the *Amern* people, but I find my way to get along with all that. I have some privations as to comfort and elegance, and am separated from all the friends of my past life, except my friend William, but I do not dwell on the shadow side. Some pleasant acquaintances I have formed and, no doubt, shall more, quite as fast as I have time to attend to them.

I rejoice to hear that your situation is improved. I hope to pass a day or two with you next summer, if you can receive me when I can come. Meanwhile, I want to hear from you, now and then, if it be only a line to let me know the state of your health. Love to Miss G. tell her I have her cologne bottle on my mantle-piece now. I sent for the little things I had from my friends that my room might look more like home.

My window commands a most beautiful view, for we are quite out of town in a lovely place on the East River. I like this, as I can be in town when I will, and *here*, have much retirement. Ever affecy, dear Aunt Mary, yours

MARGARET

How can I send you my book when it comes out? You are right in supposing my signature is the Star.

(MH: fMS Am 1086 [9:114])

111. To James Nathan

Saturday, Feby 22d [1845]
My dear friend, for the memory of the frank words of yesterday makes it impossible for me to address you more distantly.— I feared, when you went away, that you believed I, too, did not sympathize with you, or I could not have said I was so happy when you had just been telling me of your deep wants. You seemed repelled by this; but, indeed, it was not because I did not feel. It is difficult for me to put into words what was in my mind, but you will understand it when you know me more. Yet let me say to you that I think it is great sin even to dream of wishing for less thought, less feeling than one has. Let us be steadfast in prizing these precious gifts under all circumstances. The violet cannot wish to be again imprisoned in the sod, because she may be trampled on by some rude foot. Indeed our lives are sad, but it will not always be so. Heaven is bound to find for every noble and natural feeling its response and its home at last. But I cannot say much, only I would have you remember yesterday with pleasure as does

*

The birds this morning were in full song, like April.

Should you like to go with me on *Monday eveg* to hear the Messiah? If so,

will you come to tea to Mr Cranch's at 6 or a little later and take me.[1] You
may be engaged, or you may not love Handel's music, in either case, let
me know by note and I can find another guardian without difficulty. They
will send a note from the Tribune office, if you wish, but, if it be your desire to go, that is not necessary.

(MB)

1. The New-York Sacred Music Society performed *Messiah* on 24 February. Christopher
Pearse Cranch (1813–92) graduated from the Divinity School in Cambridge in 1835 but became a painter and poet.

112.   To Eugene Fuller

N. Y. 9th March, 1845.

Dearest Eugene,

Your Arkansas letter was received with great joy. It was long since I had
heard from yourself and, as usual, I cannot obtain much information
from the family. It is true I deserve not from them, as the necessity of doing so much other writing makes me a bad correspondent to them and to
every one.

I am glad too to hear of your health, and that, with the ennui of so long
a journey at such a time, you were able to make some profit. Profit always
sounds like your coming back to us, which, amid the whirl of a busy life, I
cannot cease to wish, and which Mother has only too much leisure to
dream about.

I do not know much of the family, except that Mother is still troubled
with dyspepsea, but, in other regards, not sick. Ellen well, and the child,
they say most lovely, Richard doing well. For me, I have never been so well
situated. As to a home the place where we live is old and dilapidated but
in a situation of great natural loveliness. When there, I am perfectly secluded, yet every one I wish to see comes to see me, and I can get to the
centre of the city in half an hour. The house is kept in a Castle Rackrent
style, but there is all affection for me and desire to make me at home, and
I do feel so, wh could scarcely have been expected from such an arrangement. My room is delightful; how I wish you could sit at its window with
me and see the sails glide by!

As to the public part; that is entirely satisfactory. I do just as I please,
and as much or little as I please, and the Editors express themselves perfectly satisfied, and others say that my pieces *tell* to a degree, I could not
expect. I think, too, I shall do better and better. I am truly interested in

this great field which opens before me and it is pleasant to be sure of a chance at half a hundred thousand readers.

Mr Greeley I like, nay more, love. He is, in his habits, a slattern and plebeian, and in his heart, a nobleman. His abilities, in his own way, are great. He believes in mine to a surprizing extent. We are true friends.

It was pleasant you should see that little notice in that wild place. The book is out, and the theme of all the newspapers and many of the journals. Abuse public and private is lavished upon its views, but respect expressed for me personally. But the most speaking fact and the one wh satisfies me, is that the whole edition was sold off in a week to the booksellers and $85 handed to me as my share. Not that my object was in any wise money, but I consider this the signet of success. If one can be heard that is enough! I shall send you 2 copies one for yourself and one to give away, if you like. If you noticed it in a N. O. paper, you might create a demand for it there; the next edition will be out in May.[1] In your next letter tell me your address, that I may know what to do when I wish to send parcels to you.

I wish you would write a series of letters about what you have seen in Arkansas and the S. West, that I might use in the Tribune, if I thought best. I think you would do this well. Write one, at least, about this late tour as a sample and tell about Wild Cat &c *out full.*

I hear a great deal of music, having free entrance every where from my connection with the paper. Most of the Italian Opera corps is now at N. O. and I hope you will hear them perform Semiramide, with which I was enchanted I am glad you love music as well as ever. Farewell, and Heaven bless my dear brother is always the prayer of

MARGARET.

I am almost perfectly well at present.

If you see the Weekly Tribune you will find all my pieces marked with a Star. I began 1st Decr.

(MH: fMS Am 1086 [9:116])

1. Despite its success, *Woman in the Nineteenth Century* did not have a second American edition in her lifetime.

113. To James Nathan

Waverly Place
Sunday aftn 6th April 45

Can my friend have a doubt as to the nature of my answer? Could the heart of woman refuse its sympathy to this earnestness in behalf of an injured woman? Could a human heart refuse its faith to such sincerity, even if it had accompanied the avowal of error![1]

Heaven be praised that it does *not!* Some of your expressions, especially the use of the word *"atonement,"* had troubled me. I knew not what to think. Now I know all, and surely all is well.

The first day we passed together, as you told me of your first being here, when you came to the telling the landlord so ingenuously that you had no money, and said "the tears ran down my boyish cheeks"— my heart sprang towards you and across the interval of years and I stood beside you and wiped away those tears and told you they were pearls consecrated to Truth. You said you "would not do so now" but I believed you *would* act now with the same truthfulness, though in a different manner as becomes *the man,* according to the degree in which circumstances should call on you. And so it is,—there are no tears nor cause to shed any. I need not approach so tenderly as I might have to the boy, but if it be of avail to bless you, to express a fervent hope that your great and tender soul may harmonize all your nature more and more and create to itself a life in which it may expand all its powers; this hope, this blessing take from the one in whom you have confided, and never again fear that such an experiment may fail.

Indeed I have suffered much since receiving the letter. I came into town yesterday with that winged feeling that often comes with the early sunshine. When the letter came, I could not wait, though there was only time for a glance upon it. Then a cold faintness came upon me. I took off the flowers I had put on, expressive of my feelings a little hour before, and gave them to the blind girl, for I almost envied her for being in her shut up state less subject to the sudden shocks of feeling. For there I read at once the exact confirmation of what had been told me of your position, and could not read the whole to be soothed by its sense and spirit. For this day had been given to others, and the evening to a circle of new acquaintance. Not till I went to my room for the night was there any peace or stillness and all things swam before me. For I felt the falsity of the position in which you had placed yourself, that you had acted a fiction and though from honorable nay heroic motives, had entered the path of intrigue I felt too, that he had, probably, been somewhat tempted by the romance of the position, and with a firmer clearer determination to act always with simplicity, might have found some other way. He will tell me whether I was wrong in this. But I placed the letter next my heart and all day it seemed to comfort me, and assure me that when I could be once alone, peace would come; and it has come.

I do not see, my friend, how you can feel thus secure against this being generally[?] known. It came to me through the mistress of a lodging house wherever you are, must you be subject to such transmission. I cannot say more in my case, being bound by a promise, but only repeat what I before told you, that the way in which I heard was so purely accidental as not to argue any publicity *now*. But you say you use your own name, and if you did not your personality is too remarkable to fail of being recognized, beside do some of your male friends know where or how you live?

I say this because you say disclosure might be a source of misery to your afterlife in ways I do not know of; what ways? say all to me—

As to our relations, I wish these circumstances to make no difference in them, private or as to being together in public. Now that I know all and have made up my own mind, I have no fear nor care. I am myself exposed to misconstruction constantly from what I write. Also there have been circumstances in *my* life, which if made known to the world, would judged by conventional rules, subject me as probably to general blame, as these could you. They will, probably, never be made known, but I am well prepared for the chance. Blame could not hurt me, for I have not done wrong, and have too much real weight of character to be sunk, unless by real stones of offense being attached to me: As I feel for myself, so do I for a friend. You are noble. I have elected to abide by you. We will act, as if these clouds were not in the sky. The case in which I asked your counsel was of another sort. I had proposed going about with the lady, not from any strong feeling of affinity or regard, but merely as a matter of convenience. On hearing afterwards that such public odium had been thrown upon her, I thought it might be more advisable for me to choose another escort, and I asked you, thinking thus to be enabled to judge. But *as to you* I *have* judged and have chosen.

But Oh, I wish nothing so grave had come up between us for judgement, thus early. My feeling with you was so delightful; it was a feeling of childhood. I was pervaded by the ardor, upborne by the strength of your nature gently drawn near to the realities of life. I should have been happy to be thus led by the hand through green and sunny paths, or like a child to creep close to the side of my companion listening long to his stories of things unfamiliar to my thoughts. Now this deeper strain has been awakened; it proves, indeed, an unison, but will the strings ever vibrate to the lighter airs again?—

And now farewell. Come to see me so soon as you will and may. The golden time is past, in which a female friend could so much have aided you, but tell me if there still remains any need in which such aid could benefit your charge. Farewell and love ever your friend—

I stay here today but go back to the Farm tomorrow morning. As to your letter I cannot yet part with it; at present it is safe as myself and before you go, shall be disposed of as you desire. I feel as if I had not expressed enough my deep interest in what you have done, but it was because of beginning with a sense that you must know *that* and the wish to satisfy you as to myself. You will read, I believe, what was left unwrit.

(MB)

1. The details are unclear, but Fuller apparently had recently discovered that Nathan was involved with a young "English maiden." He appears to have claimed that he had assumed responsibility for "rehabilitating" her, though she must have been his mistress. Other letters show that she accompanied Nathan when he left New York.

114.   To James Nathan

Monday April 14th [1845]

My dear friend,

What passed yesterday seems not less sad to day. The last three days have effected as violent a change as the famous three days of Paris, and the sweet little garden, with which my mind had surrounded your image lies all desecrated and trampled by the hoofs of the demon who conducted this revolution, pelting with his cruel hail-stones me, poor child, just as I had laid aside the protections of reserve, and laid open my soul in a heavenly trust. I must weep to think of it, and why, O God, must eyes that never looked falsehood be doomed to shed such tears? It seems unjust, as other things in my life have seemed, though none so much as this.[1]

Yet in that garden must be amaranths flowers "not born to die."[2] One of these should be a perfect understanding between us, and as "spirit identity", on which you relied, did not produce this, we will try words. For I perceived yesterday in you a way of looking at these things, different from mine, more common sense, and prudent, but perhaps less refined, and you may not, even yet, see my past as truly as I do myself, *now.*

I have felt a strong attraction to you, almost ever since we first met, the attraction of a wandering spirit towards a breast broad enough and strong enough for a rest, when it wants to furl the wings. You have also been to me as sunshine and green woods. I have wanted you more and more, and became uneasy when too long away. My thoughts were interested in all you told me, so different from what I knew myself The native poetry of your soul, its boldness, simplicity and fervor charmed mine, of kindred frame.

But this is *all* that can be said of my feelings up to receiving your confidential letter a week ago. I enjoyed like a child the interest with which a growing personal interest clothes common life, and the little tokens of outward nature. You enjoyed this with me, and the vibrations were sweet.

I received, indeed, with surprize the intelligence that you would go away. It startled me for the moment, with a sense that you did not prize me enough. I had felt that I could be so much to you to refine, expand, and exalt, could it be I thought you did not feel this? But then your words assured me that you *did* feel it, and I easily forgot pride and self-love. I was thinking more of you than of myself, and I hoped the travel was, indeed, just what you wanted.

But when I received from you the mark of truth so noble, and that placed your character in so striking a light, also seeming to attach so religious an importance to my view of it my heart flew open, as if with a spring, and any hidden treasure might have been taken from it, if you would. I can never resist this kind of greatness. I may say, it is too congenial. At such times I must kneel and implore ever God to bless with abundant love the true heart that consoles me for the littleness I must see in my race, elsewhere.

Afterwards I thought of you with that foolish tenderness women must to men that really confide in them. It makes us feel like mothers, and we wish to guard you from harm and to bless you with an intensity which, no doubt, would be very tiresome to you, if we had force to express it. It seemed to me that when we should meet I *should* express to you all these beautiful feelings, and that you would give me a treasure more from your rich heart. You know how we *did* meet; you seemed dissatisfied. I had an undefined anxiety to do something, and I spoke of being as a bark that fears to leave the shore. This was partly in reply to what you had said, so beautifully, in your letter, of never recalling my thoughts when they naturally rested on you, and of trusting to nature and providence. I wanted to do so, but felt afraid lest pain should ensue, such as has already ensued and which my heart, born for the most genial confidence, knows not well how to bear from a cherished hand.

When you approached me so nearly, I was exceedingly agitated, partly because your personality has a powerful magnetic effect on me, partly because I had always attached importance to such an act, and it was asked of me so as to make me conscious, and suddenly, partly because this seemed the moment to express all I had felt for you, but I could not. As to what I said of a brother, I felt distaste to the use of the word; I have seen too much of these *brothers*. I do not doubt they think for awhile like brothers, but they do not always, and I think it is fairer to have a nameless relation, which cannot be violated and may grow to what it will.

Truly the worldly and *manly* way in which you spoke of circumstances so delicate and which had moved me so much, was sad for me to hear, yet was I glad to know what could pass in the mind even of the dear one who had claimed,— *and merited,* so large a trust. My guardian Angel must take better care of me another time, and make me still more timid, for truly nothing but perfect love will give a man patience to understand a woman, even such a man as you who have so much of feminine sweetness and sensibility.

After receiving your little note of Saturday, I again looked to you to make my feelings perfectly tuneful when I saw you. I do not think any human being ever felt a lovelier confidence in the pure tenderness of another than I did when we left the church. When you said what you thought necessary to say, it struck upon my heart like a blow. Something in your manner seemed to mark it *for me,* and yet I *could not believe it,* yet the weight pressed and I could not rest till our final conversation made all clear.

O was *that* like angels, like twin spirits bound in heavenly unison, to think that any thing short of perfect love, such as I myself am born to feel, and shall yet, in some age and some world, find one that can feel for me, could enslave my heart or *compromise* a lover?

My friend! believe what I say, for I am self-conscious now. You have touched my heart, and it thrilled at the centre, but that is all. My heart is a large kingdom.

But *your* heart, your precious heart! (I am determined to be absolutely frank,) *that* I did long for. I saw how precious it is, how much more precious may be. And you have cruelly hung it up quite out of my reach, and declare I never shall have it. O das ist hart. For *no* price! There is something I am not to have at *any* price. Das ist hart. You must not give it away in my sight at any rate, but you may give away all your prudence and calculations, and arrangements, which seem so unlike your fairer self, to whomsoever you like.

It seemed the work of an evil angel making you misread a word in my letter, but since it could lead you to think it needful so to act, I am glad you did since I thus became apprized of these things in your mind, else my little birds might have flown to you in too thick flocks. You said; "what shall our relation be now?" I say, most friendly, for we are really dear to one another; only it is like other earthly relations, poison plants will sometimes grow up in the night. But we will weed them out so soon as possible, and bear with them, since only perfect love casteth out fear. Think of me with love and honor. I deserve them. So do you, and shall ever have them from me. To the inspirer of all just thoughts and holy hopes commending you, farewell, my friend.

For the sake of every thing dear, dont misread any words in *this* letter. I must tell you why I was so slow to understand you yesterday, it was because you made use of the word *hope.* "Has any circumstance led to a *hope*" etc. Ah, Gretchen! has thy really proud and sacred life only led to such an episode where thou are supposed and by a most trusted friend to be *"hop-*

ing" about such things? Where is the fault in thee, that can lead to conclusions so humiliating? Thy own mind does not appreciate it.

Yet again I am glad my friend used the very word that could come into his mind. Truth is the first of jewels,— yet let him feel that if Margaret dared express herself more frankly than another it is because she has been in her way a queen and received her guests as also of royal blood. *What* her vanity was you may see if you read how ingenuously it was said "Tell me and I will love you" as if promising a boon. Alas alas she must go to Heaven. And the journey is long.

(MB)

1. Again the details are unclear, but Nathan apparently made an overt sexual overture to Fuller, having been emboldened by her acceptance of the "English maiden." Her political reference is to the 1830 July Revolution, which led Charles X of France to abdicate in favor of the duc d'Orléans, who became the "citizen king," Louis-Philippe.

2. Fuller may have taken the phrase from Fitz-Greene Halleck's best-known poem, "Marco Bozzaris" (1825), "One of the few, the immortal names,/That were not born to die." Perhaps she remembered Octavius in *Julius Caesar*, V.i.58–59: "So I hope;/I was not born to die on Brutus' sword."

115. To Caroline Sturgis

17th April. 45

My dear Caroline,

You will remember Honora Sheppard whom you talked with in the hospital at Sing Sing.[1] You may see by the accompanying letter what Georgiana has been doing for her and proposes to do. G. went up to Albany last Saty and got her pardon from the governor at once. I can hardly tell you how much I feel the generosity of G. to be willing to take with her such a charge into her new field of action wearied out as she is, craving rest and freedom for herself. It is an act of which myself would be wholly incapable. G. is now anxious to get some money for Honora's travelling expenses, and can you aid a little and would Anna Shaw and perhaps Ellen help? Ten or even five dollars would help. Anna Ward will get a little for me here, but I do not myself know many people with purses, and Mr Greeley is prejudiced against Honora. G. will go, probably by the 25th, if you can do any thing, write to your affece

MARGARET.

A letter from Sarah Clarke but nothing special in it. Ah it is most lovely here now; whole beds of violets and mountain myrtle all starred with its blue flowers, trees just leaving out.

how many associations with these days last Spring. The dates speak powerfully even to me.

I enjoy much being with Anna Ward now; she is in a beautiful tone— We go every Sunday together to church. At Miss Lynch's was introduced to me Headly author of those letters from Hamilton County with quick glancing eye and hawk nose, you would like him a little[2] O Sullivan, too, whom I like and another pleasant man, unknown to fame![3] I am a good deal interested in Miss Lynch. Winty Whitemore is in town and remembers you *with force.* I hear you are "lovely" now Heaven help you!

(MH: bMS Am 1221 [248])

1. Honora Shepherd, a convict in whom Fuller took an interest, was pardoned by Governor Silas Wright. A child of a family of forgers, she had previously escaped from jail disguised as a man.

2. Anne Charlotte Lynch (1815–91) began her literary career in Providence and then settled in New York. Her gatherings attracted Poe, Bryant, Greeley, and Parke Godwin. Joel Tyler Headley (1813–97) was a prolific writer, two of whose works Fuller reviewed for the *Tribune.*

3. Probably John Louis O'Sullivan.

116.   To James Nathan

Friday evening.
[2? May? 1845]

You come not, dear friend. The day was full of golden sunlight, and kind words and deeds as well, for the thought of you stood at the end— but you come not. My head has ached ever since you were here, and needed you to take away its pain— but you come not. You said once I was too sensitive and that such little disappointments would affect me; it is, indeed, the absence of the light, but would never affect me any other way, where I am sure of love as I am of yours, but that absence is sad. The shadows and damps of evening settle down upon me as they do upon the earth, for where is the torch that was to cheer the indoor retirement? You come not— and now I realize that soon will be the time, when evening will come always, but you will come no more.

We shall meet in soul; but the living eye of love; that is in itself almost a soul, and that will beam no more.

O Heaven, O God, or by whatsoever name I may appeal; surely, surely O All Causing thou must be the All Sustaining *All-fulfilling* too. I, from thee sprang, do not feel force to bear so much as one of these deep impulses— *in vain!* Nor is it enough that the heavenly magic of its touch throws open all the treasure chambers of the Universe, if these enchanted doors must close again.

My little rose-tree casts its shadow on the paper. They bade me *cut it down to make it blossom,* and so have I done, though with a reluctant hand. So is it on this earth; but not so will it always be; the soul protests against it and sometime, somewhere claims its own *in full.*

Wilt thou search out such mysteries in the solitude of thy cave? Wilt thou prepare for men an image fair and grand enough of *hope!* Give that to men at large, but to me send some little talisman that may be worn next the secret heart. And let it have a diamond point that may pierce when any throb swells too far to keep time with the divine frame of things. We would not, however, stifle one natural note, only tune all sweet.

My head aches still and I must lean it on the paper as I write, so the writing goes all amiss. Ah I really needed you tonight and you could not come yet you are not away from me;— are you?

I long to hear whether the most wearisome part of your winding up is not now over. May [day] morning, after thinking it was unfit to send the flowers; I changed my mind for it seemed perhaps they might not be uncongenial in the evening after the fret and dust of the day were over. Farewell.

(MB)

117.   To James Nathan

Thursday evening.
5th June, 1845

I will no longer delay my letter of regrets for one such, I feel must be written, before the mind can shake off its weight of sadness and turn to brighter things. To be sure, before you can receive it, these hours will be past with you, yet come back with me, and sit down here by my window, and share the feelings of this hour.

Ever since you went, it has been the most beautiful weather, such as *we* never had at all. I do not think, my friend, fate smiled upon us; how much cold and storm there was; how little warm soft air when we could keep still out of doors in peace, how much interruption throughout from other affairs and relations, and the cloud of separation threatening from the distance from the very first. One good month, containing unbroken days of intercourse, and with no thought of the future would have been worth, in happiness, these five that we have known each other in such a way. But then, as we have met in common life, and amid all its cares and interruptions, all we do possess from one another is a more precious possession, for it is tested gold.

Yet I do wish we might have had together these glowing hours of the season's pride. Everything is so rich, so full, and fragrant with the warm breeze sighing all the time in excess of happiness. The roses are all out now, and the enchanting magnolia, too, and oriental locust. All the fruit is turned red in the sunlight; that on my tree, to which you so sweetly likened yourself, glances like cornelians and corals among the leaves. All is full and lustrous, as it has not been and will not be again, for these first days of June are the bridal days of the year, but through all breathes to me a tone of sorrow, over all droops a veil, for I have lost my dear companion, the first I ever had who could feel every little shade of life and beauty as exquisitely as myself, whose strength gladdened and whose gentleness soothed me, and wanting this finishing note, Nature herself pleases no more. It will not be so long, I trust, but *it is so now.*

Morning of the 6th,— When I had written the last words, I could write no more; all seemed too sad and heavy, and I went to take counsel of my pillow. Here I never fail to find comfort. Night seems to me the gentlest mother. We are taught, in our childhood, verses to which I know not if you have anything corresponding in German they begin

"Receive my body, pretty bed,
Dear pillow, thou receive my head."

And this feeling of trust in the confidential, gentle Night, that she will drive away dusky thoughts and needless cares, and bring sweet counsel and hope for the morrow, deepens in me year by year. It pleased me much when you told of your Father taking the flowers to bed with him; he must have had the same feeling. And I was not disappointed, but awoke brightly this morning. But it is daily a sadness to me again to go to the town and know I shall not find the little messenger with your letter. Out here I want you to enjoy the beauty of the solitude, in the city I feel alone among the multitude of men, because you are gone. Strange that there should be just one with whom I could hold deep sympathy, and just that one of all the thousands must go as I came. Ah well! I will fret as little as I can, but this sighing is of some use just to exhale one's—

The day you went, I was interrupted by visits all the time. At night I had promised to accompany Mrs Child and Mr Benson to the Park Theatre.[1] There an actress, once beautiful and celebrated, whom Mrs Child had raised from the most degrading fall was to reappear before a N. Y. audience[2] Mrs C., after attending her as a sister till she learnt to love her as one, had secured her engagements in the other cities, and from the gutter (as one may say,) she had come into the enjoyment of an honorable independence and respectable relations. But she had never revisited N. Y. which was the scene of her former degradation till now, and was very nervous in the fear of being hissed. Mrs C. had engaged me and other friends to be present to sustain her by our sympathy. But we were there only to heighten her disgrace; the poor woman, unable to sustain her anxiety, took some stimulant, and it set her quite beside herself. It was the saddest sight to see her robed in satin, and crowned with roses, ruining with every word all her hopes of future ease or peace, till no resource seemed left her but suicide, (for she is unfit for any thing but her profession to which she was educated,) and dealing such blows on hearts which had shown her real disinterested love. Although I had felt averse to going, because it was the day of your parting, and it would have been best to be alone and still, I became painfully interested. But in the very midst my heart beat suddenly, your image rose before me. I could think of nothing else for a long time; you must, I think, have called me that evening as you looked out on the blue waters. Afterwards as I witnessed Mrs C's trouble I thought of you, and that your labor of love to which you have sacrificed so much and me and this summer among others, was at least likely to end well. That is a rare blessing in this tangled world, to bring a good to fulfilment, even by great sacrifices. Write me all you can about this, for I feel deeply interested. Since you went I have been looking over the "The Crescent and the Cross" a book of Eastern travels; there are in the *Appendix "Hints to travellers in the East"* you may possibly not know all he mentions. Mr Delf will easily get you the book, and it is worth your looking at.[3]

Mrs Greeley thinks a great deal about you; she was left with a perfectly sweet feeling in which I rejoice. She has been in these days very tranquil

I take Josey out with me; he is very gay, but does not mind me well. I cannot get him to go into the water at all; last night I had to ask some boys to throw him in. I shall not *cross my letters much, though you did ask it,* because I know you will enjoy reading them more if I do not. I have arranged all yours in company with the white veil and the memorandum book and some dead flowers that once bloomed sweetly in hours of sweet life, but have not had courage to read them yet. To our Father's care commending you lebewohl.

After all I forgot to say to you what I meant about Mrs C's marriage. And it comes apropos to this event. It was this that with great affectionateness and love of disinterested action, she had not the surest instincts as to selecting objects or occasions, so that much she has done, has been of no good except to her own heart. I know not, however, that in either of these cases, she had much choice; she married very young, before she knew much of herself, and in the case of the actress, she could not choose but do all she could for one whom none else would help, and so she did it nobly, with the whole heart!

Please mention the receipt of each of my letters that I may be sure none of them are lost.

(MB)

1. Lydia Maria Francis (1802–80), an author and abolitionist, had known Fuller from her youth. In 1828 she married David Child. In New York she edited the *National Anti-Slavery Standard,* the Garrisonian abolitionist newspaper, but she resigned in May 1843 because of internal politics in the organization. Though Fuller writes "Benson," she probably refers to Edmund Benzon (d. 1873), a German businessman who contributed to Child's abolitionist causes.

2. Anne Henry Barrett (1801–53) was an actress who first performed in New York City in 1824. She was an alcoholic who had been rehabilitated, as Fuller says. On 2 June she played the role of Lady Gay Spanker in Dion Boucicault's *London Assurance.* She did not continue past the first evening that Fuller describes.

3. Eliot Warburton, *The Crescent and the Cross; or, Romance and Realities of Eastern Travel* (1845). Thomas Delf was an Englishman who worked for the publishing firm of D. Appleton.

118.   To Caroline Sturgis

New York, 10th July 1845.

Dear Caroline, I begin now to wish much for some words from yourself, (of your whereabouts I have heard all along from others) But as I have been silent so long I shall have no right to complain if you feel no immediate readiness to answer when at last I call. Yet do so if you can.

I hardly know, now that I feel inclined to write, what to say to you, so much has passed in my mind since we met. A flood has passed over the country; it was a mild and warm one, but it has uprooted some objects that used to be landmarks there, has planted the seeds of new growths and effected some change in the climate though the main features of the country I suppose are still the same.

All this passes, as deep passages of inward life have with me, without making any show outwardly. My activity, so far as necessary to secure leave of stay in this world, has been continued independent of it. Separation from all old habits and intimacies has saved from all casual and partial confidences; all has passed in a beautiful seclusion.

I believe this true life will never with me take form in art or literature The more its treasures accumulate the less am I inclined to do any thing with them in such ways. Sometimes I wonder they do not so express themselves, for I feel that these shadows, so precious to others, would not injure their substance in its vitality. But there is no impulse to it, and I do not care, and never shall care any more. I believe I am the mother of a genius, more than a genius. It seems as if I was learning every thing, that every element of beauty and power was being reproduced in my frame, but only in my son shall they appear not in me, his unknown but happy mother.

Do you remember that night last summer when we fell asleep on the bed and we were like Elizabeth and Mary.[1] I have often wanted to express what appeared to me that night, but could not, only every day I understand it better. I feel profou[nd]ly bound with you and hope you wear my ring.

My days pass at present in the most tranquil sweetness. You cannot think how beautiful it is in this place; the winter-sight gave no idea of what it is in its nuptial robes. I very seldom go away, and never wish to for a day. You know I thought of travelling to many places but shall not to any this summer, for we may not be able to keep the the place another, and I feel as if it were appointed me for a brief repose from my werinesses and wanderings. My room is delightful with its side view to the water and the great willow which contains the other windows. This is far more beautiful than the one we saw at Mr De Windt's and the waving of its boughs— whether in sunlight, moonlight,— or best in starlight only, has been to me more than the speech of any other tree ever.[2] The branches fall and make a bower trailing on the ground like the fringes of a tent. I have most charming places on the edge of the rocks; in one a wall of some forty feet of rock rises behind me; it is the best place I ever had to sit in. I have a fine Newfoundland dog, who is my companion on the rocks; he is as much to me as the willow.

Shall you not be here this summer? I should like to have you see these places, and have your spirit touch them too. Do you like your new abode? I should think you might be having a good time there. You will write, if you can to

MARGARET.

Intelligens has silenced Aspirans for the present. But I feel afraid the time of peace will vanish now it has been spoken of. But the spirit prompted so to do.

(MH: bMS Am 1221 [249])

1. Elisabeth, mother of John the Baptist, and her kinswoman Mary, mother of Jesus.
2. John Peter De Windt (1787–1870), whom Fuller met during her vacation in 1844.

Caroline Sturgis. Courtesy of Daphne Brooks Prout.

119. To James F. Clarke

[14 August 1845]

My dear friend James,

With a start came to me the thought this evening; if you wish to write to James at Chicago; you must do it at once, for this is the 14th August. Indeed, it *is* "in my heart" to write. Your letter was of cordial sweetness to me, as is ever the thought of our friendship, that sober suited friendship, where the web was so deliberately and well woven, and which wears so well.

I was pleased with your sympathy about The Tribune; I do not find much among my old friends. They think I ought to produce something excellent, while I am well content for the present to aid in the great work of mutual education in this way. I never regarded literature merely as a collection of exquisite products, but as a means of mutual interpretation. Feeling that many are reached and in some degree aided the thoughts of every day seem worth writing down, though in a form that does not inspire me. Then I like to feel so fairly afloat in mid-stream, as I do here. All the signs of life appear to me at least superficially, and, as I have had a good deal of *the depths,* an abode of some length in *the shallows* may do me no harm. The sun comes full upon me.

Mr Greeley is all you say. He is in other ways interesting for me to know, "A born and thorough Plebeian" as he declares himself to be, he teaches me many things, which my own influence on those who have hitherto approached me, as also that we attract in mutual relations those congenial with ourselves, has prevented my learning. He and I are in business and friendly relations there is a solid good will and natural respect without intimacy. I think him the most disinterestedly generous person, except my own Mother, that I have ever known.

You speak justly of Rousseau too.[1] With earliest instincts he was so prized by me, all development has confirmed the feeling. But natures so earnest and with the central fire so deeply enkindled will never be believed in by the world in general till men have far more manhood than now. Some of us, James, were not unlike the personages of Rousseau, the children of his Soul. We never tampered with our feelings we never falsified their expression, nor borrowed an unworthy help from false pride.

I wish you joy of your little one.[2] Your marriage is a good one, and I feel as if your children would be of value. I can congratulate you, which I could few persons. Since Anna Parsons discovered the name, it must be the right one, else I should say W. Eliot is not good enough to be associated with W. Channing. I am not pleased with much that I have heard and the little I have seen of him these later years. He seems to have grown narrow and conceited in the absence of equal and superior minds that might have checked him.

I was very sorry for those poor conscientious people that left you last winter except that foolish vain George Channing.[3] He ought to go through the water cure, no less would eradicate the taint from his system. I could not help feeling Poor Jesus! it seemed so much more sacrilegious to utter such meannesses in his name than all the crimes of the Jesuits. I declare that nothing in the world is to me so revolting as religious vanity.

Dear James, I do not want to write much more. I go to Rockaway tomorrow for sea air, as I am not strong and have preparations to make Have been today over the Great Britain; it is a majestic sight; as fine as I expected. But I would rather cross in a smaller boat; she cannot be very manageable.

Tell Sarah Mr Emerson has just been here a delightful visit. He enjoyed my rocks with free heart. Tell me what is Sarah painting; she never tells Adieu ever affecy

Your friend

MARGARET.

(MHi)

1. Though Clarke and Fuller had read Rousseau together many years before, he was reading *La Nouvelle Héloïse* for the first time.

2. Eliot Channing Clarke (1845–1921) was born on 6 May.

3. Clarke announced to his congregation that he was going to exchange pulpits with Theodore Parker, whose radical views had made him virtually ostracized by his fellow Unitarian clergy. A group of Clarke's people, including George Channing (1789–1881), Dr. Channing's brother, objected and then withdrew to form the Church of the Savior.

120.   To Ellis and Louisa Loring

New York, 22d
August 45

To Mr and Mrs Loring
Dear friends,

Mr Greeley has recd a letter from a slave-holder in Kentucky making this proposal. This person, Lindsay by name, is the owner of a mulatto girl, who, being hired out to service in the City, became a mother at a very early age of a little girl now 4 or 5 years old. This child, he says, is very handsome and sprightly, and by all strangers considered a white child. He says "as it is impossible she should here be brought up in a virtuous manner, or, in fact, receive any education at all, I am anxious to give up all right or title to her, pay her expenses on to the East and there give her up to the care of some one who will furnish evidence of being able and willing to act toward her as a parent or guardian and see that she has a fair chance of education for whatsoever place in society her abilities may fit her to occupy."

Foreseeing natural suspicions that may arise, he offers "any amount of evidence to show that this offer is entirely disinterested, and that I stand in no other relation either to Mother or child than that of Master, and shall not that long to either." He furnishes references at to his general character.

He is desirous the origin of the child should not be made known, but that she should be educated as white, and it would, I think, be an interesting task to one who feels or wishes to settle doubts as to the tendencies of African blood, of Amalgamation &c. I wished myself, much, to try a half-breed child of white and Indian descent, to ascertain how far the common objections to such unions are founded, but I am not in a situation to undertake any such charge. Do you know of any one who is? Mrs Child recommended that I should apply to you as the persons most likely to know of some place for her and to take an interest in inquiring. She also mentioned *Mary Chapman,* as one likely to take such an interest. Wd you answer soon, if you can, with convenience.[1]

Mrs C. showed me a note from Anna, which says you think of coming here this Autumn; that will be in Septr I hope, for the last days of that month or the first of Octr I go to Mass on a visit and want to see you both there and here. I want much that Anna should pass a day with me here, and see my beautiful rocks, where I have been so happy and which I shall not have next summer.[2] Do come in Septr.

In haste but always Affecy Yours

S. M. FULLER.

(MWelC)

1. Mary Chapman (1799?-1874), daughter of Henry and Sarah Green Chapman of Boston, was a Garrisonian abolitionist, as were her brother and sister-in-law.

2. Their daughter, Anna (1830–96), whom Fuller's brother Richard had loved, but who married Otto Dresel, a musician, in 1863.

121.   To Mary Rotch

New York, 9th Jany
1846.

Very dear Aunt Mary,

How shall I get done thanking your two letters, the first such a nice long one, and then the New Year's fount of ruby wine, open for me as if I were a Prince of the blood!

You must not think me disobedient though, if I turn some of the wine into a new dress. Having but one of the class Mrs Farrar calls *tightum* and being much invited out now I am in town, I was grudgingly reflecting on the necessity of getting another Grudgingly,— for you have no idea how much, in this dirtiest of cities, it costs a poor scribe (what it costs the Pharasees Imagination shrinks from counting) who is far from all aid of unpaid affection in the line of sewing getting up clothes &c even to keep herself neat in the tightum line. [ ]

Mrs Child will not go out at all, either to evening party or morning call. She says she cant afford the time, the white gloves, the visiting cards or the carriage hire. But I think she lives at disadvantage by keeping so entirely apart from the common stream of things. I shall never go out when busy, or to keep late hours, but to go sometimes is better and pleasanter for me. I find many entertaining acquaintances and some friends. So I mean to steal from your money at least ribands and lace for the inevitable dress, and that will leave me more of the grape juice than I should drink betwixt now and another Christmas.

I talk of gaieties, but shall not have much of them, if I do not get well. I have had for a fortnight a very bad cold, which has ended in abesses or boils in the glands of one cheek and side of the throat. From these I suffer much, from the pain and because it is of a burning, irritating kind that I cannot forget a minute. I have thought much of you, how patiently you bear an infliction of a similar kind all the time, while I think it hard for a week or two,— and then I fret not. You probably have observed how little I write, for the paper. I have felt really unable to write or do any thing, but better times are coming I hope.

You ask if my pieces in the paper will be published in a volume. I hope sometime they may, or at least those worth preserving, but know not when. My Miscellanies would fill several volumes, if collected, but nobody thinks it worth while to propose this. Whether they ever will depends on how far M. may win the favor of the public (without making it her object as most of the others do!)[1]

The boarding-house is a very good one, neat, orderly, still. They have been kind, as people generally are to me, urging my having my meals sent to my room &c instead of thinking, because I kept up and exerted myself, that I could not be sick, as so many would have thought.

Farewell! I look forward to the Spring visit. I hope there will be Italn Opera then and Miss Gifford and I will go together. Give much love to her A Miss Wells has called on me who was with Mrs Rotch, Frank and Maria in Rome. She gives very pleasant accounts of both the jeuveniles, but liked Frank best. I ought to tell you also that Mrs and Miss Dewey propose to call on me.[2] With patience great mercies may be expected! Affecy ever

MARGARET F.

(MH: fMS Am 1086 [9:123])

1. Her plans were fulfilled with the publication of *Papers on Literature and Art* in September.

2. Louisa Farnham (1794–1884) married Rev. Orville Dewey in 1820. He became the minister of the Church of the Messiah in New York City. The daughter was probably Mary Elizabeth (1821–1910).

122.   To Evert A. Duyckinck

4 Amity Place
N Y.
2d Feby 1846.

To Mr Duyckinck,
Dear Sir,

Mrs Ellett tells me that you lent a willing ear to a plan for the publication of some of my essays.[1] This would be very agreeable to me, as copies of them are continually borrowed and I think, if more accessible, they would command a good deal of sympathy. I should be glad if this took place under your auspices, for I have thought from what I observed that your ideas, as to movements in the literary world, are what I can truly respect. I should like an opportunity to talk with you fully: can you call upon me? If you will, by a note sent through the Tribune Office, appoint an hour I will be at home and most happy to receive you.

With respect yours

S. M. FULLER.

(ViU)

1. Elizabeth Lummis (1812?–77), who married William Henry Ellet, was a writer and a rival of Frances Osgood for Poe's attention.

123.   To Evert A. Duyckinck

[ca. 5 February 1846]

To Mr Duyckinck,
Dear Sir

I was so much interrupted last eveg, as not to be able earlier to send you the list you desired. I have made out as fully as I could an account of the pieces I wish to publish. I may alter or enlarge somewhat as limits suggest or permit.

Among the earlier pieces there is not one that has not excited a good deal of interest in this country and many of them have in England. I judge of this from the correspondence and acquaintance they have brought me. Of the degree of interest the portion that is to be taken from the Tribune may have for your public yourself can judge as you have seen them.

Should Messrs Wiley and Putnam desire or incline to make these a part of their series I should like to know as soon as may be what terms they offer and at what time they would wish to bring out the book, for I should have a good deal to do in arranging the materials and writing some new morceaux.

I request your acceptance of the illustrated copy of Summer on the Lakes and the Engh copy of my volume on Woman.

With respect yours

S. M. FULLER.

Mr Emerson informed me that the terms offered by you to him, for his poems, with every desire to be liberal on your side, were inferior to what he could make for himself in N. England.[1]

(NN-M)

1. Emerson had protracted negotiations with Duyckinck, who offered 6 cents royalty on a book of poems to sell for 31 cents. Emerson declined and gave it to Munroe & Company in Boston, with whom he published at his own risk and paid Munroe a 30 percent commission.

124.   To Samuel G. and Anna Barker Ward

New York.
3d March, 1846.

My ever dear friend,

I was glad, indeed, to get your and Anna's letters after the long silence. Indeed, of your health and outward life I had heard in other ways, but my heart had often turned towards you and wished for sight of your handwriting at least.

Yet I do not feel able to answer the good part of your letter, I mean the thinking part, unless I do so in the Tribune. I may, very likely, take it as text, if I can find a suitable form for my reflections.

At present I am not fit to write a good letter. I cannot spare time or feeling. All the month of January I was sick in a way that unfitted me for any serious effort. Ever since I have been toiling in vain to make up at the same time for my forced derelictions and to meet new demands. *Now* I am on the point, in addition to my usual work of getting out two vols of my Miscellanies (pieces from Dial and Tribune wh will require a good deal of revision; they are to be published in Wiley and Putnam's series) and getting ready to go to Europe in August, wh will be hard work, as Mr Greeley is to be absent most of the summer and I have promised to stay by the Tribune till the last. Add to this the perplexity and grief as to home affairs that Ellery's last freak has brought upon me—[1]

But it is not of this I want to speak, but of my going to Europe. It is now ten years, since I was forced to abandon the hope of going at the time when I felt that my health and mind required it as they never could again. Still more I felt that in not going with you at the time when our minds were so in unison, and when I was drawn so strongly towards your peculiar province, I lost what life could never replace. I feel so still.

At every step I have missed the culture I sought in going, for with me it [was] no scheme of pleasure but the means of needed development. It was what I wanted after my painful youth, and what I was ready to use and be nourished by. It would have given my genius wings and I should have been, not in idea indeed, but in achievement far superior to what I can be now. Fate or Heaven, or whatever we may call it, did not will it so, and in entering other and less congenial paths, I do feel that I have tried to make the best of life in every sense I could. Many sweet fruits has it brought me, fruits of spiritual knowledge and a liberal communion with the woful struggling crowd of fellow men. I have accepted my lot, such as it was, and while I have not cast over it any veil of commonplace resignations I have not complained inwardly or outwardly. I have, indeed, had my periods of morbid suffering, because the perpetual stress upon me has been beyond my strength to bear, and at this present time I feel threatened with one, because the day is thronged a great deal too thick with tasks and perplexities and I have not the chance for repose that I ought.

I hope however to avoid it, for I have grown wise and now seek physical remedies for irritated nerves, rather than struggle with them mentally, which I formerly augmented the ill by doing.

I do not look forward to seeing Europe now as so very important to me. My mind and character are too much formed. I shall not modify them much but only add to my stores of knowledge. Still, even in this sense, I wish much to go. It is important to me, almost needful in the career I am now engaged in I feel that, if I persevere, there is nothing to hinder my having an important career even now. But it must be in the capacity of a journalist, and for that I need this new field of observation.

I want to go in a way not too laborious for my strength and it is with this view that I apply to you. I have about a thousand dollars secured for my absence. But from all calculations I seem likely to want five hundred more. Can I through you or your father have a credit abroad to that amount, in case I need it.[2] I wish to be in debt to a friend, that in case I live and return, I may pay it gradually as I earn it and not feel oppressed by it. I should like it to be a debt in regular form, and pay suitable interest for the use of the money. If I live I could probably earn that sum soon, if I die, the lender would not eventually be a loser, as seven or eight hundred dollars will come to me when Mother leaves this world from which she seems likely to be driven prematurely, though truly I wish I might go first.

I think I remember something of your saying you never meant to *lend* money If you have any vow or resolution of that kind that will interfere, or if I am mistaken in thinking that yr fathers relations abroad would make this easier to you than any one else, write soon, dear Sam, and say so, and I shall apply elsewhere. If I cannot get it otherwise I can take upon me correspondences with periodicals here, only too much of that will give me so much labor as in good measure to deprive me of the benefit of the journey

Dearest Anna, I thank much for the sweet picture of your life It will be repose to think of it, in dust and rush of a different one. I have no time to answer except about my visit. I wish *very* much, to come but do not feel sure of being able and if I am, the visit must be short. I should like much however to come, if I can, and should be glad to meet Cary as else I cannot see her again. Will you ask her for the last of June or first of July and I will come then, if possible. I am glad we saw so much of each other last summer, we may not meet much again for a good or bad while.

I feel sorry not to have the books you name, they came out in my sick time and not being noticed by my hand do not belong to me by rules of the office I send such as I have.

Dear Sam I look to see you. Shall be here 4 Amity place, Mrs Elwell's till 12th March, after that time inquire at Tribune office. I have been interrupted forty times while writing and now am so again, but ever yours

MARGARET.

(MH: bMS Am 1465 [927])

1. Despite (or because) Ellen was pregnant with their second child, Ellery suddenly decided he must see Europe. He solicited money from family, friends, and acquaintances, and sailed on 3 March for Rome, where he stayed only sixteen days.

2. Both Ward and his father were employed by the prestigious Baring Brothers bank.

125.   To Evert A. Duyckinck

June 28th [1846]

private

To Mr Duyckinck

I received a note yesterday from Mr Wiley, requesting that I would omit the article on Festus from the forthcoming volumes and "all other matter of a controversial character or likely to offend the religious public."[1]

Now you well know that I write nothing which might not offend the so-called religious public. I am too incapable of understanding their godless fears and unhappy scepticism to have much idea of what would offend them. But there are probably sentences in every piece, perhaps on every page, which, when the books are once published, will lead to censure.

I consented to take counsel as to the selection of pieces with *you,* because you can understand. As there is a superabundance of matter, and whatever is not published now will be hereafter I was willing to take counsel as to the selection from the pieces. But I hope it is clearly understood that in those I *do* publish, I shall not alter a line or a word, on such accounts They will stand precisely as they were originally written and if you think Mr Wiley will not be content to take the consequences you had better stop the transaction now.

Also in the department of Foreign literature I must be guided by my own judgment. The articles on Goethe and others, probably contain things far more likely to offend than those in the piece on Festus, but I will not omit them, if I publish at all, for they are some of my best pieces, and I do not wish the volumes to be made up of indifferent matter.

I could not, if I would, act in this temporizing manner; it is too foreign to my nature. But I do not believe in it as a matter of policy. The attractive force of my mind consists in its energy, clearness and I dare to say it, its catholic liberality and fearless honor. Where I make an impression it must be by being most myself. I ought always to ignore vulgar prejudices, and I feel within myself a power which will sustain me in so doing and draw to me sufficient and always growing sympathy.

I do not believe it is *wise* to omit the piece on Festus or that on Shelley.[2] Those who care for what I write at all, will care most for such pieces. It seems unhandsome towards Mr Bailey, who is now the first of the younger living English poets, to omit him and name others. There is only one consideration that makes me willing in that case, which is that, on looking the piece over, I find the extracts make it too long and could not well be omitted. I consent then in the case of those two pieces.— I would also like to have you if you think it desirable hold counsel with Mr Wiley, as to the articles on Swedenborgianism and the Wesleys.[3] There is nothing in them controversial as, of course, there could not be in any thing I write, viewing all sects, as I do merely as expressions of human opinion and character. But they are on matters theological, though not viewed from a theological point. I wish to publish them because they have some merit, but I do not care particularly about it. Only make Mr Wiley understand that where I *do* care I shall insist, and that I give him no vouchers that there shall be nothing to offend his religious public in the book. I shall publish the articles just as they stand, without any attention to such considerations or not at all. If he is not content with that, we had better stop now. If we do, however, I shall publish an account of this transaction for I wish in every way to expose the restrictions upon mental freedom which threaten to check the progress of genius or of a religious sentiment worthy of God and man in this country.

I have read the play with great pleasure. The view of character and statements of magnetic influence from soul to soul is truly noble. The accounts by the girl of her love are fine poetry, so are those of the sympathizing aspects of nature with those dark mental seasons. There is *no metre,* rhythm though the poem assumes to be written in it. Tell the author's name; is it yours? I shall prize it.

I have recd only two proofs, as yet. I shall expect a note from you tomorrow night.

If we go on, (and I suppose we shall, only I want it to be on a firm and honorable basis) I can supply all the rest of the Engh lite[rature] part on Tuesday. Farewell, my good friend, for I feel as if you were such to me, though we have not seen much of one another yet. But I know your soul is truly liberal and fair.

S. M. F.

(NN-M)

1. John Wiley (1808–91) had taken over the firm, which had been established in 1803, at his father's death. His partner was George Palmer Putnam.

2. Despite her fondness for both writers, Fuller did not reprint her essay on Philip James Bailey's poem *Festus,* which she wrote for the *Dial,* or the review of Shelley written for the *Tribune* of 27 December 1845.

3. Her essay "Swedenborgianism," originally published in the *Tribune* on 25 June 1845, was included in volume 2, as was "Methodism at the Fountain," a review of a biography of Charles Wesley.

126.   To Richard F. Fuller

Birmingham
27th Septr 1846.

Very dear Richard,

I am pausing here for a day or two on my way to London. After passing ten days very delightfully in Westmoreland and Cumberland, where, beside the enjoyment of that most beautiful scenery, I made several very agreeable acquaintance and even friends, we went on to Edinburgh There we passed a week on our way to the Highlands, and three days on return. We were fourteen days on the Highland excursion, days of ever varying enjoyment. On the lofty Ben Lomond, I got lost, and passed the night out on a heathery Scotch mountain, alone, and only keeping my life, by exertions to ward off the effects of the cold and wet, to which I should have feared my bodily strength and mental patience alike unequal, *if* I had not tried. I was rather ill for a few days after it, and the Springs suffered much from anxiety and excitement, for they were up and had a crowd of shepherds out searching the mountain all the night, but, since I have got off without eventual injury, we are all glad of the experience for it was quite a deep one. You will find a sketch of the externals of the affair in the Tribune, but when I can have time, I shall try to write it in a form that will be more interesting to my intimates.

On leaving Scotland, we passed by Melrose and Abbotsford to Newcastle There I descended into the coal mine, a somewhat rare feat for a lady. Thence to York and Sheffield and yesterday here, arriving about 2 this morn.

I find pleasure in every step of the way. There is every thing to see. My companions are most kind and we get on harmoniously. I find a surprising number of persons who not only receive me warmly, but have a preconceived strong desire to know me. This is founded mostly on their knowledge of "Woman in the 19th &c" Among these a number of intellectual and cultivated men of whom I shall hereafter speak to you. I may add that from their habits of conversation so superior to those of Americans, I am able to come out a great deal more than I can at home, and they seem to be proportionately interested.

So much for self, such particulars as I cannot write to others and know to be most interesting at home. This letter is necessarily a short one, as I write in the only hour of leisure I shall have before the steamer of 4th Octr I am very anxious to hear from you all again now and hope to find letters waiting in London. I want most to hear of dear Mother's arm, whether all is doing well; with her Next to that of yourself. My feeling is rather a hope that you may not go to the [West?] yet am not sure but I am wrong about it. I am partly selfish, unwilling that you should go away. Of the two other alternatives, it does seem that, if you should must be disappointed with Henry it *may* lead more to your happiness, as the country is so much more congenial to you than Boston.[1] I do not, however, feel able, at this distance to have a decisive view, but leave all in confidence to destiny believing that *no way* will it turn out *ill* with one like you. Shall however be anxious to know the result. Get *thin paper* when you write; letters are paid for by weight and the next may have to follow me in my journies.

My next will be to Mother. Love to Ellen Arthur and Lloyd. Heaven bless and keep yourself, dear Richard prays always your sister

M.

(MH: fMS Am 1086 [9:136])
1. Henry Holton Fuller (1790–1852), their uncle, in whose office Richard was working.

127. To Evert A. Duyckinck

London
30th Octr 1846.

Dear Mr Duyckinck,

The letter which I intended to write you dwindles into a note, for many as were my interruptions in N.Y. they scarcely enabled me to form a notion of those inevitable to a London life. The only way of escape is *to hide*,— this is what I tried to do today in order to writing some notes by Mr Welford, yet here it is three o clock before I can put pen to paper.[1]

Yet I like London, like England *very* much and have already formed so many interesting connections that I do not feel that I could be content to return to the U. S. without passing some time here again. Indeed I may come and pass some time here for the purpose of writing. Several fine openings have been made for me where I might have taken up important subjects and published my view in excellent places, but I cannot now possibly get time to write without sacrificing many valuable opportunities of learning. A year hence will not be too late.

I have been recd here with a warmth that surprized me; it is chiefly to Women in the 19th &c that I am indebted for this; that little volume has been read and prized by many. It is a real misfortune to me that Mr Wiley took the course he did about my miscellanies; the vols have been kindly recd but every one mentions their being *thin*; the arrangement, too, that obliged me to leave out all I had written on Continental lite[rature] was very unfortunate for me. I have reason to feel daily how much use it would have been to me if these essays and others of a radical stamp were now before the readers and that a false impression has been given here of the range and scope of my efforts. However it is of some use to have those that are printed with me now, though I have constantly to regret the absence of some I intended to insert as now is just the time for them to make their mark here. I have seen some persons of celebrity and others that will attain it ere long. I wish I had time to write of this, but, as it is, must refer to the Tribune for such slight and public sketches as there is now time to make. Mr Mathews made me promise to write to him of those to whom he gave me letters, but I have seen none of them except Mr Horne and him only once, as he has been almost all the time in Ireland.[2] Miss Barrett has just *eloped* with Browning; she had to elope, Mr Horne says, from a severe hard father.[3] The influence of this father seems to have been crushing. I hope she may now be happy and well; perhaps I shall see them (i e her and Browning) in Italy. Mr Tupper I missed through an unlucky misunderstanding as to the time of his visit.[4] The others are, probably, out of town.

If you see Mr Godwin, please tell him that Hugh Doherty is here and that I see much of him and Dr Wilkinson of Swedenborgian celebrity and like them exceedingly.[5] In connection with the Howitts I see very pleasant persons and they, themselves, are very pleasant.

Now I must stop for lack of time, though much there is to say. Will you write to me at Paris. I shall be there in a week, your brother, if there, can hear of me at Galignani's. I shall leave my address there, and shall stay a month or more. In Rome Torlonia is our banker. Will you be so kind as to send three sets of the "Papers on Literature and Art" to *Richard F. Fuller, 6 State St. Boston.* I will write him what to do with them. Please give my best regards to Mr Mathews. I should like much to hear from him, too, if he has time Letters are a true favor to me, now when *I* have no time to earn them.

Very truly yours

MARGARET FULLER.

Pray tell me a great deal if you write or rather let me say *when* you write

There are some copies of "Summer on the Lakes" still at Graham's Tribune Building could you not induce Mr Wiley to send some of them here on sale with my other book. I have given away two or three here and people seem interested in the book.

Tell me if there is anything special about which I might inquire for you or do any thing for you in *my* way.

Tell me if Mr Murdock is succeeding.[6] I see something of a young actress here who would be worth catching for America, if there were any Goethe to train her. She has great natural resources.

(NN-M)

1. Charles Welford (1815?–85) was a book importer in London.

2. Cornelius Mathews (1817–89) was a member of the Young America group of writers, associated with Duyckinck. Fuller published part of his play *Witchcraft* as an appendix to *Papers on Literature and Art,* though she did not identify its author. Richard Henry Horne (1803–84) was a playwright and poet, who, like Mathews, was a friend of Elizabeth Barrett.

3. Elizabeth Barrett married Robert Browning on 12 September and left for Italy on the 19th. Fuller had reviewed her work and included the essay in *Papers.* Barrett's father, Edward

Barrett Moulton-Barrett, was indeed an unforgiving man. In 1851 he returned all the letters his daughter had written him with the seals unbroken.

4. Martin Farquhar Tupper (1810–89) wrote a very popular volume, *Proverbial Philosophy* (1838).

5. Parke Godwin (1816–1904), a writer, editor, and translator, was William Cullen Bryant's son-in-law. Fuller knew and liked him in New York City. Hugh Doherty was a British writer and editor of the *London Phalanx,* a Fourierist newspaper. James John Garth Wilkinson (1812–99) was a homeopathic physician, a disciple of Swedenborg, a friend of both the elder Henry James and Emerson.

6. James Edward Murdoch (1811–93) was an actor and teacher.

128.   To Caroline Sturgis

[16? November 1846]

[ ] I find how true for me was the lure that always drew me towards Europe. It was no false instinct that said I might here find an atmosphere needed to develope me in ways *I* need. Had I only come ten years earlier; now my life must ever be a failure, so much strength has been wasted on obstructions which only came because I was not in the soil most fitted to my nature, however, though a failure, it is less so than with most others and the matter not worth thinking about. Heaven has room enough and good chances enough in store, no doubt, and I can live a great deal in the years that remain.

As soon as I got to England, I found how right we were in supposing there was elsewhere a greater range of interesting character among the men, than with us. I do not find, indeed, any so valuable as three or four among the most marked we have known, no Waldo, none so beautiful as William when he is *the angel,* more like Charles on the Egyptian side, none so beauty-ful as S. was when he *was Raphael,* but so many that are strongly individual and have a fund of hidden life.

In Westmoreland I knew and have since been seeing in London, a man such as would interest you a good deal; his name is Atkinson, some call him the "Prince of the English Mesmerizers" and he has the fine instinctive nature you may suppose from that.[1]

He is a man about thirty, in the fulness of his powers, body and mind. He is tall and firmly formed, his head of the Christ-like sort as seen by Leonardo, mild and composed, but powerful and sagacious. He does not think, but perceives and acts. He is intimate with the artists, having studied architecture himself as a profession, but has some fortune on which he lives, sometimes stationary and acting in the affairs of other men, sometimes wandering about the world and learning. He seems bound by no tie, yet looks as if he had children in every place.

I saw also a man, an artist, severe and antique in his spirit; he seemed burdened by the sorrows of aspiration, yet very calm, as secure in the justice of Fate. What he does is bad, but full of a great desire. His name is Scott. I saw also another, a pupil of De la Roche, very handsome, and full of a voluptuous enjoyment of Nature; him I liked a little in a different way.[2]

By far the most beauteous person I have seen is Joseph Mazzini. If you ever see "Sanders People's Journal," you can read articles by him that will give you some notion of his mind, especially one on his friends the two Bandieras and Rufini, headed "Italian Martyrs.—He is one in whom holiness has purified, but nowhere dwarfed the man. I shall make a little sketch of him in a public way for the Tribune. I do not like to say more of him here now. I can do it better when I have seen him more, which I shall do in the course of time.

I saw some girls in London that interested me. Anna Howitt, daughter of W. and Mary Howitt about 22 has chosen the profession of an artist; she has an honorable ambition, talent, and is what is called a sweet pretty girl.[3] Margaret Gillies is older; she has given up many things highly valued by English women to devote herself to Art, and attained quite a high place in the profession; her pictures are full of grace, rather sentimental, but that she is trying to shake off.[4] For the rest she is an excellent, honest girl. But the one whom I like *very* much is Eliza Fox, only daughter of the celebrated W. J.[5] She is about five and twenty; she also is an artist and has begun a noble independent life. she seems very strong and simple, yet delicate in the whole tissue of her. I could not find time to talk with her as I wanted but whenever I did she grew upon me. Whenever I did I thought of you and Jane and lamented that you did not embark on the wide stream of the world as artists, then all that has been so beautiful in your lives would have been embodied for others, too, who needed it so much. Eliza has a friend, also an English woman, now living at Rome of whom she spoke with such cordial esteem that I shall look for her when there. they both have had a great deal to contend with. They say men *will not* teach girls drawing with any care, and beside they find it so difficult to get chances to draw from living models.

I saw another fine girl; she was not an artist, but has a great deal of life, and she is so tall, strong and beautiful, like the nymphs. But there is not room to tell you about *her* or much about any thing.

The three months in England were months of the most crowded life, especially the six weeks in London. I came here, resolved to rest, for I am almost sick. A strange place to rest, some would think, but till my letters are presented no one knows me, and I shall not send them for some days. We are *getting dressed* (I do not wonder as I look around me here at the devotion of a French woman to her *mise* it is truly *deliceuse* as they call it with

that absurd twinkle of their pretty eyes.) Rachel is acting.[6] I have a letter
to her and one to George Sand, but I do not want to see them, till I get to
speaking French a little. Today we have come to our private lodging a very
cheerful elegant apartment in the Hotel Rougement, where I shall speak
French all the time, beside taking a master, and I hope to improve a good
deal in a few days. Goodnight, as this must wait till next Steamer I shall
add to it just before sending.

(MB)

   1. Henry George Atkinson (1812–84), a phrenologist and mesmerist, was long a friend of
Harriet Martineau.
   2. David Scott (1806–49) was a Scottish artist. Hippolyte Paul Delaroche (1797–1856), a
French painter, founded the Eclectic school. His pupil whom Fuller met was probably
Edward Armitage (1817–96), later known for his frescoes.
   3. Anna Mary Howitt (1824–84) was a writer, artist, and spiritualist.
   4. Margaret Gillies (1803–87) worked in watercolors. She did portraits of Wordsworth
and Dickens.
   5. William Johnson Fox (1786–1864), a liberal Unitarian reformer, was prominent as an
orator for the Anti-Corn Law League.
   6. Rachel (1820–58), born Élisa Félix, excelled in tragic roles. The most celebrated actress of her time, she restored the Comédie-Française to prominence.

129.   To Mary Howitt

Rome
18th April, 1847.

My dear Mrs Howitt

   A letter received from you just before leaving Paris, ought to have been
answered much earlier, but the truth is I have not known exactly how to
answer. The biographical sketches you asked of me, it would be highly
agreeable to me to make and had I recd the letter long enough before
leaving Paris, I should have made the attempt. I did not know but there
might again here be intervals whether of bad weather or from any other
cause which might give me the leisure and chance for concentrating my
interest on these subjects. But such do not come, and I begin to feel that
they will not till I am settled again next winter

   I have such opportunities now of learning and seeing what may never
be before me again that I cannot bear to lose them and I feel that I shall
be so much better fitted to write after them that I am hardly willing to at
present.

   Especially as to the memoir of George Sand I have learned and thought

so much about her position while in France and find the subject to in-
volve so much and so difficult to be treated exactly to my mind that I cannot do it except just at the right moment and when circumstances favor
my being undisturbed to fix my mind full and strong upon it. It is a thing
I shall do, no doubt, but I may be too late for you, as you want it in connexion with these translations of Miss Hays.[1]

All this being so uncertain as to time, on my part, you will, probably,
prefer to ask some other person. But, if you do not find one that suits you,
and, of course, you will not want a sketch of a figure so important to our
era unless you like it much, I can say that it is my present plan to return to
Paris next winter and that then I shall probably be willing to engage for
sketches of George Sand, La Mennais, and, if you wish, them Beranger
and Le Roux.[2] I have some ideas which please me in relation to all four.
But I do not care to express them unless I can do so to my mind, and in
consecutive sketches.

In case you ask another, the best engraved portrait of George Sand is
from the picture by Charpentier but none of them are good.[3] They all
make her face too coarse or too tragic. She has really a noble face, and
not tragic at all.

Of La Mennais David the Sculptor owns the best engraving.[4] I was told
it is now needful to apply to him by writing, if you want a copy. This is hear
say. I could not find in the shops a good one for myself and had no time
to write to M. David after receiving yr letter before leaving Paris.

At the same time that you wrote to me first about your Journal, Mazzini
wrote to me about the Peoples I thought at first it was the same request as
his name was on your list of contributors and answered in the affirmative.
I suppose it makes no difference to you as the two journals have, of
course, different sets of readers. If I find any thing to write about Italy that
might seem of value to Mazzini, I will send it to him, if any thing more
likely to interest you, it shall be yours. But I hardly hope to write any
thing, the impressions are too numerous and important. I may not be
able to write of them at all till I am elsewhere.

Remember me to Mr Howitt and to Anna Mary. I hope happy hours in
Rome are in store for her. Please tell Miss Fox I have seen Miss Raincock,
but not yet her pictures.[5] Mr and Mrs S. and Eddie send much love, all are
very well now We always think in connection with you of others of your
friendly circle, of Dr Smith, the Misses Gillies, of Gertrude.[6] Will you write
a line to let me know how you all are and whether you shall ask another to
write the sketch of Me Sand and, if so, who it shall be. I am anxious
England should have one in the true feeling I should be proud and
pleased if it were for me to give it. Me Sand personally inspired me with

warm admiration and esteem; she would have done so, if I had read no word of hers. Adieu yours with friendliest faith and good will

MARGARET FULLER

I gave Mr Nicauel a French gentleman an introduction to you. If he delivers it you will find him possessed of valuable and accurate information as to the Parisian world.

Could you ascertain for me, whereabouts Mrs Browning, Elizh Barrett, is in Italy If I go near I am anxious to see her. Address me here Care Torlonia and Co.

(MeHi)

1. Matilda Hays's translation of Sand's *The Last Aldini*.
2. Félicité-Robert de Lamennais (1782–1854), whom Fuller met on the trip, was an ultramontane priest who became a Christian socialist. Pierre-Jean de Béranger (1780–1857), whose poetry Fuller had long admired, was also a liberal politician and a poet. Pierre Leroux (1797–1871) was a philosopher, journalist, and politician with whom Sand founded *La Revue indépendante*.
3. Auguste Charpentier (1813–80) was best known for his paintings of such writers and actors as Alexandre Dumas père, Sand, Rachel, and Sir Walter Scott.
4. Pierre-Jean David d'Angers (1788–1856), a sculptor, was known for his busts of Jeremy Bentham, Goethe, and Victor Hugo and for his medallions of contemporary writers.
5. Sophia Raincock, a painter, lived in Rome from 1847 to 1873.
6. Thomas Southwood Smith (1788–1861) was an Edinburgh minister, doctor, philanthropist, and reformer to whom Jeremy Bentham left his body. Smith kept the skeleton fully dressed in his office. Mary Leman Gillies (1800–1870) was a writer. Gertrude Hill (1837–1923), Smith's granddaughter, married George Henry Lewes's son.

130.   To Mary Rotch

Rome
23d May 1847.

Dear Aunt Mary,

it is very long since I have written, but very often that I think of you. This is such a rich book, this of Europe, I know not how to spare time from studying it to write to my friends at home. Yet I hope their love and thoughts follow me. I know yours do. Beside your two letters, I have heard of you through W. Channing, Mother and others; very sweet to me was your little intercourse with Mother; it gave her a great deal of pleasure; do see her again if you go to Boston.

The only thing wanting in your letters has been that you should speak more particularly of your health. Although I know it must be better or you could not do the things I hear of your doing, I want to know particularly about it. Will you not write to me of that and our other topics of mutual interest and direct to care of *Greene and Co* Paris. I think now I shall remain abroad another year. I cannot content myself without;— a single year is so entirely inadequate to see all which I wish to see.

All winter in Paris, although my life was rich in novelties of value, I was not well; the climate was too damp for me, and then I had too much intellectual excitement of the same kind as at home. I need a respite, a long leisure of enjoyment, a kind of springtime to renovate my faculties. But Paris is the very focus of the intellectual activity of Europe, there I found every topic intensified, clarified, reduced to portable dimensions: there is the cream of all the milk, but I am not strong enough to live on cream, at present. I learned much, I suffered to leave Paris, but I find myself better here, where the climate is so enchanting, the people so indolently joyous, and the objects of contemplation so numerous and admirable, that one cannot pass the time better than by quietly *looking* one's fill. It is entirely the [ ] of the Past. The tendency of the present Pope to Reform gives an interest by drawing out the feelings of the people, but it is not sufficient to affect importantly the state of things in Italy which presents the most striking contrast to that of our country, and, *as* a contrast, is for the time desirable especially for me who find invitation to a trance of repose here.[1] Its influence is so good that I have had the headach only twice during a two months' abode in Rome and I am really strong now.

How I wish, dear Aunt Mary, that you could come to Europe with Mary and, if it was not for the voyage, the rest would not be difficult. When Mary does come, let it be with very sure friends. My travelling companions are extremely amiable, else should I suffer, for the friction of travelling is very great upon the temper.

Of the gorgeous pageant of the Roman church, I have now seen enough to be thoroughly sated It is imposing often, but oftener frivolous, and must I think be very oppressive to the present Pope, who seems truly a thoughtful noble minded man. I shall tell one or two good anecdotes of him in my next letter to the Tribune.

And now adieu, dear Aunt Mary, and Mary. I had but a quarter of an hour today to write this letter just to say dont forget to think affectionately of yours in the distance

MARGARET.

(MH: fMS Am 1086 [9:131])

1. Giovanni Maria Mastai-Ferretti (1792–1878) became Pope Pius IX in 1846 and immediately raised hopes for liberal political reforms. Fuller wrote: "He is a man of noble and good aspect, who, it is easy to see, has set his heart upon doing something solid for the benefit of Man." Her early enthusiasm made her later disgust with Pius all the more severe.

131.   To Richard F. Fuller

Casa Greca
via Sa Apollonia
Florence,
1st July 1847

My dear Richard,

I cannot remember when I wrote last, but it must have been some weeks ago; the two months passed at Rome seemed but a moment; the five weeks since have been equally crowded; my utmost strength and spirits suffice only to seize a very small portion of what each day presents; the riches of Italy seem immeasurable and I cannot endure to go away without my fair share.

I have here recd and answered a letter from Arthur giving the family news. By some mistake our letters by the last steamer have not been sent here. I hope to find them at Venice where I shall arrive the 10th or 11th of this month, taking Ravenna, Bologna and Ferrara by the way. I hope much there will be one from you and one from Mother. I begin at moments to feel a yearning for the loved familiar faces, but I shall not yield to it.

My first object in this letter being business, I will write about that first as it is very important to me now and there is no knowing how many interruptions may occur to prevent my finishing the letter as I would.

Mr and Mrs Spring think now they shall go into Germany for only a few weeks. I do not wish to go in that hurried way, am equally unsatisfied to fly through Italy and shall therefore leave them in Switzerland take a servant to accompany me, and return hither and hence to Rome, for the autumn, perhaps the winter. I should always suffer the pain of Tantalus thinking of Rome, if I could not see it more thoroughly than I have as yet even begun to, for it was all *outside* the two months, just finding out where objects were. I had only just begun to live with their life when I was obliged to leave.

This prospect presents many charms, but it leaves me alone in the midst of a strange land. While with Mr S. he managed all my little affairs and, if my own money had failed, I could not have been at a loss. But now any failure in that way would place me in a desolate condition and I want to be *"forehanded"* and quite tranquil, at least on that side, for there is no one in Italy to whom I should feel entitled to go for aid. Arthur has written me that the death of Uncle Abraham makes it possible to raise some money for me soon if I want it.[1] If you can now get five hundred dollars for me, either advanced by Mother or otherwise, I want it remitted direct to *Greene and Co Bankers, Paris*. I say if you *can*, but truly I depend upon it, and I believe dear Mother will let me have it, if there is no better way. You will receive this letter early in August. I want you to remit by the steamer of 15th August [the] money to Greene and Co and have a credit sent to me here at

Florence to care of J. Mozier Esq. Sculptor.[2] I shall come to his house when I return here in Septr. And write to me yourself, dear R. at the same time.

I say no more but rely on your affection and business habits that I shall not suffer anxiety and annoyance here alone amid strangers A credit from Greene and Co is the same as money. There are other ways, but I want the most simple taken, as I have not much head for these things.

I find myself happily situated here in many respects. The Marchioness *Arconati Visconti*, to whom I brought a letter from a friend of hers in France has been good to me as a sister and introduced me to many interesting acquaintance.[3] But this Me Arconati is herself the most interesting The sculptors Greenough and Powers I have seen much and well, other acquaintance I possess less known to fame, but not less attractive.[4] Florence is not like Rome; at first I could not bear the change, yet for the study of the fine arts, it is a still richer place. Worlds of thought have risen in my mind, some time you will have light from all these stars. Meanwhile I must pause it is almost dark. I have no more time. Write now on single sheets like this and without envelope; they charge in Italy enormous postage and not by weight but on each piece of paper. Adieu my beloved brother; all the family be specially remembered if I have not room to say Love. Forgive all omissions now in my letters; they are inevitable My next will be to Mother.

Ever yours

MARGARET

(MH: fMS Am 1086 [9:138])

1. At his death on 6 April, Abraham Williams Fuller had an estate exceeding $80,000, but Margaret received only $214.28.

2. Joseph Mozier (1813–70) was a Vermont businessman turned sculptor, who permanently settled in Italy in 1845. Though he and Fuller were friendly, he besmirched her memory to Hawthorne years later.

3. Costanza Trotti Bentivoglio (1800–1871) married the marchese Giuseppe Arconati-Visconti (1797–1873) in 1818. She was devoted to Italian independence and was Fuller's closest European friend.

4. Hiram Powers (1805–73), a sculptor, moved to Italy in 1837. Fuller came to know him well.

132. To Caroline Sturgis

Bellagio,
Lake of Como, 22d August 47.

Dearest Carrie,

I am sorry you never write. I often wish to hear from you and then I am afraid you will get out of the habit of telling me any thing. It may be so long before we meet again.

I remember I wrote to you from Rome in the first weeks, when I was suffering terrible regrets and could not yet find myself at home in Italy. I do not know whether you ever received that letter, but if not, I could not go back upon those things.

Rome was much poisoned for me so, but, after a time; its genius triumphed and I became absorbed in its peculiar life. Again I suffered from parting, and have since resolved to return there and pass at least a part of the winter

People may write and prate as much as they like about Rome, they cannot convey thus a portion of its spirit. It must be inhaled wholly, with the yielding of the whole heart. It is really something transcendant, both spirit and body.

Those last glorious nights in which I wandered about amid the old walls and columns or sat by the fountains in the Piazza del Popolo, or by the river, seem worth an age of pain both after and before only one hates pain in Italy.

Tuscany I did not like so well; it is a great place to study thoughts, the history of character and art. Indeed there I did really begin to study as well as gaze and feel. But I did not like it. Florence is more in its spirit like Boston, than like an Italian city. I knew a good many Italians, but they were busy and intellectual, not like those I had known before. But Florence is full of really good, really great pictures. There first I really saw some of the great masters. Andrea del Sarto, in particular, one sees only there, and he is worth much. His wife, whom he always paints, and for whom he was so infatuated, reminds me of Mrs Greeley; she has just the same bad qualities, and in what is good the same wild nature, the same of what is called deviltry.[1]

Bologna charmed me. This is really an *Italian* city, one in which I should like to live, full of hidden things and also the wonders of art are very great there. The Caracci and their friends had vast force, not much depth, but enough force to occupy for a good while, and Dominichino, when great at all, is very great.[2]

At Bologna I saw a man who seems to me the type of some of George Sand's characters he knows her well.

Venice was a dream of enchantment! *there* was no disappointment, art and life are one, there is one glow of joy, one deep shade of passionate melancholy. Giorgione, as a man, I care more for now than any of the artists though he had no ideas.[3]

At Venice, the Springs left me, and it was high time, for I had become qui[te] insupportable I was always out of the body, and they, good friends, were *in*. I felt at times a wicked irritation against them for being the persons who took me away from France, which was no fault of theirs. Since I have been alone I ha[ve] grown reasonable again; indee[d] in [the] first week floating about in [a] go[nd]ola, I seemed to find myself again

I was not always alone in Venice, but have come through the fertile plains of Lombardy and counted its treasures seen the Lakes Garda and Maggiore, and a part of Switzerland alone, except for occasional episodes of companionship sometimes romantic enough. Especially [ ] takes me to heart in Europe, and more than ever in Italy.

In Milan I staid awhile and knew some radicals, young and interested in ideas. Here, on the lake, I have fallen into contact with some of the high society, duchesses, marquises and the like. My friend here is a marchioness who bears the name of *Visconti,* by my side I have formed connection with a fair and brilliant Polish lady, born princess *Radzivill,* it is rather pleasant to come a little on the traces of these famous histories, also both these ladies take pleasure in telling me of spheres so unlike mine and do it well. The life here on the lake is precisely what we once at Newbury imagined as being so pleasant; these people have charming villas and gardens on the lake, adorned with fine works of art; they go to see one another in boats; you can be all the time in a boat, if you like. If you want more excitement or wild flowers you climb the mountains. I have been here sometime and shall stay a week longer. I have found soft repose here. Then I return to Rome seeing many things on the way. Do write to me *Care of Greene and Co Paris.* I want a letter from you and am ever yours in love

MARGARET.

I shall go back to Paris by and by, but do not yet know precisely when. If you write soon after receiving this I shall get the letter in R[ome].

(MH: bMS Am 1221 [252])

1. Fuller had long admired the work of Andrea del Sarto (1486–1531), who married Lucrezia del Fede (1490?–1570). Fuller knew of her through Giorgio Vasari's spiteful description of her.

2. The Carracci were a family of Bolognese painters—Agostino, Annibale, and Ludovico—who founded the Accademia degli Incamminati. Their exploration of "eclecticism" influenced such painters as Il Domenichino, Guido Reni, and Claude Lorrain.

3. Il Giorgione (Giorgio Barbarelli) (ca. 1478–1511) was a Venetian painter who influenced Titian.

133. To Margarett C. Fuller

Rome, 514 Corso.
2d etage.
16th Octr 1847.

Dearest Mother,

Here I am, fairly installed in a home that promises to be permanent for six months. You cannot guess how rejoiced I am! During the three months I travelled in the north of Italy, was upon the lakes and in Switzerland— my enjoyments were great and many, my privileges extraordinary, but my sufferings were commensurate. On the bright side the weather was beautiful and the heat less than is usual in an Italian summer. I made many and ardent friends, of all ranks, from the very highest to the lowest; the Italians sympathize with my character and understand my organization, as no other people ever did; they admire the ready eloquence of my nature, and highly prize my intelligent sympathy (such as they do not find often in foreigners) with their sufferings in the past and hopes for the future. It will take me weeks when I return to give you sketches of the persons and stories I learnt at that time. I also learnt a vast deal of the history and art of Italy. I found myself far better situated to be travelling alone, as now I was thrown constantly with foreigners who would tell me what I wanted to know, and with whom I made progress in the language. My mind made a vast stride in these three months, and my perception of beauty was all the keener for the sickly nervous state I was in. Yet that sickliness was the darkest shade on the other side. I had continually attacks of cholera which prostrated my strength as nothing ever did before. I could find no medicine, no food that suited me. When I rose up if I took any thing to sustain me, it caused fever. One time I was so ill that I was afraid I should die on the road, and nobody know it but my courier, a brutal wretch who robbed and injured me all he could under the mask of obsequiousness. He wasted a good deal of money for me, before I could learn how to prevent it. At present I understand well, all that is needed for Italian travel and can never be so situated again. When I leave here I shall take precautions of which once I did not dream.

I felt often very anxious about money. Grateful as I am for Uncle A's bequest, and for its coming just when needed to save me from a check in all my plans which would have been so bitter, it was not enough. If he had left me ten or even five thousand dollars I should have been so happy, for money now is all I want, firm health I see I cannot have; it is too late. I have been sometimes much encouraged, but am sure now that my health will never stand against shocks and difficulties. But more money would, in a great measure, free me from them. Let me thank you here for your prompt attention to my wishes about money. You are always the same. I received the five hundred dollars in Florence There I was detained for a time by illness, the sequel of all I had in the north. But I was with good friends who nursed me with refined care and tenderness, and when I began to revive, saw that I had repose, proper nourishment and gentle exercise, and did for me those little things needed before I could come away. The name of these friends is Mozier they were originally from Ohio. Mr M. is a man of fortune, who has taken to sculpture from love, and shows promise of much excellence; his wife a very good and sweet woman.

I arrived here some days ago, having seen the Tuscan vintage, which disappointed me; it is delightful to eat the grapes fresh from the vines, and the mild-eyed Tuscan peasants seem very pleasant and joyous but the Italian landscape in autumn is so sere and brown, so different from ours or even that of England, I longed for the accustomed shows of earth, beneath these serene heavens, in this lovely light. I saw also Sienna, one of those true Italian towns, where the old charm is unbroken. I came here some days ago, and after a good deal of search, have taken charming rooms. They are on the Corso, so that I see all that goes on in Rome, near the Pincian Mount, Piazza del Popolo, and Villa Borghese, so that I have for every day the pleasantest walks of Rome. The rooms are elegantly furnished, everything in the house so neat, more like England than Italy, service excellent, every thing arranged with a reasonable economy, and at fixed prices for all the six months. I have my books, my flowers, every thing leads me to hope the six months of quiet occupation I want, here is glorious Rome, where all the pleasures I most value, so rich and exalting, are within my reach. The only drawback is a little danger from the character and position of my hostess. She was formerly the mistress of a man of quality who loved her so much that she made him marry her before his death, so that she is a Marchioness, but not received into society. The bankers who chose my apartments with me thought this no objection, nor will it be, if she lets me alone enough, but she is a most insinuating creature and disposed to pet me too much. I am a little afraid of her going too far, so that if I should be obliged to decline any overture from her, she will be angry and hate me. But if we can get along I like her much; she has black eyes and red hair like Aunt Martha, a pretty color and fine skin, very graceful manners, and speaks Italian beautifully, which is a good practice for me. She has introduced to me her present lover. He is a distinguished Italn artist, who has been devoted to her for some years. He is an officer of note in the newly organized Civic guard, and will bring all the news to the house, he is also very agreeable.[1] Of course I seem to ignore all these circumstances; he appears here merely as a friend and visitor, and if she observes strict good sense and propriety in her relations with me, all will go on well, but the ground is a little delicate I hope however all will go well; every thing else promises so sweetly. I am now very well, and the air of Rome seems to agree with me, as it did before. I shall not write to my family oftener than once a month, as I must apply all my strength now to gather the fruit of my travels, but hope you will not put too great an interval between your letters. I am very glad you are at Cincini and hope from you some detailed acct of Wm and

Fanny and their little ones. Remember me most affecy to them and feel me ever with warmest love your daughter

M.

P.S.

I ought to observe to give you a clearer idea of my position with the Marchioness, that the custom of Rome is to take your apartment, and live entirely separate from the family to whom the house belongs. The house is divided into suites; they occupy one, each tenant, or family of tenants another. I did not expect even to see [her] except when I paid my bills. But it is her pleasure to come in and arrange my flowers, and serve me at table, which she does standing! and yesterday when I had the headach to attend me. I think she will do this less, when I cease to be a new toy, and she sees how seriously I am occupied, and then matters will arrange themselves.

A flood of joy came over me when I was able at last to see Rome again. To live here, alone and independent, to really draw in the spirit of Rome, Oh! what joy! I know so well how to prize it that I think Heaven will not allow anything to disturb me! My protecting ang[els] have been very tender of late and led me carefully out of every difficulty.

Do not fail when you write to tell me how your arm is. I have not heard this great while

(MH: fMS Am 1086 [9:140])

1. The creation of a civic guard was central to self-rule for the citizens of Rome. It was regarded as among the most important reforms of Pius's early career.

IV

A Time Such as I Always Dreamed Of

1848–1850

It is a time such as I always dreamed of, and for long secretly hoped to see.

We know little of Fuller's return to Rome in the autumn of 1847 save that by January 1848 she was undoubtedly pregnant, though perhaps not yet married. Coincident with her state was the eruption of revolution, not only in the Italian states but across all of Europe. In January and February several Italian states began to create constitutions, Pius publicly supported the movement, and then, on 24 February, the French revolted and deposed Louis-Philippe. On 13 March, Metternich was overthrown in Austria, and even the German states showed signs of revolution. Milan ousted the Austrians and Charles Albert declared war, so the spring had brought an unbroken series of triumphs for the liberal and radical reformers.

Fuller documented these developments in her *Tribune* letters, providing an American audience with a firsthand account written by a woman who spoke the languages and knew some of the participants in the revolutions. As her pregnancy developed, so did the aspirations of the Italians, but crises were quick to come: on 29 April 1848 Pius publicly denounced the war on Austria and made it clear that he would not support a war or go further in reforms, and Charles Albert soon lost decisive battles to the Austrians. Thus the momentum was lost just as Fuller had to leave Rome for the Abruzzi mountains to have her child. She had told no one of her condition, and she was completely alone, save for occasional visits by Ossoli, who could not absent himself from Rome for long.

On 5 September Angelo Eugene Ossoli was born. Fuller stayed through the fall with him in her retreat in Rieti, but in November she left the child with a nurse and returned to Rome. Shortly after that, Pius fled Rome for the Kingdom of Naples, and a Roman republic was formed by the election of a constituent assembly, which asked Mazzini to become its leader. In the spring of 1849 Fuller not only was in the midst of a revolution, she

255

knew personally the man at its head. Not surprisingly, the pope appealed to the European powers to restore him, and the French, despite their status as a republic, responded with an assault against Rome. Fuller served as a nurse in a hospital, tending the wounded, while Ossoli fought with the Civic Guard. It was a harrowing time, for the French bombarded Rome severely, and by the first of July 1849 they crushed the resistance.

Fuller and Ossoli fled, first to Rieti, where they found Angelo half dead of neglect, and then to Florence, where the political life under the grand duke of Tuscany was moderate. There Fuller and Ossoli had their one all-too-brief period of normal married life, living openly as a family. When Fuller broke the news about Ossoli and Nino to her family and friends in the United States, she caused a sensation, for the inevitable speculation and gossip quickly blossomed. Florence brought Fuller friendship with Robert and Elizabeth Browning, whose poetry she had reviewed in her earlier writing. She also completed a history of the Italian revolutions, a manuscript based on her participation, on her knowledge of history, and on her friendship with many of the participants in Rome and elsewhere. She made some attempt to publish it in London but decided that it must wait for an American publisher.

The Ossolis were destitute and politically suspect: he, of course, was estranged from his family, who were in the papal service; Fuller was a foreigner. By early 1850 she decided to take the family to the United States and resume her career as a writer. Though deathly afraid of ocean travel, she booked passage on a sailing ship, for the safer steamers were prohibitively expensive. She made her good-byes and set sail with her husband and child, first for Leghorn and then for New York, on the barque *Elizabeth,* Captain Seth Hasty in command. After leaving Leghorn, Hasty fell ill with smallpox and died, leaving the command to the mate, Henry Bangs. After burying Hasty at sea at Gibraltar, Bangs sailed on, arriving off the coast of New York on 19 July 1850.   In a heavy storm, he misjudged his location; the ship struck a sandbar off Fire Island during the night. Several of the passengers and crew survived the high seas, but the next day Margaret, Ossoli, and Angelo were drowned. Only the child's body was recovered. The book manuscript disappeared.

These letters capture the most intense time of Fuller's life: pregnancy, birth, war, and departure. Readers can here follow her emotions and health as she approaches the birth of her son; we can see how traumatic the subsequent separation was, and we can know at first hand the dangers she and Ossoli faced during the siege. After that ordeal, their stay in Florence seems almost idyllic, even if it was a harsh, unusually cold winter. Letters to Carrie Sturgis, to her sister, Ellen, and to her mother show Fuller as mother and wife, roles she gladly assumed. Finally, the letters show Fuller's hopes of resuming her career, hopes that were ended only by a stroke of fate.

134. To Richard F. Fuller

Rome, 17th March, 1848.

My very dear Richard,

Today I receive your letter of 6th Feby. I had already answered that of 31st Jany, but not sent my letter to the post, and now I will condense its substance into this.

Your view of your relation with Henry seems to me just and corresponds with what I have known of him.[1] I do not think it can be for your interest to remain there. Yet do not for my sake break quite yet. I am anxious you should for a few months remain in Boston, and secure of your own subsistence. I should feel very desolate here, if I had not you to write to, able to do what is needful for me there. I will not be a restraint upon you long, but should like to feel sure you will be in Boston up to December of this year.

As to your going to the West, my instinct is not in favor of your doing so. From what I know of the west and of you it does not seem to me your true sphere. Yet I may be wrong, and if *you* were *entirely sure* it were best for you, I could have nothing to say against it.

With regard to my living with you on a farm, it is a project that presents great charms to my imagination. Amid the corrupt splendors of the old world, I begin to pine for the pure air of my native land. Near sight of potentates and powers, the achievements of talent and great events only makes the very private simple sphere seem more attractive. I should be more likely to be content with such a life as you propose than ever before. I should like very much to live with you. And I agree that it is most undesirable for me to remain in a field, where the excitements of the hour use up my strength and prevent my doing any thing of permanent value, where I am ill paid, and where I *could* live but a very little longer, for my strength is almost spent. I would give almost any thing else for freedom from care and the most simple, congenial life. Or if not wholly congenial, yet at least unconstrained.

But could we *have* such freedom? I do not know enough about these farming affairs to judge *why*, but, of the many in our country who try these experiments, almost all fail. It seems to me that devotion to the interests of a farm, and much physical force in the members of a family are necessary to a tolerable economic result. In the last of these no persons, accustomed to an intellectual life, are rich. As to money, apart from the world, if I could earn enough to provide for my own personal expenses, and a stout servant for us both, it would be all I could expect. As to personal exertion I could order the accounts, give an air of comfort to the house, but as to *work*, that could not be I was never educated to it, and my natural delicacy is greatly increased now. A little exercise, a few arrangements are all to which I am equal. (I keep writing words wrong speaking and hearing constantly Italian I much forget my English.)

Thus it stands with me. Should I live, should I return to my native country and free, and you were satisfied on these points I think *I* should like the plan.

But there are reasons why I cannot answer positively till the autumn of this year.[2] There are circumstances and influences now at work in my life, not likely to find their issue till then. If you still wish it, I think [I] shall [b]e able to answer by October of this year. Meanwhile you can keep the subject before you and write to me from time to time, what you think.

I feel afraid you may sometime love in a quarter that will make you regret having made choice of this narrow path when it is too late to change. Try fully to weigh this chance also.

I remember once when we lived in the Brattle house I was with Eugene in the garden and he said, "Our family star has taken an unfavorable turn; father had always luck in aid of his efforts till now; now his fortunes begin to decline and we shall never be lucky any more." I thought of this the other day after after reading Arthur's letter and yours. We are never wholly sunk by storms, but no favorable wind ever helps our voyages to surprising good results. Eugene, I do hope, has found, after all his tribulation, the humble content he craves, but a little ill health, or unfavorable crisis in affairs could give him great trouble. Wm gets along, but seems likely never to do more. Ellen has wed herself to difficulties from which only the death of her husband could free her. Arthur, I had thought would have outward prosperity, but his calamity hangs on him like a cloud. Fortune does not yet favor you. I doubt your life like mine will be a battle. May you have greater physical energy to sustain it. My courage has at last given way, beneath a three months headach and the deep disappointment of my plans for the employment of my [winter at Rome I] have earned no money I have done nothing. My plans are at a stand. I am tired of life and feel unable to face the future. But this last four or five days I am free from headach and cough; the physician assures me I shall be better so soon as the rains cease, which they seem resolved never to. Rain we have had from 16th Dec till now this 17th March. But when I *do* feel better, I will write again; no doubt things will look differently. I have learnt an immense deal, if ever I could have the force to make use of it. Meanwhile my dear brother, living or dying your affec sister and friend

M.

When you write to Mother say I am anxious to hear from her particularly and shall write soon. When does she return to N. England?

(MH: fMS Am 1086 [9:147])

1. As usual, Richard was quarreling with their uncle Henry Holton Fuller.
2. Fuller was at this time several months pregnant and knew the child was due in the autumn.

135. To Richard F. Fuller

Rome 20th May, 1848.

My dear brother,

I have been hoping to receive a letter from you, before leaving Rome, but if it does not come today, I shall not hear, perhaps for a fortnight. Tomorrow I go into the mountains, and, in those remote country towns, shall be able to get my letters only at irregular intervals. I shall employ a friend to get them from the banker here and send them to me when he can.

My health is much revived by the spring, here as gloriously beautiful as the winter was dreary. We know nothing of spring in our country; here the soft and brilliant weather is unbroken, except now and then by a copious shower which keeps every thing fresh. The trees, the flowers, the bird-songs are in perfection. I have enjoyed greatly my walks in the Villas here whose grounds are of three or four miles in extent, and like free nature in the wood glades and still paths, while they have an added charm in the music of their many fountains and the soft gleam here and there of sarcophagus or pillar. I have also been a few days at Albano, and explored its beautiful environs alone to much greater advantage than I could last year in the carriage with my friends. I have been to Frascati and Ostia with an English family who had a good carriage and were kindly intelligent people, who could not disturb the Roman landscape.

Now I am going into the country, where I can live very cheaply, even keeping a servant of my own, without which I should not venture alone into the unknown and wilder regions. I do not travel this summer, though I have recd several good invitations for several reasons, a sufficient one is the agitated state of Europe. I hope the pure air of the mountains will strengthen me and that I shall be able to write, but we can only know by trying. I have been so disappointed in my Roman winter, I dare not plan and hop[e] decisively again. I have suffered much with Rome, and her enervating breath still paralyzes my body, but in soul I know and love her profoundly and do hope, my dear Richard, you will see her sometime. The expression "City of the Soul" does indeed designate her and her alone.[1]

jects that have engaged my attention for some time back. But who knows?
The disturbances of the times, or an unfavorable state of health may mar
my purpose as has often happened before.

You will have seen my account of the measures by which the Pope has
lost all substantial influence in Italy and Europe.[2] There is something fatal
in a priestly environment: he remained a layman to so late an age one
might have hoped he would not get stupified by the incense of the
church, but remember how things looked beneath the open heavens. But
the influence of the crafty priests that surrounded him was unhappily too
much for his strength. However God has blessed his good intent and a
work is begun which his failure cannot check.

I hear often from Waldo; he sees much, learns much always but loves
not Europe.[3] There is no danger of the idle intimations of other minds al-
tering his course more than of the moving a star. He knows himself and
his vocation.

Goodbye, dear Aunt Mary, if I live, you will always hear from me now
and then. Give my love to Maria Rotch Tell her there is not a Jesuit in Italy
that would venture to give so plausible a version of Catholicism as
Coolidge Shaw: he is quite sincere, but not to be trusted as a thinker.[4]
Love to Mary. Best wishes ever for the continuance of peace and the increase of joy to both from

.   MARGARET.

(MH: fMS Am 1086 [9:145])

1. Andrew Robeson (1787–1862) was a wealthy New Bedford businessman; Martha Robeson Tucker (1820–52) was also from New Bedford.

2. On 29 April, the pope had issued an allocution in which he disavowed the war and refused to become the head of a republic. The announcement completely ended his influence
as a reformist.

3. Emerson, who was in England for an extended lecture tour, had visited France to see
the new republic at first hand.

4. Joseph Coolidge Shaw (1821–51), brother of Fuller's close friend Frank Shaw, was
then studying in Rome. In 1850 he became a Jesuit.

137. To Charles King Newcomb

22d June 48

My dear Charles,

It was a very pleasing surprize this morng to see your hand writing. You
speak of you and your Mother having written, but I have never recd any
letter from either, nor any answer to the questions I have asked our mutual friends about you. I remember just about the time you wrote 15th

May, I sent a message to your Mother in a letter written to America and thought at the same time I wish I could know about Charles now.

You ask if I never feel home-sickness. I have at times fits of deep longing to see persons and objects in America. At times my ear and eye grow weary of the sound of a foreign tongue, and the features of a foreign race. But then my affections and thoughts have become greatly interested in some things here, and I know if I once go to the U. S. I can never come back.

Then you know, dear Charles, *I* have no "home," no peaceful roof to which I can return and repose in the love of my kindred from the friction of care and the world. My Mother has love enough and would gladly prepare me such an one, but I know she has not money. Returning to the U. S. seems return to a life of fatigue, to which I feel quite unequal, while I leave behind many objects in whose greatness and beauty I am able for a time to forget these things. Thus I prize the present moment and get what I can from it. I may be obliged to return ere long, for nothing in outward life favors my plans, nor do any letters bring any but bad news.

At present my outward environment is very beautiful. I am in the midst of a theatre of mountains, some of them crowned with snow, all of very noble shapes. Along three sides run bridle paths, fringed with olive and almond groves and vineyards; here and there gleams a church or shrine. Through the valley glides a little stream, along its banks here and there little farm houses; vegetation is most luxuriant in this valley. This town is on a slope of one of the hills, it is a little place, much ruined, having been once a baronial residence, the houses of these barons are gone to decay; there are churches now unused, with faded frescoes over the arched portals, and the open belfry and stone wheel-window that are so beautiful. Out of town sweet little paths lead away through the fields to Convents, one of Passionists, another of Capuchins, both seem better than the monks found near great cities; it looks very peaceful to see their drape[d] forms pacing up the hills, and they have a healthy red in the cheek, unlike the vicious sallowness of monks of Rome. They get some life from their gardens and birds, I suppose. In the churches still open are pictures, not by great masters, but sweetly domestic, which please me much. There is one of the Virgin offering the nipple to the child Jesus; his little hand is on her breast, but he only plays and turns away; others of Santa Anna teaching the Virgin, a sweet girl of ten years old, with long curling auburn hair to read, the Virgin leans on her mother's lap; her hair curls on the book. There is another of the Marriage of the Virgin, a beautiful young man, one of three suitors, and like her as if her cousin, looks sadly on while she gives her hand to Joseph. There is often sweet music in these churches, they are dresst with fresh flowers, and the mountain breeze sweeps through them so freely, they do not smell too strong of incense.

Here I live with a lively Italian woman who makes me broth of turnips and gets my clothes washed in the stream. I shall stay here some time, if the beautiful solitude continue to please. The country people say "Povera, sola, soletta," poor one, alone, all alone! the saints keep her," as I pass. They think me some stricken deer to stay so apart from the herd. But the cities are only 3 days off, if I wish to go, full of wars and the rumors of wars and all sorts of excitements, which have proved beyond my strength to share for the present. Good bye, dear Charles. I have written little, you know it is but little one can write in a lctter. Address always Greene and Co. thcy will forward the letter. My love to your Mother and sisters. I was pleased you mentioned Cary. I wish she would write

Ever yours

MARGARET.

(MB)

138.   To Giovanni Angelo Ossoli

Martedi 27th [juigno] 48

Mio Caro,

Anche oggi non viene niente, adesso due settimane che non ricevo i giornali, da te viene nulla righa in risposta a mie due ultime. Non so niente delle cose chi m'interessan; mi sento tutta sola, imprigionata, troppo infelice

Credo bene che non è tuo defetto;—che tu hai scritto o inviato, ma non mi fa di bene, come per qualche ragione non ricevo.

Non mancate venire il Sabato; io morro esser lasciato cosi Fa un gran calore qui; non piove, e io non prendo piu piacer sortire. Come mia testa era molto sturbata, ho fatta cavare sangue. Son debole e soffro nel petto, altro non sto male.

Un parte delle truppe, de questi bimbini chi son ritornati da Lombardia sta nel Castello, uno dei loro Ufficiali in questa locanda, sovente molti di loro vengon qui pel pranzo, fan grande romore.

Addio, non ho coraggio dire niente più. Il giorno che tu vieni, si non hai già mie lettere dalla Banca invia questa e cercale. Dio ti benedica mio amico,

Tuesday 27th [June] 48

My dear,

Also today I received nothing, now for two weeks I have not received any papers, nor have I heard from you in reply to my last two letters. I

Giovanni Angelo Ossoli. By permission of the Houghton Library, Harvard University (MS Am 1806, Box A-pictures folder).

know nothing about the things that I am interested in; I feel lonely, imprisoned, too unhappy.

I am sure it is not your fault;—certainly you have written and sent them, but I am sorry since for some reason I do not receive anything.

Do not fail to come on Saturday; I will die if left so It is very hot here; it does not rain and I do not like to go out anymore. As I suffered from a terrible headache, I had a bloodletting. I am weak and suffer in my chest, the rest is not bad.

A part of the troops of these infants who have come back from Lombardia are living in the castle, one of their officers is often in this inn, many of them come here for lunch, they make a lot of noise.

Good bye, I have no more spirit to tell you more. The day that you come, if you have not yet gotten my letters from the bank, send this one and look for them. God bless you, my friend.

(MH: fMS Am 1086 [9:181])

139.   To Giovanni Angelo Ossoli

Sabato 22d luglio [1848]
Aquila.

Caro mio
    questa mattina ho tua lettrina del 20 e i giornali.

Martedi avevo tua altra con quella per Giuditta &—

Si, davvero questi son giorni terribili per Roma, io non posso pensare come le cose torneran.

La debolezza deplorabile del Papa a fatta più di male a Italia che il tradimento del Re di Napoli.

Penso un poco venire da Rieti. Decidero martedi prossima, si ricevo, come spero per te una risposta dal banchiere. Ma le cose stan si retardate; io non so che aspettare. La lettera pel banchiere ti ho inviata martedi passata, dopo sua risposta dicedero anche che fare pel denaro.

Non sto bene, mi duole adesso molto la testa ma questa settimana non più i denti e va bene perchè la medicina provista per tua affezione non arriva.

ho fatta conoscenca per accidente cogli Marchesi de Torres, due fratelli, e signori principali qui. Non era molto prudenti per qualchi ragioni ma come la cosa e fatta, si voglio partire domanderò consiglio di loro.

Scrivero più martedi spero molto che posso decidere allora e che tu recev[e]rai per tempo mia lettera Sempre tua

Saturday, 22d July [1848]
Aquila

My dear,

I have this morning your dear letter of the 20th and the newspapers.

Tuesday I had your other with the one for Giuditta &c— Yes, indeed these are terrible days for Rome, I cannot think how these things will turn out.

The deplorable weakness of the Pope has caused more troubles to Italy than the King of Naples' betrayal.[1]

I am thinking about coming to Rieti. I will make up my mind this coming Tuesday, if I receive, as I hope, an answer by you from the banker. But these things are going on very slowly; I do not know what to expect. I sent you last Tuesday the letter for the banker, after receiving his answer, I will also decide what to do about the money.

I am not well, now my head is hurting me but not my teeth this week and this is good because the medicine by your affection has not arrived

I met by accident the Marchesi de Torres, two brothers, and outstanding personalities here. It was not too prudent for various reasons but since it has happened, if I want to leave I will ask advice of them.[2] Tuesday I will write again[;] I very much hope that I can decide then and that you will receive my letter in time. Always your

(MH: fMS Am 1086 [9:199])

1. Ferdinand II (1810–59), the Bourbon monarch of the Kingdom of the Two Sicilies, was the most repressive of the Italian heads of state. Though he had been forced into liberal concessions, he withdrew his troops from the war against Austria on 18 May, a move that Fuller in the *Tribune* called "the first great calamity of the war."

2. Probably Ferdinando de Torres (1790–1861) and his younger brother Bartolomeo. Ferdinando was a poet and author of several books.

140. To Giovanni Angelo Ossoli

Rieti
2 agosto 48

Mio caro,

Ricevo questa mattina la tua, scritta ieri, cosi mi trovo davvero più vicino da te e spero sicuro rivederte domenica la mattina

Quanto m'ha fatta allegra la tua notizia di una vittoria, ma mi sorprende che l'Epoca del 31 luglio non parla del bulletino. Aspetto ansiamente un altro giornale.

Ho trovata un apartamento che mi conviene si bene, è sopra la fiume, e un veduta che ti piacera molto anche, pare fresca e più ariosa che a Aquila, e senza questa romore terribile; si sente solamente il fiume, qui posso trovare piacere davvero stare con te, vieni la domenica e stai lungo come e possibile.

Sento cura di sapere, si tu recevi mia lettera scritta la domenica 30 luglio, contiene ordine sul banchiere pel denaro, di che adesso sto in bisogno, e per mie lettere &c per star sicura ho fatto ordine *per te in persona prendere questo denaro*. Addio, caro, non manca la domenica, tu arriverai di bon ora, e io vedo passare la dilligenza sul ponte. Sto in casa di un certo Fassetti, strada Vendana, questo uomo e cancelliere del vescovo, ma si altro non mi trovi, domandi del albergo Campana, e vieni vieni presto alla tua affa

Rieti

2 August 48

My dear,

This morning I received the letter you wrote yesterday, so now I feel really closer to you and hope to see you surely on Sunday morning.

How glad I was in hearing from you the news of a victory, but I am surprised that the Epoca of July 31 does not mention the bulletin.[1] I am anxiously waiting for another newspaper.

I have found an apartment that suits me well, it is along the river, and has a view that you will surely like[;] it seems cool and more airy than in Aquila, and there is not that terrible noise; you can only hear the river, here I can really enjoy being with you[;] come on Sunday and stay as long as you can.

I am anxious to know if you received the letter I wrote you on Sunday July 30[;] it contains an order to the banker for the money I need now, and for my letters &c to be on the safe side I made out an order so that *you personally can take this money*. Good bye my dear, do not miss next Sunday, you will arrive early and I will see the stagecoach passing across the bridge. I live in the house of a certain Fassetti, Vedana street, this man is the bishop's chancellor, but if you do not find me there, ask for hotel Campana, and come come soon to your affectionate

(MH: fMS Am 1086 [9:182])

1. Charles Albert suffered a decisive defeat at the hands of Radetzky's Austrian army at Custoza on 25 July. The "victory" of which Ossoli wrote was perhaps a rear-guard action as Charles Albert retreated toward Milan.

141. To Giovanni Angelo Ossoli

Rieti
domenica 13 Agosto 48.

Mio caro,

Pare miracolo come tutte cose van contrarie a noi. Che la Bologna [h]a
rcsistita va bene, ma che questo farebbe probabile per te partire precise a
questo momento!

Ma fai che è bene per tuo onore. Io non credo molto che il Papa de-
cidera inviare la Civica, ma si questo si fa e si cè, di bisogno per tuo onore,
parti e io cercerò sostenermi.

Non trovo niente di alterazione in mio stato, avanti di ricever tua lettera
pensava scriverti che non credeva sarebbe di bisogno per ti venire avanti il
Sabato. Adesso lascio al tuo giudizio quando venire si davvero tu puoi
venire mai più. In tutto evento spero sentire qualche cosa martedi la mattina e io allora scrivero un altra volta. Tua visita m'ha fatta di bene son
stata dopo più tranquilla. E almeno noi abbiam avuti alcune ore di pace
insieme, si adesso è tutto terminato

Addio, amore, t'abbraccio sempre e prego per tuo bene.

Un addio affettuosissimo

Rieti
Sunday 13 August 48.

My dear,

It seems very strange how everything is going against us. The fact that
Bologna has resisted is good, but that this would make it likely for you to
leave at this very moment![1]

But do what is right for your honor. I do not really think that the pope
will decide to send the Civic Guard, but if it happens, and if it is necessary
for your honor, leave and I will try to be strong.[2]

There is no change in my health, before receiving your letter I intended to write you that I did not think it was necessary for you to come
hcre before Saturday. But now I leave to your judgment when to come if
really you can ever come again. In any case I hope to hear something on
Tuesday morning and then I will write you once again. Your visit did me
good and afterward I was calmer. And at least we have had some peaceful
hours together, if now everything is over.

Goodbye my love, I always embrace you and pray for your well-being.

A very warm goodbye

(MH: fMS Am 1086 [9:183])

1. On 6 August, Radetzky entered Milan, ending the war with Piedmont. Two days later a detachment of his army invaded the Papal States and attacked Bologna, which successfully resisted.

2. Pius, however, had no intention of opposing Austria and did nothing save extend a papal blessing to the guard.

142.   To Giovanni Angelo Ossoli

Rieti
15 agosto 48

Per nostro conto, amore, sarò molto grata si tu non stai d'obbligo partire, ma ah! come è indegno il Papa! Pare adesso uomo senza cuore: è questo traditore di Carlo Umberto: Saran maladetti per tutti i secoli avvenire.

In mio condizione non e ancora cambio importante; ho fatto cavare sangue; il medico mi piace; penso che è una persona in che posso fidare per curarmi bene si viene da difficolta. Lui dice che è impossibile fissare un giorno per mi ma pensa fra poco. Io apparecchio tutto quanto e possibile.

Adesso spero molto rivederti domenica la mattina, m'incresce per ti viaggiare in quello carrettino, ma tu avrai il tempo riposare dopo. Si e possibile tu starai ancora la settimana. Si vivo si sto bene, spero in pochi giorni dopo l'evento essere capace governare miei affari, ma allora starei molto più tranquilla averti al mio lato.

Ma ancora ridico che ho detta in mia ultima tu farai che è meglio per te, si un dovere previene da venire qui, io cercherò curarmi; voglio tuo bene in questi giorni[è] importante, più che tutt'altro. La luna e stata si bella queste ultime sere, m'ha indollorata non avere tua compagnia Ma speriamo un poco ancora,

sempre tua con molta affezione

Rieti
15 August 48

For our sake, my love, I will be very grateful if you are not obliged to leave, but ah! how contemptible is the pope! He seems now a man who has no heart: and this betrayer of Charles Albert: they will be cursed for all ages to come.[1]

There is not yet any important change in my condition; I was bled; I like the doctor; I think he is a person whom I can trust to take care of me if something goes wrong. He says that it is impossible to settle a day for me But he thinks soon. I will arrange as much as possible.

Now I really hope to see you on Sunday morning, I am sorry that you have to travel in that little coach, but then you will have time to rest afterward. If it is possible please stay here for a week. If I live and if I am well, I hope a few days after the event to be able to manage my affairs, but then I would be much calmer having you at my side.

But I repeat what I told you in my last letter[;] do what is better for you, if a duty hinders your coming here I will try to take care of myself; in these important days I want your good above all. The moon was very beautiful these last nights, it grieved me not to have your company. But let us hope a little more.

Always yours with much love

(MH: fMS Am 1086 [9:184])

1. Charles Albert abandoned Milan to the Austrians and barely escaped the enraged Milanese, who wanted to resist Radetzky. His action earned him the epithet Re Tentenna (King Wobble) and led Fuller to write in the *Tribune*, "Had the people slain him in their rage, he well deserved it at their hands."

143.   To Richard F. Fuller

Mountains of Southern
Italy, 16th August 48

My dear brother,

In a letter recd from you about the middle of June, you say you are going to Lennox to make a visit, and after that and previous to going into Ohio you shall write to me. But I suppose you did not. This is the only letter I have from any member of my family for near four months. Indirectly I heard that Arthur was ordained at Manchester in April and that Mother had returned from the West.[1]

I wrote to Mother and to E. Hoar by a Mr Page who left Rome early in May. By Dr Gardner of Boston who expected to be there in June, I sent Ellen her Cameo and the coral cross for Greta. By Mr Hillard a mosaic to Mother. I want to know if these things have come safe.

In an evil hour, wishing to save you pressure I trusted for the expenses of the summer to a remittance from Mr Greeley, which up to this hour has never arrived. I begin to believe I shall never receive it, as in a letter dated the 27th June, he says he supposes I have it long since. He does not say how it came. Meanwhile not only my mind has been harassed, but much of the benefit of my summer has been forfeited by this failure. I have been unable to procure reference books which would have been most precious to me, and of which I can never again make use to this same advantage. I have been prevented from making the most interesting excursions among others the want of a few dollars prevented my seeing the birth-place of Ovid and Lake Facino.

Now I do not know what will become of me, if I do not, in the course of Septr receive the money either from you or Mr G. I shall not have the means to leave Italy, nor even to return to Rome, if indeed I could still have food and lodging here. It makes me heart-sick to think how long I have waited and of the uncertainty of correspondence at this distance.

Sometimes it seems to me I have no friend, or some one would divine how I am placed and find the means to relieve me. Yet I know I *have* friends better than the average of human nature supplies.

As to Mr Greeley he shows no disposition to further my plans. Liberality on the part of the Tribune would have made my path easy. And I feel that if any one in America had been interested to enable me here to live and learn on my own way, I could have made, at least, a rich intellectual compensation. But people rarely think one like me worth serving or saving. Still I must not be ungrateful having to thank 1st the Springs 2d the Mannings who volunteered a loan, 3d Mrs Farrar who has now offered to lend me a hundred dollars and 4th and most you, who, amid your own difficulties, have never forgotten me. And I feel sure that if you have recd my last letter I shall be relieved before the end of Septr. Hoping it may be so I try to keep my mind tranquil and make as much use as possible of the present moment.

I have changed place since I wrote last and am now in a spot less rich in historic association, yet of the ancient Umbrian dominion and enchanting in its natural beauty. The house is upon a rapid river. I occupy its upper apartment, containing a chamber for my servant a little room for eating, and mine, a large brick paved room of the simplest finish and furniture but with a *loggia* upon the river with its whispering willows. This *loggia* a wooden terrace is long enough for an evening walk, and these glorious moonlight nights, I pass many hours there, uninterrupted by a sound except the rush of the stream and occasionally a soft bell from a convent of Cappucins high among the mountains. A rich vineyard is opposite my window, and there the contadini work a little sing and play more. I see too an ancient villa with its cypress plantations and a distant cleft among the mountains leads on the eye and fancy. I never in my life had a room I liked as I do this. I can open the whole apartment and let the breeze draw through. Below my servant washes the clothes on a large stone in the running water which leaves them white as snow. For the apartment I pay nine dollars a month. Figs, grapes, peaches the most delicious I can have enough for the day for five or six cents. The best salad enough for two persons for one cent a day. Here I make the nearest approach to economical living I have been able to in Italy. My servant is from Rome. I could not live without her; the country people are too dirty, and she cooks sews and irons for me but it is rather a bore to have her she does not like so much solitude and wonders I do not "go mad writing"

Goodbye, my dear Richard, much shall I have to say, if ever we meet again, but three sheets of paper (and I pay eighty cents to get *one* to you) come to an end in a moment. Hoping to hear much from you and with love to dearest Mother your sister

M.

I do not say anything of public affairs, but all goes wrong. My dearest friends are losing all, and the Demon with his cohort of traitors, prepares to rule anew these heavenly fields and mountains. But I do not quite despair yet. France may aid.[2] If not Italy [w]ill be too hot or too cold to hold me.

(MH: fMS Am 1086 [9:152])

1. Arthur Fuller was ordained on 29 March at Manchester, New Hampshire, where he served until 1853.

2. On 7 August the Piedmontese ambassador at Paris asked the French for 60,000 troops, but France refused the request.

144. To Giovanni Angelo Ossoli

la domenica 20th Agosto [1848]

Mio caro,

ti aspettavo un poco questa mattina, e aveva tuo caffè tutto pronto ma credo tu hai ragione aspettare. Si trovi niente al contrario, vieni il sabato sera prossimo.

Miei notti divengon più e più sturbati, e questa mattina stavo d'obbligo fare un altro sanguigno, dopo mi trovo sollevata ma debole e non capace dire altro che son sempre tua affeza

Inchiudo un altra ordine pel banchiere, si tu vieni il sabato Scrivo lo adesso non essendo sicura che posso scrivere molti giorni più. T'abbraccio.

Sunday
20th August [1848]

My dear,

I was waiting for you this morning, and I had your coffee ready but I think you are right to wait. If nothing prevents you, come this Saturday evening.

My nights become more and more disturbed, and this morning I had to have another blood letting, afterwards I feel better but weak and I am not able to say more than I am always your affectionate

I enclose another order for the banker, if you come on Saturday. I write it now because I am not sure I can write in the next few days. I embrace you.

(MH: fMS Am 1086 [9:204])

145.   To Giovanni Angelo Ossoli

Rieti 7 Settembre 1848

Cmo Consorte

Io sto bene molto meglio che io sperava. Il Bambino anche va bene ma piange molto ancora, e spero che sarè più tranquillo quando tu vieni. Per altro voglio che per me sii tranquillo, e ti darò spesso mie nuove scrivendoti di nuovo ben presto. La mia lettera che hai per Parigi potrai affrancarla alla Posta.

Tutti di questa famiglia dove io mi trovo ti salutano. Dandoti un abbraccio, ed un bagio in questo caro Pupo che ho nelle braccia sono Tua Affma

MARGHERITA

Rieti 7 September 1848

Dearest Husband

I feel much better than I hoped.[1] The child is doing well too but he still cries a lot, and I hope he will be calmer when you come. As for the rest I want you to be reassured, and I will often give you my news writing again very soon. The letter of mine you have for Paris you can stamp at the post office.

All the people in the family where I am staying send their regards. Embracing you and kissing you in this dear baby I have in my arms I am Your Affectionate

MARGARET

(MH: fMS Am 1086 [9:185])

1. Angelo was born on 5 September.

146. To Giovanni Angelo Ossoli

Sabato
[9 settembre 1848]

Mio bene,

Scrivo nel letto alcune parole solamente. Ricevo tuo questa mattina, e spero altro per domani. Son stata male col febbre di latte ma oggi meglio e spero tutti i giorni stare più forte. C'e di bisogno; son d'obbligo oggi inviare Giuditta in Roma; lei non può fare niente adesso. Io prendo una che ha anche latte si mio non basta.

Il bambino e molto bello, tutti dicon cosi io prendo molto piacere riguardarlo. Lui ti da un bacio come anche tua

M.

Saturday
[9 September 1848]

My love,

I write only a few words in bed. I receive[d] yours this morning, and I hope for another one to-morrow. I have been sick with nursing fever but today I am better and I hope I will grow stronger every day. There is need for it; I must send Giuditta to Rome today; she cannot do anything now. I [will] take one who can also breastfeed since my milk is not sufficient.

The child is very beautiful, everybody says so[;] I enjoy very much looking at him. He sends you a kiss as does also your

M.

(MH: fMS Am 1086 [9:210])

147. To Giovanni Angelo Ossoli

Rieti
sabato 23 settembre [1848]

Mio caro,

ricevo questa mattina il giornale e tua lettrina.

Io sento la verità di che tu dici che bisogna per prendere una balia la grandissima cautela; io aspettero per tutto consultare con ti. Pensi solamente si il bambino sta fuori di Roma, tu non puoi vederlo sovente. Altro, l'aria della campagna sarebbe meglio, senza dubbio, per sua salute

È si caro; mi pare qualche volte, per tutte le difficolta e le disgrazie, che si vive, si sta bene può divenire un tal tesoro per noi tutti due, e un compenso per tutto. Io voglio molto per ti rivederlo; ma bisogna per ti avere pazienza sentirlo strillare sovente; è un ostinato. Anche per tua venuta io spero che mia spalla può essere guerita ancora e io forte assai sortire un poco con ti.

Adesso fa bel tempo e io sorto sulla loggia. Ser Giovanni e buono per me, ma sue sorelle son de[te]stabi[li] mescolando in tutto, e si avare, si interressate, si vogliono risparmian mi mi denaro, vogliono riprenderlo per loro. Ma anche cerco io tenere la pace con loro; si trovan cattivi gent[i] [ ] tutta parte, e questi, si interressati e volgare, almeno non sono perfide come la Giuditta. Addio, amore, abbracceandoti son la tua

M.

Dimmi si stai meglio in salute co[ ] spero di si, perche e più caldo.

Rieti
Saturday, 23 September [1848]

My dear,

I receive this morning the newspaper and your dear letter.

I feel the truth in what you say that we must be very cautious in hiring a nurse; I will wait about everything to take counsel with you. Only think that if the baby is out of Rome, you can not see him very often. Furthermore, without doubt the air of the country would be better for his health

He is so dear; sometimes I think that for all the misfortunes and difficulties, if he lives, if he is well, he can become a great treasure for the two of us, and a compensation for everything. I want you very much to see him; but you must be very patient when you hear him scream often; he is obstinate. Also, when you come I hope my shoulder will be well and that I can be strong enough to go out with you for a while.

The weather is beautiful now and I go out on the loggia. Mr. Giovanni is good to me, but his sisters are detestable, meddling in everything and so stingy and self-centered; they want me to save money, so that they can have it for themselves. Anyway I try to keep the peace with them; one can find bad people [ ] everywhere and these, if greedy and vulgar, at least are not as perfidious as Giuditta. Goodbye my love, embracing you I am your

M.

Tell me if you feel better [ ] I hope yes because it is warmer.

(MH: fMS Am 1086 [9:205])

148. To Giovanni Angelo Ossoli

Rieti
Martedi 26, Settembre [1848]

M'incresce tanto, amore, sentire che non stai bene ancora; è allora qualche cosa seria che hai. Se non stai bene, non vieni qui la notte nel maledetto carrettino, aspetta per la diligenza; è vero che ho bisogno vederti presto e lungo come possibile ma aspettero piutosto che esporre tua salute.

Ma il giovedi scrivi precise quando posso aspettarti; voglio stare pronta. Invio qui giù un ordine sulla banca pelle mie lettere; tu puoi inviarlo il giorno che vieni. Anche cerchi a la grande posta, e *posta restante* si non c'è niente per mi, e dimando una volta ancora a la posta del Dottore dove è andato e quando ritorna in Roma. E m'apporti questa volta mia Cologne e miei guanti.

Scusa tutto l'incommodo.

Adesso noi commenciamo stare davvero bene, mio bambino e io. Lui dorme tutta la notte, e mia spalla, l'ultima notte, non m'ha tormentata; cosi io anche ho dormita. Lui è sempre si grazioso come è possibile per mi mai, mai lasciarlo? Sveglio la notte, lo riguardo, e penso ah, è impossibile lasciarlo. Addio, amore, si senti come io tu sei impaziente venire; allora noi possiamo parlare e avere ancora alcuni felici momenti di più La tua

M.

Rieti
Tuesday 26, September [1848]

I am very sorry, my love, to know that you are not well yet; it is then something serious that you have. If you are not well do not come here in the night by that cursed small cart but wait for the stagecoach; it is true that I need to see you soon and as long as possible but I will wait rather than to expose your health.

But on Thursday write exactly when I can expect for you; I want to be ready. Enclosed here I send another order on the bank for my letters; you can send it the day you come. Also look at the main post office and the *Posta Restante* if there is something for me and ask once again at the post office about the doctor; where he is gone and when he will come back to Rome. And this time bring me my cologne and my gloves.

Excuse all the inconveniences.

Now we are beginning to be really well, my baby and myself. He sleeps all night long, and my shoulder did not hurt me last night, so that I could have some sleep too. He is always so nice, how would it ever be possible for me to leave him? I wake up in the night, look at him, and I think ah, it is impossible to leave him. Goodbye my love, if you feel like me, you are very impatient to come; then we can talk and have more happy moments together Your

M.

(MH: fMS Am 1086 [9:206])

149. To Giovanni Angelo Ossoli

Rieti
15 Ottobre, 48

Mio amore,

una della lettere che tu hai inviata, mi fa conoscere la morte della vecchi Siga mia amica di che ti ho parlata sì sovente. Ho pianto tanto, mi ho fatta malatta, ma non potevo altro; non era nel Mondo persona piu buona, nè più affettuosa per me. Ho perduta una ottima amica

Le altre lettere sono importanti, ti dirò quando vieni.

Pensa sempre in cercando casa per mi non compromettermi stare in Roma, mi pare sovente non posso stare lungo senza rivedere il bambino, è si caro e la vita mi pare sì incerta; non so come lasciar miei cari. Prendi l'appartamento per poco di tempo, bisogna che starò in Roma almeno un mese scrivere e anche stare vicino di te, ma voglio stare libera ritornar qui, si sento troppo ansiosa per lui, troppo soffrente.

O Amore come e difficile la vita! Ma tu, tu sei buono, Si mi era solamente possibile farti felice!

Il bachiere mi ha dato ricevute in sua lettera. Anche vuole ricevere subito l'inchiuso; vedi tu che l'ha subito; e mia firma per cambio in Parigi dice piu presto l'invio il meglio può fare per mi.

Non pensi un momento di Giovanni come compare Sarebbe, mi pare, fidare troppo in lui; io non lo credo degno. E meglio per ti fidare in qualche tuo eguale, chi come gentil'uomo guardera tuo segreto. Pi- un altra volta da tua

M.

Ho qualche cosa curiosa dirti di Giovanni quando vieni. Ieri il bambino pareva soffrire e era cattivo ma oggi sta bene e sì bello! Scrivi subito che tu hai ricevuto queste

Rieti
15 October, 48

My love,

one of the letters that you sent let me know about the death of the elderly lady, my friend of whom I often spoke to you.[1] I cried so much that

I became ill, but I could not help it; no one in the world was better and more affectionate to me than she was to me. I have lost a very good friend

The other letters are important, I will tell you when you come.

Always remember in looking for a house for me not to commit me to living in Rome; often I think that I could not stay for a long time without seeing the baby again, he is so dear and life seems so uncertain; I do not know how to leave my dear ones. Take the apartment for a short time; I need to stay in Rome for at least one month to write and to be close to you, but I want to be free to come back here if I am too anxious and grieved about him.

Oh dear, how hard life is! But you are so good, if it were only possible for me to make you happy! In his letter the banker sent me the receipts. He also wants to receive the enclosed at once; take care that he has it at once; about my signature for the exchange in Paris, he says that the quicker I send it the better it will be for me.

Do not think for a moment about Giovanni as godfather. It would be, I think, to trust too much in him; I do not think he is worth it. It is better for you to trust in someone your equal who as a gentleman will protect your secret. More another time from your

M.

I have something curious to tell you about Giovanni when you come. Yesterday the child seemed to suffer and was bad, but today he is well and so beautiful! Write to me as soon as you receive these

(MH: fMS Am 1086 [9:189])

1. Mary Rotch died on 4 September.

150.   To Giovanni Angelo Ossoli

venerdi 27—[ottobre 1848]

Mio amore,

m'incresce molto che tuo zio è il solo Italiano che non osserva feste, giusto per nostra noja. Sarà molto freddo il 4, per ti venire la notte, anche suppongo piovera allora e tutti i giorni di tua visita qui e il giorno di nostro ritorno. Adesso son begli giorni.

Altro mi piace stare una settimana più con mio bambino. Sta tutti i giorni più interessante. Altro sento il bisogno stare un pezzo con ti, e andare una volta più nel mondo da che son stata aparte adesso 5 mesi. Ma non voglio fissarmi in Roma cosi che non posso lasciare si son troppo infelice separata dal bambino o per altra ragione voglio. Sarebbe meglio prendere un peggiore appartamento o una camera sola che fare grande spese o m'obbligarmi per lungo tempo. Cosi è meglio non decidere avanti la mia venuta in Roma.

Per mia salute non va male, solamente non guadagno forza e son sovente rinfreddata alzando la notte col bambino. Starò bene quando ho viaggiato, passeggiato un poco. Pel innesto noi faremo nostro possibile e si non può farsi, io spererò che lui stara sicuro nel inverno, e io stesso cercerò materia la primavera senza fidando in nul Rietino.

Son due, tre begli passeggi che spero fare con ti si per miracolo noi abbiamo sole quando tu stai qui.

Quanto m'incresce non sentire che Milano si leva contro Radetzky a questo momento importante. Io teme fideran in questo maladetto cattivo Carl Alberto troppo lungo e che Italia sia perduta quando era ancora possibile per lei stare felice.

Inchiudo un ordine alla Banca pegle mei lettere, che voglio ancora una volta e t'abbracciando con grande affezione come fa anche nostro caro tua

M.

Friday 27th— [October 1848]

My love,

I am really sorry that your uncle is the only Italian who does not observe the holidays, just for our aggravation. It will be very cold on the 4th, for you to come at night, I suppose it will also rain then as well as for the whole time of your visit and on the day of your return. Now the days are beautiful.

On the one hand I am happy to spend another week with my baby. He becomes more interesting every day. On the other hand I feel the need to spend some time with you and to go once again into the world from which I have been apart now for 5 months. But I don't want to settle in Rome so as not to be able to leave if I am too unhappy away from the baby or for any other reason. It would be better to take a worse apartment or only a room rather than making great expenses or committing myself for a long time. So it is better not to decide before my coming to Rome.

My health is not bad, only I am not gaining any strength and I often have a cold from getting up at night with the baby. I will be well after having travelled, walked a bit. As for the immunization we will do our best and if it cannot be done I will hope that he will be safe during the winter and I myself will look for the material in the spring without relying anymore on this person from Rieti.

There are two or three walks which I would like to do with you if by a miracle we have some sun when you come here.

How much I regret not to hear that Milan revolts against Radetzky at this important moment. I am afraid that they will trust in this cursed and bad Charles Albert for too long and that Italy will be lost when it was still possible for her to be happy.

I enclose an order to the Bank for my letters, which I want once again, and embracing you with great affection as does also our dear one your

M.

(MH: fMS Am 1086 [9:210])

151. To Emelyn Story

Rome,
28th Novr 1848.

Here I am again, my dear Emelyn. I passed the road and meadows over-flowed because the Tiber was swollen by recent rain; Rome was all reeking with the same cold mist that made me suffer so much last winter, and yet— how beautiful and dear it seemed to be here again, to hear the voices of the many fountains, to see in that pale struggling moonlight the obelisks and ruins more eloquent than ever!

O Rome, *my* country bad as the winter damp is, and lazy as the climate makes me, I would rather live here than any where else in the world.

The scarlet abomination, as our Puritan ancestors deemed it, has had a good dip in the stream of progress, since you were here and the red certainly looks spotted and *streaky*. I am living in a Rome without Pope or Cardinals.[1] Some old persons weep the desecration. But Rome in general takes it very coolly, though ignorant where the "immortal", now, alas! immortally contemptible, Pio is gone, and to what measures he may suffer himself to be led against her.

But the Romans had grown weary of being duped and so sure that they had nothing to hope from him, that the universal feeling seems to be "Let go" at any rate.

My fear is that Rome cannot hold together in her present form against innovation and that we are enjoying the last hours of her old solemn greatness. Will you not return then to see her once more! Florence, full of beautiful things as it is, is, to my mind, just nothing compared with Rome, and, in its intellectual atmosphere, no Italy at all.

Write to me of what and whom you find. I want to know if Wm takes as much pleasure in Powers and his works as he expected and how he is. I heard he was not well. And the children how fare they? and are they very happy? I hope yes, and that Edith enjoys being in the city of flowers, only I suppose there are few now. In June, when I was there first, the flowers are enchanting! And Uncle Tom?[2] is he happy? and does he not want to take a palazzo and a villa here, instead of his nice house in Boston?

"Crodie" has a most sweet place; it is fine that any one can have such apartments, such a garden, and such a view for only 240 dollars a year only I wish you had them instead of her, especially as I am not far off. in Piazza Barberini I suppose you could take them for the year they are to be absent, if you wished, studio and all.

I am almost alone in Rome, there is hardly a person I know here, I have screwed my expenses down to the lowest possible peg; at least it seems so now, but I dont know;— that art seems to be capable of gai[ ] indefinite perfection in Italy. Meanwhile I have a room I like very [m]uch and two nice old people to take [ca]re of me, as clean and "smart" and less cunning than the Marchesa. My rooms in her house are still free if you know any single gentle man coming on from Florence that want such, indeed now is accomodation for two single gentlemen, if *not* rolled into one, as she has made a pretty bedroom of her little parlor, and the whole may be had very cheap as indeed may rooms of any description in this present Rome; should the Assembly for the Constituente be held here, they may be filled up, but the Murray guide book mob fight shy, which makes it quite delightful for me to be here now.

Do you see much of the Greenoughs? Mrs G. is a woman of the world, and does not interest me, but is sweet tempered and kindly.[3] Greenough, in the right mood, I think a delightful companion; he has a vein of delicate wit, and is a poet when he speaks of birds and animals; he can describe their looks and motions with almost Shakspearean power. Are the Brownings still in Florence and have you made their acquaintance? if not, should you like to do so through a note from me. Goodbye, dear Emelyn, again write quick and tell me if you hear anything of Amern friends, especially Caroline, Jane and the Lorings. I know nothing; people in U. S. are fast forgetting me. Affecy

What is become of the Blacks?[4]

Crodie says Mrs Ames is really a mother, pray write if you know any thing about *that.*[5]

(NNC)

1. On the evening of 24 November the pope, dressed as an ordinary priest, slipped out of a secret exit from the Vatican and left Rome for Gaeta, just over the border in the Kingdom of Naples, where he remained until after the fall of the Roman Republic.

2. Edith Marion Story (1844–1917), oldest of the Story children. Thomas Wetmore (1794–1860), William Story's uncle, was traveling with them in Italy.

3. In 1837 Horatio Greenough married Louisa Ingersoll Gore (1813–91), daughter of John Gore of Boston.

4. Charles Christopher Black (1809–79) later became curator of the South Kensington Museum in London and was for a time on the staff of the Victoria and Albert Museum.

5. Sarah Fisher Clampitt (1817–1901), a sculptor, married the painter Joseph Alexander Ames.

152.   To Richard F. Fuller

Rome.

19th Jany 1849.

My dear Richard,

With my window open looking out upon towards St Peter's and the glorious Italian sun pouring in, I was just thinking of you. I was just thinking how I wished you were here that we might walk forth and talk together under the influence of these magnificent objects. I was thinking of the proclamation of the Constitutional Assembly here a measure carried by courageous youth in the face of age sustained by the prejudices of many ages.[1] The ignorance of the people and all the wealth of the country. Yet courageous youth faces not only these, but the most threatening aspect of foreign powers, and dares a future of blood and exile to achieve priveleges which are our (American) common birthright. I thought of the great interests which may in our country be sustained, without obstacle by every able man, interests of humanity, interests of God.

I thought of the new prospects as to wealth opened to our country men by this acquisition of New Mexico and California the vast prospects of our country every way, so that it is in self a vast blessing to be born in America, and I thought how impossible it is that one like Richard, of so strong and generous nature shall, if he can but patiently persevere, be defrauded of a rich, manifold, powerful life. Perhaps I should have written much of hopes, but Mr Hooker, my banker entered and obliges me to abandon the future for the annoyance of the present.

I wrote you that no doubt several letters from you were lost among them one containing the first of exchange on Brown Shipley and Co. Now it seems some one, intercepting that letter, has forged my signature and taken the money. They B. S. and Co have protested the second of exchange saying they had paid the first.

I am no longer responsible having sold the bill to the bankers here and paid commission still it will be very unpleasant for me, if they have difficulty about it. When you write let me know if your letter was not sent as usual through *Greene and Co* I cannot doubt *it was* as all your letters are, but answer to this, and tell if you know any circumstance elucidating this affair.

I was disturbed enough before to lose letters containing, I suppose, some important part of your mental history. Just so with dear Eugene the letters were lost in which he spoke of his acquaintance with and growing love for Eliza.[2] My apparent silence made him silent, the precious habit of intimacy was broken. Some peculiar aspect of my star indicates misfortune from the loss of letters. What I have had to endure at different periods from this cause would if written down make a romance. Now when I am to be separated from a friend I begin at once to fear to lose him quite from such a cause.

To have another summer all poisoned by cares and embarrassments as last was would be dreadful. I had reduced my expenses to the lowest possible amount and done without every thing hoping at least thus to feel free and not think about money. Now I do not feel pleasantly because, if the bank is called on to give me much money and does not receive it they will be annoyed So, dear R. tax your memory to know whether you ever sent letters without posting them yourself, or through any channel other than Greene and Co, and answer by next steamer after receiving this.

I will wait and not close up this leaf till the last moment, perhaps there will be something important to say.

Thursday eveg 25th Jany. This has been a most beautiful day and I have been a long walk out of town. How much I should like to walk sometimes with you again!

I went to the Church of St. Lorenzo, one of the most ancient in Rome, rich in early mosiacs also with spoils from the temples, marbles, ancient sarcophagi with fine basso relievos, magnificent columns. There is a little of every thing but the medley is harmonized by the action of time and the sensation induced is that of homely repose. It has the public cemetery and there lie the bones of many poor; the rich and noble lie in lead coffins in the church vaults of Rome Rome.

But St Lorenzo loved the poor When his tormentors insisted to know where he had hid his riches "There" he said pointing to the crowd of wretches who hovered near his fiery bed, compelled to see the tyrants of the earth hew down the tree that had nourished and sheltered them

Amid the crowd of inexpressive epitaphs one touched me erected by a son to his father. He was, says the son, an angel of prosperity, seeking our good in distant countries with unremitting toil and pain. We owe him all. For his death it is my only consolation "that in life I never left his side."

Returning I passed the Pretorian Camp, the Campus Scelesadus[?], where Vestals that had broken their vows were buried alive in the city whose founder was born from a similar event, such are the usual, the frightful inconsistencies of mankind.

From my windows I see the Barberini Palace. In its chambers are the portrait of the Cenci, and the Galatea so beautifully described by Goethe. In the garden are the remains of the [*illegible*] of Servius Tullius.

Yesterday as I went forth I saw the house where Keats lived in Rome where he died. I saw the Casino of Raphael. Returning I passed the Villa where Goethe lived when in Rome; afterwards the houses of Claude and Poussin.

Ah, what human companionship here, how everything speaks!

I live myself in the apartment described in Andersen's "Improvisatore" which get you and read as scene of the childhood of Antonio.[3] I have the room, I suppose, indicated as being occupied by the Danish Sculptor. Read also Goethe's Year in Rome and Romish Elegies, Brownings "Bells and Pomegranates" at least those whose scene is laid in Italy and a book of late production (I mean within these past two or [three] years)[4] We shall talk to better advantage on my return if you know these books

The inclosed letters, being written on very thin paper I want you to inclose seal and send to their respective addresses. I have prepared the packet in this way to save postage, even so I pay two or three dollars, so grudge not thy trouble

The note to Mrs Ames I wish you would take yourself and make her acquaintance. Miss Peabody will tell you where she lives. She was with m[e] much in Rome, could tell you much abou[t] me, and I think you will like her. She may seem to you frivolous at first as she says every thing good or bad without distinction that comes into her head, but she has a beautiful character, entirely simple and generous.

[Te]ll me with whom you associate now. I [kn]ow nothing, having lost those letters. Tell all you can. I always fear to seem flimsy in speaking of your feelings. You say none can thread my mind and destiny that is true, even if with you and knowing as much as one can of another I could still only hope to offer good suggestions, and now I have not seen you so long your character is doubtless developed on other sides, presents new features *I* am no longer young, yet still so often new and surprizing to myself, you are at a more growing age.

28th As usual I have to send of the packet before receiving my letters, The mails are now so arranged that I can never answer to the latest intelligence But Mrs Crawford has a letter giving account of the suicide of Emerson.[5] When he was here though in such florid youth, it struck me he would not live long there were in his face signs of his fate

Adieu dear R. dont die you, prays your sister and friend

MARGARET

(MH: fMS Am 1086 [9:156])

1. On 29 December the provisional junta that ruled Rome called for an election on 21 January 1849 to create a national assembly. It was to be elected by universal male suffrage and a secret ballot, and was to meet on 5 February.

2. Eliza Rotta, whom their brother Eugene married in 1846.

3. Hans Christian Andersen (1805–75), whose *Improvisatore; or Life in Italy* had been translated by Mary Howitt in 1845.

4. Goethe published his *Italienische Reise* in 1816–17 and *Römische Elegien* in 1795. Fuller had reviewed the eighth number of Browning's *Bells and Pomegranates* in the *Tribune* and included it in *Papers on Literature and Art.*

5. Thomas Crawford (1813?–57), a sculptor, married Louisa Ward (1823–97), Julia Ward Howe's sister, in 1844. George Samuel Emerson (1825–48), son of George Barrell and Olivia Buckminster Emerson, killed himself on 19 December.

153.   To Emelyn Story

Rome
27th Jany 1849

My dear Emelyn

I was quite disappointed by the reading of your letter. Though I wrote you as well as I could both pros and cons, I had hoped very much you would come. And I still hope your doubts will end so. Now I shall write with that view because if I should have a chance to talk with you about your further plans and projects writing is superfluous.

Mr. Wetmore says he shall persist in asking you to come, and I wish it might be so as to arrive by the 5th Feby. They are making great preparations here for opening the Constitutional Assembly. Then, after that, begins the Carnival on the 10th. It will not be brilliant, as masks in the day time are forbidden, still you might like to see it again.

I write in the expectation that all will remain tranquil, as there is every reason to expect it will unless the incredible treachery now surmized of the French President should be actuated In any event, we do not think that you need apprehend any annoyance.[1]

I have been to look at Poussin's house for you and also the *Casa del Scimia!!* in Quattro Fontane. I prefer the monkey apartment, it is large, sunny, a beautiful saloon, two very large bedrooms two good size, 7 beds in all, a good dining room, abundant linen and table service, a small kitchen. The entrance is fine. The back windows look on the Barberini gardens, and they have a garden of their own. The walks from this part of Rome would be comparatively new to you; the air is the best. This apartment I think you can have for 40 a month, perhaps for 30 or 35, while Poussin would not come down below 70, and *I* should, at any rate, like monkey house better. Then for me; I like the name; it presents a refreshing contrast to the glories and classicalities so eternal in eternal Rome. There is something so original in the sign; it befits the house of *Barberini*.

I flatter myself that when this arrives William will have finished his model (he is not firm of health enough to stay in a studio damp as you describe) the fit of content with Florence gone off, for to my mind 'tis only a paroxysm, and the trunks ready to be packed for here. Come on at once, if you can. It would be only a night at the Hotel d'Angleterre if the lodgings were not taken. I would go with you next morning and you would be sure of being content with them which is more than any person the most desirous of studying the tastes of another can feel in taking rooms for a friend.

I have a letter from Mrs. Browning in which she expresses their pleas[ure] in making your acquaintance. I am very glad for both. Since I cannot see them now, I want some of their thoughts and, think you, not they be so candid as to lend me a copy of Bells and Pomegranates. I want so much to read again the poems about Italy and can't get them. I would easily find an oppory to send them back.

I am not at all surprised at what you say of Keats. I always thought with Byron "Strange that the mind, that very fiery particle, could let itself be snuffed out by an article."[2] Anna Parsons, dwelling in her trance on a private letter of his (Keats's) was much distressed at finding a degree of self-seeking unworthy of his genius.

I would be glad for William to call with the inclosed letter on Madame Arconati. He will thus, if she is at home, see one who is considered by many the most distinguished woman in Italy and who would be distinguished where there was a far greater number of worthy competitors If she is not at home will he leave his card and address, provided you still expect to stay some days in Florence. I have left her free to call or not. At an earlier period she would not have failed so to do on a friend of mine, but now cares and sorrows are accumulated upon her and I ask her to do as she feels, but if she does not call, she may send me something by you. Have you Murray's Hand Book of Southern Italy, if so, bring. I cannot find it in Rome. I trouble you much, dear Emelyn, but you know I would gladly do as much for you. Affecy yr friend

MARGARET.

M. Arconati speaks English well. A beautiful presence is fled. Ellen Hooper! did you know her well?

When William calls on Madame A, he will send her in the letter first, with his card and then she will come into parlor having read it and knowing about him. She knew and liked Julia Howe when in Milan.[3] Remember that she is a Milanese.

If you come and take an apartment large enough I might pass two or three weeks with you in April, when I have done working and we could run about to see pikters. I think monkey house has no couch for me, however it would be very near this one, if I keep this room then We would talk of that when you come. If you think of the Grecian expedition, would not William naturally meet Mr Black here?

(TxU)

1. Louis Napoleon (1808–73) had been elected president of the French Republic on 10 December. Despite his previous anticlerical stand, he worked against the Roman Republic for the restoration of the pope's temporal power.
2. *Don Juan,* canto 11, stanza 60, slightly misquoted.
3. Julia Ward Howe visited Milan in 1843 on her wedding trip.

154.   To Giuseppe Mazzini

Rome
3 March, 1849.

Dear Mazzini,

Though knowing you occupied by the most important affairs, I again feel impelled to write a few lines. What emboldens me is the persuasion that the best friends,— in point of perfect sympathy and intelligence the only friends,— of a man of ideas and of marked character, must be women. You have your mother; no doubt you have others, perhaps many; of that I know nothing; only I like to offer also my tribute of affection.

When I think that only two years ago, you thought of coming into Italy with us in disguise, it seems very glorious, that you are about to enter Republican Rome as a Roman Citizen. It seemed almost the most sublime and poetical fact of history. Yet, even in the first thrill of joy, I felt, "He will think his work but beginning now"

When I read from your hand these words "il lungo esilio testè ricominciato, la vita non confortata fuorchè d'affetti lontani e contesi, e la speranza lungamente protratta e il desiderio che commincia a farmisi supremo di dormire finalmente in pace, dachè non ho potuto vivere in terra mia"[1]

When I read these words they made me weep bitterly and I thought of them always with a great pang at the heart. But it is not so, dear Mazzini. You do not return to sleep under the sod of Italy, but to see your thought springing up all over her soil. The gardeners seem to me, in point of instinctive wisdom or deep thought, mostly incompetent to the care of the garden, but an idea like this will be able to make use of any implements, it is to be hoped will educate, the men by making them work. It is not this, I believe, which still keeps your heart so melancholy, for I seem to read the same melancholy in your answer to the Roman assembly. You speak of "few and late years," but some full ones still remain; a century is not needed, nor ought the same man, in the same form of thought, to work too long on an age. He would mould and bend it too much to himself, better for him to die and return incarnated to give the same truth aid on yet another side. Jesus of Nazareth died young; but had he not spoken and acted as much truth as the world could bear in his time? A frailty, a perpetual short-coming, motion in a curve line, seems the destiny of this earth. The excuse awaits us elsewhere; there must be one, for it is true, as said Goethe, that "Care is taken that the trees grow not up into heaven."[2] Then, like you, appointed ministers, must not be the less earnest in their work, yet to the greatest, the day, the moment is all their kingdom. God takes care of the increase.

Farewell! For your sake I would wish at this moment to be an Italian and a man of action. But *though an American,* I am not even *a woman of action;* so the best I can do is to pray with the whole heart. Heaven bless dear Mazzini, cheer his heart and give him worthy helpers to carry out its holy purposes!

(MH: fMS Am 1086 [11:105])

1. "The long exile that has just recommenced, the life unconsoled unless by affections that are remote and contested, and the long-protracted hope and the desire that has become deep of sleeping in peace at last since I could not live in my land."

2. Goethe's motto for the third part of *Dichtung und Wahrheit.*

155. To Marcus Spring

Rome
9th March, 1849.

Dear Marcus,

I wish you had written by this last steamer. I confidently expected to hear. Am anxious to know how Rebecca fared and, beside, it would have put me in the humor for writing, which, unluckily, I seldom am, when, as now, I have a private popportunity.

I send you by some poppo a pair of screens, selected principally because Eddie liked so much this pin-pricked St Peters and now he can keep it constantly between him and the light, if he likes.

I am anxious you should send this letter direct to my friend Caroline. I believe she is at Newburgh. You can detect her address through Dr Hull, who is her physician. She always forgets to send it to me. I send you also 1 no of Roman Advertiser, that you may see how we go on at Rome. You will see our good friends, the Stralts, edit. They deserve credit for being quite alone among the English in showing fairness towards Italy and have lost many a subscriber in consequence. I say they; it is the young man that guides the team, but Ma and Pa help push a little. The paper presents a refreshing contrast to the nauseous adulations and catholic out catholicized sentimentalities with which Hemans[?] used to stuff it.

But what I write for now is to tell that last night Mazzini came to see me. You will have heard how he was called to Italy, and received at Leghorn like a Prince as he is. Unhappily, in fact, the only one, the only great Italian. It is expected that if the Republic lasts he will be President. He has been made a Roman Citizen, and elected to the Assembly, the labels bearing in giant letters *Giuseppe Mazzini Cittadino Romano,* are yet up all over Rome. He entered by night on foot to avoid demonstrations, no doubt, and enjoy the quiet of his own thoughts at so great a moment. The people went under his windows next night and called him out to speak, but I did not know about it. Last night, I heard a ring, a German artist who lives here opened, the people of the house being out, I heard somebody say my name, the voice struck upon me at once I rushed. He looks more divine than ever, after all his new strange sufferings. He asked after all of you, lamented that he had never written. I told him you knew how impossible it was for him in these times, that you held him dear and would value his message of remembrance.

If he comes here again before I send this letter I shall get him to write his name for Rebecca, as she used to wish, but I felt last night, perhaps this is all he will be permitted to give me. He staid two hours and we talked through rapidly of every thing. He hopes to come often, but the crisis is tremendous and all will come on him, as, if any one can save Italy from her foes, inward and outward, it will be he. But it is very doubtful whether this be possible, the foes are too many, too strong, too subtle. Yet heaven helps sometimes. I only grieve I cannot aid him, freely would I give my life to aid him, only bargaining for a quick death! I dont like slow torture. I fear that is in reserve for him to survive defiant. True he can never be utterly defeated, but to see Italy bleeding prostrate once more will be very dreadful for him.

What would I not give that my other two brothers, Mr Emerson and William Channing could see him. All have in different ways the celestial fires, all have pure natures. They may have faults, but no base alloy. To me they form a triad. I know none other such.

Mickiewicz is a great poet, an inspired man, but he belongs to a different order of spirits from them.[1]

All this I write to you, Marcus, because you said when I was suffering to leave Mazzini, "you will meet him in heaven".

This I believe will be, despite all my faults. My other brothers will meet him, too.

17th Another steamer and no letter from you, do write Marcus, I feel disappointed. O if I could possibly have some good news some word to cheer me from any body on earth. You cant think how much I have had to suffer since we parted.

I have only seen Mazzini again in the Assembly; he has sent me tickets twice to hear him speak: it was a pure commanding voice, but when finished he looked very exhausted and melancholy. He looks as if the great battle he had fought the past year had been too much for his strength, and that he was only sustained now by the fire of his soul.

This little picture is for Jeanie; her mother can tell her the story. Ever affecy yrs

MARGARET

I have not got the autograph. he is overpowered with affairs at this moment; if I ever get, I shall keep it for Rebecca.

(CSt)

1. Adam Mickiewicz (1798–1855) was a Polish poet and revolutionary patriot who lived in Paris. Fuller met him there, and they corresponded when she was in Italy.

156.   To Ellen Fuller Channing

Rome
13th March, 1849.

My dear Ellen,

It is more than a year since I heard from you, and more than a year since I sent your pin and the little cross for Greta. I rather wonder you have never written a word, to tell me whether you liked them or not. I never even knew whether they reached you. I sent your pin by Mrs. Gardiner, a mosaic for Mother by Mr. Hillard.

I never recd from you money to buy you engravings!

I am now so neglected by my old friends that it quite takes away disposition on my side to write to them. Perhaps some letters are lost but I cannot know.

When I do get a letter there is generally forgetfulness how little I am likely to know of details as to your affairs in U. S. Of you I know nothing, except, as Charles Newcomb mentioned you were not at home when he was in Concord, I suppose you were then well.

I inclose some little pictures for Greta; if I were there, I could tell her stories about them all, and teach her to pronounce the Italian names.

All these costumes I have seen often; they animate the streets and squares of Rome on festival occasions. The Eminente is the Roman Transteverini, the descendant of the old blood, many of these women are very handsome and proud. The first autumn I was here I went often to see them dancing with their tamberines, and hear them sing their frank love-songs. I am now [r]id of all these women; [th]ey are so very unintellectual; at first one likes the naiveté but people always tire, when it is impossible to draw them one single step beyond their habitual limits. I have passed in Rome a winter nearly as lonely as you can in your little brown cottage, but then how different, when I can always have the delight of going into the galleries or among the great remains, and every day the public events bring so much excitement. Yet now I mean to seek people a little. Sometimes I go apart because in their faces there is so little comfort, in their hearts so little warmth, but after awhile I must always return for it is my nature to expe[rience] and love a great many [hum]an beings, and I feel blighted in a narrow life.

The Crawfords take you this. Mrs. C. thinks herself very poor because she has only three thousand dollars a year and cannot keep a carriage; she comes here into my garret to tell me these distresses; how they must economize severely to have a thousand dollars in pocket when they leave Rome. They are going through France and by steamer. I fear when I come, it must be by sail-ship. I dread the voyage exceedingly so long an one would be very terrible to my poor head. However I hope 'tis far enough off. I shall not come this year unless driven, yet dont let people forget me quite, twould be sad to come home and find nobody to greet poor affectionate

MARGARET.

(MH: fMS Am 1086 [9:174])

157.   To Caroline Sturgis Tappan

16th March, 1849.

My loved Caroline

Your letter received yesterday, so full of sweetness and acquainting me so well with the facts of your life brought true consolation: forgive, if in the inclosed, I utter something like a reproach, that I knew through others first this great fact in your life.[1] I ought not to have felt so, But all the while I was hoping myself, I thought of you too, and expected this news from your next letter. When it told me nothing, I thought it was not so, then when others came and told me, I felt sad. Since I have had this troubled feeling, I will not suppress it, but send the inclosed letter, otherwise not of worth, that you may know me no better than I am.

Now then your little one is there. Will not William write me the day and hour and what kind of weather there was when it came. I hope to hear soon.

I am very glad to hear how your life is likely to be and that you will be with your baby among mountains. Mine too saw mountains when he first looked forward into the world. Rieti, not only an old classic town of Italy, but one founded by what are now called the aborigines, is a hive of very ancient dwellings with soft-colored red brown roofs, a citadel and several towers. It is in a plain twelve miles in diameter one way, not much less the other, entirely encircled with mountains of the noblest form, casinos and hermitages gleam here and there on their lower slopes. This plain is almost the richest in Italy and full of vineyards. Rieti is near the foot of the hills on one side, the rapid Velino makes almost the circuit of its walls on its way to Terni. *I too had my apartment, shut out from the family on the bank of this river. I too saw the mountains,* as I lay on my restless couch. I had a *piazza, or as they call them here loggia which hung over the river,* where I walked most of the night, for I was not like you, I could not sleep at all those months. I do not know how I lived.

In Rieti the ancient Umbrians were married thus. In presence of friends the man and maid received together the gifts of *fire and water.* The bridegroom then conducted to his house the bride. At the door he gave her the keys and entering threw behind him nuts as a sign that he renounced all the frivolities of boyhood.

But I intend to write all that relates to the birth of Angelino in a little book, which I shall, I hope, show you sometime. I have begun it and then stopped; it seemed to me he would die. If he lives, I shall finish it, before the details are at all faded in my mind.

Rieti is a place where I should have liked to have him born, and where I should like to have him now, but 1st the people are so wicked, the most ferocious and mercenary population of Italy. I did not know this when I went there. I expected to be solitary and quiet among poor people. But they looked on *the marchioness* as an ignorant *Inglese,* and they fancy all *Inglesi* have wealth untold. Me they were bent on plundering in every way; they are so still. They made me suffer terribly in the first days and disturb me greatly still in visits to my darling. To add to my trouble, the legion Garribaldi is now stationed there, in which so many desperadoes are enlisted. The Neapolitan troops 6 miles off are far worse, and in case of conflict I should fear for the nurse of Angelino, the loveliest young woman there. I cannot take her from her family. I cannot change him to another place without immense difficulty in every way. That I could not nurse him was owing to the wickedness of these people, who threw me into a fever the first days. I shall tell you about it sometime. There is something very singular and fateful in the way all has wrought to give me more and more sorrow and difficulty. Now I only live from day to day watching the signs of the times; when I asked you for the money I meant to use it to stay with him in Rieti, but now I do not know whether I can stay there or not. If it proves impossible, I shall at all risks, remove him. I may say every day is to me one of mental doubt and conflict; how it will end, I do not know. I try to hold myself ready every way body and mind for any necessity.

You say no secret can be kept in the civilized world and I suppose not long, but it is very important to me to keep this, for the present, if possible, and by and by to have the mode of disclosure at my option. For this, I have made the cruellest sacrifices; it will, indeed, be just like the rest, if they are made of none effect.

After I wrote to you I went to Rieti. The weather was mild when I set out, but by the fatality that has attended me throughout, in the night changed to a cold, unknown in Italy and remained so all the time I staid. There was, as is common in Italy, no fireplace except in the kitchen. I suffered much in my room with its brick floor, and windows through which came the cold wind freely. My darling did not suffer, because he was a little swaddled child like this and robed in wool beside, but I did very much. When I first took him in my arms he made no sound but leaned his head against my bosom, and staid so, he seemed to say how could you abandon me, what I felt you will know only when you have your own. A little girl who lived in the house told me all the day of my departure he could not be comforted, always refusing the breast and looking at the door; he has been a strangely precocious infant; I think it was through sympathy with me, and that in that regard it may be a happiness for him to be with these more plebian, instinctive, joyous natures. I saw he was more serene, that he was not sensitive as when with me, and slept a great deal more. You speak of my being happy; all the solid happiness I have known has been at times when he went to sleep in my arms. You say when Ellen's beautiful life had been so wasted, it hardly seemed worthwhile to begin another.[2] I had all those feelings too. I do not look forward to his career and his manly life; it is *now* I want to be with him, before passion, care and bafflings begin. If I had a little money I should go with him into strict retirement for a year or two and live for him alone. This I cannot do; all life that has been or could be natural to me is invariably denied. God knows why, I suppose.

I receive with profound gratitude your thought of taking him, if any thing should happen to us. Should I live, I dont know whether I should wish him to be an Italian or American citizen; it depends on the course events take here politically but should we die, the person to whom he would naturally fall is a sister of his father a person of great elegance and sweetness but entirely limited in mind. I should not like that. I will think about it. Before he was born I did a great deal having the idea I might die and all my spirit remain incarnated in him, but now I think I shall live and carry him round myself as I ride on my ass into Egypt. We shant go so mildly as this yet

You talk about your mangers, Carrie, but that was only for a little, presently came Kings with gold cups and all sorts of things. Joseph pawned them; with part of the money he bought this nice donkey for the journey; and they lived on the rest till Joseph could work at his trade, we have no donkey and it costs a great deal to travel in diligences and steamers, and being a nobleman is a poor trade in a ruined despotism just turning into a Republic. I often think of Dicken's marchioness playing whist in the kitchen.[3] So I play whist every where.

Speaking of the republic, you say do I not wish Italy had a great man. Mazzini is a great man; in mind a great poetic statesman, in heart a lover, in action decisive and full of resource as Cesar. Dearly I love Mazzini, who also loves me. He came in just as I had finished this first letter to you. His soft radiant look makes melancholy music in my soul; it consecrates my present life that like the Magdalen I may at the important hour shed all the consecrated ointment on his head. There is one, Mazzini, who understands thee well, who knew thee no less when an object of popular fear than now of idolatry, and who, if the pen be not held too feebly, will make that posterity shall know thee, too.

Ah well! what is the use of writing, dear Caroline. A thousand volumes would not suffice for what I have to say. Pray for You? oh much I have, for my love for you is deep, I trust immortal. May you hold a dear one safe in your arms! and all go sweetly as it has gone

> I could not wish thy better state
> Was one of my degree
> But we may mourn that evil fate
> Made such a churl of me.

Could I envy it would be this peace with the own one, but God grant it to Carrie, since thou wert such a niggard as to steal it from me. At least make some good use of it; don't give it to fools only.

Adieu, love, my love to William your husband with the fair noble face.

You can always show him my letters if he cares to read them, then burn—
and when you are once more able [ ] to

[M]ARGARET

Although I think y[r]emember that I shall be [ ] for it is, indeed, a
great physical crisis.

No American here knows that I ever was in Rieti. They suppose I passed
the summer at Subiaco.

(MH: fMS Am 1086 [9:170])

1. Ellen Sturgis Tappan (1849–1924) was born on 11 February.
2. Tappan's sister, Ellen Sturgis Hooper, who had an unhappy marriage.
3. Charles Dickens, *The Old Curiosity Shop*, chap. 57.

158.   To Anna Barker Ward

Rome, 18th March,
1849.

My dear Anna,

I thought of you in your mountain home, enjoying life peacefully with
Sam and your children when a letter comes to tell me that you have for
months been separated from them, and are under a physician's care in
New York.

Thus some strange worm comes in every bud; there is nothing quite un-
touched and wholesome in this world.

You will receive this about May and then I want Sam to make for me the
yearly bulletin of your affairs, and be more particular as to details than
heretofore. For of you especially I should like to know exactly how you
fare and what are the prospects of recovery.

Caroline writes me that she too is likely to live in Lenox, so, if you are
well enough to be there and I ever come there, I shall see several of my
friends near together. But it must not be as it was in a dream I had here
in Rome. I dreamed that I came to your house; the place seemed quite
beautiful to me and I saw the mountains from the window. While I was
looking, you and Sam came in with a number of persons I did not know.
You all talked of things about which I knew nothing and nobody spoke to
me or drew me from my window. At last I suggested that I had been gone
a long time and you replied carelessly "O yes, I think I have not seen you
since Wednesday."— You must not be so indifferent when I *do* come, for
it is really a long time since we have met and your home I have never
seen.

Ellen Hooper is gone to a fitter sphere. I hope, more equal compan-ionship. Is not Sam sorry to miss her? She cared a great deal for him.

I have passed the sunny winter in Rome, beset by cares and perplexities in strange combination, yet ransoming many hours when I could forget myself and learn from every part and live in the whole. I know not how I shall find myself in America separated from objects that have been so much to me. Rome as an abode has taken the strongest hold on my affec-tions. Could I live here very simply with one or two objects of affection and what it is always so easy to find here two or three intellectual companions, sometimes publishing a few thoughts or impressions selected from the many, I should be content. But every plan I have made to secure by my own exertions the slender means needed for such a life has failed owing to the negligence of those to whom I trusted in the distance. This seems to me very sad. I am here at a most important crisis. I am fitted to observe and communicate my observations. Yet owing to the carelessness of those who had made me every vow of love and service, I have suffered cruel suspense and at last more cruel disappointment,—I cannot tell you how weary I am of striving in the world. More weary than I ought, but my strength was pre-maturely exhausted, and the baffling of hope all through life will sadden the most ardent nature at last so that it gives smoke easier than flame.

Adieu! these lines I send by a private hand. They will not reach you be-fore the 1st May; then I hope you will write, you or Sam to your friend

MARGARET.

Should I be able to remain, you will not see me before the Summer of 1850. Important objects as well as my wishes urge my remaining here a year more.

(MH: bMS Am 1465 [930])

159. To Giovanni Angelo Ossoli

Rieti,
4th Avrile 49.

Mio caro,

Quanto e strana che noi non possiamo passare questo giorno insieme. Bisogna pregare essere piu felici un altro anno. Ieri avevo comprato uc-celletti per nostra cena e speravo molto vederti come non sei venuto non mangiavo io. Ma oggi non mi dispiace che non sei venuto perche ancora piove forte, e Angelino, che e stato avanti si felice, si grazioso che volevo tutti i momenti per ti vederlo oggi sta male. Ha sofferto tutta la notte cogli denti, e oggi, poverino, non puo trovare pace. Speriamo che stara bene quando hai potete venire.

Mi pare che ero inviato per Dio proteggerlo in questi giorni terribili. Niccola stavo pazzo più che quaranta ore, Chiara sempre piangendo disperata. Ieri notte Niccola ha dormito e oggi sta in suoi sensi.

Garribaldi non ha passato la frontiere, altro son venuti più truppe Napolitane in Aquila e qui vengon adesso piu truppe Romane da Terni rinforzare Garribaldi. Ma non si crede qui che Napolitani pensan entrare, ma che fan questi dimostrazioni per levare una parte delle forze Romane da Terracina, che probabile van entrare per Terracina

Garribaldi non ha nul comando sopra questi desperati di sua banda, la Domenica amazzavan un frate, due cittadini e fra se nove, si dice. Due corpi eran trovati nel fiume. La presenza della truppa regolare puo prevenire questi eccessi. Ma io adesso non ho, sicuro, coraggio sorfire sola. Sta vicino da qui un piccolo giardino dove vado con Angelino negli begli giorni, in strada non sorto mai.

Domandi di Antonia si qualche persona mi ha cercato e fa mi piacere mettere questa lettrina subito a la posta per Firenze. Quanto mi dispiace che tu hai questo servizio terribile per la notte. Sara una rovina per tua salute e quanto e fatta scioccamente e senza calcolo come tutte le cose di Roma come si cercavan disgustare. Prendi per mi subito il foglio di Mazzini, si tu hai denaro per un mese si non pel sei mese. Son perfettamente disgusta con questa Epoca è divenuto foglio reazionario. Addio, mio bene, Dio ti benedica e ti conserva prego questo 4 Avrile la tua

M.

Aspetto tue nuove Venerdi.

Non vieni qui la notte, vieni per la diligenza e prendi posta in cabriolet, di bon ora.

Rieti,
4th April 49.

My dear,

How very strange it is that we cannot spend this day together.[1] We must pray to be happier another year. Yesterday I had bought little birds for our dinner and I hoped very much to see you[;] since you did not come, I did not eat. But today I am not sorry that you did not come because it is still raining hard, and Angelino, who was before so happy, so nice that I wanted you to see him every moment is not well today. He suffered all night because of his teeth and today, poor baby, he cannot find any peace. I hope he will be well when you are able to come.

I think I was sent by God to protect him in these terrible days. Niccola was crazy for more than 40 hours, Chiara always crying with desperation. Last night Niccola slept and today he is no longer delirious.

Garribaldi has not crossed the frontier, but more Neapolitan troops went to Aquila and more Roman troops are coming here from Terni to reinforce Garribaldi.[2] Nobody here believes that the Neapolitans think to enter, but they are making these maneuvers in order to move a part of the Roman forces from Terracina, and probably they are going to enter through Terracina.

Garribaldi has no control over these desperados of his band, it is said that on Sunday a friar, two citizens and 9 of their own were killed. Two bodies were found in the river. The presence of the regular troop can prevent these excesses. But now I surely do not have courage to go out alone. Near here there is a small garden where I go with Angelino on nice days, I never go out into the street.

Ask Antonia if someone has looked for me and please do me the favor to put this letter quickly into the mail for Florence. I am so sorry that you have that terrible night duty. It will ruin your health and it is done as foolishly and senselessly as everything else in Rome[,] as if for the purpose to try to disgust. Get Mazzini's paper for me at once, if you have money for one month if not for six months. I am really disgusted with this Epoca[;] it has become a reactionary's paper. Goodbye my dear, on this 4 April God bless and protect you prays your

M.

I forward your news on Friday.

Do not come here in the night, come by stagecoach and take a seat in the carriage early.

(MH: fMS Am 1086 [9:196])

1. Their commemoration of the date strongly suggests that it was their wedding anniversary.

2. Charles Albert had again attacked the Austrians and again lost. The Romans thought the war likely to continue even though Charles Albert abdicated, and so they sent Garibaldi's troops to the mountains, where they remained until 26 April.

160.   To Giovanni Angelo Ossoli

[guigno 1849]

Quanto m'incresce, amore, mancar ti ieri e possibile anch, oggi, si tu puoi venire. Vado a Casa Diez, si possibile cerchi la, ultimo piano, si sto la ancora o son andato al spedale. Dio ti conserva Quanto ho sofferta a vedere i feriti, e non posso conoscere si qualche cosa ti accade, ma bisogna sperare. Ho ricevuta la lettera di Rieti, nostro Nino sta perfettamente bene, grazia per questo.

[M]i fa di bene che almeno i Romani han fatto qualche cosa, si solamente tu puoi stare. In evento del morte di tutti dui ho lasciata una carta
col certificato di Angelino e alcune righe pregando i Sto curare per lui. Si
per qualche accidente io moriro tu puoi riprendere questa carta si vuoi da
me, come da tua moglie. Ho voluta per Nino andare in America, ma tu
farari come ti pare. Era nostro dovere combinare questo meglio. Ma speriamo che non sara bisogno. Sempre benedicendo la tua

MARGHERITA

Si tu vivi e io moro, stai sempre devotissimo per Nino. Si tu ami mai un
altra, ancora pensi primo per lui, io prego, prego, amore.

[June 1849]

How sorry I am, love, to miss you yesterday and possibly also today, if
you can come, I [will] go to Casa Diez, if possible inquire for me there, on
the last floor, if I am still there or if I went to the hospital. God keep you
How much I suffered at the sight of those wounded people, and I have no
way of knowing whether something happens to you, but one must hope. I
received the letter from Rieti, our Nino is perfectly well, thanks for this.

It does me good that at least the Romans have done something, if only
you can survive. In the event of the death of both of us I have left a paper
with Angelino's birth certificate and a few words praying the Sto[rys] to
take care of him. Should I by any chance die you can take back this paper
from me, if you want, as from your wife. I wanted Nino to go to America,
but you will do as you wish. It was our duty to arrange this better, but let's
hope that there will not be need for it. Always blessing you your

MARGARET

If you live and I die, be always very devoted to Nino. If you ever love another woman, always think first of him, I beg you, beg you, love.

(MH: fMS Am 1086 [9:215½])

161.   To Richard F. Fuller

Rome
8th July, 1849.

My dear Richard,

I received two or three weeks ago your letter of the 4th May. Probably I
shall answer it, sometime, if I should ever again find myself tranquil and
recruited from the painful excitements of these last days. But amid the ru-

ined hopes of Rome, the shameful oppressions she is beginning to suffer, amid these noble bleeding martyrs, my brothers, I cannot fix my thoughts on any thing else.

I write that you may assure Mother of my safety, which in the last days began to be seriously imperilled. Say that so soon as I can find means of conveyance, without an expense too enormous, I shall go again into the mountains. There I shall find pure bracing air and I hope stillness for a time. Say she need feel no anxiety if she does not hear from me for some-time. I may feel indisposed to write, as I do now, my heart is too full.

Private hopes of mine are fallen with the hopes of Italy. I have played for a new stake and lost it. Life looks too difficult. But, for the present, I shall try to waive all thoughts of self, and renew my strength.

Say to dear Eugene when you write that the hour is not yet come for me to write to him as I would.

On the last page is the answer to Mr E. B. Clarke about the engraving it is put apart so that you can tear it off and give it him.[1] I do not feel as if I could write any more. Your affectionate sister

M.

I have found a conveyance and hope to be in the country tomorrow. Radetsky is expected here on Sunday.[2]

(MH: fMS Am 1086 [9:160])

1. Probably Elijah Pope Clark (1791–1859), a Boston bank cashier who had long been in-terested in Thomas Carlyle and who acted as his American agent after 1847.

2. Though the Austrians controlled all of the northern Papal States, they did not contest the French for Rome. Radetzky did not enter the city.

162.   To Lewis Cass, Jr.

Rieti
19th July, 1849.

Dear Mr Cass,

I seem to have arrived in a different world, since passing the mountains. This little red-brown nest, which those we call the aborigines of Italy made long before Rome was, lies tranquil amid the net-work of vineyards, its casines and convents gleam pleasantly from the hillsides, the dirt accumu-lates undisturbed in its streets, and pigs and children wallow in it, while Madonna-veiled bare-legged women twirl the distaff at every door and win-dow, happy if so they can earn five cents a day. We have not been able to find an apartment, so we have rooms at the rustic *locanda*, which is on the piazza, clean and airy and where may be studied all the humours of the place. There is the fountain where come the girls in their corset, long shift-sleeves, and coloured petticoat, the silver needle in their fine hair, attractive they look from my window for the dirt disappears in distance. Near, it not dismays their lovers, who help them to adjust the water-vase on their heads. (N. B. no husband does this.) All the dandies of Rieti in all kinds of queer uniforms are congregated below, at the barber's the druggists, the caffé, they sit and digest the copious slander, chief product of this, as of every *little* hive of men. The Baronesses and Countesses, in the extreme of Italian undress, are peeping through the blinds, at half past seven, if the band plays, they will put on their best dresses, (alas! mongrel French fashions prevail here,) and parade on foot, fanning themselves whether the weather be hot or cold, on foot, for the Corso of Rieti is nominal. At present the scene is varied by the presence of the Spanish force, who promise to stay only three days, and I hope they will not, for they eat every thing up like locusts. For the moment it pleases to see their foreign features, and hear the noble sounds of their language. We have performed our social duties, have called on the handsome doctor's wife, whom we [fo]und ironing in her antichamber. [Mad]ame, the Gonfaloniere's sister, who had just had a child, and recd us in her chamber, and on the father guardian of the beautifully placed monastery of St Antonio, who insisted on making us excellent coffee, which we must take under the shade of the magnificent cypresses, for women must not enter, "only" said he chuckling, "Garribaldi obliged us to let his enter, and I have even seen them braiding their hair!" Maria of the Episcopal garden has left her card in the form of a pair of pigeons. I could find much repose for the moment in these simple traits of a limited life and in this pure air, were it not for the state in which I find my baby. You know, my dear Mr Cass, I flattered you with the thought you would be happy in having a child, may you never know such a pang as I felt in kissing his poor pale little hand which he can hardly lift. He is worn to a skeleton, all his sweet childish graces fled; he is so weak it seems to me he can scarcely ever revive to health, if he cannot, I do not wish him to live; life is hard enough for the strong it is too much for the feeble. Only, if he dies, I hope I shall, to[o.] I was too fatigued before, and this last shipwreck of ho[pes] would be more than I could bear.

Adieu, dear Mr Cass, write when you can; tell me of the world, of which I hear nothing here, of suffering Rome, always dear, whatever may oppress me, and of yourself. Ever yours

M. O.

(MB)

163. To Samuel G. and Anna Barker Ward

Florence
21st Octr 1849.

My dear Sam,

I saw with great pleasure your writing on one of the letters brought by Mr Mozier and opened that one first; it was a disappointment to find only a few lines about the money, though I thank you much for your affectionate thoughtfulness of me which induced your sending that; it was welcome at this period, though I am sorry to need such aid and should not but for the violation of pledges in those who had not only promised but offered to secure me employment ample for my maintenance in remaining abroad. But I will not stain this brief page with any notice of the bitter cares and disappointments I have been made to suffer at a time when a little peace would have been so precious. Ere reading this you will know that I am married and that my husband is not better situated than myself; indeed worse for he must be for the present separated from his natural friends and career. He will have by and by a little money from the paternal estate, but, in the present condition of the Roman dominion, it is not easy to raise, we may have to wait several years. Every thing has turned against us; we are not disposed to complain amid the desolation of other homes, and the deep griefs the noblest we know are suffering, yet our causes for anxiety are great, the rather as we have a little tender one to care for, and I confess I do not feel much courage when I think of privation for him. I would wish him the shelter of a secure roof, good care and a serene environment in his earliest days. I thought I had loved the children of others as much as I could love a child, but find the thrill far more vital with my own; You may perhaps look for me to say something of my companion and to you I should like to, but it is too difficult; you are among the very few of my friends who I think may be able to see why we can live together, and may appreciate the unspoiled nature and loveliness of his character; he is entirely without what is commonly called culture, educated by a tutor and that tutor an old priest, he knows readin ritin and rithmetic, but the first I think he never used to go through with a book; nature has been his book; of that some lines he has spelled thoroughly. To me the simplicity, the reality, the great tenderness and refinement of his character make a domestic place in this world and as it is for my heart that he loves me, I hope he may always be able to feel the same, but that is as God pleases. It seems to us now that, if we were sure of a narrow competency, we could have a good deal of happiness together in what remains of life; however it is not worth-while to trouble too much, life itself is so uncertain; we both had a narrow escape during the seige of Rome; our little one has since been very near death, and now the Cholera is as near as Bologna.

I will now turn to Anna from whom I have a letter since receiving yours—you speak dear Anna of my not having answered some letter, probably some one has been lost, as many were in the more convulsed days; here five have come to me that have been *perdus* in some corner for more than a year but none was from you; it was I know not how long since I had heard. Now I thank you for this one which gives me the real facts as to your health, Sam's new life &c. I had heard before that you bore your imprisonment beautifully but had been led to fear you would not be able to walk any more, but lose the benefit and joy of free motion entirely as Mrs Spring did when I knew her; you do not say positively, but I infer from your letter it is nothing so, for you talk of climbing the hills with me. Your hills and all objects in America look very far off to me; at times I cannot realize that I shall ever see the old familiar faces again; very dear and lovely they seem in the distance, especially now as in the sad reflux of that great tide of life in which my heart had gone forward with as much force as was left it I have more time to think of lang syne. It makes me weep to think of it; life was so fatiguing then and is so now, beyond my strength; happy are those who have a childhood of play beneath the trees; I hope your little ones will have it in their mountain home, and that if I do not see you or them there we shall meet in Elysium— But perhaps we shall meet in some very different place; I have some vague idea of returning next summer, though ways means and prospects are yet to be discovered. At present we are moored in Florence, I hope till April or May. I wrote to you the day I recd your letter, but before finishing, the Police began to trouble us, and I have been uncertain if we should not have to go away. Now we have permission to stay for two months and I suppose they will make no difficulty about renewing it. So I hope you will write here to Margaret Ossoli, care J. Mozier Esq. Although a green retirement and still country life seem now to me so sweet, I felt glad to hear that Sam is to leave it for a time; it is better to mix often with the struggling suffering crowd; it is a more generous life and culture. Happy those who can alternate the two lives at pleasure. I like to see Dante as he stands here on the wall of the Cathedral Heaven and Hell are in the near view, he touches the walls of Florence. Yet it is not Florence I would have chosen to touch. Florence is a kind of Boston: it has not the poetic greatness of the other Italian cities; it is a place to work and study in; simple life does not seem so great. I feel reconciled to be here now as the place most economical and convenient and where I still have two or three friends. I begin to feel interested again in looking at Art and I like walking on the heights, beside the air agrees with the baby; who seems to grow better every day; still this place will never charm me as have (I do not speak of Rome, which was my *home*) but Venice, Milan Bologna, Brescia in fact almost all Italian towns. The end of my sheet bids me come to an end; you asked me to write a *real* letter. I fear this will give you no satisfaction, if so, pardon dear Anna, so great has been the passion of my life since you knew me, it is difficult to speak. My friends remain in their place I seem to have more clue to their state than they to mine. Across the stream I see them; they look fair and tall, but I must go to them; they cannot come to me. Farewell.

(MH: bMS Am 1465 [931])

164. To Elizabeth Barrett Browning

Casa Libri
Thursday 6th Decr [1849]

Dear Mrs Browning,

Thanks for sending me the names. I find I had already the same cap pattern, but it looked so pretty on your baby's head I did not recognize it.[1]

I am very sorry the nurse did not come upstairs with him; if you send her again will you tell her to do so, that he may exchange a few looks with mine. I think babies seem amazed at one another, they are not in haste to make acquaintance, probably they still feel what a world lies hidden in each person, they are not not yet made callous by those habits of hasty unfeeling intercourse soon formed by what is called society.

It seemed to me when I was last at your house, as if a curtain fell down between us. A great sadness fell upon me, just after Mr Browning came in; it did not seem to come from him; he seemed cheerful and glowing after his walk, but some cause changed suddenly the temper of my soul, so that I could hardly realize what was passing and the cloud did not leave me for several hours. Did you share any such influence. I think probably it was confined to me, but have noted the day and hour in my diary, in case any interpretation should later be tendered.

Those fragments expressed the almost universal feeling towards Poe; several women loved him, but it seemed more with passionate illusion which he amused himself by inducing than with sympathy; I think he really had no friend.[2] I did not know him, though I saw and talked with him often, but he always seemed to me shrouded in an assumed character. Still as I did not know him, and do not accept the opinions of others till my own impressions have confirmed them, as I did know he had much to try his spirit I always treated him cordially. He seemed to feel that *I* was not prejudiced against him; he once said that he had faith in me, that he thought me not only incapable of baseness, but incapable of understanding it; that this was from him a strong expression of esteem, shows what his life had been. He said in a sketch he published of me that he thought me capable of great affection.[3] Now, seeing these bitter waters poured out even upon his tomb, I have remembered these things and regretted that I never tried whether more friendliness from me might have been useful to him; but it is only the millionth time I have let occasions pass where suffering fellow men might have been soothed or helped Pardon that the leaf is soiled.[4] I had not observed it. Ever truly yours

M. OSSOLI

(VtMiM)

1. Robert Wiedeman Barrett Browning (1849–1912), called "Pen" or "Penini," later became a painter and sculptor.

2. Fuller was evenhanded in her assessment of Poe. She praised his fiction and pointed out the strengths and weaknesses of the poetry. She reviewed him in the *Tribune* but left him out of her essay on American literature in *Papers on Literature and Art.*

3. After calling *Woman in the Nineteenth Century* "a book which few women in the country could have written, and no woman in the country would have published, with the exception of Miss Fuller," Poe said her face showed "profound sensibility, capacity for affection, for love."

4. In October 1849 Rufus Griswold, Poe's literary executor, published a defamatory article in the *Tribune.*

165. To Ellen Fuller Channing

Florence.
11th Decr 1849

My dear Ellen

I find myself in the novel position of having no less than 3 letters of yours to answer, the one written after your visit to Mother, one by Mr Mozier (with Napoleon, contribution of 2 dimes from my little loves of the rising generation, their hair and the Daguerrotype) and one a year and a half old which came to light with 3 dollars worth more of the same date tother day. This is the second time of my unexpectedly finding the gaps in correspondence filled up, in consequence of some bankers clerk feeling an unexpected twinge of conscience. I wish the fit would come upon them oftener than once a year. The Daguerrotype is beautiful. Mr Horatio Greenough was delighted with it; he says it is a true picture, another person of fine taste observed that the position and sentiment of the child are truly Raphaelesque. Several have observed that she looks like my Angelino. I do not see that it is so.

You are anxious, my dear Ellen, to know some details of my past history and I should like to gratify you, but I hardly know how. There are some reasons which I cannot explain, further than by the remark that Ossoli is still a member of the Roman Catholic church, why I do not go into all the matter of fact history. I cannot, at least at present, tell exactly the facts, so I choose to say nothing. I should be glad if he disengaged himself entirely from the Roman ritual, but I doubt he never will; his habitual attachment to it is strong, and I do not trouble myself about it as no priest has any influence over his mind.

About him I do not like to say much, as he is an exceedingly delicate person. He is not precisely reserved, but it is not natural to him to *talk* about the objects of strong affection. I am sure he would not try to describe me to his sister, but would rather she would take her own impression of me, and, as much as possible, I wish to do the same by him. I expect that to many of my friends Mr Emerson for one, he will be nothing, and they will not understand that I should have life in common with him. But I do not think he will care; he has not the slightest tinge of self-love; he has throughout our intercourse been used to my having many such ties; he has no wish to be anything to persons with whom he does not feel spontaneously bound, and when I am occupied is happy in himself. But *some* of my friends and my family who will see him in the details of practical life, cannot fail to prize the purity and simple strength of his character, and, should he continue to love me as he has done, to consider his companionship an inestimable blessing to me. I say *if*, because all human affections are frail, and I have experienced too great revulsions in my own not to know it, yet I feel great confidence in the permanence of his love. It has been unblemished so far, under many trials, especially as I have been more sick, desponding and unreasonable in many ways than I ever was before and more so, I hope, than I ever shall be again. But at all such times, he never had a thought except to sustain and cheer me; he is capable of the sacred love, the love passing that of women, he showed it to his father, to Rome, to me, now he loves his child in the same way. I think he will be an excellent father, though he could not speculate about it, or in fact about anything

Our meeting was singular, fateful I may say. Very soon he offered me his hand through life, but I never dreamed I should take it. I loved him and felt very unhappy to leave him, but the connexion seemed so every way unfit, I did not hesitate a moment. He, however, thought I should return to him, as I did. I acted upon a strong impulse. I could not analyze at all what passed in my mind. I neither rejoice nor grieve, for bad or for good I acted out my character Had I never connected myself with any one my path was clear, now it is all hid, but in that case my development must have been partial. As to marriage I think the intercourse of heart and mind may be fully enjoyed without entering in this partnership of daily life, still I do not find it burdensome. We get along very well and I find have our better intercourse as much as if we did not buy (unhappily we have nothing to sell) together. The friction that I have seen mar so much the domestic life of others does not occur with us, or at least has not. Then there is the pleasure of always being at hand to help one another. Still all this I had felt before in some degree. The great novelty, the immense gain to me is my relation with my child. I thought the mother's heart lived in me before, but it did not. I knew nothing about it. Yet before his birth I dreaded it. I thought I should not survive but if I did and my child did, was I not cruel to bring another into this terrible world. I could not at that time get any other view. When he was born that deep melancholy changed at once into rapture, but it did not last long, then came the prudential motherhood, then came Mrs Edgworth, Mrs Smith. I became a coward, a caretaker not only for the morrow, but impiously faithless twenty or thirty years ahead. It seemed very wicked to have brought the little tender thing into the midst of cares and perplexities we had not feared in the least for ourselves. I imagined every thing; he was to be in danger of every enormity the Croats were then committing on the babies of Lombardy. The house would be burned over his head, but if he escaped, how were we to get money to buy his bibs and primers. Then his father was to be killed in the fighting and I t[o] die of [ ]. Your hazarding the opinion dear Ellen, [tha]t it would have been best to tell Mother any part of th[is] till I arrived at some "clearing" however fruitless, and [w]aterless, only shows the impossibility of judging for others in these great trials. I have borne Mother much love, and shown her some, and never more than by standing quite alone, in those strangely darkening days. I grieve she should have suffered now, but that is nothing in comparison with anxiety she might have been made to feel.

During the siege of Rome I could not see my little boy. What I endured at that time in various ways not many would survive. In the burning sun I went every day to wait in the crowd for letters about him Often they did not come. I saw blood that had streamed on the wall close to where Ossoli was. I have here a piece of bomb that burst close to him. I sought solace in tending the suffering men. But when I saw the beautiful fair young men bleeding to death, or mutilated for life, I felt all the wo of all the mothers who had nursed each to that full flower to see it thus cut down. I felt the consolation too for those youths died worthily. I was the Mater Dolorosa, and I remembered that the midwife who helped Angelino into the world came from the sign of the Mater Dolorosa. I thought, even if he lives, if he comes into the world at this great troubled time, terrible with perplexed duties, it may be to die thus at twenty years, one of a glorious hecatomb indeed, but still a sacrifice. It seemed then I was willing he should die But when I really saw him lingering as he did all August 2d and July 1st between life and death, I could not let him go unless I would go with him. When I saw his first smile, his poor wan feeble smile and more than four weeks we watched him night and day before we saw it, new resolution downed in my heart, I resolved to live day by day and hour by hour for his dear sake and feed on ashes when offered. So if he is only treasure lent, if he must go as sweet Waldo did, as my little Pickie, as *my* children do,[1] I shall at least have these days and hours with him. Now he is in the highest health and so gay— We cannot but feel happy in him, though the want of money is so serious a thing. I wish we had a little money, since we *have* lived, or knew better how to earn it. I suppose we shall find ways The governor of the world must have his alms days every now and then; we will eat the charity soup ourselves and buy pap for Nino. If I can but be well, there's the rub, always.

[G]ive love and kisses to the dear children, tell Marnie and Ittie I keep the dimes for Angelino.[2]

He plays a great deal with their hair, talks to it, says *poor*, I hope they may all meet next summer, and Eugene's little one, too. My love to dear Elizh I wish she and Mr Emerson would write to me, but I suppose they dont know what to say Tell them there is no need to say anything about these affairs if they dont want to. I am just the same for them I was before and yr affect sister

M.

(MH: fMS Am 1086 [9:171])

1. Arthur Young Greeley (1844–49), called Pickie, was the son of Horace and Mary Greeley.

2. The Channings' two daughters: Margaret Fuller (1844–1932) and Caroline Sturgis (1846–1917).

166. To Caroline Sturgis Tappan

[ca. 17 December 1849]

[ ] I do not know what to write about him; he changes so much; has so many characters; he is like me in that, his father's character is simple and uniform though not monotonous more than are the flowers of spring,

flowers of the valley. He is now in the most perfect rosy health, a very gay impetuous, ardent, but sweet tempered child. He seems to me to have nothing in common with the first baby with its exstatic smiles, its exquisite sensitiveness and a distinction in the gesture and attitudes that struck every body. His temperament seems changed by taking the milk of these robust women. His form is robust but the feet and [ ] quite any [ ] make him some prettier dresses.

He is now come to quite a knowing age (fifteen months.) In the morng, so soon as dressed, he signs to come into our room, there draws our curtain, kisses me, rather violently pats my face, says *poor*, stretches himself and says *bravo*, then expects as a reward to be tied in his chair and have his play things. These engage him busily, but still he calls to us to sing and drum to enliven the scene. Sometimes he calls me to kiss his hand; he laughs very much at this. Enchanting is that baby laugh, all dimples and glitter, so strangely arch and innocent. Then I wash and dress him; that is his great time. He makes it as long as he can insisting to dress and wash me the while; kicking, throwing the water about full of all manner of tricks that I think girls nere dream of. Then is his walk; we have beautiful walks here for him, Lung-Arno by the bridges, or the sunny walk at the Cascine protected by fine trees always warm in mid-winter the band playing in the distance and children of all ages walking and sitting with their nurses. His walk and sleep give me about three hours in the middle of the day, then at [nig]ht he goes to bed and we have the [ ] otherwise I am always engaged [with] him. Indeed I often walk [with] him, as Italn servants are [not] to be trusted and I feel now [the] need of seeing him at each [mo]ment.

[I] feel so refreshed by his young life. Ossoli diffuses such a peace and sweetness over every day, that I cannot endure to think yet of our future. Too much have we suffered already trying to command it. I do not feel force to make any effort yet. I suppose that very soon now I must do something. I hope I shall feel able when the time comes. I do not yet.

My constitution seems making an effort to rally by dint of much sleep. I had slept so little for a year and a half, during the last months of pregnancy never an hour in peace, after the baby's birth, such anxiety and anguish, when separated from him, I was consumed as by nightly fever. I constantly started up seeming to hear him call me. The last two months at Rome would have destroyed almost any woman then when I went to him, he was so ill and I was constantly up with him at night, carrying him about, feeding him. At Perugia he began to get better. Then w[hen] we arrived here the Police [ ] to send us away; it was as [ ] as three weeks before we coul[d] [get] permission to stay. Now for th[ree] months we have been tranquil; a[nd] have resolved to repose and enjo[y] being together as much as we cou[ld] in this brief interval, perhaps all we shall ever know of peace. It is very sad we have no money; we could have been so quietly happy awhile. I rejoice in all Ossoli did but the results in this our earthly state, are disastrous, especially as my strength is now so much impaired This much I do hope, in life or death to be no more separated from Angelino. Last winter I made the most vehement efforts at least to redeem the time hoping thus good for the future. But of at least two volumes written at that time, no line seems of any worth.[1] I had suffered much constraint, much that was uncongenial, harassing, even agonizing, but this kind of pain found me unprepared. The position of a mother separated from her only child is too frightfully unnatural.

I do think to see you and your baby this coming year. You two I wish to see and some other friends and Mother. Eugene hopes to come to N. England. I have not seen him for 9 years and may not again if I do not take this oppory. There are many difficulties but I think we shall come. If we cannot place ourselves well there, it will be time to think where to go, when I have seen you all, and know whether Ossoli can learn English and to live with those of English blood. Perhaps I shall see you in your Lenox home. But what you say of the meddling curiosity of people repels me. It is so different here When I made my appearance with a husband and a child of a year old nobody did the least thing to annoy me. All were most cordial, none asked or implied questions. Yet there were not a few that might justly have complained that when they were confiding to me all their affairs and doing much to serve me, I had observed absolute silence to them. Others might for more than one reason be displeased at the choice I made. All have acted in the kindliest and most refined manner. An Italian lady with whom I was intimate who might be qualified in the court Journal as one "of the highest rank sustained by the most scrupulous decorum"!! when I wrote "Dear friend, I am married. I have a child There are particulars as to my reasons for keeping this secret I do not wish to tell. This is rather an odd affair, will it make any difference in our relations?" She answered "What difference can it make, except that I shall love you more now that we can sympathize as mothers?" Her first visit here was to me; she adopted at once Ossoli and the child to her love Emelyn Story wrote me that William was a little hurt at first that I did not tell him even in the trying days of Rome, but left him to hear it as he unluckily did at the table d'hote in Venice. But his second and prevailing thought was regret that he had not known it so as to soothe and aid me, to visit Ossoli at his post, to go to the child in the country. Wholly in that spirit was the fine letter he wrote me, one of my treasures. His character has come out beautifully at times in Europe; he has had his ordeals. The little Amern society here have been most cordial and attentive; one lady who has been most intimate with me dropped a tear or two over the difficulties before me but she said "Since you have seen fit to take the step all your friends have to do now is to make it as easy for you as they can."

I am sorry it is known that I had written to you for one thing; it might give pain to Mother to know I had told any one in America before her. I had a letter from her in the Summer, when speaking of the fact that she had never been present at the marriage of one of her children, she said with a kind of sigh, "I think if Arthur were engaged he would tell me, but perhaps not" A great pang came of remorse and I thought if Angelino dies I will not give her the pain of knowing that I have kept this secret from her. She shall hear of this connection as if it were something new. When I found he would live I wrote to her; it half killed me to write those few letters, and yet I know many are wondering I did not write more letters and more particularly. As soon as they were done, I went into bed, but soon had to rise for the baby cried

"Ah che giorni"! I often see Rossini here and think I could teach him to make a better Semiramide![2] But Mother received my communication in the highest spirit. She said she was sure a first object with me had been now and always to save her pain She blessed as she rejoiced that she should not die feeling there was no one left to love me with the devotion she thought I needed. She expressed no regret at our poverty she offered me her feeble means to stead me. Her letter was a noble crown to her life of disinterested purifying love. I should be inexpressibly grieved now, if there is the least thing more to give her pain. Richard, too, never writes. I suppose he is deeply hurt at my silence, but he is young and strong and will feel differently when he has seen me.

29th An absurd number of days have passed without my getting time even to finish this little letter. Generally I go out little, but have taken my part in the Christmas holidays. They interest me now through my child as they never did for myself. I like to go out and watch the rising generation who will be his contemporaries. On Sunday I went with the Italian friend I mentioned in her carriage to the Cascine, after we had taken the drive we sat down on a stone seat in the sunny walk, to see the people walk by. The Grand Duke and all his children, the elegant Austrian officers who will be driven out of Italy when Angelino is a man, Princess Demidoff with her hussars, Harry Lorrequer (Lever) and his absurd brood, M de Corceilles who helped betray Rome, many lovely children, many little frisking dogs with their bells.[3] The sun shone brightly on the Arno, a bark moved gently by All seemed good to the baby, he laid himself back in my arms, smiling, singing to himself, dancing his feet. I hope he will retain some trace in his mind of the perpetual exhilarating picture of Italy. You say you would like your child to have it; I hope she will, while yet a child walk in these stately gardens full of sculpture and hear the untiring music of the fountains. It is to childhood it must be most important. Christmas eve we went to the Annunziata for midnight mass, but it is not splendid here like Rome. Still we enjoyed it, sitting in one of the side chapels, at the foot of a monument, seeing the rich crowd steal gently by, every eye gleaming every gesture softened by the influence of the pealing choir, of the hundred silver lamps, swinging their full light in honor of the abused Emmanuel. But the finest thing was passing through the Duomo, no one was there, only the altars lit up, the priests who were singing could not be seen, by this faint light, the vast solemnity of the interior is really felt. The hour was worthy of Brunelleschi. I hope he has walked there so. You will love the Duomo, it is far more divine than St Peters, worthy of Genius, pure and unbroken. St Peters is like Rome, mixture of sublimest God, with corruptest Earth. I adore the Duomo, though no place can now be to me like St Peters, where has been the splendidest part of my life. My feeling was always perfectly regal, on entering the piazza of St Peters, the calmest intoxication, no spot on earth is worthier the sun light, on none does it fall so fondly. Christmas day I was just up and Nino all naked on his sofa, when came some beautiful large toys that had been sent him a bird, a horse, a cat that could be moved to express different things. It almost made me cry to see the kind of fearful rapture with which he regarded them, legs and arms, extended, fingers and toes quivering, mouth made up to a little round O, eyes dilated; for a long time he did not even wish to touch them, after he began to he was different with all the three, loving the bird; very wild and shouting with the horse, with the cat pulling her face close to his, staring in her eyes, and then throwing her away. Afterwards I drew him in a lottery at a child's party given by Mrs Greenough a toy of a child asleep on the neck of a tiger. The tiger is stretching up to look at the child; this he likes best of any of his toys. It is sweet to see him when he gets used to them and plays by himself, whispering to them, seeming to contrive stories. You would laugh to know how much remorse I feel that I never gave children more toys in the course of my life. I regret all the money I ever spent on myself or in little presents for grown people, hardened sinners. I did not know what pure delight could be bestowed. I am sure if Jesus Christ had given, it would not have been little crosses. You must not show this letter to William he would certainly think it far funnier than yours. There is no use for me to write any more, I could write on all kinds of things a month, but I am very tired this very minute. There is snow all over Florence in our most beautiful piazza. La Maria Novella, with its fair loggia and bridal church is a carpet of snow and the full moon looking down, I had forgotten how angelical all that is, how fit to die by. I have only seen snow in mountain patches for so long, here it is the even, holy shroud of a desired peace. God bless all good and bad tonight and save me from despair

I must not write any more. I am very glad I will have some money to buy you things, and I shall be pleased indeed if I can get the engravings for Elizh. I had one for her once, and was so silly as to give it away. I want you to specify how high I may go for your cameo, some of fine workmanship are as much as thirty dollars, the one I should once have liked to get for you was only six. There are many grades of excellence as to the cutting. Such an one as my Apollo that you remember may sometimes be got for three or four dollars. Rome is the cameo place, still I hope to be able to please you here. You did not specify any other objects; I suppose you will when you send the money. Goodnight, I leave a little place open, if more words be needed on steamer day.

30th Decr I see I have been writing with the most shameful ink; your eyes will be quite put out. This is Sunday I suppose you have been playing with your baby (you on your side do not tell me her age, but I suppose it 9 months,) mine has been walking to day. I have taken such pleasure in watching his little foolish legs. I am sorry to say he seems timid and yet a great bully. I hope these faults may be evoked up into respectable virtues by dint of steady maternal reasoning. We have got your frightful news from Boston. Certainly there is no place like Boston for unexpected horrors. Imagination cowers, faints and dwines away in the attempt to depict Dr Parkman being murdered, Dr Webster murdering.[4] Mr Browning was here yesterday and inspired by this occasion we exchanged our chronicles of the kind. When you first showed me *Pippa passes* I did not foresee what pleasant hours I should pass with the writer, only that writer I never see. We talk too fast; he is too entertaining for us to get really acquainted You ask am I sorry for Sam's being in business. No! I had all my sorrow out about Sam when he gave up being an artist. His life can never be wholly fit, nor ever fail to be full of acquisition. How does he look now? Dear Carrie I wish it was any use to ask you to write at once. Will you see this letter and note rightly delivered for love of

MARGARET.

(MH: fMS Am 1086 [9:166])

1. Fuller was writing a history of the recent revolutions in the Italian states. The manuscript was lost in the shipwreck that took her life.

2. "Ah! quel giorno ognor rammente," an aria in act 1 of Rossini's *Semiramide*.

3. Leopold II (1797–1870) was the grand duke of Tuscany; Matilde Bonaparte (1820–1904), daughter of Jerome Bonaparte, married Prince Anatoly Nikolaevich Demidov (1813–70); Claude-François Tircuy de Corcelle (1802–92) was an author who became the

French envoy to Rome; Charles James Lever (1806–72), an Irish novelist, wrote *The Confessions of Harry Lorrequer* (1839).

4. Dr. John White Webster (1793–1850) was convicted and executed for the murder of Dr. George Parkman (1790–1849), an uncle of the historian. Both men were prominent Boston physicians, and Webster was on the Harvard faculty.

167.   To Margarett C. Fuller

Florence
6th Feby 1850.

Dearest Mother

After receiving your letter of Octr I answered immediately, but, as Richard mentions in one dated 4th Decr that you have not heard, I am afraid by some post-office mistake it went into the mail-bag of some sail-ship instead of steamer and so you were very long without hearing. I regret it the more as I wanted so much to respond fully to your letter, so lovely, so generous, and which of all your acts of love was perhaps the one most needed by me and which has touched me the most deeply.

I gave you in that a flattering picture of our life and those pleasant days lasted till the middle of Decr but then came on a cold unknown before to Italy and has lasted ever since. As the apartments are not prepared against such; we suffered a good deal, beside both O. and myself were taken ill at New Year's time and were not quite well again all Jany. Now we are quite well; the weather begins to soften, though still cloudy damp and chilly so that poor baby can go out very little. On that account he does not grow so fast and gets troublesome by evening, as he tires of being shut up so much in two or three little rooms where he has examined every least object hundreds of times. He is always pointing to the door. He suffers much with chilblains as have other children here; however he is with that exception in the best health and great part of the time very gay, laughing, dancing in nursemaid's arms and trying to sing and drum in imitation of the bands which play a great deal in the piazza.

Nothing special has happened to me. The uninhabitableness of the room in which I had expected to write and the need of using our little dining room the only one where is a stove for dressing baby taking care of him, eating and receiving visits and messages has prevented my writing for six and seven weeks past. In the eveg when baby went to bed about 8 I began to have time, but was generally too tired to do other than read. The four hours, however from 9 till 1 beside the bright little fire have been very pleasant. I have thought a great deal of you remembering how you suffer by cold in the winter and hope you are in a warm comfortable house, have pleasant books to read and some pleasant friends to see One does not want many only a few bright faces to look in now and then and help thaw the ice with little rills of genial converse. I have fewer of these than in Rome, but still several. It is odd how many old associations have turned up here, mostly connected with Father There are the Greenoughs you knew their mother, and Father used to keep locks of their sisters' hair in his desk. Mr Horatio Greenough is married to Miss Gore, whom I first saw at Dr Freeman's Mr Henry Greenough to Miss Boott who was a friend of Amelia Greenwood's.[1] They are all very friendly in their conduct towards me. Then Horace Sumner youngest son of Father's Mr Charles Sumner lives near us and comes every evening to read a little while with Ossoli.[2] They exchange some instruction in Engh and Italn. He has been much ill and is too slow and old in his ways for one of his age, so that those who know him slightly do not like him, but he has solid good in his heart and mind; we have a true regard for him and he has shown true and steadfast sympathy for us. When I am ill, or in a hurry he helps me like a brother. He often speaks of Lloyd whom he knew at Brook farm, and appreciated the grain of gold that is mixed up with so much sand to incumber it. Then who should come along but Anna Breck (Mrs Aspinwall) rich in California gold, with a daughter that seemed much older than herself and a son of 15 named Lloyd.[3] Her husband I found pleasant, herself not more congenial than of old, though still pretty, simple and smiling in the way father used to like so much. She enraged one or two persons here that are quite fond of me, by not echoing at all when they praise me. She was very civil, but I suppose thought I was just as odd and disagreeable as ever. Indeed, not one of Father's friends ever became mine, in fact I was an odd and unpleasing girl to people generally. However, it matters not. One thing seems *odd to me,* dear Mother, as I see so much money flow by, that none of us ever gets any. It is quite a destiny. Here has been a fat round-eyed old lady who had taken seven thousand dollars, just for pocket money to buy pictures and engravings. I thought, now if you could just spare me fifty dollars of that to buy little common engravings to illustrate lessons on Italy, if I want to give some when I go home. But the round-eyed can get such a mass of things she cant use, while I have never had a dollar I could spare for what I could make so interesting to others as well as myself.

I wanted too so much to buy several little objects connected with the early days of the baby that in case I do not return with him, now as I hope, would be so precious for him in after life. However! we must not think too much of these clippings and repressions on every side, but just be thankful if we can get our dinner of herbs and love therewith

I am very anxious to hear from you, to know how you are, and Arthur, if any thing new has occurred, and especially if Eugene is fixed to come to the North this summer. I hope and expect to come, but baby has not yet his teeth, cannot walk and help himself much and we have not yet the money. Mr Mozier wants me not to return yet, but so far all looks to me as if it were important and desirable to delay no longer. I shall see you and all my friends; you especially I feel the need of sccing now. I want to talk with you and know for myself how you are and have you see the baby. Then I would not on any account miss seeing Eugene, if he comes, who knows when another chance might occur. If I am to publish, I had best be there, and I hope to make some arrangement by which we may pass together at least three or four years of our lives. Ossoli looks forward with great desire to seeing you he lost his own mother when very little and now exercises himself much in saying *Mother.* I cannot boast he says it very well. If you have not written, pray do, suddenly on getting this. With love to Arthur, Aunt Abba, Cousin Ellen ever yr affecte

MARGARET.

(MH: fMS Am 1086 [9:176])

1. The Greenough sisters, daughters of David and Elizabeth Bender Greenough, were Louisa (1809–92), Laura (1811–78), Ellen (1814–93) and Charlotte (1815–59). Frances Boott (1809–97) married Henry Greenough (1807–83) in 1837.

2. Horace Sumner (1824–50) died with the Ossolis in the shipwreck.

3. Anna Breck (1812–94), daughter of George and Catherine Breck, married William Henry Aspinwall in 1829. Her daughter was Anna Lloyd Aspinwall (1831–80); the son was Lloyd (1830–86), later a Union general in the Civil War.

168.   To Arthur Hugh Clough

Florence
16th Feby 1849. [1850]

Dear Mr Clough,

I am going to write, principally with the view of getting a letter back, so you must not disappoint me.

You wrote that you might see me here, might come every now and then to Italy. But you must come to America rather. I think I shall go there this summer. Dearly as I love Italy and incomplete as is my acquaintance with her yet, I do not like to be here at this time of incubus. Often I forget it, but on reawaking to a sense of the realities round me it is crushing to think, to feel all that is smothered down in mens minds. I care least for these cowed and coward Florentines; they are getting only what the[y] deserve, but do not like to be among them.

The judicious conduct of the Austrians here is quite admirable. One would not think that men installed where they are not wanted and ought not to be could seem so gentlemanly The troops are kept in great order, still from the very nature of the case the Tuscans gather with each day fresh cause for gloomy brooding. The Austrians at this moment seem in great dread of an outbreak, but I suppose it could only be some trifling street fuss as yet

Yes I shall like to go back and see our "eighteen millions of bores," with their rail-roads, electric telegraphs, mass movements and ridiculous dilet-tant phobias, but with ever successful rush and bang.[1] I feel as if I should be the greatest bore of all when I get home, so few will care for the thoughts of my head or the feelings of my heart, but there will be some pairs of eyes to see, and a sense of fresh life unknown here.

I have recd an offer from an Amern publisher for my book, but it is not satisfactory and I think to wait till I go myself, perhaps to burn meanwhile. I am not at all sorry it was not to be published in England, (indeed now I see the question whether foreigners can hold copy right is quite decided against us) and I shall not care if prevented from publishing at all. I dare say the experiences if left for seed corn will grow to something better.

As to money I have not got any yet, but probably should not by the book; if it succeeded tolerably, I should get cheated somehow out of the penny fee.

Casting aside the past and the future, and despite the extreme cold which has tormented me much in an Italn apartment, fit only for May and June, I have enjoyed many bright and peaceful hours this winter. My little baby flourishes in my care; his laughing eyes, his stammered words and capricious caresses afford me the first unalloyed quiet joy I have ever known. Tis true! he must grow up to sorrow and to strive and have less and less the sweet music that seems to flow around him now, if like his mother he will be full of faults and much unreasonable, but I hope there will be in him a conquering, purifying energy too. What we call God seems so very near in the presence of a child; we bless the love that gave this soul to put an end to loneliness, we believe in the justice that is bound to provide it at last with all it needs. I like also much living with my husband. You said in your letter you thought I should at any rate be happier now because the position of an unmarried woman in our time is not de-sirable; to me on the contrary it had seemed that in a state of society where marriage brings so much of trifling business arrangements and var-ious soporifics the liberty of single life was most precious. I liked to see those I loved only in the best way. With Ossoli I liked when no one knew of our relation, and we passed our days together in the mountains, or walked beautful nights amid the ruins of Rome. But for the child I should

have wished to remain as we were, and feared we should lose much by entering on the jog-trot of domestic life. However, I do not find it so; we are
of mutual solace and aid about the dish and spoon part, yet enjoy our free
rambles as much as ever. Now I have written a good deal of me, will you
write some sincere words of you, at least as much so as you have put in
your print. Which makes me always so sorry I threw away the chance of
knowing you in Rome. Had I known you before we could have talked
then, but I was so pressed with excitements, I had not the soul to make a
new acquaintance

Is Mazzini in London; have you seen him? if so, do write me how he is
and whatever you may know of him. I think of him with unspeakable affection, but do not wish to write.

Adieu, dear Mr Clough, your friend

MARGARET

(Bodleian Library)

1. Thomas Carlyle's Smelfungus, in the recently published "Latter-Day Pamphlets," says
that Americans "have begotten, with a rapidity beyond recorded example, Eighteen Millions of the greatest *bores* ever seen in this world before,—that hitherto is their feat in
History!"

169.   To Richard F. Fuller

Florence
24th Feby 1850.

My dear Richard,

I take the oppory of sending under cover to S Ward, to write you a little
note just that the family may hear from you, how I am. Now that I pay 25
cents here on every single sheet instead of a dollar as I used to through
the banker I find my letters do *not* go so swiftly and surely and even of this
postage I must be chary

I hoped by this time to say decisively when I come home, but do not yet
know, we not being sure yet we can get the money. The voyage, made in
the cheapest way we can, must cost us about 150 dollars as, even if we
brave the length and discomforts of voyage by a merchant-man, and go
without any help for care of the baby in case of being sick, we must still
buy stores and have a cow or goat to insure him proper food. We *may* have
in this way two months on the ocean. I have always suffered much in my
head at sea. However to go by France would be more than double the ex-

pense. Happy the fowl of the air who dont have to think so much about these things. I hope by hook (we shant try by crook) to get the means and come somehow.

Days have come here already such as was the May day on which you wrote to me last year, glorious days that expand the heart, uplift the whole nature. Walks here are very charming, because in whatever direction you move on leaving the gates, you immediately find yourself climbing a height, while below lies gently nestled the brown first home of many an eagle, many a song bird, too. You are very sublime and stern, my dear Richard, in your disownings of the lures and ambitions of this life, as well as amazed at the *worldliness* of your sister, who on her side, was not a little surprised, to say nothing of other feelings, at such accusations, more than once repeated, too. At the risk of confirming this dark view of her character, she must observe, she has at times hoped much you would sometime have dollars enough to traverse land and waves and see some beauteous sights that will be to her memory a joy forever. But the little bit of paper ends so only more love to all from

MARGARET.

Admire this war steed I intend to have a donkey engraved with some motto and in this same style beauty. Motto Fier mais soumis

(MH: fMS Am 1086 [9:135])

170.   To Samuel G. Ward

Florence
24th Feby 1850

I ought, dear Sam, to have acknowledged by last steamer the receipt of the money but an accident made me miss the day for writing from here. I lost eighteen dollars here by the exchange; if Caroline (Tappan) comes to you to send me a little sum to buy her engravings, tell her there is now this loss, and the banker says likely to be worse Perhaps her father could send in some way by which I would have all the money to spend for her, a note direct on Leghorn, or the like, or it might be arranged for me to take it direct from Mr Mozier and something bought or done for him in U. S. If she sends fifty dollars, I would not like to have only forty five, for example, to buy her things.

We have had a winter incredibly cold for Italy, and it is very bad here where houses are not prepared. I had attached no importance to having

fire-places in the sleeping rooms and we have really suffered, in consequence, our *sala,* where I had expected to write could not be warmed, we
have had nothing but a little dining room, to dress, eat, take care of the
baby &c; that generally smoky the coldest days; we have scarce had more
comfort, and retirement than one might in a Western log cabin. But now
begins glorious Spring weather, like the (few) good days of May in N. England. Not withstanding the bad weather, my health has been constantly
improving. Since my father's death (which you may remember took place
just after we were acquainted,) I have never been so well as at present. I
have always looked back to the few weeks we passed on that journey as the
last period of tranquillity in my life. During those weeks the persons with
whom we were were kindly towards me, and even their defects not uncongenial. Mrs Farrar protected me with a great deal of thoughtful affection,
for which I have never ceased to be grateful; in my growing acquaintance
with you I found a kind of home, my enjoyment of nature and my own
mind was profound. Afterwards I had always griefs or cares to beset me,
and allow me free life only for hours or days at a time. In Europe I have
had countless plagues all along; many rich joys and grand opportunities,
but generally snatched away half known or shut up half tried by failure of
health or want of money to do as I wished. This winter there were cares
enough, but I have put them aside; we began with the resolve that, having
planned our life for these few months as prudently as we could; we would
enjoy it as much as we could and leave the rest to Him that careth for the
least birds, though He does let so many of them get shot. We are not shot
yet, nor frozen, nor starved My little boy on the contrary is very fat though
I am afraid he will not do so well after he is weaned from his great stout
Roman mother in the flesh. He grows every way; except hair, and people
rather jeer at me, for having only a *bald* child. I piously wish them the fate
of the scoffers who did not prize that peculiarity in a Prophet, and beside
flatter myself that being in temperament so unlike Absalom he will show
the opposite conduct towards a fond parent.[1] Now in these fine days I
have begun to go sometimes to the galleries; in winter the Uffizi are too
cold. I feel works of art more than I have ever yet. I feel the development
of my own nature as I look on them; so many hid meanings come out
upon me. Two new (old) Raphaels have of late been discovered under the
paint. One seems to me only a copy; the other is a lovely Madonna in the
earlier manner. Jesi is making an engraving of the Raphael (Last Supper)
discovered in the coach-house. It would be good for you to have as companion to Leonardo's. The contrast of mind in the two ways of treating
the subject as you see them together speaks like a dialogue. With love to
Anna ever yours

M.

(MH: bMS Am 1465 [934])

1. As the prophet Elisha was going up to Beth-el, he was mocked by a group of children, who said, "Go up, thou bald head; go up, thou bald head." The enraged prophet cursed them and "there came forth two she bears out of the wood, and tare forty and two children of them." King David's son Absalom, known for his beauty and luxuriant hair, raised a rebellion against his father but was captured and then killed after his hair caught on the branch of an oak tree.

171. To Lewis Cass, Jr.

Florence
2d May, 1850.

Dear Mr Cass,

I shall, most probably, leave Florence and Italy the 8th or 10th of this month and am not willing to depart without saying adieu to yourself. I wanted to write the 30th April, but a succession of petty interruptions prevented. That was the day I saw you first and the day the French first assailed Rome. What a crowded day that was! I had been in the morning to visit Ossoli in the garden of the Vatican, just after my return you entered. I then went to the hospital and there passed the night amid the groans of many suffering, some dying men. What a strange first of May it was as I walked the streets of Rome by the first sunlight of next day! Those were to me grand and impassioned hours. Deep sorrow followed, many embarrassments many pains! Let me once more at parting thank you for the sympathy you showed me amid many of these. A thousand years might pass and you would find it unforgotten by me. I shall be glad however if you have destroyed, or will destroy, letters I wrote you during that period. I was heartsick, weary; the future seemed too difficult, and I too weak to face it. What I felt, what I wrote then is below the usual temper of my mind, and I would be glad to cancel all trace of those weaker moods—

I leave Italy with profound regret and with only a vague hope of returning. I could have lived here always, full of bright visions, and expanding in my faculties, had destiny permitted. May you be happy who remain here! it would be well worth while to be happy in Italy.

I had hoped to enjoy some of the last days, but the weather has been steadily bad since you were in Florence. Since the 4th April, we have not had a fine day and all our little plans for visits to favorite spots, and beautiful objects from which we must long be separated, have been marred!

Adieu! I do not feel like writing much. You will, probably, not have time to answer now, but if you feel inclined sometimes to address me in our country, a permanent address would be to care of S. G. Ward, Boston

I sail in the bark Elizabeth f[or] New York. She is laden with mar[ble] and rags, a very appropriate companionship for wares of Italy. She carries Powers's statue of Calhoon.[1] Adieu, remember that we look to you to keep up the dignity of our country; many important occasions are now likely to offer, for the American, (I wish I could write the *Columbian*) man to advocate, more, to *represent* the cause of Truth and Freedom, in face of their foes, and remember me as their lover and your friend

M. O.

(MH: fMS Am 1086 [9:169])

1. The city of Charleston commissioned Hiram Powers in 1845 to make a statue of John Calhoun. It was salvaged from the wreck of the *Elizabeth* but later destroyed when the city burned in the Civil War.

BIBLIOGRAPHICAL ESSAY

In addition to my six-volume edition of *The Letters of Margaret Fuller,* readers will want to read others of Fuller's writings. Selections may be found in these anthologies: Bell Gale Chevigny, *The Woman and the Myth: Margaret Fuller's Life and Writings,* rev. ed. (Boston: Northeastern University Press, 1994); Jeffrey Steele, *The Essential Margaret Fuller* (New Brunswick: Rutgers University Press, 1992); and Mary Kelly, *The Portable Margaret Fuller* (New York: Penguin, 1994). Larry J. Reynolds has edited *Woman in the Nineteenth Century* (New York: W. W. Norton, 1998). Judith Mattson Bean and Joel Myerson have edited *Margaret Fuller, Critic: Writings in the* New York Tribune, *1844–1846* (New York: Columbia University Press, 2000). Reynolds and Susan Belasco Smith edited Fuller's European essays for the *Tribune* in *"These Sad, but Glorious Days"* (New Haven: Yale University Press, 1991).

Many biographies of Fuller have been written. A good one-volume life is Joan Von Mehren, *Minerva and the Muse* (Amherst: University of Massachusetts Press, 1994). A more comprehensive study is Charles Capper, *Margaret Fuller: An American Romantic Life,* vol. 1 (New York: Oxford University Press, 1992); the second volume is in preparation. Joel Myerson edited a collection of essays devoted to Fuller, *Critical Essays on Margaret Fuller* (Boston: G. K. Hall, 1980). Full-length critical studies are Margaret Vandenhaar Allen, *The Achievement of Margaret Fuller* (University Park: Pennsylvania State University Press, 1979), and Christina Zwarg, *Feminist Conversations: Fuller, Emerson, and the Play of Reading* (Ithaca: Cornell University Press, 1995). Other discussions of Fuller may be found in Joel Myerson, *The New England Transcendentalists and the "Dial": A History of the Magazine and Its Contributors* (Rutherford, N.J.: Fairleigh Dickinson University Press, 1980); Julie K. Ellison, *Delicate Subjects: Romanticism, Gender, and the Ethics of Understanding* (Ithaca: Cornell University Press, 1990); Larry J. Reynolds, *European Revolutions and the American Literary Renaissance* (New Haven: Yale University Press, 1988); and Thomas R. Mitchell, *Hawthorne's Fuller Mystery* (Amherst: University of Massachusetts Press, 1998).

Finally, a complete bibliography of Fuller's writing may be found in Joel Myerson, *Margaret Fuller: A Descriptive Bibliography* (Pittsburgh: University of Pittsburgh Press, 1978) with a supplement in *Studies in the American Renaissance 1996* (Charlottesville: University Press of Virginia, 1996, 187–240). A bibliography of works about Fuller is Myerson, *Margaret Fuller: An Annotated Secondary Bibliography* (New York: Burt Franklin, 1977) with a supplement in *Studies in the American Renaissance 1984* (Charlottesville: University Press of Virginia, 1984, 331–85). A discussion of earlier work on Fuller may be found in Robert N. Hudspeth, "Margaret Fuller," in *The Transcendentalists: A Review of Research and Criticism,* ed. Joel Myerson (New York: MLA, 1984).

INDEX